LESBIAN SUBJECTS
A Feminist Studies Reader

edited by Martha Vicinus

Indiana University Press

Bloomington and Indianapolis

© 1996 by *Feminist Studies*

All rights reserved

The paper used in this publication meets the minimum requirements of American
National Standard for Information Sciences—Permanence of Paper for Printed
Library Materials, ANSI Z39.48-1984.

Manufactured in the United States of America

Library of Congress Cataloging-in-Publication Data

Lesbian subjects : a feminist studies reader / edited by Martha Vicinus.
p.   cm.
Includes index.
ISBN 0–253–33060–2 (cloth : alk. paper). — ISBN 0–253–21038–0
(pbk. : alk. paper)
1. Gay and lesbian studies—United States.   2. Women's studies—
United States.   I. Vicinus, Martha.
HQ75.16.U6L47   1996
305.48'9664—dc20   95-45054

1   2   3   4   5   01   00   99   98   97   96

Contents

13

The Gender Closet: Lesbian Disappearance under the Sign "Women"
Cheshire Calhoun *209*

14

"They Wonder to Which Sex I Belong": The Historical Roots
of the Modern Lesbian Identity
Martha Vicinus *233*

Introduction

Martha Vicinus

IN 1980 THE pioneering lesbian historian Blanche Weisen Cook wrote of "The historical denial of lesbianism [which] accompanies the persistent refusal to acknowledge the variety and intensity of women's emotional and erotic experience."[1] This "historical denial" has been overtaken by a cacophony of voices; the growth in cultural studies in the academy has brought the study of homosexuality from its suspect position to the center of work on gender and sexuality. The lesbian is an accepted subject for scrutiny—she exists, but how are we to define her history, who do we include, and when did it begin?

This anthology includes essays published in *Feminist Studies* from 1980 to 1995, as well as one ground-breaking essay from *Gender and History*. As such, it is both a historical document, tracing the development of lesbian studies from its present-day beginnings, and a summation of work to date. The essays represent no teleological movement from simple generalizations to sophisticated complexities, but rather a series of repeated themes and concerns. "Lesbianism" was never defined solely as "bedroom sex," or as "intense friendship." Rather, the difficulties involved in defining a lesbian perspective and a lesbian past—a culture, social milieux, even states of mind—were recognized from the beginning. This collection provides an overview of the field, past and present. Two aspects of lesbian studies remain fundamental, and are implicit or explicit in each of the essays that follow: the biographical and the bodily. Who is the "I" in this body? What is the body that I possess, or that I want to possess? If this body is a constructed artifice whose desires are learned and shaped by complex social and cultural forces, can we understand that construction in any way outside metaphor and language? However unstable the lesbian subject may appear, however much a "learned performance," none of the authors doubts her existence. There may be no core, no fixed definition, but lesbian subjects exist.

But with so many critics rushing into the field of lesbian studies, what are the main issues at the moment? The study of homosexuality is popular now, but despite this popularity—or perhaps because of it—something that ought to be happening in lesbian studies is not happening. Rather than rehearsing the contents of *Lesbian Subjects*, this introduction reviews the main ideological currents in recent work on lesbian sexuality and culture; it questions some of the assumptions and definitions that have become common parlance, and suggests possible alternatives.

Too many people, whether experts or beginners, remain excessively concerned with knowing-for-sure.[2] Lesbian history has always been characterized by a "not knowing" what could be its defining core. More than a decade ago I pointed out a paradoxical tendency: writers appeared to be both reticent to name women's same-sex desire and overeager to categorize and define women's sexual behavior; unfortunately this still remains true.[3] Our own literalism, a paucity of sources, and what Judith Bennett has called "definitional uncertainty" have inhibited all too many of us from undertaking the painstaking excavational work necessary to understand the variety of women's sexual subjectivities, and the ways in which different societies have permitted, forbidden, and interpreted these experiences.[4] Alternatively, the current emphasis upon playful gender instability has led to a wholesale embracing of sexual polymorphism, without sufficient concern for the distinctiveness of lesbian behavior, past or present. Our current models in the United States privilege either the visibly marked mannish woman or the self-identified lesbian; romantic friendships, once the leading example of a lesbian past, are now either reconfigured in terms to fit these categories or labeled asexual. We seem to accept only what is seen and what is said as evidence. These limitations have shaped both how we know and how we imagine the lesbian.

I want to argue for the possibilities of the "not said" and the "not seen" as conceptual tools for lesbian studies. Recognizing the power of not naming—of the unsaid—is a crucial means for understanding a past that is so dependent upon fragmentary evidence, gossip, and suspicion. Moreover, a contemporary perspective that is limited to the visible, self-identified lesbian will reduce an understanding of both the daily life of the homosexual and her multiple relationships with the dominant heterosexual society and its cultural productions. A more open definition of women's sexual subjectivity, and of the nature of lesbian desire, will enable us not only to retrieve a richer past, but also to understand the complex threads that bind women's public actions with their private desires.

The binaries that have dominated the conceptualization of sex and gender have been rigorously questioned recently, but too often this questioning has yielded either polymorphous play or an unstable "third sex" defined by cross-dressing and marginal sexuality.[5] I maintain that the lesbian is never absent from any definition of woman, whatever her avowed sexual preference. I am arguing here for the primacy of a continuum of women's sexual behaviors, in which lesbian sexuality can be both a part of and apart from normative heterosexual marriage and child-bearing. This does not mean a return to Adrienne

Rich's notion of a continuum of "woman-identified experience," in which all-female bonding is defined as unproblematic nurturance and love in opposition to the divisions wrought by compulsory heterosexuality.[6] Rather, we must recognize the permeability of women's sexual boundaries, the continuum of their sexual experiences that also contains an irreducible sense of the dangerous difference implicit in homosexuality. Perhaps no image—a continuum, circle, or margin—can embody a subject as pervasive and as central as sexual desire. But I contend that the lesbian is an intrinsic part of the modern, western sexual imaginary. Women's same-sex love always remains a dangerous affront to male sexual prerogatives; but, as Elizabeth Wilson notes in this volume, it is also a dangerous act that can unite and divide two women. Lesbian studies is not a marginal preoccupation of lesbians only, but is pivotal to our understanding of women; by implication, this must include men, for we live in a gendered world in which the subordinate gender can never escape the dominant.

It is ironic that "lesbianism" continues to depend upon the evidence of sexual consummation, whereas heterosexuality is confirmed through a variety of diverse social formations. For example, we know of several unconsummated marriages among middle-class British intellectuals; the Ruskins, the Carlyles, and George Bernard Shaw and Charlotte Payne Townshend are well-known examples. These spouses may be failed heterosexuals, but they are not stripped of their sexual identity. Conversely, even when we have evidence of homosexual practices, it has often been reinterpreted as asexual sentimentality or non-genital cuddling. The American sculptor Harriet Hosmer (1830–1908) made a specific distinction in her letters between kissing her close friends and the pleasures of "Laöcooning" in bed with her woman lover, but her most recent biographer insists that Hosmer was not like her lesbian friend Charlotte Cushman (1816–76), the internationally admired American actress.[7] However difficult it may be to interpret the flowery language of letters written between friends by both women and men during the nineteenth century, are we not relying too much on a literal language of either sex or sentimentality? Why is an explicit statement seen as a truth statement, and elision as uncertainty?

As Eve Kosofsky Sedgwick has said in regard to male homosexuality, ignorance is not an empty box waiting to be filled by knowledge.[8] Ignorance now and in prior times can be willed. I want to suggest that a lesbianism can be everywhere without being mentioned; the sustained withholding of the name can actually be the very mechanism which reinforces its existence as a defined sexual practice.[9] In effect, we have what is unnamed now and in the past, as well as our own reluctance to name; a determined ignorance reinforces homophobia and impoverishes lesbian studies.

This insistence upon explicitness has led to a privileging of an identity model of the lesbian. We have focused on two obvious categories of same-sex love: romantic friendships and butch-femme role playing. The former depends upon our present-day identification of these friendships as homoerotic, if not homosexual, while the latter depends upon self-identification by the women themselves. Romantic friends can be called the "good girls"—educated, monogamous, and gently loving of women. Numerous examples of these Sapphic loves can be documented throughout European and American history, for they were an established phase of a young girl's initiation into emotional maturity. As a result, it has been repeatedly claimed that "once upon a time" women could love each other and society approved.[10] This rosy picture of social acceptance, while never fully endorsed by historians, has seemed boringly asexual to many lesbians of today. They preferred, in Alice Echols's phrase, the "bad girls" from an immediate, retrievable past.[11] 1950s working-class butches drank, fought, and had fun; among lesbians, a romantic nostalgia for the bar-dyke culture of this period is common. Self-identification as either butch or femme has become the defining sign of one's true identity.[12]

I want to suggest that limiting lesbian sexuality to these two categories, romantic friendships and butch-femme roles, has led to a dreary narrowing of conceptual possibilities. Both are defined so as to leave little room for women who might behave differently at different times, or who might belong to both categories of romantic friendship and butch/femme passion—or neither. How are we to define a married woman who falls in love with a woman? Or a lesbian who falls in love with a man?[13] Charlotte Cushman fashioned for herself a visibly mannish appearance, while writing letters to her lovers in a romantic friendship style. She and her partners wore matching jackets and dresses, so that they looked alike, but different from heterosexual women.[14] The "randy widow" of medieval literature seems to have disappeared from the lesbian overview, perhaps because, with historical primness, we have refused to call anybody a lesbian before the late nineteenth century, arguing that the word was not used before then. Actually, if we wish to be literal-minded—which I am arguing strenuously against—"lesbian" is used in its modern sense as early as 1736, in a virulent attack on the widowed Duchess of Newburgh.[15]

Present-day concerns with self-identification have led to a fetishization of *difference* visibly inscribed on the physical appearance of a woman, and its seemingly inevitable accompaniment, the coming-out story. One might say that scholars of romantic friendships, such as Carroll Smith-Rosenberg and myself, have "outed" forgotten nineteenth-century middle-class women whose diaries and letters so eloquently describe their erotically charged emotional involvements with women.[16] Elizabeth Lapovsky Kennedy and Madeline D. Davis pioneered interviewing women who participated in the bar community of Buffalo in the 1940s and 1950s; numerous local studies of lesbian-dominated softball leagues, bars, and other venues have followed their efforts.[17] Anthologies of coming-out autobiographies have given ordinary women of all ethnicities an opportunity to speak their sexual preference.[18] However important these political gestures have been—and I do not wish to minimize them—they all depend upon a notion of lesbian visibility—of recognition *and* then the speaking what has previously been suppressed, ignored, or denied.

Given the conceptual impasse of lesbian history by the mid-1980s, it is hardly surprising that "queer theory," based in cultural studies, has come to the fore as the most exciting way to think about sexual object choice. It posed a new set of questions that could be more easily answered—or deployed—than a history dependent upon certifiable homoeroticism. The queer perspective is most eloquently argued by Eve Kosofsky Sedgwick in *The Epistemology of the Closet,* which is based upon the premise that "an understanding of virtually any aspect of modern Western culture must be, not merely incomplete, but damaged in its central substance to the degree that it does not incorporate a critical analysis of modern homo/heterosexual definition."[19] Queer theorists, led by the philosopher Judith Butler, have fought vigorously against the notion of homosexuality as a miming of heterosexuality—as if the latter were the legitimate original and homosexuality an imitation. Moreover, as Lisa Duggan has pointed out, "queer theories" refuse the marginality of both civil-rights–style liberal gay politics and the ghettoizing of gay studies. They provide a means of analyzing the here and now, giving fresh impetus to political action at a time when many left-leaning academics have felt the lack of any viable political arena.[20] These are heady claims for a subdiscipline just gaining academic credibility. But they have freed lesbian studies from previously reductive notions of sexual identity, as well as the tedious essentialist (sexual identity rooted in biology) versus social construction (sexual identity determined by social factors) debate that agitated homosexuals in the late 1980s.[21]

Few queer theorists have been centrally concerned with historical questions; instead they have focused upon the cultural construction of gays and lesbians at the present time. One of the new questions the queer theorist Judith Butler asked was, "Does gender exist?" Her answer is "yes and no," because all gender is performance. Revising the psychoanalytic notion first advanced by Joan Rivière, that femininity itself is a masquerade, she argues that no one can be defined by or limited to a single gendered identity; even the process of speaking as a lesbian is, in her words, "a production . . . an identity which, once produced, sometimes functions as a politically efficacious phantasm," but which, as an "identity category," suggests "a provisional totalization."[22] For Butler the performance of gender, and especially the practices of butch/femme and drag,

offers a more viable politics in our postmodern world than identity-based politics, which depends upon privileging one identity over another.[23] In effect, she
has taken the definitional uncertainty about "what is a lesbian" and argued for
its radical potential. If all gender is a performance, then we need not seek a coherent lesbian identity in the past or present. Lesbians are a social construct produced in the process of relating to others. This is, of course, an immensely freeing notion.

Nevertheless, as Kath Weston has pointed out, butch and femme roles today
may be a "playful, irreverent, anti-essentialist approach to gender, but this association is confined to a limited number of 'players' in relatively specialized
historical circumstances."[24] For her, sexual performance is a class privilege of
educated, white American women. People do not always experience themselves
as being in control of gendered representations, which involve their immersion
in social and material relations.[25] For Weston, a troubling residue of an essentialized, intrinsic role remains in lesbian sexuality. Given the limited number of
roles played by lesbians and lesbian-like women in history, as I document in my
essay in this anthology, critics may be poised now to reconsider the limits of
gender mutability, and to reconsider the ways in which we act out our sexual
desires within a finite number of scripts.[26]

Biddy Martin has argued that much queer theory posits a dichotomy between race and sexuality, whereby race becomes the stable identity in opposition to a playful, postmodern sexual sensibility.[27] In effect, it places sexuality
outside such variables as race and class, giving it a kind of false independence.
Martin, like Weston, points to the impossibility of sustaining a metaphoric performance independent of the social context that shapes and constrains all of us,
whatever our current sexual choice. But for Martin, and implicitly, I would argue, for anyone who studies the lesbian, Butler's argument about the performative nature of gender "underscores the importance of rendering visible complexities that already exist but are rendered unthinkable, invisible, or
impossible by discursive/institutional orderings with deep investments in defining viable subjects."[28] It is precisely these "discursive/institutional orderings" that scholars need to examine—to render visible—for they reveal the pervasive denial of lesbian practices.

My own criticism of "queer theory" as defined by Judith Butler and Sue-Ellen Case rests in part on its ahistorical nature. The wholesale embracing of a
theatrical metaphor ignores the historical contingencies within which lesbian
roles are constructed, and their specific meanings at different historical times—
indeed, even the possibility of their non-existence in the past.[29] Modern sexual
behavior cannot be divorced from its intersection with race, nation, class, and
other social variables, nor can it be wholly a matter of fashionable, presentist

metaphorizing. Moreover, the focus of queer theory upon performance is also a privileging of the visible, which returns us to some of the same difficulties that have characterized identity-based history. It is as if "what is gender?" is still confined to "what is *visibly* gendered?" From its very inception, lesbian studies has been concerned with "making visible" the lesbian of the present and the past. This process of reclamation has focused almost entirely upon the mannish woman because she has been the one most obviously different from other women—and men. What does this insistence on visibility do to notions of both femininity and feminism? Are we fixated on visibly marked difference, whether it be a "performed" gender or a gendered identity, because the explicitness of our age demands clear erotic signals?

Historicizing lesbian roles may help to problematize the privileging of the visible as sexual sign. External physical signs were the crucial referent for the nineteenth-century medical profession. Early sexologists argued that a born invert could be identified by her enlarged clitoris or her excessive body hair, or by similar physical "deformations."[30] Freud's theory of sexual difference depends directly upon the male child's *seeing* its mother's lack of a penis.[31] But if only the visual marker of mannishness could signify sexual preference, a so-called femme could be distinct from a heterosexual woman only by her performance of an extreme form of femininity, as if to counteract Havelock Ellis's claim that such women were the homely leftovers rejected by men. Teresa de Lauretis has tackled "what cannot be seen" in her analysis of Radclyffe Hall's *The Well of Loneliness* (1928). The mannish Stephen's lover, Mary, "in most representations" "would be either passing lesbian or passing straight," for she can be seen as lesbian only on the arm of her lover.[32] Recently self-identified political femmes have refused an identity based solely on their relationship to a butch lover. As Lisa M. Walker has said, "because subjects who can 'pass' exceed the categories of visibility that establish identity, they tend to be peripheral to the understanding of marginalization." Like Biddy Martin, she too criticizes the implicit racism of writers who reify marginalization in terms of "the visible signifier of difference," whether it be race, class, or "mannishness."[33]

Even a cursory glance at lesbian history shows that many couples dressed alike in a manner that would repel men, and remind onlookers of their distinct interest in each other. I have already mentioned Charlotte Cushman; she and her partner Mathilda Hays in 1852 were described by Elizabeth Barrett Browning as a couple who had "made vows of celibacy & of eternal attachment to each other—they live together, dress alike . . . it is a female marriage."[34] The famous late-eighteenth–early nineteenth-century Ladies of Llangollen wore identical Irish riding habits and powdered wigs. Observers repeatedly sought to differentiate the two women; a scurrilous journalist described the fifty-one-year-old, dumpy Lady Eleanor Butler as "tall and masculine" and "in all respects a young man."[35] His preconception of their relationship demanded a visible differentiation between the two women, even if they themselves eschewed such marking. Seemingly a popular model of "inversion" predates the sexologists, though this has not yet been sufficiently explored by historians. Sartorial sameness, as practiced by the Ladies and Cushman and Hays, may well have been an upperclass defense against the well-known lower-class "female soldier," or it may have been a means of resisting the stereotypes of what we would now call "butch/femme."

I wish to problematize not only the emphasis upon visibility as an essential marker of the lesbian, but also the necessity of a language of homosexuality as a precursor to a lesbian sexual identity. Some feminists have found Jacques Lacan's theory of the construction of the subject through language to be an especially powerful way to theorize feminine desire, however much they may disagree with his notion of desire for the phallus. By concentrating on the psychological importance of the child's entry into a socially constructed language, he has drawn our attention to the ways in which language is an intrinsic part of our sexual selves. Moreover, Lacan's notion that the individual subject is constituted in a world of language and symbols eliminates a strict boundary between the self and society—a potentially invaluable starting point for lesbian studies, a field defined by its lack of clear boundaries.

Language theories remain a powerful means for understanding the formation of the individual self, but I want to suggest that we may be in danger of magnifying their importance in lesbian studies. For both Lillian Faderman and Esther Newton, the late-nineteenth-century sexologists' language of genital sex made women sexually self-conscious. For Newton, this "new vocabulary built on the radical idea that women apart from men could have autonomous sexual feeling" and thereby freed lesbians from the asexuality of romantic friendships.[36] Radclyffe Hall seemed to confirm Newton's generalization; her heroine, Stephen, in *The Well of Loneliness* (1928), cannot understand what is wrong with her until she stumbles upon an annotated copy of the sexologist Richard von Krafft-Ebing in her father's study. For Faderman, this provision of a sexual language was a misfortune that took away the innocence of romantic friends. She describes late-nineteenth-century women as "fledgling human beings" who lacked the self-confidence to resist the sexologists' language of neurosis.[37] Both interpretations, though diametrically opposed, give inordinate power to language as either a freeing or a disabling means of self-identification for lesbians. They also reinforce a sense that until middle-class women had a sexual vocabulary, their relationships were either asexual or guiltily furtive.

These two influential critics both deny homosexual agency to pre-twentieth-century women. It is therefore no surprise that many lesbians greeted with pleasure and relief the 1988 publication of excerpts from the diary of the early nineteenth-century English gentlewoman Anne Lister (1791–1840). Lister had developed a vocabulary to define her lesbian behavior, including such words as "kiss" to describe her orgasms and those of her partners. Entries written in code are quite explicit about what she did in bed, as well as what she suspected numerous other women of doing. At last we had evidence that women in the past not only knew what to do in bed with each other, they actually did it—and then created their own sexual vocabulary. Lister also found other women who enjoyed sexual relations with each other; she may not have inhabited a modern lesbian subculture, but she knew that other women of her own social class shared her proclivities. Karen V. Hansen's essay in this collection confirms the sexual base of many romantic friendships, across racial, class, and national lines. She examines the correspondence between two mid-nineteenth-century African-American women. Like Lister, Addie Brown and Rebecca Primus spoke a language of explicit sexual love, speaking of "bosom sex" as indicative of their passion.

Yet I don't believe that scholars need similar diaries or letters, however valuable, in order to read the past. Indeed, I want to caution against focusing on what is said—either by others or by a woman herself. By doing so we may fall into the trap of the same literalism that has characterized our search for the visible markers of lesbian sexuality. The analysis of romantic friendships in particular has been bedeviled by the assumption that because Victorian women from upper-class backgrounds did not use the language of sex, they could not know what to do in bed.[38] Just because Anne Lister reverses this widespread generalization, it does not free us to assume unproblematically—and unhistorically—that every time two women slept together they were disporting themselves. The time has come to stop concentrating on what might have been said or done in private and to focus on other issues.

As Terry Castle has noted, the lesbian is repeatedly treated as if she were a ghost, whose sexual activities cannot be defined, and yet she repeatedly reappears, haunting the heterosexual imaginary. This ghosting of lesbian desire has made possible a denial of its reality for too long. Readers can learn from Castle that the "apparitional lesbian" is not absent from history, but is to be found everywhere, and as she suggests, "to focus on presence instead of absence, plenitude instead of scarcity."[39] As part of that plenitude, I return to my earlier argument: if we begin with a continuum, a range, of sexual behaviors as possible for all women, then the lesbian is not marginal or phantasmic, but pivotal. We need to remind ourselves again—as queer theorists have claimed—that all sexual behavior is polymorphous, changeable, and impossible to define absolutely;

it can be understood only in relation to the multifarious elements that make up a human identity. Many more women will be part of that continuum, temporarily or permanently, when we recognize the sheer variety and richness of women's sexual desires—and actions. Truth-claims cannot be made, but a fuller lesbian studies can be constructed.

Martha Vicinus
University of Michigan

Notes

Special thanks to Judith Bennett, Annamarie, Susan S. Lanser, and Claire G. Moses for reading various versions of this introduction. I am indebted to the National Endowment for the Humanities for a fellowship that made possible the completion of this book. I also wish to thank the many editors of *Feminist Studies* who freely gave of their time in order that these essays, when they were first published, would be an enduring contribution to lesbian studies. Brenda Ruby was an invaluable production assistant; many thanks for her prompt and efficient help. This introduction is a revised and shorter version of "Lesbian History: All Theory and No Facts or All Facts and No Theory?" *Radical History Review* 60 (Fall 1994), 57–75.

1. Review of *Doris Faber, The Life of Lorena Hickok: ER's Friend* (New York: Morrow, 1980), in *Feminist Studies* 6/3 (Fall 1980): 510.

2. Sheila Jeffreys makes this point from a different political perspective from mine in "Does It Matter If They Did It?" in *Not a Passing Phase: Reclaiming Lesbians in History, 1840–1985,* ed. Lesbian History Group (London: The Woman's Press, 1989), 19–28.

3. "Sexuality and Power: A Review of Current Work in the History of Sexuality," *Feminist Studies* 8 (Spring 1982): 150–51.

4. Judith Bennett, "The L-word in Women's History," unpub. paper (October 1990). I have not mentioned bisexuality. As Elisabeth D. Daümer has recently said, for a bisexual, falling in love with a woman does not seem like "a truer, more authentic self ha[s] surfaced," but instead it is "the exhilaration of being offered a choice that she had not known—or felt—to exist." See her "Queer Ethics, or The Challenge of Bisexuality to Lesbian Ethics," *Hypatia* 7/4 (Fall 1992): 99.

5. The most influential critics for these perspectives have been Judith Butler in *Gender Trouble: Feminism and the Subversion of Identity* (New York: Routledge, 1990) and Sue-Ellen Case, "Towards a Butch-Femme Aesthetic," *Discourse* 11/1 (1988–89): 55–73. For a discussion of the importance of "the third sex," see Marjorie Garber's *Vested Interests* (New York: Routledge, 1991).

6. Adrienne Rich, "Compulsory Heterosexuality and Lesbian Existence," *Signs* (5/4 (Summer 1980): 648–49.

7. Doris Sherwood, *Harriet Hosmer: American Sculptor, 1830–1908* (Columbia: University of Missouri Press, 1991), 169–71, 270–73.

8. Eve Kosofsky Sedgwick, *Epistemology of the Closet* (Berkeley: University of California Press, 1990), 7–8.

9. Annamarie Jagose, "Springing Miss Wade: *Little Dorrit* and a Hermeneutics of Suspicion," unpub. paper (1993).

10. The best-known argument for this position is Lillian Faderman's in *Surpassing the Love of Men: Romantic Friendship and Love between Women from the Renaissance to the Present* (New York: William Morrow, 1981), and her essentially unchanged position in *Odd Girls and Twilight Lovers: A History of Lesbian Life in Twentieth-Century America* (New York: Columbia University Press, 1991). See also the ways in which these generalizations have been unproblematically accepted by literary critics such as Tess Cosslett, *Woman to Woman: Female Friendship in Victorian Fiction* (Brighton: Harvester, 1988), and Betty T. Bennett, *Mary Diana Dods: A Gentleman and a Scholar* (New York: William Morrow, 1991).

11. See her *Daring to Be Bad: Radical Feminism in America, 1967–75* (Minneapolis: University of Minnesota Press, 1989).

12. A sense of finding one's "true identity" as a butch or a femme, particularly in opposition to 1970s feminism characterizes many of the "coming-out" stories in *The Persistent Desire: A Femme-Butch Reader*, ed. Joan Nestle (Boston: Alyson Publications, 1992).

13. See Jan Clausen's "My Interesting Condition: What Does It Mean When a Lesbian Falls in Love with a Man?" *Outlook* 2/3 (Winter 1990): 10ff.

14. Joseph Leach, *Bright Particular Star: The Life and Times of Charlotte Cushman* (New Haven: Yale University Press, 1970), 188 and passim.

15. William King's *The Toast*, a mock-heroic epic written after he had lost a debt case to the Duchess, is discussed by Emma Donoghue, "Imagined More Than Women: Lesbians as Hermaphrodites, 1671–1766," *Women's History Review* 2/2 (1993): 210.

16. See Smith-Rosenberg's ground-breaking "The Female World of Love and Ritual: Relations between Women in Nineteenth-Century America," originally published in 1975, and reprinted in her *Disorderly Conduct: Visions of Gender in Victorian America* (New York: Alfred Knopf, 1985), 53–76, and my "Distance and Desire: English Boarding School Friendships, 1870–1920," originally published in 1984, and reprinted in *Hidden from History: Reclaiming the Gay and Lesbian Past*, ed. Martin Bauml Duberman, Martha Vicinus, and George Chauncey, Jr. (New York: New American Library, 1989), 212–29.

17. *Boots of Leather, Slippers of Gold: The History of a Lesbian Community* (New York: Penguin, 1993).

18. See especially the highly influential *This Bridge Called My Back: Writings of Radical Women of Color*, ed. Cherríe Moraga and Gloria Anzaldúa (Watertown, Mass.: Persephone Press, 1981). See also the critique of coming-out stories by Biddy Martin, "Lesbian Identity and Autobiographical Difference[s]," in *The Lesbian and Gay Studies Reader*, ed. Henry Abelove, Michèle Aina Barale, and David M. Halperin (New York: Routledge, 1993), 274–93.

19. Sedgwick, p. 1.

20. Lisa Duggan, "Making It Perfectly Queer," *Socialist Review* 22/1 (Jan.–March 1992): 26–27.

21. This debate is summarized in the introduction to *Hidden from History: Reclaiming the Gay and Lesbian Past*, ed. Martin Duberman, Martha Vicinus, and George Chauncey, Jr. (New York: New American Library, 1989), 1–13. Eve Kosofsky Sedgwick suggests that most of us hold two contradictory notions of homosexuality simultaneously, both an essential identity and a socially constructed sense of "gayness." She labels these "minoritizing" and "universalizing." See Sedgwick, 1, 9, 86–87.

22. Judith Butler, "Imitation and Gender Insubordination," in *Inside/Out: Lesbian Theories, Gay Theories*, ed. Diana Fuss (New York: Routledge, Chapman & Hall, 1991), 13–15. The running head to this essay gives a better sense of its contents than the title: "Decking Out: Performing Identities."

23. See not only "Imitation and Gender Subordination," but also her *Gender Trouble*. See also Sue-Ellen Case.

24. Kath Weston, "Do Clothes Make the Woman?: Gender, Performance Theory, and Lesbian Eroticism," *Genders* 17 (Fall 1993): 7.

25. Weston, 13.

26. This point has been made earlier by Stephen Epstein, "Gay Politics, Ethnic Identity: The Limits of Social Constructionism," *Socialist Review* 93/94 (May–August 1987): 9–54; Carole Vance, "Social Construction Theory: Problems in the History of Sexuality," in *Homosexuality, Which Homosexuality?* ed. Dennis Altman et al. (London: Gay Men's Press, 1989), 13–34; and Teresa de Lauretis, "Sexual Indifference and Lesbian Representation," *Theatre Journal* 40/2 (May 1988): 155–77.

27. Biddy Martin, "Sexual Practice and Changing Lesbian Identities," in *Destabilizing Theory: Contemporary Feminist Debates*, ed. Michèle Barrett and Anne Phillips (Stanford: Stanford University Press, 1992), 106–107. I am indebted to Marlon Ross for reminding me of Martin's argument.

28. Martin, "Sexual Practice," 104–105.

29. In "Critically Queer," *GLQ* 1/1 (1993): 17–32, Butler partially responds to critics who have called her work ahistorical.

30. See George Chauncey, Jr., "From Sexual Inversion to Homosexuality: Medicine and the Changing Conceptualization of Female Desire," *Salmagundi* 58–59 (Fall/Winter 1982–83): 114–46.

31. For a discussion of the implications of this, see Jacqueline Rose, *Sexuality in the Field of Vision* (London: Verso, 1986), 227–28.

32. De Lauretis, 177.

33. Lisa M. Walker, "How to Recognize a Lesbian: The Cultural Politics of Looking Like What You Are," *Signs* 18/4 (Summer 1993): 868, 888. See also Shane Phelan, "(Be)Coming Out: Lesbian Identity and Politics," *Signs* 18/4 (Summer 1993): 765–90, and Daümer's critique of lesbian identity ethics from a bisexual's perspective (note 2).

34. Elizabeth Barrett Browning to Arabel Moulton-Browning, her sister, 22 October 1852. Quoted by Sherwood, 41.

35. Quoted in Elizabeth Mavor, *The Ladies of Llangollen* (London: Michael Joseph, 1971), 74.

36. Esther Newton, "The Mythic Mannish Lesbian: Radclyffe Hall and the New Woman," in Duberman et al., 286.

37. Faderman, 249. This section reprints her well-known "The Morbidification of Love between Women by 19th-Century Sexologists," *The Journal of Homosexuality* 4 (1978): 73–90.

38. See Faderman, passim, but see also my own cautious "Distance and Desire: English Boarding School Friendships, 1870–1920," in Duberman et al., 212–29.

39. Terry Castle, *The Apparitional Lesbian: Female Homosexuality and Modern Culture* (New York: Columbia University Press, 1993), 19.

PART I

Explorations

THE ESSAYS IN this section all explore forgotten, unnoticed, or neglected lesbian figures in literature, history, and literary history. The identification of lost lesbians continues to be an important part of lesbian history, as we become more sensitive to archival sources, oral history, and creative work by women who felt that they could speak only in metaphor or other code about a tabooed subject. Each essay offers a critique of our present understanding of female sexuality. Some examine how we have misinterpreted the past, so as to underplay the fear of female sexuality, or in order to create a particular, defined lesbian subjectivity. Alternatively, we have ignored the ubiquitous homophobia of so many social institutions, rather than acknowledge the pervasive fear of lesbian sexuality. The essays in "Explorations" explore the various ways in which a lesbian sexual identity can be unstable and unseen, yet be a palpable presence. Such a situation is both enabling, for women could love each other unnoticed, and disabling, for women together were always suspect. These paradoxes are explored in each of the essays that follow.

Akasha (Gloria) Hull's pioneering discussion of her discovery of the bisexuality of the Harlem Renaissance poet Alice Dunbar-Nelson opened new perspectives on the writing of biography and the world of black intellectual women. It remains a model of exploratory writing, claiming neither too much—Dunbar-Nelson was very much of her time, race, and class—nor too little—Dunbar-Nelson was neither ignorant of nor unwilling to acknowledge her passionate feelings. Her essay complements Elizabeth Meese's fantasy conversation with the modernist writers Virginia Woolf and Vita Sackville-West. Meese, like Hull, explores the implications of silence—of society's silencing—of lesbian desire. She interpolates herself into their letters, arguing that "it matters when *lesbian* is not spoken." But then she also concedes the impossibility of language ever rendering the thing known or seen.

When avant-garde women writers of the 1920s could not speak openly, we recognize the importance, and difficulty, of recuperating homosocial relations. This cannot be done effectively, as Moore, Meyer, and Cahn all demonstrate, without also acknowledging the heterosexual world within which women fashion their relationships. Leisa D. Meyer analyzes the wholesale efforts by the government and military leaders to prevent the "stigma" of lesbianism tainting the

Women's Army Corps during and immediately after World War II. Susan K. Cahn explores twentieth-century American women's sports to document the mixture of support and homophobia that characterized a world of physically proud women. Even though many self-identified lesbians were and are attracted to both the military and sports as careers, their personal choices could not, and cannot, be made apart from the pervasive homophobia within each institution. Women apart from men, especially when teamwork is essential, have been, and remain, suspect.

Lisa Moore's revisionary work on three early nineteenth-century texts demonstrates "how powerful a part the category of female sexuality played in the cultural imaginary of the period." She finds a tension between generally recognized romantic friendships and erotic intimacy between women; rather than an easy acceptance of women's emotional ties to each other, Moore documents a pervasive sense of unease. This unease is repeated in the modern detective fiction that Anne Herrmann examines. Just as Moore questions our model of a sunny past for romantic friendships, Herrmann suggests the limitations of current models of lesbian subjectivity. She demonstrates through three contemporary novels the varied ways in which lesbian eroticism is made visible to the reader, even though it is repeatedly misinterpreted or unnoticed by other characters in each novel.

1

Researching Alice Dunbar-Nelson

A Personal and Literary Perspective

Akasha (Gloria) Hull

Soon after I began teaching one of my first Black American literature courses a few years ago, a student in the class—a young Black woman—came up to me after a session on Paul Laurence Dunbar and told me that she knew a lady in the city who was his niece. While I was digesting that information, she ran on, saying something about Dunbar, his wife Alice, the niece, the niece's collection of materials about them, and ended by stressing that there was, as she put it, "a *lot* of stuff." From that unlikely, chance beginning has developed my single most significant research undertaking—one which has led me into the farthest reaches of Black feminist criticism and resulted in new literary scholarship and exhilarating personal growth.

This essay is a description of that process of researching and writing about Alice Dunbar-Nelson. It is only my own, one Black woman's experience, but in a certain limited sense, it can also be regarded as something of a "case study" of Black feminist scholarship. We need to uncover and (re)write our own multi-storied history and talk to one another as we are doing so. I emerged from (not to say survived) this particular experience with insights relevant to myself, to Dunbar-Nelson as woman and writer, and to the practice of Black women's literary criticism.

At the end of that first conversation, the student promised to introduce me to Ms. Pauline A. Young—Dunbar's niece by his marriage to her mother's sister—but somehow this never happened. A year or so passed, and I finally met Ms. Young after she saw me on a local television program during which I discussed her "Aunt Alice," and she afterwards called the producer. By this time,

Feminist Studies 6, no. 1 (Summer 1980). © 1980 by Gloria T. Hull. This essay is from *Black Women's Studies*, ed. Gloria T. Hull, Patricia Bell Scott, and Barbara Smith (Old Westbury, N.Y.: The Feminist Press, 1981).

I had begun a serious study of early twentieth-century Black women poets, including Alice Dunbar-Nelson, and was convinced that she was an important and fascinating figure who warranted more than the passing attention which she had heretofore received.

A good deal of this attention focused upon her as the wife of Paul Laurence Dunbar (1872–1906), America's first nationally recognized Black poet. Nevertheless, on her own merits, Alice Dunbar-Nelson was an outstanding writer and public person. She was born in New Orleans in 1875, grew up and taught school in the city, and was prominent in its Black society, especially in musical and literary circles. She moved north, finally settling in Wilmington, Delaware in 1902 where she remained until shortly before her death in 1935. From this base, she achieved local and national renown as a platform speaker, clubwoman, and political activist. She associated with other leaders such as W. E. B. DuBois, Mary Church Terrell, and Leslie Pinckney Hill. In addition, she was a writer all through her life. She poured out newspaper columns, published many stories and poems, the bulk of which appeared in two books and in magazines like *Crisis* and *Collier's*, and edited two additional works.

Knowing what I had already learned about Dunbar-Nelson, I was more than eager to become acquainted with Ms. Young and her materials. When I did, I was astounded. There in the small cottage where she lived was a trove of precious information—manuscript boxes of letters, diaries, and journals; scrapbooks on tables; two unpublished novels and drafts of published works in file folders; clippings and pictures under beds and bookshelves. I looked at it and thought—ruefully and ironically—of how, first, word-of-mouth (our enduring oral tradition) and, then, sheer happenstance accounted for my being there. I also thought of how this illustrated, once more, the distressing fact that much valuable / unique / irreplaceable material on women, and especially minority women writers, is not bibliographed and / or publicized, is not easily accessible, and is moldering away in unusual places.

In order to use this collection, I had to impose myself and become a bit of a nuisance. Being a Black woman certainly helped me here; but, even so, Ms. Young was understandably careful about her documents. She never told me exactly everything she had (indeed, she may not have remembered it all herself) and allowed me to see it a little at a time until gradually I gained her confidence, got the run of the house, learned what was there, and began to use it. As I did so, my good fortune became even more apparent. This was the only place where some of these materials existed. They will probably be willed to the Moorland-Spingarn Research Center at Howard University in Washington, D.C., and then scholars will have to wait some years before they are sorted, catalogued, and readied for public use.

Ms. Young herself is a retired librarian and Delaware historian—which partly accounts for her consciousness of the worth of her holdings. Her years of trained habit also, no doubt, resulted in her adding many of the dates and sources on what would otherwise have been tantalizingly anonymous pictures and pieces of newsprint. In general, Ms. Young proved to be one of the biggest resources of all. With her memories and knowledge, she could share family history, identify people and references, and give invaluable information about their relationship to her aunt which no one else could provide. Once I puzzled for two days over the name of a companion in Alice's diaries only to learn finally from Ms. Young that it was the family dog.

Our personal relationship was even more charged and catalytic in ways which benefited us as individuals and further enhanced the work that we were doing. Interacting, we moved from cordiality to closeness. Several factors could have hindered or even stopped this development—the most elemental being Ms. Young's instinctive protectiveness of her aunt and family. Although her feelings probably encompassed some ambivalence (and possibly more difficult unresolved emotions), these had been softened by time until her most powerful motivations were admiration and the desire to see her aunt get her due. Other complicating factors could have been the generational differences of perspective between us, and whatever undercurrent of feeling could have resulted from the fact that my writing on her aunt fulfilled a wish which unpropitious external circumstances had made it harder for Ms. Young herself to realize.

What tied us together was our common bond of radical Blackness and shared womanhood. We were two Black women joined together by and for a third Black woman / writer whose life and work we were committed to affirming. Our building of trust and rapport was crucial to this whole process. Despite some rough spots, it enabled us to relate to each other in a basically honest, usually up-front manner, and to devise means (both informal and legal) for apportioning the labor and the credit.

The episode which most challenged—but ultimately proved—our relationship was the question of how her aunt's sexuality should be handled. When I discovered while editing Dunbar-Nelson's diary that her woman-identification extended to romantic liaisons with at least two of her friends, I imparted this information to Ms. Young. Her genuinely surprised response was "Oh, Aunt Alice," and then immediately, "Well, we don't have to leave this in!" The two of us talked and retalked the issue. I assured her over and over again that these relationships did not besmirch Dunbar-Nelson's character or reputation or harm anyone else, that there is nothing wrong with love between women, that her attraction to women was only one part of her total identity and did not wipe out the other aspects of her other selves, and that, finally, showing her and the

diary as they in fact were was simply the right thing to do. I knew that everything was fine when at last Ms. Young quipped, "Maybe it will sell a few more
books," and we both laughed. Inwardly, I rejoiced that, at least, this one time,
this one Black woman / writer would be presented without the lies and distor-
tions which have marked too many of us.

Studying Dunbar-Nelson brought many such surprises and insights. Their
cumulative meaning can be stated in terms of her *marginality*, on the one hand,
and her *power*, on the other—a dual concept which suggests a way of talking not
only about her, but also about other Black women writers singly or as a group.
First of all, Dunbar-Nelson has usually been seen as the wife of America's first
famous Black poet who incidentally "wrote a little" herself. This is a situation
which those of us who research minority and / or women writers are familiar
with—having to rescue these figures from some comfortable, circumscribed
shadow and place them in their own light. Furthermore, Dunbar-Nelson's basic
personal status in the world as a Black woman was precarious. On the economic
level, for instance, she always had to struggle for survival and psychic necessi-
ties. That this was so graphically illustrates how the notion of her, and other
individuals, as "genteel" and "bourgeoise" needs revision. Generally, Black
women occupy an ambiguous relationship with regard to class. Even those who
are educated, "middle-class" and professional, and who manage to become
writers almost always derive from and / or have firsthand knowledge of working or "lower"-class situations. Also, being Black, they have no entrenched and
comfortable security in even their achieved class status (gained via breeding,
education, culture, looks, etc., and not so much by money). And, being women,
their position is rendered doubly tangential and complex. Dunbar-Nelson revealed these contradictions in the dichotomy between her outward aristocratic
bearing, and the intimate realities of her straitened finances and private fun.

Her determination to work in society as a writer also made her vulnerable.
Things were not set up for her, a *Black woman*, to make her living in this way.
This had to do with the avenues of publication that were open to her and the
circles of prestige from which she was automatically excluded. When she
needed one most, she was not able to get a job with even *Crisis* or the National
Association for the Advancement of Colored People, of a Black newspaper or
press service—her excellent qualifications notwithstanding. She was compelled
to always accept or create low-paying employment for herself, and to carry it
out under the most trying conditions.

Only the power emanating from within herself, and strengthened by certain external networks of support, enabled Dunbar-Nelson to transcend these
destructive forces. Her mother, sister, and nieces in their inseparable, female-
centered household constituted a first line of resistance (sometimes in conjunc-

tion with her second husband). Then came other Black women of visible achievement such as Edwina B. Kruse, Georgia Douglas Johnson, and Mary McLeod Bethune with whom she associated. In varying ways, they assured each other of their sanity and worth, and collectively validated their individual efforts to make the possible real. Yet, in the end, Dunbar-Nelson had to rely on her own power—the power of her deep-seated and cosmic spirituality, and the power that came from the ultimately unshakable inner knowledge of her own value and talent.

Everything I have been saying illustrates the Black feminist critical approach which I used in researching Dunbar-Nelson. Having said this much, I am tempted to let the statement stand without further elaboration because, for me at least, it is much easier to do this work than to talk about the methodological principles undergirding it. There is the danger of omitting some point which is so fundamental and / or so integrally a part of the process and of oneself as to feel obvious. And, with so much feminist theory being published, there is the risk of sounding too simple or repetitive.

Very briefly, then, the most basic tenets are: 1) everything about the subject is important for a total understanding and analysis of her life and work; 2) the proper scholarly stance is engaged rather than "objective"; 3) the personal (both the subject's and the critic's) *is* political; 4) description must be accompanied by analysis; 5) consciously maintaining at all times the angle of vision of a person who is both Black and female is imperative, as is the necessity for a class-conscious, anticapitalist perspective; 6) being principled requires rigorous truthfulness and "telling it all"; 7) research and criticism is not an academic or intellectual game, but a pursuit with social meanings rooted in the "real world." I always proceeded from the assumption that Dunbar-Nelson had much to say to us and, even more importantly, that dealing honestly with her could, in a more-than-metaphoric sense, "save" some Black woman's life—as being able to write in this manner about her had, in a very concrete way, "saved" my own.

It goes without saying that I approached her as an important writer and her work as genuine literature. Probably as an (over?) reaction to the condescending, witty, but empty, British urbanity of tone which is a hallmark of traditional white male literary scholarship (and which I intensely dislike), I usually discuss Dunbar-Nelson with level high seriousness—and always with caring. Related to this are my slowly-evolving attempts at being so far unfettered by conventional style as to write creatively, even poetically, if that is the way the feeling flows. Here, the question of audience is key. Having painfully developed these convictions and a modicum of courage to buttress them, I now include/visualize everybody (my department chair, the promotion and tenure committee, my mother and brother, my Black feminist sisters, the chair of Afro-American studies, lovers, colleagues, friends) for each organic article, rather than write sneaky, schizophrenic essays from under two or three different hats.

In the final analysis, I sometimes feel that I am as ruthlessly unsparing of Dunbar-Nelson as I am of myself. And the process of personal examination is very much the same. For a Black woman, being face-to-face with another Black woman makes the most cruel and beautiful mirror. This is as true in scholarly research as it is on the everyday plane. Once I was dissecting an attitude of Dunbar-Nelson's, of which I disapproved, to a dear friend who has known me all of our adult lives. He gave me a bemused look and said, "You can't stand her because you're too much like her." I had never thought of it in quite those exact terms. Then, I rose to her / my / our defense.

However, it is true that Dunbar-Nelson and I are locked in uneasy sisterhood. On the one hand, I feel identity, our similarities, and closeness. On the other, there are differences, ambivalence, and critical distance. Superficially, one can see such commonalities as the facts that we were both born in Louisiana, lived in Delaware, wrote poetry, engaged in social-political activism, put a lot of energy into our jobs, appreciated our own accomplishments, did needlework, liked cats, and so on down a rather long list. External differences are equally obvious.

On a deeper level (as my friend perceptively pointed out), our relationship becomes most strenuous when I am forced to confront in Dunbar-Nelson those things about myself which I do not relish—a tendency toward egoistic stubbornness, and toward letting oneself get sidetracked by the desire for comfortably assimilated acceptance, to divulge but two examples. Seeing my faults in her and, beyond that, seeing how they relate to us as Black women, fuels my efforts at self-improvement. Nevertheless, her most enduring role-model effect is positive, inspirational. I think of her existence from its beginnings to the eventual scattering of her ashes over the Delaware River and know that she was a magnificent woman.

Now that most of my work on her is over, she is no longer as strong a presence in my life, although she remains a constant. Hanging in the hall is a painting that she owned (a small watercolor given to her by a woman who was her friend-lover), and two of her copper mint-and-nut plates sit among the dishes on a pantry shelf. Alice herself has not deigned to trouble me—which I take as a sign that all is well between us.

2

"Something More Tender Still than Friendship"

Romantic Friendship in Early-Nineteenth-Century England

Lisa Moore

THE GENEALOGY OF contemporary lesbian identities and practices is sharply
attenuated: we know much more about the emergence in the early twentieth century of the term "lesbian" in sexology and popular accounts, and the
women, communities, and texts through which its current meaning has been
constructed, than we do about the historical lineages that made that emergence
possible. Indeed, we have been cautioned by feminist historians not to look for
"lesbians" in the eighteenth and nineteenth centuries; curiously, however, this
caution against anachronism has most often taken the form of an ahistorical
prohibition against reading sex between women in history. In insisting upon
such a reading—upon reading lesbian sex—this essay does not attempt to find
"lesbians" in the early-nineteenth-century texts it examines; rather, these texts
demonstrate how powerful a part the category of female homosexuality played
in the cultural imaginary of the period. Such images, although not representations of "lesbians" as we now understand the term, are nevertheless part of
the history of those representations and as such warrant our careful scrutiny.
The conflicts these texts express and contain have their legacies in the construction both of current lesbian identities, practices, and communities and in the
history of the specific forms of homophobia we struggle with today. As a conceptual category in the early nineteenth century, the possibility of sex between
women played a constitutive role in the three texts examined below: in a domestic novel, in the diary of an early-nineteenth-century British woman who
recorded her sexual intimacies with other women, and in a Scottish legal case

Feminist Studies 18, no. 3 (Fall 1992). © 1992 by Feminist Studies, Inc.

in which two women teachers were accused of "indecent behavior." By reading the tension between "romantic friendship" and female homosexuality
across both fiction and nonfiction, this essay seeks to establish the status of that
tension as a basic, if sometimes unstated, cultural assumption—a linchpin in
the rise to power of both the bourgeois "private" and the bourgeois "public"
spheres. As such, it formed an important part of the construction of specifically
modern versions of sexuality, gender, the body, and the family, and of class and
colonial relations, public order, and the rule of law. By implication, then, if bourgeois culture has a stake in effacing the symbolic role played by female homosexuality in its own rise to power, contemporary feminism has a stake in expos-
ing that role.

The constitution of the category of female homosexuality in these texts is
necessary to two historical processes at work within and outside them: the rise
of domestic fiction over the eighteenth century and its establishment as a ca-
nonical literary genre in the nineteenth century, and the coterminous shift from
an eighteenth-century idea of the self as social and socially obligated to the Romantic investment in the unique individual. Over the course of the eighteenth
century (from Defoe to Richardson to Austen, for example), the novelistic heroine changed from the subject of picaresque and ribald adventures to a more
clearly psychological and moral entity, the repository of the novel's charactero-
logical realism and the guarantee of its virtuous and didactic status. The novel
also begins to focus, not on economically and morally marginal figures like
Moll Flanders but on the middle-class family with the domestic woman at its
center. The genre of domestic fiction thus became the story the bourgeoisie told
about itself, the fable that made its rise to power seem the natural and legitimate
result of its greater virtue when compared with the poor or the aristocracy.

The ideological struggle represented by both these processes is visible in
the texts below as a problem of interpretation. Questions of writing, reading,
knowledge, and self-knowledge are the arenas in which this struggle is played
out. Romantic friendship poses a problem of reading in these texts. Although it
is invoked to render relationships between women transparent and accessible
to the purposes of bourgeois patriarchy—heterosexual compassionate marriage,
class and colonial relations, the disciplinary rule of law—it surfaces again and
again as an ambiguous term that raises anxieties in the act of attempting to contain them. At this crucial juncture in the emergence of modern notions of sexual
identity and the self, women's texts (often novels) and women themselves are
linked in the representation of romantic friendship. Both are seen as dangerous
and hard to read in spite and because of their status as marginal, unknowable,
and possibly sexual.

The relationships represented in these texts exemplify what the major feminist historian of intimacy between women, Lillian Faderman, calls "romantic

friendships." According to Faderman, this is the eighteenth-century term for the "love relationships between women" that were known as "Boston marriages" and "sentimental" friendships by the late nineteenth century.[1] Although I find her term useful, my account of how romantic friendship was viewed at the turn of the eighteenth century differs markedly from Faderman's. She claims that romantic friendships were widely approved of and idealized and therefore were never conceived of as sexual, even by romantic friends themselves. My argument, on the other hand, emphasizes the conflict between approving accounts of the chastity of these relationships, virulent denunciations of the dangers of female homosexuality, and self-conscious representations of homosexual desire by women. Faderman's book shares with the other well-known feminist study of the history of women's intimacy, Carroll Smith-Rosenberg's article, "The Female World of Love and Ritual: Relations between Women in Nineteenth-Century America,"[2] the assumption that intimate female friendship of the past, far from being a problematic or contested category, was straightforwardly valued and encouraged by the middle-class society in which it was found. Faderman claims, for example, that romantic friendship in the eighteenth century" signified a relationship that was considered noble and virtuous in every way" (p. 16), and Smith-Rosenberg stresses the extent to which these friendships were "socially acceptable and fully compatible with heterosexual marriage" (p. 34). Such accounts, I would argue, draw very partially on the evidence of how these relationships were viewed by contemporaries. Faderman's and Smith-Rosenberg's studies obscure the wariness and even prohibition that sometimes surrounded women's friendships, leaving us with a flattened notion of contesting constructions of female sexuality in late-eighteenth-century and early-nineteenth-century England.

Many of the limitations of Faderman's and Smith-Rosenberg's arguments spring from their reliance on the category of gender to the exclusion of a systematic consideration of sexuality in their efforts to understand women's intimate friendships. For Faderman, sexuality is a "limited" vantage point from which to regard these relationships, for it is only "in our century that love has come to be perceived as a refinement of the sexual impulse" (p. 19). By dismissing sexuality from her account of romantic friendship, Faderman can forge a link between the women she is studying and the particular lesbian feminist community out of which she is writing—a link that paradoxically refuses to see lesbian community as importantly constituted by sexuality. "In lesbian-feminism," she writes,

> I found a contemporary analog to romantic friendship in which two women were everything to each other and had little connection with men who were so alienatingly and totally different. . . . I venture to guess that

had the romantic friends of other eras lived today, many of them would
have been lesbian-feminists; and had the lesbian-feminists of our day lived
in other eras, most of them would have been romantic friends. (P. 20)

Their (gendered) difference from men, then, rather than their (sexual) desire for
women, draws romantic friends and lesbian feminists to one another. This polemical interpretation of contemporary lesbian-feminist communities and relationships, Faderman makes clear, is an attempt to intervene in the misogynist
medicolegal view, found, for example, in Freud's "Psychogenesis of a Case of
Homosexuality in a Woman,"[3] that lesbians relate to women in the same way
men do, as failed and ridiculous pseudomen. But important as such interventions have been in feminist theory, Faderman's approach serves feminism
poorly. Faderman purports to offer an account of lesbianism as woman-cen-
tered, having nothing to do with men or masculinity (although paradoxically,
it is their difference from men that defines lesbians) and everything to do with
feminism. In such an account, gender becomes the primary analytic category
and sexuality is seen at best as a subcategory of gender and certainly completely
determined by it.

Smith-Rosenberg's argument, although more careful and less polemical,
nonetheless shares this basic analytic grid. She argues that the "emotional segregation of men and women" in nineteenth-century U.S. society produced "a
specifically female world . . . built around a generic and unself-conscious pattern of single-sex or homosocial networks" (p. 35). For her, the basic pattern of
women's interactions was "an intimate mother-daughter relationship" (p. 41),
and she frequently describes the relationships between the women she studies
in familial terms, for example as "sisterly bonds" (p. 39). Thus, although she
takes pains to point out the "intensity and even physical nature" (p. 32) of
women's intimate friendships, Smith-Rosenberg ultimately wants to locate that
physicality within a set of nonsexual, familylike interactions between women.
Like Faderman, Smith-Rosenberg opposes an account of same-sex relationships
that sees them only "in terms of a dichotomy between normal and abnormal."
Instead, she suggests an approach that "would view [these relationships] within
a cultural and social setting rather than from an exclusively individual psychosexual perspective" (p. 28). This relocation from the individual to the social,
for Smith-Rosenberg, is a move from analyses of sexuality to those of gender.
This conceptual reframing, however, obliterates the possibility of an analysis of
sexuality as a phenomenon both distinct from gender and social in its production and effects.

My own exploration of the early-nineteenth-century discourse of romantic
friendship gives priority to the ideological work of sexuality as a social category

related to but distinct from gender. I offer Maria Edgeworth's 1801 novel, *Belinda*, as a symptomatic representation of the contradictory status of the ideology of romantic friendship in the period. Following an examination of the novel, this analysis turns to the diary account of Regency Yorkshire-woman Anne Lister's numerous sexual affairs with women in order to clarify the ways in which women readers of domestic fictions like *Belinda* may have found spaces among the contradictory imperatives of romantic friendship within which to construct themselves as female homosexual characters.[4] Finally, *Woods and Pirie v. Dame Cumming Gordon*, an 1811 Scottish legal case in which two female teachers were accused of having a sexual relationship by one of their pupils, establishes one instance of the way in which this ideology shaped notions of public virtue and legal truth.

Belinda and the "Man-Woman"

Like many eighteenth-century novels[5] of heterosexual love and marriage, Maria Edgeworth's 1801 *Belinda* is named for its heroine. Despite this conventional marker of the marriage plot, however, Belinda's relationships with her suitors are relatively marginal: the men are often absent, relegated by the narrative to the Continent or belatedly summoned by it from the West Indies. Belinda's romantic friendship with Lady Delacour, the rakish woman of the world who launches her into society and finally, precariously, into marriage with Clarence Hervey, pushes the marriage plot to the margins. But the implicit pleasures and explicit dangers of romantic friendship cluster most clearly around the figure of Harriot Freke, the crossdressing "man-woman"[6] whom Belinda supplants as Lady Delacour's intimate friend in the novel's second chapter. This brief discussion of the novel, then, focuses primarily upon this emblematic figure and not upon the more conventional relationship between Lady Delacour and Belinda. For Harriot Freke's displacement from Lady Delacour's affections fails to banish her from the narrative itself. Her several reappearances work to expose the political and moral ruin threatening young ladies who trust too much to intimacy with other women and the grave consequences for society of such relationships. Thus, Belinda's judgment of Mrs. Freke also defines one of the chief didactic aims of the novel itself; she provides "a lesson to young ladies in the choice of female friends" (p. 230).

Lest her functions in the novel be misunderstood, Harriot Freke's name itself signals her unnatural status in the novel's terms. The most important clue to and symptom of her freakishness is her dress. From her first appearance at a masquerade, during which Lady Delacour looks for her dressed as "the widow Brady, in man's clothes" (p. 14), until her final defeat when she is mistaken by

Lady Delacour's gardener for "the fellow . . . who has been at my morello cherry-tree every night" (p. 282) and caught and wounded in the gardener's "man-trap," Harriot Freke exults in dressing like a man. Wearing men's clothes also allows Mrs. Freke to adopt gestures implicitly coded in the novel as "masculine": polishing a pistol on the sleeve of her coat (p. 46), throwing her hat upon the table (p. 204), striking the sole of her boot with her whip (p. 205). An early scene sets up her masculinized position with regard to the heroine as well. Desiring Belinda's presence in her house, Mrs. Freke attempts to "carry her off in triumph" from the home of the virtuous Percivals. All the activity of the attempted elopement is seen to be what Belinda calls the "knight-errantry" of Mrs. Freke; Belinda, whom her would-be rescuer calls a "distressed damsel," can only "draw back" from the spectacle of an active woman. Her masculine activity, of course, is the kind conventionally ridiculed in the domestic novel: Mrs. Freke's movement through a room is the inattentive bluster of the vain buck, like that of Austen's John Thorpe in *Northanger Abbey*.

The chapter in which this scene appears is entitled "The Rights of Woman," and in it Mrs. Freke produces several mutually inconsistent "plump assertions" purporting to represent arguments for the equality of women with men. These "assertions," culminating in her cry of "I hate slavery! Vive la liberté! . . . I'm a champion for the Rights of Woman" (p. 208), are firmly and reasonably opposed by Mr. Percival, who claims to be "an advocate for [women's] happiness" instead of their rights. Harriot Freke's clothing is linked in this chapter to her freedom of movement and her opposition to the "slavery" of women. All are coded as the ineffective dandyism of the failed suitor, and all are made to seem ridiculous and unnatural in a woman.

By ridiculing Harriot Freke, Edgeworth vividly satirizes a whole cluster of proto-Romantic Jacobin ideas—feminism, domestic and political revolution, opposition to slavery, sexual freedom. Harriot Freke's male-parodic behavior, however, links these ideas to the possibility of a female erotic agency directed, not at men but at other women. Harriot Freke is the "wrong" suitor for Belinda, true; but that she could be represented as a suitor at all raises fundamental problems in the novel's attempt to construct the sexuality of the domestic woman. Thus, although Harriot Freke is figured as a joke here, she also poses a danger to Belinda, the danger of inappropriate female friendship. Clearly, to associate with such a woman would compromise Belinda in the eyes of her host and of her suitor, Mr. Vincent, who is also present during the scene. Thus, when Mr. Vincent asks if she is not afraid of making an enemy of Mrs. Freke, Belinda replies, "I think her friendship more to be dreaded than her enmity" (p. 211). Belinda has successfully learned and reproduced the novel's most important stricture about female friendship—that women who attempt to usurp the position of men are not just inappropriate but dangerous friends for young ladies hoping to marry well.

The novel opposes Harriot's freakish courtship of Belinda with Lady Delacour's ladylike attentions, establishing romantic friendship between "normal" feminine women as an appropriate relationship within which the women can express intense romantic feeling. But the passionate language of romantic friendship fails to uphold a stable distinction between the two kinds of intimacy between women. For example, Lady Delacour asks herself: "What was Harriot Freke in comparison with Belinda Portman? Harriot Freke, even whilst she diverted me most, I half despised. But Belinda!—Oh, Belinda! how entirely have I loved—trusted—admired—adored—respected—revered you!" (p. 164). The rivalry and comparison set up here between Harriot and Belinda suggests a troubling equation between two characters who are supposed to represent moral opposites.

The public stakes of "the choice of female friends" become clear in a scene early in the novel. Lady Delacour recounts the many adventures in which she has been involved with Harriot Freke, adventures which culminate in Lady Delacour's being challenged by another woman, Mrs. Luttridge, to a duel. The occasion is an election, in which Lady Delacour and Mrs. Freke are canvassing for one candidate and Mrs. Luttridge for his opponent. Incensed by a caricature Lady Delacour has drawn of her, Mrs. Luttridge is heard to say that "she wished . . . to be a man, that she might be qualified to take proper notice of [Lady Delacour's] conduct" (p. 44). Significantly, the social problem begins with one of reading: Harriot Freke has read an essay by Clarence Hervey on "The Propriety and Necessity of Female Duelling," the argument of which she uses to convince Lady Delacour to duel. Lady Delacour tells Belinda that she is persuaded by "the masculine superiority, as I thought it, of Harriot's understanding," as well as by Harriot's assurance that she "should charm all beholders in male attire." Both Mrs. Luttridge and her second appear in men's clothes as well. As the crossdressed women fire into the air, a mob of the local electorate pours on to the scene. Lady Delacour suddenly realizes that "an English mob is really a formidable thing," especially when she herself is the object of its wrath. She says she is "convinced that they would not have been half so much scandalized if we had boxed in petticoats" (p. 47) rather than dueling in boots and jackets. Their danger increases until Clarence Hervey arrives, driving a herd of pigs; he convinces the mob to follow him in order to race a French man driving a flock of turkeys and diverts the crowd's attention to this nationalistic contest. Lady Delacour's improperly loaded pistol backfires and she sustains a wound to her breast. Everyone else escapes without physical harm, but the political consequences are more serious. "The fate of the election turned upon this duel," Lady

Delacour says. "With true English pigheadedness, they went every man of them and polled for an independent candidate of their own choosing, whose wife, forsooth, was a proper behaved woman" (p. 49).

The force of this scene depends upon the centrality of the novel's—and the period's—anxieties about how improper female friendship can lead women to usurp the positions of men, resulting not only in confused gender and sexual boundaries but also in personal and political violence. These anxieties underscore the simultaneous necessity and impossibility of policing the boundaries of romantic friendship. For although, on the one hand, such a friendship could be argued to guarantee female virtue, because it fixed women's desires and attentions upon one another rather than upon possibly sexual relations with men; on the other hand, female friendship could also result in a dangerous female autonomy from men, even an attempt to take the place of men (in this case by dressing like them or dueling like them).[7] The usurpation of male-gendered clothing and behavior by women, then, produces a dislocation in the social organization of sexuality. The sexual agency made possible by romantic friendship disrupts heterosexual norms, calling into question the gendered terms within which the domestic space is organized. "Masculinity" and "femininity" are revealed as arbitrary social codes rather than as the given essences argued for by domestic fiction. And in the context of the domestic novel, wrenching sexuality from gender in this way sets in motion a whole set of political upheavals that threaten to collapse the tightly knit interrelations of gender, class, nation, and sexuality upon which the novel's authority depends.

Belinda is one of those eighteenth-century novels that uneasily condemn the reading of novels themselves on the grounds that they give their young women readers dangerous ideas about how to act in the world.[8] This self-undermining anxiety spills over into ambivalence about all acts of writing and reading—about who writes, who reads, and what effects these activities have on the susceptible minds of women. In this scene, women reading—Harriot Freke's and Lady Delacour's response to Hervey's essay—has indeed produced women rioting, or women *and* rioting. And this nexus—of autonomous, indecent women and an enraged popular mob—is a potent threat in this novel and, I would argue, in the definition of romantic friendship as well. If inappropriate friendships between women can throw an election and rouse the common people of an English county to protest *en masse*, then the stakes of separating off "virtuous" romantic friendship, in which women's reading is controlled by propriety, from "indecent" female intimacy, which fails to distinguish appropriate texts for women, are high indeed. The explicit anxiety in this scene might be political unrest, but such public consequences were shadowed by the possibility of privatized, sexual indecency between women as well. Both spectacles of rebellion are linked to the fear that in order to mark the boundary betweeen "virtuous" and "indecent" female friendships, one might have actually to represent an indecent character like Harriot Freke in order to condemn her but that such a representation might also have the power, as it does within the text,[9] to entice women to imitate her rather than to turn from her in horror. Such representations, in short, might give female readers access to the very acts and attitudes that the category "romantic friendship" exists to suppress.

Harriot Freke, significantly, is not a duelist here. Throughout the novel, her distanced agency places her outside the world of conventional femininity in which the heterosexual plot of the novel takes place. Appropriately, then, the character who most clearly recognizes her as a transgressor of gender boundaries, bestowing upon her the epithet "man-woman," is the Black slave Juba, whom Mr. Vincent, one of Belinda's suitors, has brought with him from Jamaica. Indeed, it is in her interactions with Juba, placed late in the novel, that the wider ramifications of Mrs. Freke's aberrant status are clearest. Her relationship with Juba pivotally establishes the importance of female sexual "normality" in anchoring not only domestic and familial relations but also class and colonial ones.

The major incident in which Juba takes part begins with a reference to Harriot Freke's characteristically distanced agency in the sexuality of the women around her: "It is somewhat singular that Lady Delacour's faithful friend, Harriot Freke, should be the cause of Mr. Vincent's first fixing his favourable attention on Miss Portman." Juba parks his master's carriage in Mrs. Freke's space. Next,

> Mrs Freke, who heard and saw the whole transaction from her window, said, or swore, that she would make Juba repent of what she called his insolence. The threat was loud enough to reach his ears, and he looked up in astonishment to hear such a voice from a woman. . . . Mr Vincent, to whom Juba, with much simplicity, expressed his aversion of the *man-woman* who lived in the house with him, laughed at the odd manner in which the black imitated her voice and gesture. . . . (Pp. 199–200)

Of course, this scene establishes not only Mrs. Freke's inappropriate masculinity but Juba's appropriate or normal masculinity as well. In retelling the incident to Mr. Vincent, Juba is clearly a man among men, for this moment at least.

Juba's account is the only utterance in which the novel makes Harriot Freke's masculinity explicit; the narrator and other characters allude to qualities which are read, in the context of the novel's conventional construction of femininity, as masculine, but it takes Juba, a character as "freakish" (in the novel's world) as Mrs. Freke herself, to name what is so shocking about her. This pas-

sage draws attention first to his "simplicity," the uncivilized propensity for seeing right to the heart of things manifested in his "astonishment" at hearing a
woman swearing. Because he has not been perverted by the metropolitan fashion that makes Harriot Freke's oddities tolerable in the polite world, he can identify them as repulsive and oxymoronic by demonstrating an instinctual "aversion of the *man-woman*." But equally important is Juba's affinity with her. His
ability to imitate "her voice and gesture" indicates not just the racist notion that
Africans are imitative, monkeylike, but also suggests that, because of his own
"odd manner," Juba can successfully parody Mrs. Freke's. Juba, then, is as freakish in his colonial simplicity as is Harriot Freke in her metropolitan decadence.
Both primitiveness and decadence help define the boundaries of the middle-
class female virtue that is the novel's ideological ground.

At the moment when Juba and Mrs. Freke clash, all the alternative possibilities for representing female sexuality that are being generated and unsuccessfully contained in Belinda's world of female domestic power break out
into the larger national and international space.[10] The incident underscores the
importance of publicly identifying and repudiating Harriot Freke's aberrant
power. Thus, she is punished by being brutally mangled in a "man-trap" set
to catch garden thieves, and the novel insists that as a result of her wound "the
beauty of her legs would be spoiled, and . . . she would never more be able to
appear to advantage in man's apparel" (p. 284). Harriot Freke's body is torn
from the narrative when its compelling power as a freakish spectacle threatens
to overwhelm its exemplary function. We see no more of Harriot when she can
no longer wear men's clothes.

Because the novel's heterosexual plot has been so problematized, the act of
ending the narrative becomes a problem as well. The last lines of the novel are,
paradoxically, not part of a novel at all but a heroic couplet, the kind of summary
statement that often concludes eighteenth-century plays: "Our tale contains a
moral; and no doubt/You all have wit enough to find it out." It is significant that
the final couplet should refuse to identify the novel's "moral." This gesture indicates both the novel's overt concern with moral questions and its inability to
deal coherently with the central ones it raises. The absence of a moral from the
novel's conclusion signals the possibility that these questions have not been
fully recuperated by its awkward and incoherent version of heterosexual clo-
sure. For the linchpin of the novel's moral universe is the purity of its heroine,
a purity guaranteed by the reformation of her intimate friend. Central to this
reformation is Lady Delacour's rejection of Harriot Freke and the sexual irregu-
larity she represents. The novel tries to make this process unproblematic by having Lady Delacour cast off her friend in the second chapter. But because the
novel places the issue of female friendship at the center of so many other sys-

tems of authority, Harriot Freke must be constantly summoned back into the story to demonstrate the threat posed by inappropriate female friendship to gender relations, sexual norms, nationalism, and race and colonel relations—to establish these relations by constructing their opposites in the world in which Harriot Freke might be desirable and powerful.

Reading Novels: A "Fearful Rousing"

Such a fictional world, in which the ridiculed and marginalized female "suitor" has the power to threaten and disrupt the heroine's progress toward heterosexual marriage, has clear links with emerging Romantic notions of the antihero as social outcast. The Jacobin Harriot Freke holds political, social, and sexual views remarkably similar to those of a historical person, Anne Lister, who might have been one of her readers. Lister's diary provides an example of how eighteenth-century ideas about the potential threat of novel reading to female virtue, combined with a Rousseauist investment in individual emotional and sexual singularity, could come together to produce female homosexual desires, practices, and texts. Lister, born in 1791 in West Yorkshire, kept voluminous diaries that recorded details—often in code—of her numerous sexual affairs with women, most frequently with a married woman named Marianne Lawton with whom she was involved for several years. Lister's struggles to understand and justify her own desires are most often struggles over literary interpretation—that is, struggles over reading and the sexual effects of texts.

The effect of domestic fictions like *Belinda* proves most problematic for Lister. In recording her response to such fiction, Lister clearly participates in turn-of-the-century assumptions that inappropriate reading will allow women access to information that might threaten their virtue. She habitually reads novels, sometimes aloud to her friends, sometimes alone. Following an afternoon of reading aloud, Lister notes that the company agreed "that Lady Caroline Lambe's novel, *Glenarvon*, is very talented but a very dangerous sort of book."[11] The danger seems to increase when Lister is alone:

> From 1 to 3, read the first 100pp. vol. 3 *Leontine de Blondheim*. . . . It is altogether a very interesting thing & I have read it with a sort of melancholy feeling, the very germ of which I thought had died forever. I cried a good deal . . . Arlhofe reminds me of of C—[Marianne Lawton's husband], Leontine of M—[Marianne], & Wallerstein of myself. I find my former feelings are too soon awakened & I have, still, more romance than can let me bear the stimulus, the fearful rousing, of novel reading. I must not indulge it. I must keep to graver things and strongly occupy myself with other thoughts and perpetual exertions. I am not happy. I get into what I have

been led with . . . Anne [a woman with whom she had had an affair she kept secret from Marianne]. Oh, that I were more virtuous and quiet. Reflection distracts me & now I could cry like a child but will not, must not give way. (P. 146)

One of the dangers of novel reading, then, is that it might lead one to compare the fictional situation too closely with "real life" and thus create a heightened emotional and sexual state that might work against virtuous determinations like Lister's vow to see no more of Anne. In order to remain "virtuous and quiet," then, one must avoid "the stimulus, the fearful rousing, of novel reading."

Nonfiction, however, seems to produce for Lister a less problematic—although paradoxically more socially disruptive—form of identification. In attempting to explain to her own satisfaction her continuing devotion to Marianne, Lister claims that, like Rousseau, she must follow her own genius: "Je sens mon coeur, et je connais les hommes. Je ne suis fait comme aucun de ceux que j'ai vus; j'ose croire n'être fait comme aucun de ceux qui existent. Rousseau's *Confessions*, volume and page, first."[12] Instead of producing confusing sensory and emotional responses, as did fiction, Rousseau's memoir allows Lister a more respectable form of identification with a "moral" nonfictional text. Significantly, fiction is coded as both female (inasmuch as Lady Caroline Lamb is the only novelist mentioned) and morally dangerous in Lister's diary. By distancing herself from the dangerous femininity of fiction and instead strategically rereading Rousseau's masculinist memoir, Lister is able to align her desires with those of a central cultural figure, genre, and text. Like Harriot Freke's reading of Hervey's essay on female dueling, Lister's appropriation of male-authored texts allows her to produce a self-representation that exceeds the limits on female behavior these texts themselves work to produce. Lister's account of her desire for Marianne assumes that female homosexuality, as something that can be explained with recourse to Rousseau's notion of the true and unique self, lies at the heart of mainstream cultural concerns.

Crucially, then, Lister's most explicit statement of self-conscious identity, a statement that has the force of a Romantic manifesto, involves an even more concrete rearrangement of a male-authored text. In 1821, she writes:

Burnt . . . Mr Montague's farewell verses that no trace of any man's admiration may remain. It is not meet for me. I love, & only love, the fairer sex & thus beloved by them in turn, my heart revolts from any other love than theirs. (P. 145)

Like Harriot Freke adopting men's clothes in order to proposition the heroine, Lister (who also crossdressed) skillfully pillages the male-authored texts available to her in order to authorize her desires, transforming these masculine accoutrements into something else altogether: the conditions of production of female homosexual character. Whether swearing off literature, quoting it, or burning it, Lister's interaction with texts, as manifested in her own writing, produces and defines female homosexuality as an early-nineteenth-century conceptual category.

Significantly, Lister herself is skeptical of the theory that romantic friendship was completely determined by the ideology of female sexual passivity. When Marianne writes to ask her, after a visit to the famous Ladies of Llangollen,[13] whether she thinks that relationship "had always been platonic," Lister records the following reply:

> I cannot help thinking that surely it was not platonic. Heaven forgive me, but I look within myself and doubt. I feel the infirmity of our nature & hesitate to pronounce such attachments uncemented by something more tender still than friendship. (P. 210)

For Lister, sexual love between women was not only possible but also likely in the context of romantic friendship.

"Hindoo Laws": Female Homosexuality and the Colonial Body

The social importance of the category romantic friendship is made explicit in a Scottish legal case that was tried in 1811, just ten years after the publication of *Belinda*. The facts of the case are briefly these: Jane Pirie and Marianne Woods met in 1802 in Edinburgh and became intimate friends immediately.[14] In 1809 they opened a boarding school for young gentlewoman. In November 1810, the grandmother of one of their pupils and one of Edinburgh's most influential noblewoman, Lady Cumming Gordon, withdrew her granddaughter, Jane Cumming, from the school for what she called "very serious reasons" ("State of the Process," p. 135) and recommended that several other families do the same. Within a few days, the school was emptied. In May 1811, Pirie and Woods brought a charge of libel against Lady Cumming Gordon. When the hearings began, Lady Cumming Gordon's lawyer, George Cranstoun, submitted a statement that accused Pirie and Woods of "indecent and criminal practices" ("Petition for Lady Cumming Gordon," p. 2). The central piece of evidence was the following testimony from Jane Cumming, in which she describes what happened one night while she was in the bed she shared with her teacher, Miss Pirie.

> She wakened one night with a whispering, and heard, Miss Pirie say, "O do it darling [punctuation *sic*], and Miss Woods said, "Not to night;" . . . then Miss Pirie pressed her again to come in, and she came in, and she

lay above Miss Pirie . . . Miss Woods began to move, she shook the bed, and she [Cumming] heard [a noise like] . . . putting one's finger in the neck of a wet bottle. . . . [Finally] she heard Miss Woods say to Miss Pirie, "Good night, darling, I think I have put you in the way to get a good sleep to-night." ("State of the Process," pp. 70, 73.)

The libel case was ultimately decided, by a margin of one vote, in favor of Miss Pirie and Miss Woods—that is, the judges decided that they were innocent of the "indecent and criminal practices" of which they had been accused. However, Dame Cumming Gordon successfully petitioned Parliament to excuse the teachers' claims for damages. Unable to support themselves over the nine-year course of the trial, Woods and Pirie had separated, reduced from flourishing businesswomen to the ranks of the genteel poor.

The case turned on the problem of defining romantic friendship. Witnesses were repeatedly asked if they had ever seen the teachers "kissing, caressing, and fondling each other, more than . . . could have resulted from ordinary female friendship" ("State of the Process," p. 49). The lawyer for the two women played heavily on the outrage to virtuous friendship that the charges represented.

> They little thought, that that warm and interesting mutual regard, which springs from the finest and purest feelings of the human heart, and can only exist in pure and virtuous breasts, should be to them the source of the foulest condemnation, or be converted into the means of fixing upon them an imputation of the blackest and most disgusting atrocity. ("Petition of Miss Marianne Woods and Miss Jane Pirie," p. 3)

The heavy stress on notions of fineness, purity, and virtue in these statements indicates the importance of a naturalized norm of emphatically nonsexual friendship between women to which the relationship between Woods and Pirie is implicitly compared. This is the view to which Faderman and Smith-Rosenberg refer in their analyses. The language used to invoke this norm reveals that one of its major functions is to make "virtue" a quality "natural" to women—that is, to render women's sexuality and sexual agency *un*ordinary, complicated, devious, unnatural, impure, and vicious. But the necessity of reiterating these terms, often within the same sentence, points to the lawyer's anxiety over the instability of the norm that he must nonetheless invoke as stable and unproblematic.

The very possibility that sexual acts could occur between women in the absence of a man dislodged a whole system of interpreting women's "ordinary" acts and desires. Lord Meadowbank, indeed emphasizes what poor strategy it was for teachers to sleep with pupils, rather than each other, during the school term if they really wanted to have sex together. This argument rests on the assumption that for teachers to sleep in the same bed would have been a perfectly ordinary occurrence that would raise no suspicions—yet it also reveals the capacity of acts of "ordinary" female friendship to mask the indecent acts that were supposed to be their antithesis. Lord Meadowbank points out that

> under the unsuspected state of female intercourse and habits in this country, they could have been under no difficulty, had it so pleased them, so to have arranged the household, as to have afforded them ample opportunity of every possible indulgence, without suspicion of any impropriety. ("Speeches of the Judges," p. 9)

Inadvertently, this statement demonstrates the impossibility of successfully scrutinizing female friendship, because its "unsuspected state" makes its sexual status unknowable, at least to the male judicial observer. If you can't tell from the outside whether "female intercourse and habits" might be masking "every possible indulgence," how can you rely upon the "unsuspected state" of such habits as the basis for a legal decision?

This challenge to cultural assumptions about sexless female friendship posed an interpretive problem for the judges—the problem of how to read women's representations of female homosexual desires. In their speeches, the judges repeatedly figure the very existence of this problem and the ambiguities it raises about female heterosexual virtue as threats, not just to the students in the boarding school but also to society itself. Lord Meadowbank asserts that besides the students, the teachers, and Lady Cumming Gordon,

> there is a fourth party whose interest is deeply at stake, I mean the public: for the virtues, the comforts, and the freedom of domestic intercourse, mainly depend on the purity of female manners, and that, again, on their habits of intercourse remaining, as they have hitherto been,—free from suspicion. [Thus your Lordships] have taken every precaution within your power, though necessarily with small hopes of success, to confine this cause by the walls of the Court, and keep its subject and its investigation unknown in general society. ("Speeches of the Judges," p. 2)

The difficulty for the judges was to try to determine which was the more unlikely: that a schoolgirl had imagined her teachers acting together in such a way as to "supply the absence or neglect of males" ("Speeches of the Judges," p. 16) or that the teachers themselves had not only imagined but carried out such acts. Thus, the question of the "truth" of the case comes to rest on a choice between, not women's sexual passivity and their agency but on two equally problematic forms of that agency.

This impasse threatened to disrupt a system of cultural authority in which women's sexual virtue held in place and legitimated the very forms of gender, class, and national power which authorized the court's investigation itself.[15] In an attempt to shore up the "natural" status of passive female sexual virtue and hence guarantee their own authority, the judges looked to factors other than gender to shift the origin of the no-win choice between Jane Cumming's "truth" and that of her teachers. Thus, evidence that women could imagine or carry out sexual acts without the presence of a man placed an added burden on the explanatory powers of race and coloniality to locate the origins of the problem of stable female virtue.

Significantly, Jane Cumming, the pupil who first described the teachers' relationship to her grandmother, had been born in India of an Indian mother and a Scottish father, Lady Cumming Gordon's son. Dark-skinned and illegitimate, she spent the first several years of her life in India with her mother's family. Several of the judges felt that her "Hindoo" background was the source of her story. Lord Meadowbark refers to "two Hindoo laws" which, in his mind, establish the strictly foreign character of sex between women by marking out the activity of the deviant foreign body.

> There is no sort of doubt, that women of a peculiar conformation, from an elongation of the *clitoris*, are capable both of giving and receiving venereal pleasure, in intercourse with women, by imitating the functions of a male in copulation; and that in some countries this conformation is so common, that circumcision of the *clitoris* is practised as a religious rite . . . and I dare say, it is also true enough, that as a provocative to the use of the male, women have been employed to kindle each other's lewd appetites. Nor is it to be disputed, that by means of tools, women may artificially accomplish the venereal gratification. . . . But if tools and tribadism [clitoral penetration] are out of the question, then I state as the ground of my incredulity . . . the important fact, that the imputed vice has been hitherto unknown in Britain. ("Speeches of the Judges," pp. 7, 8)

Ultimately, most of the judges were to use this argument—that race determines sexuality more importantly than does gender, at least in the case of deviance—to acquit the two Scottish teachers. Of course, Pirie and Woods were never examined to determine whether they bore the "peculiar conformation" that would make it possible for them to have sex together, according to this theory: rather, their "normality" was assumed on the basis of their race. The possibility that British female bodies or British female erotic imaginations were capable of sexual congress with each other was thus diverted in the trial through recourse to a racist myth of a deviant, sexualized Eastern woman's body which, like her sexual conversation, was unnaturally similar to a man's.

Conclusion: Frekish Friendship

The formal and ideological difficulties posed by the necessary function Edgeworth's character Harriot Freke plays in defining domestic female virtue arise from the capacity of the category "romantic friendship" not only to manage and contain women's nonmarital desires and their representations but also to incite and sometimes fulfill them. In the context of the Scottish judges' fears about public safety and Anne Lister's potent construction of herself as a sexual agent, Edgeworth's novel cannot convincingly dismiss Harriot Freke's power and example through satire and ridicule. The figure of Harriot Freke invokes both the spectacle raised by the Woods-Pirie case, the spectacle of the sexual recolonization of British women's intimate relationships by subaltern "indecency," and the potential, made manifest in Anne Lister's diaries, that women's reading and writing could create a homosexual agency for women. The dangerous appeal of Harriot Freke's presence in *Belinda*, both for the women within the narrative and the women readers outside it, is marked by the novel's attempts to mask her freedom and power by mediating her agency in the chaotic actions she is nonetheless blamed for causing. Nancy Armstrong argues that in eighteenth- and nineteenth-century culture, the domestic woman "exercised a form of power . . . the power of domestic surveillance."[16] Harriot Freke, as the figure for indecent female friendship, plays the necessary Other to bourgeois women in the privatized domestic space where they hold and exert this power. However, she also threatens the sanctity of that space by revealing the conflict of the several systems of authority based on gender, class, and race that make it possible.

Significantly, it is the production of specifically sexual figures within this female-gendered space that disrupts these systems. It is only by reading these sexual figures—reading them precisely as sexual—that this important tool in the bourgeoisie's story about the legitimacy of its own rise to power becomes visible. Female homosexuality, at once produced and banished in the invocation of romantic friendship, provides a unique category with which to analyze a specific moment in the transition from eighteenth-century notions of "character" to the Romantic investment in identity that continues to shape homosexuality and homophobia today. The case of female homosexuality as a specific problem for reading and interpretation has a history distinct both from that of male homosexuality and from that of "women," a history fascinating and important in its own right and crucial to our understanding of the stakes of the wider historical processes that produced it and which it exposes.

Notes

I wish to thank all those whose comments on drafts of this essay helped shape my ideas about Edgeworth, romantic friendship, and lesbian theory: Laura Brown, Mary Jacobus, Laura Mandell, Biddy Martin, Terry Rowden, Charlotte Sussman, and Alok Yadav.

1. Lillian Faderman, *Surpassing the Love of Men: Romantic Friendship and Love between Women from the Renaissance to the Present* (New York: William Morrow, 1981), 16. All references are to this edition; subsequent citations appear in parentheses in the text.

2. Carroll Smith-Rosenberg, "The Female World of Love and Ritual: Relations between Women in Nineteenth-Century America," in *The Signs Reader: Women, Gender, and Scholarship*, ed. Elizabeth Abel and Emily K. Abel (Chicago and London: University of Chicago Press, 1983). References will be included parenthetically in the text. Despite Smith-Rosenberg's focus on nineteenth-century American women, I consider her account useful for a study of the earlier turn-of-the-nineteenth-century British discourse of romantic friendship for both empirical and theoretical reasons. First, she uses several eighteenth-century examples, and some of the women whose letters and diaries she quotes traveled or lived in England. Second, she uses these case histories to support more general claims about "the long-lived, intimate, loving friendship between women" and its relation to female sexuality more generally (pp. 27, 54).

3. In "Psychogenesis of a Case of Homosexuality in a Woman," Freud says of his patient that "in her behaviour towards her love-object she had throughout assumed the masculine part. . . . She had thus not only chosen a feminine love-object, but had also developed a masculine attitude towards that object." More generally, he ends the essay by describing a "female homosexual" as "a woman who has felt herself to be a man, and has loved in masculine fashion." See Philip Rieff, ed., *Sexuality and the Psychology of Love* (New York: Macmillan, 1963), 141, 159.

4. I use "character" here as a term historically antecedent to what we would now call "identity."

5. Marilyn Butler points out that Edgeworth based her account of London fashionable life in *Belinda* on the stories of her father, Richard Lovell Edgeworth, who had lived in London during the 1770s. Maria Edgeworth had never actually visited the metropolis at the time she wrote this novel in 1800. In the sense that *Belinda* describes the 1770s as if they were the present, it is more clearly an eighteenth-century novel than, for example, the contemporary works of Jane Austen. See Marilyn Butler, *Maria Edgeworth: A Literary Biography* (Oxford: Clarendon Press, 1972), 149.

6. Maria Edgeworth, *Belinda*, Pandora Press Edition (London: Routledge & Kegan Paul, 1986), 200. All references are to this edition; subsequent citations appear in parentheses in the text.

7. The crowd shifts its attention from the duel to the race because Clarence plays on their Gallophobia, exhorting them to help on his pigs "for the love of Old England." Significantly, Harriot Freke had explained their predicament to him in French, presumably so that the crowd wouldn't understand that she was appealing for help. Mrs. Freke is linked to things French at other points during the novel as well, as for example, when she declares herself a champion

for the Rights of Woman with the slogan "Vive la liberté!" And the Frenchness of Lady Delacour's name, as well as her position at the head of a salon of wit and fashion and her independence from her husband, underline the novel's equation between the inappropriate agency
these women wield and their aristocratic, "Frenchified" notions of social relations. Such a rejection of French ideas, always a strain in English popular thinking, was particularly acute for
the bourgeois English in the period following the French Revolution. The middle class distanced itself from both the popular violence of the French lower classes and the luxurious ex-
cesses of the aristocracy in an attempt to reassure itself that such an event would not happen
in England. As Louis Crompton notes, "nowhere did English Francophobia find more impas-
sioned expression than in attitudes toward sex." See his *Byron and Greek Love: Homophobia in
Nineteenth-Century England* (Berkeley: University of California Press, 1985), 4.

8. Janet Todd notes that "the corrupting power of books was a commonplace of eighteenth-century thought" (Janet Todd, *Women's Friendships in Literature* [New York: Columbia
University Press, 1980], 210 n. 16). Nancy Armstrong discusses how, in their moral and educational writings, Maria Edgeworth and her father "accept the view that prevailed during the
eighteenth century, which said fiction behaved subversively and misled female desire" (15).
The danger not just of reading but of reading novels had become so conventional by midcentury that satirizing it could form the major narrative structure of Charlotte Lennox's *The Female
Quixote* (1752) as well as Jane Austen's better-known *Northanger Abbey* (1818), written in the
1790s.

9. After Belinda's rejection of her, Harriot Freke reappears in the novel with another
young lady in her thrall.

10. Thanks to Terry Rowden for helping me formulate this connection.

11. Helena Whitbread, ed., *I Know My Own Heart: The Diaries of Anne Lister, 1791–1840*
(London: Virago Press, 1988), 296. All references are to this edition; subsequent citations appear
in parentheses in the text.

12. Whitbread, 283. Whitbread translates these lines thus: "I know my own heart & I
know men. I am not made like any other I have seen. I dare believe myself to be different from
any others who exist" (frontispiece).

13. Lady Eleanor Butler and Sarah Ponsonby eloped from their matchmaking families in
1778 and lived together in Llangollen, Wales, until Butler's death in 1829. They became something of a tourist attraction and were often held up by contemporaries such as Burke,
Wordsworth, and Southey as exemplars of selfless (because nonsexual) love. However, an account entitled "Extraordinary Female Affection," which appeared in a local Welsh newspaper
in 1790, ridiculed Butler's masculinity and cast doubts on the respectability of the Ladies. Less
public accounts of the relationship, then, tended to be more skeptical of its chastity. See Elizabeth Mavor, ed. *A Year with the Ladies of Llangollen* (London: Penguin Books, 1984).

14. *Miss Marianne Woods and Miss Jane Pirie against Dame Helen Cumming Gordon* (New
York: Arno Press, 1975). This edition is an unedited reprint of the original trial materials, in
which each portion of the testimony is paginated separately. My references will include section
title and page number and will be included parenthetically in the text. See also Lillian Faderman, *Scotch Verdict: "Miss Pirie and Miss Woods v. Dame Cumming Gordon"* (New York: William
Morrow, 1983). This volume consists of excerpts from the trial transcripts, which Faderman
claims are "edited . . . considerably, but always with a concern for the accuracy of the ideas
expressed in the original documents" (iii), interspersed with Faderman's own speculations
about the case. According to Faderman, this is the case upon which Lillian Hellman based her
1934 play, *The Children's Hour*.

15. As Nancy Armstrong points out, the creation of the domestic authority of the virtuous middle-class woman allowed for the emergence of "that middle-class power which does
not appear to be power because it behaves in specifically female ways." See her *Desire and Domestic Fiction: A Political History of the Novel* (London: Oxford University Press, 1987), 26. I would

add that one such way was that judicial authority came to operate on the model of familial authority, as a moral and protective, rather than punitive and coercive, force. Thus, safeguarding virtue—and hence necessarily defining, identifying, and *producing* it—became a matter for the courts as well as the churches.

16. Ibid., 19.

3

From the "Muscle Moll" to the "Butch" Ballplayer

Mannishness, Lesbianism, and Homophobia in U.S. Women's Sport

Susan K. Cahn

I~N~ 1934, *Literary Digest* subtitled an article on women's sports, "Will the Playing Fields One Day Be Ruled by Amazons?" The author, Fred Wittner, answered the question affirmatively and concluded that as an "inevitable consequence" of sport's masculinizing effect, "girls trained in physical education to-day may find it more difficult to attract the most worthy fathers for their children."[1] The image of women athletes as mannish, failed heterosexuals represents a thinly veiled reference to lesbianism in sport. At times, the homosexual allusion has been indisputable, as in a journalist's description of the great athlete Babe Didrikson as a "Sapphic, Broddingnagian woman" or in television comedian Arsenio Hall's more recent witticism, "If we can put a man on the moon, why can't we get one on Martina Navratilova?"[2] More frequently, however, popular commentary on lesbians in sport has taken the form of indirect references, surfacing through denials and refutations rather than open acknowledgment. When in 1955 an *Ebony* magazine article on African American track stars insisted that "off track, girls are entirely feminine. Most of them like boys, dances, club affairs," the reporter answered the implicit but unspoken charge that athletes, especially Black women in a "manly" sport, were masculine manhaters, or lesbians.[3]

The figure of the mannish lesbian athlete has acted as a powerful but unarticulated "bogey woman" of sport, forming a silent foil for more positive, corrective images that attempt to rehabilitate the image of women athletes and resolve the cultural contradiction between athletic prowess and femininity. As a

Feminist Studies 19, no. 2 (Summer 1993) © 1993 by Feminist Studies, Inc.

stereotyped figure in U.S. society, the lesbian athlete forms part of everyday cultural knowledge. Yet historians have paid scant attention to the connection between female sexuality and sport.[4] This essay explores the historical relationship between lesbianism and sport by tracing the development of the stereotyped "mannish lesbian athlete" and examining its relation to the lived experience of mid-twentieth-century lesbian athletes.

I argue that fears of mannish female sexuality in sport initially centered on the prospect of unbridled heterosexual desire. By the 1930s, however, female athletic mannishness began to connote heterosexual failure, usually couched in terms of unattractiveness to men, but also suggesting the possible absence of heterosexual interest. In the years following World War II, the stereotype of the lesbian athlete emerged full blown. The extreme homophobia and the gender conservatism of the postwar era created a context in which longstanding linkages among mannishness, female homosexuality, and athletics cohered around the figure of the mannish lesbian athlete. Paradoxically, the association between masculinity, lesbianism, and sport had a positive outcome for some women. The very cultural matrix that produced the pejorative image also created possibilities for lesbian affirmation. Sport provided social and psychic space for some lesbians to validate themselves and to build a collective culture. Thus, the lesbian athlete was not only a figure of discourse but a living product of women's sexual struggle and cultural innovation.

Amazons, Muscle Molls, and the Question of Sexual (Im)mortality

The athletic woman sparked interest and controversy in the early decades of the twentieth century. In the United States and other Western societies, sport functioned as a male preserve, an all-male domain in which men not only played games together but also demonstrated and affirmed their manhood.[5] The "maleness" of sport derived from a gender ideology which labeled aggression, physicality, competitive spirit, and athletic skill as masculine attributes necessary for achieving true manliness. This notion found unquestioned support in the dualistic, polarized concepts of gender which prevailed in Victorian America. However, by the turn of the century, women had begun to challenge Victorian gender arrangements, breaking down barriers to female participation in previously male arenas of public work, politics, and urban nightlife. Some of these "New Women" sought entry into the world of athletics as well. On college campuses students enjoyed a wide range of intramural sports through newly formed Women's Athletic Associations. Off-campus women took up games like golf, tennis, basketball, swimming, and occasionally even wrestling, car racing, or boxing. As challengers to one of the defining arenas of manhood, skilled female athletes became symbols of the broader march of womanhood out of the Victorian domestic sphere into once prohibited male realms.

The woman athlete represented both the appealing and threatening aspects of modern womanhood. In a positive light, she captured the exuberant spirit, physical vigor, and brazenness of the New Woman. The University of Minnesota student newspaper proclaimed in 1904 that the athletic girl was the "truest type of All-American coed."[6] Several years later, *Harper's Bazaar* labeled the unsportive girl as "not strictly up to date," and *Good Housekeeping* noted that the "tomboy" had come to symbolize "a new type of American girl, new not only physically, but mentally and morally."[7]

Yet, women athletes invoked condemnation as often as praise. Critics ranged from physicians and physical educators to sportswriters, male athletic officials, and casual observers. In their view, strenuous athletic pursuits endangered women and threatened the stability of society. They maintained that women athletes would become manlike, adopting masculine dress, talk, and mannerisms. In addition, they contended, too much exercise would damage female reproductive capacity. And worse yet, the excitement of sport would cause women to lose control, conjuring up images of frenzied, distraught co-eds on the verge of moral, physical, and emotional breakdown. These fears collapsed into an all-encompassing concept of "mannishness," a term signifying female masculinity.

The public debate over the merits of women's athletic participation remained lively throughout the 1910s and 1920s. Implicit in the dispute over "mannishness" was a longstanding disagreement over the effect of women's athletic activities on their sexuality. Controversy centered around two issues—damage to female reproductive capacity and the unleashing of heterosexual passion. Medical experts and exercise specialists disagreed among themselves about the effects of athletic activity on women's reproductive cycles and organs. Some claimed that athletic training interfered with menstruation and caused reproductive organs to harden or atrophy; others insisted that rigorous exercise endowed women with strength and energy which would make them more fit for bearing and rearing children. Similarly, experts vehemently debated whether competition unleashed nonprocreative, erotic desires identified with male sexuality and unrespectable women, or, conversely, whether invigorating sport enhanced a woman's feminine charm and sexual appeal, channeling sexual energy into wholesome activity.

Conflicting opinion on sexual matters followed closely along the lines of a larger dispute which divided the world of women's sport into warring camps. Beginning in the 1910s, female physical educators and male sport promoters squared off in a decades-long struggle over the appropriate nature of female

competition and the right to govern women's athletics. The conflict was a complicated one, involving competing class and gender interests played out in organizational as well as philosophical battles. It was extremely important in
shaping women's sports for more than fifty years. Although historians of sport
have examined the broad parameters of the conflict, they have paid less attention to the competing sexual perspectives advanced by each side.[8]

Physical educators took a cautious approach on all matters of sexuality, one
designed to safeguard vulnerable young athletes and to secure their own professional status as respectable women in the male-dominated worlds of acade-
mia and sport. Heeding dire warnings about menstrual dysfunction, sterility,
and inferior offspring, educators created policies to curtail strenuous competition and prohibit play during menstruation. They worried equally about the impact of sport on sexual morality. Alleging that competition would induce "powerful impulses" leading girls into a "temptation to excess" and the "pitfall of
overindulgence," educators and their allies pressured popular sport promoters
to reduce the competitive stimulation, publicity, and physical strain thought to
endanger the sexuality of their female charges.[9]

Popular sport organizations like the Amateur Athletic Union agreed that
unregulated female competition posed physiological and moral dangers. But
AAU officials countered protectionist physical education policies with a nationalist, eugenic stance which argued that strenuous activity under proper guid-
ance would actually strengthen reproductive organs, creating a vigorous cadre
of mothers to produce a generation of stalwart American sons.[10] Although making some concessions to demands for modesty and female supervision, in the
long run AAU leaders and commercial sport promoters also rejected educators'
emphasis on sexual control. Sponsors of popular sport found that sexual hype,
much more than caution, helped to attract customers and mute charges of mannishness. In working-class settings and in more elite sports like swimming, an
ideal of the "athlete as beauty queen" emerged. Efforts to present the female
athlete as sexually attractive and available mirrored the playful, erotic sensibility present in the broader commercial leisure culture of the early twentieth
century.[11]

The class and gender lines in this dispute were complicated by overlap-
ping constituencies. Female educators adhered closely to middle-class, even
Victorian, notions of respectability and modesty. But their influence spread beyond elite private and middle-class schools into working-class public schools
and industrial recreation programs. And male promoters, often themselves of
the middle-class, continued to control some school sport and, outside the
schools, influenced both working-class and elite sports. Moreover, Black physical educators advanced a third point of view. Although few in number, early-

twentieth-century African American physical education instructors generally aligned themselves with popular promoters in favor of competition and inter-scholastic sports. Yet their strong concern with maintaining respectability cre-ated some sympathy for the positions advanced by white leaders of women's physical education.[12]

On all sides of the debate, however, the controversy about sport and female sexuality presumed heterosexuality. Neither critics nor supporters suggested that "masculine" athleticism might indicate or induce same-sex love. When ex-perts warned of the amazonian athlete's possible sexual transgressions, they linked the physical release of sport with a loss of heterosexual *control*, not of *inclination*. The most frequently used derogatory term for women athletes was "Muscle Moll." In its only other usages, the word "moll" referred to either the female lovers of male gangsters or to prostitutes. Both represented disreputable, heterosexually deviant womanhood.

By contrast, medical studies of sexual "deviance" from the late nineteenth and early twentieth centuries quite clearly linked "mannishness" to lesbianism, and in at least two cases explicitly connected female homosexuality with boyish athleticism.[13] It is curious then that in answering charges against the mannish Muscle Moll, educators and sport promoters of this period did not refer to or deny lesbianism. However, the "mannish lesbian" made little sense in the het-erosocial milieu of popular sports. Promoters encouraged mixed audiences for women's athletic events, often combining them with men's games, postgame dances and musical entertainment, or even beauty contests. The image of the athlete as beauty queen and the commercial atmosphere that characterized much of working-class sport ensured that the sexual debate surrounding the modern female athlete would focus on her heterosexual charm, daring, or dis-repute. The homosocial environment of women's physical education left educa-tors more vulnerable to insinuations that their profession was populated by "mannish" types who preferred the love of women. However, the feminine re-spectability and decorum cultivated by the profession provided an initial shield from associations with either the mannish lesbian or her more familiar coun-terpart, the heterosexual Muscle Moll.

The Muscle Moll as Heterosexual Failure: Emerging Lesbian Stereotypes

In the 1930s, however, the heterosexual understanding of the mannish "amazon" began to give way to a new interpretation which educators and pro-moters could not long ignore. To the familiar charge that female athletes resem-bled men, critics added the newer accusation that sport-induced mannishness disqualified them as candidates for heterosexual romance. In 1930, an *American Mercury* medical reporter decried the decline of romantic love, pinning the blame on women who entered sport, business, and politics. He claimed that such women "act like men, talk like men, and think like men." The author explained that "women have come closer and closer to men's level," and, consequently, "the purple allure of distance has vamoosed."[14] Four years later, the *Ladies Home Journal* printed a "Manual on the More or Less Subtle Art of Getting a Man" which listed vitality, gaiety, vivacity, and good sportsmanship—qualities typically associated with women athletes and formerly linked to the athletic flapper's heterosexual appeal—as "the very qualities that are likely to make him consider anything but marriage."[15] Although the charges didn't exclusively focus on athletes, they implied that female athleticism was contrary to heterosexual appeal, which appeared to rest on women's difference from and deference to men.

The concern with heterosexual appeal reflected broader sexual transformations in U.S. society. Historians of sexuality have examined the multiple forces which reshaped gender and sexual relations in the first few decades of the twentieth century. Victorian sexual codes crumbled under pressure from an assertive, boldly sexual working-class youth culture, a women's movement which defied prohibitions against public female activism, and the growth of a new pleasure-oriented consumer economy. In the wake of these changes, modern ideals of womanhood embraced an overtly erotic heterosexual sensibility. At the same time, medical fascination with sexual "deviance" created a growing awareness of lesbianism, now understood as a form of congenital or psychological pathology. The medicalization of homosexuality in combination with an antifeminist backlash in the 1920s against female autonomy and power contributed to a more fully articulated taboo against lesbianism. The modern heterosexual woman stood in stark opposition to her threatening sexual counterpart, the "mannish" lesbian.[16]

By the late 1920s and early 1930s, with a modern lesbian taboo and an eroticized definition of heterosexual femininity in place, the assertive, muscular female competitor roused increasing suspicion. It was at this moment that both subtle and direct references to the lesbian athlete emerged in physical education and popular sport. Uncensored discussions of intimate female companionship and harmless athletic "crushes" disappear from the record, pushed underground by the increasingly hostile tone of public discourse about female sexuality and athleticism. Fueled by the gender antagonisms and anxieties of the Depression, the public began scrutinizing women athletes-known for their appropriation of masculine games and styles—for signs of deviance.

Where earlier references to "amazons" had signaled heterosexual ardor, journalists now used the term to mean unattractive, failed heterosexuals. Occasionally, the media made direct mention of athletes' presumed lesbian tendencies. A 1933 *Redbook* article, for example, casually mentioned that track and golf star Babe Didrikson liked men just to horse around with her and not "make love," adding that Babe's fondness for her best girlfriends far surpassed her affection for any man.[17] The direct reference was unusual; the lesbian connotation of mannishness was forged primarily through indirect links of association. The preponderance of evidence appears in public exchanges between opponents and advocates of women's sport.

After two decades of celebrating the female collegiate athlete, yearbooks at co-ed colleges began to ridicule physical education majors and Women's Athletic Association (WAA) members, portraying them as hefty, disheveled, and ugly. A 1937 Minnesota yearbook sarcastically titled its presentation on the WAA "Over in No Man's Land."[18] Finding themselves cast as unattractive prudes or mannish misfits, physical educators struggled to revise their image. They declared the muscle-bound, manhating athlete a relic of the past, supplanted by "lovely, feminine charming girls" whose fitness, suppleness, and grace merely made them "more beautiful on the dance floor that evening."[19]

Similar exchanges appeared in popular magazines. After *Literary Digest* published Fred Wittner's assertion that "worthy fathers" would not find trained women athletes attractive mates, AAU official Ada Taylor Sackett issued a rebuttal which reassured readers that because athletic muscles resembled "those of women who dance all night," women in sport could no doubt "still attract a worthy mate."[20] When critics maligned athletic femininity, they suggested that athletes were literally un-becoming women: unattractive females who abdicated their womanhood and fell under sexual suspicion. When defenders responded with ardent assertions that women athletes did indeed exhibit interest in men, marriage, and motherhood, it suggested that they understood "mannish" to mean "not-heterosexual."

The Butch Ballplayer:
Midcentury Stereotypes of the Lesbian Athlete

Tentatively voiced in the 1930s, these accusations became harsher and more explicit under the impact of wartime changes in gender and sexuality and the subsequent panic over the "homosexual menace." In a post-World War II climate markedly hostile to nontraditional women and lesbians, women in physical education and in working-class popular sports became convenient targets of homophobic indictment.

World War II opened up significant economic and social possibilities for gay men and women. Embryonic prewar homosexual subcultures blossomed during the war and spread across the midcentury urban landscape. Bars, night-clubs, public cruising spots, and informal social networks facilitated the development of gay and lesbian enclaves. But the permissive atmosphere did not survive the war's end. Waving the banner of Cold War political and social conservatism, government leaders acted at the federal, state, and local levels to purge gays and lesbians from government and military posts, to initiate legal investigations and prosecutions of gay individuals and institutions, and to encourage local police crackdowns on gay bars and street life. The perceived need to safeguard national security and to reestablish social order in the wake of wartime disruption sparked a "homosexual panic" which promoted the fear, loathing, and persecution of homosexuals.[21]

Lesbians suffered condemnation for their violation of gender as well as sexual codes. The tremendous emphasis on family, domesticity, and "traditional" femininity in the late 1940s and 1950s reflected postwar anxieties about the reconsolidation of a gender order shaken by two decades of depression and war. As symbols of women's refusal to conform, lesbians endured intense scrutiny by experts who regularly focused on their subjects' presumed masculinity. Sexologists attributed lesbianism to masculine tendencies and freedoms encouraged by the war, linking it to a general collapsing of gender distinctions which, in their view, destabilized marital and family relations.[22]

Lesbians remained shadowy figures to most Americans, but women athletes—noted for their masculine bodies, interests, and attributes—were visible representatives of the gender inversion often associated with homosexuality. Physical education majors, formerly accused of being unappealing to men, were increasingly charged with being uninterested in them as well. The 1952 University of Minnesota yearbook snidely reported: "Believe it or not, members of the Women's Athletic Association are normal" and found conclusive evidence in the fact that "at least one . . . of WAA's 300 members is engaged."[23] And in 1956, a newspaper account of the University of Texas Sports Association (UTSA) women's sports banquet led off with the headline, "UTSA Gives Awards," followed by a subheading "Gayness Necessary." The second headline referred to a guest speaker's talk on positive attitudes, entitled "The Importance of Being Debonair," but the lesbian allusion was unmistakable and I believe fully intentional.[24]

The lesbian stigma began to plague popular athletics too, especially working-class sports noted for their masculine toughness. The pall of suspicion did not completely override older associations with heterosexual deviance. When *Collier's* 1947 article on the Red Heads, a barnstorming women's basketball team, exclaimed "It's basketball—not a strip tease!" the author alluded to both the heterosexual appeal and the hint of disrepute long associated with work-ing-class women athletes.[25] But the dominant postwar voice intimated a differ-ent type of disrepute. Journalists continued to attack the mannish athlete as ugly and sexually unappealing, implying that this image could only be altered through proof of heterosexual "success."

The career of Babe Didrikson, which spanned the 1920s to the 1950s, illus-trates the shift. In the early 1930s the press had ridiculed the tom-boyish track star for her "hatchet face," "door-stop jaw," and "button-breasted" chest. After quitting track, Didrikson dropped out of the national limelight, married profes-sional wrestler George Zaharias in 1938, and then staged a spectacular athletic comeback as a golfer in the late 1940s and 1950s. Fascinated by her personal transformation and then, in the 1950s, moved by her battle with cancer, journal-ists gave Didrikson's comeback extensive coverage and helped make her a much-loved popular figure. In reflecting on her success, however, sportswriters spent at least as much time on Didrikson's love life as her golf stroke. Headlines blared, "Babe Is a Lady Now: The World's Most Amazing Athlete Has Learned to Wear Nylons and Cook for Her Huge Husband," and reporters gleefully de-scribed how "along came a great big he-man wrestler and the Babe forgot all her man-hating chatter."[26]

Postwar sport discourse consistently focused on women's sexual as well as their athletic achievements. As late as 1960, a *New York Times Magazine* headline asked, "Do men make passes at athletic lasses?" Columnist William B. Furlong answered no for most activities, concluding that except for a few "yes" sports like swimming, women athletes "surrendered" their sex.[27] The challenge for women athletes was not to conquer new athletic feats, which would only fur-ther reduce their sexual appeal, but to regain their womanhood through sexual surrender to men.

Media coverage in national magazines and metropolitan newspapers typi-cally focused on the sexual accomplishments of white female athletes, but post-war observers and promoters of African American women's sport also con-fronted the issue of sexual normalcy. In earlier decades, neither Black nor white commentary on African American athletes expressed a concern with "man-nish" lesbianism. The white media generally ignored Black athletes. Implicitly, however, stereotypes of Black females as highly sexual, promiscuous, and un-restrained in their heterosexual passions discouraged the linkage between man-nishness and lesbianism. Racist gender ideologies further complicated the meaning of mannishness. Historically, European American racial thought char-acterized African American women as aggressive, coarse, passionate, and physi-cal—the same qualities assigned to manliness and sport.[28] Excluded from domi-nant ideals of womanhood, Black women's success in sport could be interpreted not as an unnatural deviation but, rather, as the natural result of their reputed closeness to nature, animals, and masculinity.[29]

Within Black communities, strong local support for women's sport may also have weakened the association between sport and lesbianism. Athletes from Tuskegee Institute's national championship track teams of the late 1930s and 1940s described an atmosphere of campuswide enthusiastic support. They noted that although a male student might accuse an athlete of being "funny" if she turned him down for a date, in general lesbianism was not a subject of concern in Black sport circles.[30] Similarly, Gloria Wilson found that she encountered far less uneasiness about lesbianism on her Black semipro softball team in the late 1950s and 1960s than she did in the predominantly white college physical education departments she joined later. She explained that the expectation of heterosexuality was ingrained in Black women to the point that "anything outside of that realm is just out of the question." While recalling that her teammates "had no time or patience for 'funnies,'" Wilson noted that the issue rarely came up, in large part because most team members were married and therefore "didn't have to prove it because then too, their men were always at those games. They were very supportive."[31]

Although Black athletes may have encountered few lesbian stereotypes at the local level, circumstances in the broader society eventually pressed African American sport promoters and journalists to address the issue of mannish sexuality. The strong association of sports with lesbianism developed at the same time as Black athletes became a dominant presence in American sport culture. Midcentury images of sport, Blackness, masculinity, and lesbianism circulated in the same orbit in various combinations. There was no particular correlation between Black women and lesbianism; however, the association of each with mannishness and sexual aggression potentially linked the two. In the late 1950s, Black sport promoters and journalists joined others in taking up the question of sexual "normalcy." One Black newspaper in 1957 described tennis star Althea Gibson as a childhood "tomboy" who "in later life . . . finds herself victimized by complexes."[32] The article did not elaborate on the nature of Gibson's "complex," but lesbianism is inferred in the linkage between "tomboys" and psychological illness. This connotation becomes clearer by looking at the defense of Black women's sport. Echoing *Ebony's* avowal that "entirely feminine" Black female track stars "like boys, dances, club affairs," in 1962 Tennessee State University track coach Ed Temple asserted, "None of my girls have any trouble getting boy friends. . . . We don't want amazons."[33]

Constant attempts to shore up the heterosexual reputation of athletes can be read as evidence that the longstanding reputation of female athletes as mannish women had become a covert reference to lesbianism. By mid-century, a fundamental reorientation of sexual meanings fused notions of femininity, female eroticism, and heterosexual attractiveness into a single ideal. Mannishness, once primarily a sign of gender crossing, assumed a specifically lesbian-sexual connotation. In the wake of this change, the strong cultural association between sport and masculinity made women's athletics ripe for emerging lesbian stereotypes. This meaning of athletic mannishness raises further questions. What impact did the stereotype have on women's sport? And was the image merely an erroneous stereotype, or did lesbians in fact form a significant presence in sport?

Sport and the Heterosexual Imperative

The image of the mannish lesbian athlete had a direct effect on women competitors, on strategies of athletic organizations, and on the overall popularity of women's sport. The lesbian stereotype exerted pressure on athletes to demonstrate their femininity and heterosexuality, viewed as one and the same. Many women adopted an apologetic stance toward their athletic skill. Even as they competed to win, they made sure to display outward signs of femininity in dress and demeanor. They took special care in contact with the media to reveal "feminine" hobbies like cooking and sewing, to mention current boyfriends, and to discuss future marriage plans.[34]

Leaders of women's sport took the same approach at the institutional level. In answer to portrayals of physical education majors and teachers as social rejects and prudes, physical educators revised their philosophy to place heterosexuality at the center of professional objectives. In the late 1930s, they invited psychologists to speak at national professional meetings about problems of sexual adjustment. Such experts described the "types of people who are unadjusted to heterosexual cooperative activity" and warned women in physical education to "develop a prejudice *against* segregation of the sexes."[35] Told that exclusively female environments caused failed heterosexual development, physical educators who had long advocated female separatism in sport were pressed to promote mixed-sex groups and heterosexual "adjustment."

Curricular changes implemented between the mid-1930s and mid-1950s institutionalized the new philosophy. In a paper on postwar objectives, Mildred A. Schaeffer explained that physical education classes should help women "develop an interest in school dances and mixers and a desire to voluntarily attend them."[36] To this end, administrators revised coursework to emphasize beauty and social charm over rigorous exercise and health. They exchanged old rationales of fitness and fun for promises of trimmer waistlines, slimmer hips, and prettier complexions. At Radcliffe, for example, faculty redesigned health classes to include "advice on dress, carriage, hair, skin, voice, or any factor that would tend to improve personal appearance and thus contribute to social and economic success."[37] Intramural programs replaced interclass basketball tournaments and weekend campouts for women with mixed-sex "co-recreational" activities like bowling, volleyball, and "fun nights" of ping-pong and shuffleboard. Some departments also added co-educational classes to foster "broader, keener, more sympathetic understanding of the opposite sex."[38] Department heads cracked down on "mannish" students and faculty, issuing warnings against "casual styles" which might "lead us back into some dangerous channels."[39] They implemented dress codes which forbade slacks and men's shirts or socks, adding as well a ban on "boyish hair cuts" and unshaven legs.[40]

Popular sport promoters adopted similar tactics. Martialing sexual data like they were athletic statistics, a 1954 AAU poll sought to sway a skeptical public with numerical proof of heterosexuality—the fact that 91 percent of former female athletes surveyed had married.[41] Publicity for the midwestern All-American Girls Baseball League included statistics on the number of married players in the league. In the same vein, the women's golf tour announced that one-third of the pros were married, and the rest were keeping an eye peeled for prospects who might "lure them from the circuit to the altar."[42]

The fear of lesbianism was greatest where a sport had a particularly masculine image and where promoters needed to attract a paying audience. Professional and semipro basketball and softball fit the bill on both accounts. Athletic leaders tried to resolve the problem by "proving" the attractive femininity of athletes. Softball and basketball tournaments continued to feature beauty pageants. Although in earlier times such events celebrated the "sexiness" of the emancipated modern woman, in later decades they seemed to serve a more defensive function. The AAU's magazine, the *Amateur Athlete*, made sure that at least one photograph of the national basketball tournament's beauty "queen and her court" accompanied the photo of each year's championship team. Behind the scenes, teams passed dress and conduct codes. For example, the All-American Girls Baseball League prohibited players from wearing men's clothing or getting "severe" haircuts.[43] That this was an attempt to secure the heterosexual image of athletes was made even clearer when league officials announced that AAGBL policy prohibited the recruitment of "freaks" and "Amazons."[44]

In the end, the strategic emphasis on heterosexuality and the suppression of "mannishness" did little to alter the image of women in sport. The stereotype of the mannish lesbian athlete grew out of the persistent commonsense equation of sport with masculinity. Opponents of women's sport reinforced this belief when they denigrated women's athletic efforts and ridiculed skilled athletes as "grotesque," "mannish," or "unnatural." Leaders of women's sport unwittingly contributed to the same set of ideas when they began to orient their programs around the new feminine heterosexual ideal. As physical education policies and media campaigns worked to suppress lesbianism and marginalize athletes who didn't conform to dominant standards of femininity, sport officials embedded heterosexism into the institutional and ideological framework of sport. The effect extended beyond sport to the wider culture, where the figure of the mannish lesbian athlete announced that competitiveness, strength, independence, aggression, and physical intimacy among women fell outside the bounds of womanhood. As a symbol of female deviance, she served as a powerful reminder to all women to tow the line of heterosexuality and femininity or risk falling into a despised category of mannish (not-women) women.

Beyond the Stereotype: "Mannish" Athletes and Lesbian Subculture

Changes in American sexual practices, politics, and beliefs help account for the emerging lesbian stereotype and its impact. However, that explanation alone fails to consider lesbian agency. Was the mannish lesbian athlete merely a figure of homophobic imagination, or was there in fact a strong lesbian presence in sport? When the All-American Girls Baseball League adamantly specified, *"Always appear in feminine attire* . . . MASCULINE HAIR STYLING? SHOES? COATS? SHIRTS? SOCKS, T-SHIRTS ARE BARRED AT ALL TIMES," and when physical education departments threatened to expel students for overly masculine appearance, were administrators merely responding to external pressure?[45] Or were they cracking down on women who may have indeed enjoyed the feel and look of a tough swagger, a short haircut, and men's clothing? And if so, did mannishness among athletes correspond to lesbianism, as the stereotype suggested? In spite of the public stigmatization, some women may have found the activities, attributes, and emotions of sport conducive to lesbian self-expression and community formation.

As part of a larger investigation of women's athletic experience, I conducted oral histories with women who played competitive amateur, semiprofessional, and professional sports between 1930 and 1970. The interviews included only six openly lesbian narrators and thirty-six other women who either declared their heterosexuality or left their identity unstated.[46] Although the sample is too small to stand as a representative study, the interviews offered a rich source of information about popular sexual theories, the association of lesbianism with sport, and lesbian experience in sport. The oral histories and scattered other sources indicate that sport, particularly softball, provided an important site for the development of lesbian subculture and identity in the United States.[47] Gay and straight informants alike confirmed the lesbian presence in popular sport and physical education. Their testimony suggests that from at least the 1940s on, sport provided space for lesbian activity and social networks and served as a path into lesbian culture for young lesbians coming out and searching for companions and community.

Lesbian athletes explained that sport had been integral to their search for sexual identity and lesbian companionship. Ann Maguire, a softball player, physical education major, and top amateur bowler from New England, recalled that as a teenager in the late 1950s,

> I had been trying to figure out who I was and couldn't put a name to it. I mean it was very—no gay groups, no literature, no characters on "Dynasty"—I mean there was just nothing at that time. And trying to put a name to it. . . . I went to a bowling tournament, met two women there [and] for some reason something clicked and it clicked in a way that I was not totally aware of.

She introduced herself to the women, who later invited her to a gay bar. Maguire described her experience at age seventeen:

> I was being served and I was totally fascinated by the fact that, oh god, here I am being served and I'm not twenty-one. And it didn't occur to me until after a while when I relaxed and started realizing that I was at a gay bar. I just became fascinated. . . . And I was back there the next night. . . . I really felt a sense of knowing who I was and feeling very happy. Very happy that I had been able to through some miracle put this into place.[48]

Loraine Sumner, a physical education teacher who for several decades also played, coached, and refereed sports in the Boston area, recalled: "We didn't have anybody to talk to. We figured it out for ourselves you know." In sport she found others like herself, estimating that as many as 75 percent of the women she played with were lesbian. In such a setting Sumner put a name to her own feelings and found others to support her: "There was a lot of bonding, there's a lot of unity. You've got that closeness."[49] For these women, sport provided a point of entry into lesbian culture.

The question arises of whether lesbians simply congregated in athletic settings or whether a sports environment could actually "create" or "produce" lesbians. Some women fit the first scenario, describing how, in their struggle to accept and make sense out of lesbian desire, sport offered a kind of home that put feelings and identities into place. For other women, it appears that the lesbian presence in sport encouraged them to explore or act on feelings that they might not have had or responded to in other settings. Midwestern baseball player Nora Cross remembered that "it was my first exposure to gay people. . . . I was pursued by the one I was rooming with, that's how I found out." She got involved with her roommate and lived "a gay lifestyle" as long as she stayed in sport. Dorothy Ferguson Key also noticed that sport changed some women, recalling that "there were girls that came in the league like this . . . yeah, gay," but that at other times "a girl come in, and I mean they just change. . . . When they've been in a year they're completely changed. . . . They lived together."[50]

The athletic setting provided public space for lesbian sociability without naming it as such or excluding women who were not lesbians. This environment could facilitate the coming-out process, allowing women who were unsure about or just beginning to explore their sexual identity to socialize with gay and straight women without having to make immediate decisions or declarations. Gradually and primarily through unspoken communication, lesbians in sport recognized each other and created social networks. Gloria Wilson, who played softball in a mid-sized midwestern city, described her entry into lesbian social circles as a gradual process in which older lesbians slowly opened up their world to her and she grew more sure of her own identity and place in the group.

> A lot was assumed. And I don't think they felt comfortable with me talking until they knew me better. Then I think more was revealed. And we had little beer gatherings after a game at somebody's house. So then it was even more clear who was doing what when. And then I felt more comfortable too, fitting in, talking about my relationship too—and exploring more of the lesbian lifestyle, I guess.[51]

Like Wilson, other narrators stated that after playing together, lesbian teammates frequently went out to eat and drink or joined each other for parties at private homes. In addition, they recalled that lesbian fans regularly attended softball games and occasionally socialized with athletes over postgame meals and drinks. Outside sources confirm the interview testimony. Lisa Ben, founder of the first known U.S. lesbian magazine *Vice Versa*, moved to wartime Los Angeles thinking she was the only "girl" who preferred to "go out strictly with girls." After meeting some women in her apartment building who admitted to the same desires, she recalled, "Then they took me to a girls' softball game; of course I wasn't the least interested in sports, but it gave me a chance to meet other gay girls."[52] Women's softball provided public space for lesbians to gather when there were few gay bars or other social institutions. Lesbian activist Barbara Grier stated the point succinctly: "It was a place to go where you knew there would be dykes."[53]

Gay narrators also reported encountering lesbians in physical education, but their accounts suggest that the level of professional and personal fear in physical education circles created an intense pressure to conceal and even deny the lesbian presence among faculty and majors. As professionals concerned with propriety and reputation, many lesbian physical educators may have avoided gay bars or other public gatherings, choosing to build more secretive, privatized lesbian networks which protected them against exposure.

In an era when women did not dare announce their lesbianism in public, the social world of popular sport allowed women to find each other as teammates, friends, and lovers. Loraine Sumner explained, "Well it was very nice because you see you developed your friendships. You didn't have to go out looking for women; they were all right there." Among amateur and semipro sports, softball had the most notorious lesbian reputation, but informants noted that other sports offered similar possibilities. They also theorized that both the personal networks and the public validation gained through these sports were especially important for working-class women with limited job and educational opportunities. Sumner recalled her own options as an unmarried, working-class Catholic in Boston: "Back then you either had to go into the convent or you had to get married and that was about it. Nobody ever thought that there was anything else for women back then. So it was—Thank God we had the sports!"[54]

While lesbian narrators underscored the significance of sport in their own lives, many other former athletes concurred that lesbians were indeed recognizably present in sport. A few women remained unaware of lesbians or even the stereotype. But others recalled that although they rarely or never heard lesbianism openly discussed, all but the most naive figured it out. Some kept their comments brief, as in the case of a physical educator and star softball pitcher who curtly replied, "as far as that existing, *affirmative*." Others elaborated, explaining that over time they became aware of women "pairing off," "getting clannish" with each other, or joining others who appeared to be "on the masculine side." A Chicago softball player recalled that gay athletes, "didn't expound that they were, like they do today on television and all over. It was more of a secretive thing." Nevertheless, she concluded that "you'd have to have been pretty naive not to have known. And I was naive, too. But not that naive!"[55]

If athletics provided a public arena and social activity in which lesbians could recognize and affirm each other, what exactly was it that they recognized? This is where the issue of mannishness arises. Women athletes consistently explained the lesbian reputation of sport by reference to the mannishness of some athletes. Nebraska softball player Jessie Steinkuhler suggested that the lesbian image of sportswoman came from the fact that "they tried to act like a man, you know the way they walked, the way they talked and the things they did."[56] Rarely did informants specify whether they were referring to known lesbians or just to "mannish athletes" who might give the impression of lesbianism. The distinction was not marked, indicating a substantial overlap in how the two categories of "deviant" women were perceived.[57]

When narrators did speak specifically of lesbians, they also remarked upon hairstyles, dress, and an overall mannish appearance. Whether from personal contact or hearsay, women who came of age at midcentury had become familiar with lesbian stereotypes and fashions, and they used gender cues to assess and describe sexual identity. All-American league baseball player Dorothy Ferguson Key recalled that "tomboyish girls" who "wanted to go with other girls" signaled their mannishness "in the shoes they bought. You know, it was how they dressed. . . . In some way you could just tell they were mannish."[58] Another softball and baseball player echoed Key's claim: "I think that when people were lesbians, or whatever you want to call them, they wanted short haircuts, they wanted to wear pants, they wanted to, you know, *be* like a boy. . . . Somebody had a short haircut then, they might as well as had a sign on their back."[59]

These comments could merely indicate the pervasiveness of the masculine reputation of athletes and lesbians. However, lesbian narrators also suggested connections, although more complicated and nuanced, between athletics, lesbianism, and the "mannish" or "butchy" style which some lesbians manifested. None reported any doubt about their own gender identification as girls and women, but they indicated that they had often felt uncomfortable with the activities and attributes associated with the female gender. They preferred boyish clothes and activities to the conventional styles and manners of femininity. For example, track and softball competitor Audrey Goldberg Hull recalled her attraction to "masculine" dress and style, a preference which she experienced as being related to her sexual attraction to women. As the youngest member of a semipro softball team, she met older women whose "masculine" style made her feel she was not alone, even if she could not yet articulate her feelings or make contact with others who shared them. She had no knowledge of these women as lesbians, but described "a subjective idea that yes, these two women were masculine. They had that definite—the dress. . . . Well you know, the more masculine ones, I would think, wouldn't it be nice to know these girls. But I was so much younger. . . . Gosh, here I am, I'm playing softball with these older nice looking women."[60]

The pejorative image of the masculine lesbian has a long and harmful history. We obviously need to reject the onerous characterization of lesbians as unwomanly females who tend toward manly sexual desires and activities. However, statements like Hull's suggest that it is important to consider how gendered identities, activities, and sensibilities inform sexual identities and experiences. Societies employ gender to organize emotional experience as well as activities and physical traits. Along with Hull, other lesbian narrators confirmed a connection, although a complex one, between sexual identity and gendered structures of feeling. Several spoke of their own attraction to styles deemed

masculine by the dominant culture and their relief upon finding athletic comrades who shared this sensibility. Josephine D'Angelo recalled that as a lesbian
participating in sport, "you brought your culture with you. You brought your
arm swinging . . . , the swagger, the way you tilted or cocked your head or whatever. You brought that with you." She explained that this style was acceptable
in sports: "First thing you did was to kind of imitate the boys because you know,
you're not supposed to throw like a girl." Although her rejection of femininity
made her conspicuous in other settings, D'Angelo found that in sport "it was
overlooked, see. You weren't different than the other kids. . . . Same likeness,
people of a kind."[61]

These athletes were clearly women playing women's sports. But in the gender system of U.S. society, the skills, movements, clothing, and competition of
sport were laden with impressions of masculinity. Lesbianism too crossed over
the bounds of acceptable femininity. Consequently, sport could relocate girls or
women with lesbian identities or feelings in an alternative nexus of gender
meanings, allowing them to "be themselves"—or to express their gender and
sexuality in an unconventional way. This applied to heterosexual women as
well, many of whom also described themselves as "tomboys" attracted to boyish
games and styles. As an activity that incorporated prescribed "masculine"
physical activity into a way of being in the female body, athletics provided a
social space and practice for reorganizing conventional meanings of embodied
masculinity and femininity. *All* women in sport gained access to activities and
expressive styles labeled masculine by the dominant culture. However, because
lesbians were excluded from a concept of "real womanhood" defined around
heterosexual appeal and desire, sport formed a milieu in which they could
redefine womanhood on their own terms.

Moreover, in sport lesbian athletes found a social practice compatible with
midcentury lesbian culture. By the 1940s many lesbians participated in an urban lesbian subculture which articulated sexual identity through gendered
butch / femme styles and sexual roles.[62] Although lesbians cultivated a public
presence that encompassed elements of masculinity and femininity, in the
wider culture it was the "masculine" style that stood out as the sign for lesbianism. The "tough," "boyish," "swaggering" style some athletes adopted reso-
nated with butch styles in the broader lesbian community. It was this sensibility
that narrators referred to when they spoke vaguely of "the way they walked,
the way they dressed, and the things they did."[63] Athletic lesbians who embraced a "tough" posture, "mannish" dress, and short hair drew upon a visual
and emotional vocabulary of masculinity to create a recognizable style and
positive female identity. Narrator Loraine Sumner made this point when she described sport as particularly well-suited for lesbian recognition. "Well, I

shouldn't say you surmise, but there's something there that you recognize in others that are in the same lifestyle you are. More so than if you saw a woman walking down the street. Some you can tell and some you can't. But in sports I think there's just a way that you can pick it out."[64]

However, the connections among lesbianism, masculinity, and sport require qualification. Many lesbians in and out of sport did not adopt "masculine" markers. And even among those who did, narrators indicated that butch styles did not occlude more traditionally "feminine" qualities of affection and tenderness valued by women athletes. Sport allowed women to combine activities and attributes perceived as masculine with more conventionally feminine qualities of friendship, cooperation, nurturance, and affection. Lesbians particularly benefited from this gender configuration, finding that in the athletic setting, qualities otherwise viewed as manifestations of homosexual deviance were understood as inherent, positive aspects of sport.[65] Aggressiveness, toughness, passionate intensity, expanded use of motion and space, strength, and competitiveness contributed to athletic excellence. With such qualities defined as athletic attributes rather than psychological abnormalities, the culture of sport permitted lesbians to express the full range of their gendered sensibilities while sidestepping the stigma of psychological deviance. For these reasons, athletics, in the words of Josephine D'Angelo, formed a "comforting" and "comfortable" place.[66]

Yet lesbians found sport hospitable only under certain conditions. Societal hostility toward homosexuality made lesbianism unspeakable in any realm of culture, but the sexual suspicions that surrounded sport made athletics an especially dangerous place in which to speak out. Physical educators and sport officials vigilantly guarded against signs of "mannishness," and teams occasionally expelled women who wore their hair in a "boyish bob" or engaged in obvious lesbian relationships. Consequently, gay athletes avoided naming or verbally acknowledging their sexuality. Loraine Sumner explained that "you never talked about it. . . . You never saw anything in public amongst the group of us. But you knew right darn well that this one was going with that one. But yet it just wasn't a topic of conversation. Never."[67] Instead, lesbian athletes signaled their identity through dress, posture, and look, reserving spoken communication for private gatherings among women who were acknowledged and accepted members of concealed communities.

Although in hindsight the underground nature of midcentury lesbian communities may seem extremely repressive, it may also have had a positive side. Unlike the bars where women's very presence declared their status as sexual outlaws, in sport athletes could enjoy the public company of lesbians while retaining their membership in local communities where neighbors, kin, and coworkers respected and sometimes even celebrated their athletic abilities. The unacknowledged, indefinite presence of lesbians in sport may have allowed for a wider range of lesbian experience and identity than is currently acknowledged in most scholarship. For women who did not identify as lesbian but were sexually drawn to other women, sport provided a venue in which they could express their desires without necessarily having articulated their feelings regarding their sexual identity. It is possible that even as they started "going around" with other women, some athletes may have participated in lesbian sexual relationships and friendship networks without ever privately or publicly claiming a lesbian identity. My evidence supports only speculative conclusions but suggests that the culture of sport provided social space for some women to create clearly delineated lesbian identities and communities, at the same time allowing other women to move along the fringes of this world, operating across sexual and community lines without a firmly differentiated lesbian identity.

As they persisted in their athletic endeavors, women gained assurance that allowed them to reject derisive stereotypes of "mannish" athletes. Narrators, straight and gay, continually emphasized that athletic skill, friendship networks, and achievements heightened their confidence and self-esteem. They described a process of finding a stronger and more "authentic" self through sport.[68] One woman who was painfully aware of the lesbian athletic stigma nevertheless found that through sport: "I felt better about myself. . . . And so I guess that was my identity at that time, being very successful at sport."[69] Similarly, Loraine Sumner came to feel that through sport, she "didn't mind being different"; and Audrey Hull recalled that being a good athlete "was a fantastic feeling. . . . Sports for me was the embodiment of that little girl that could do no wrong. . . . I *was* my sports."[70]

Women in sport experienced a contradictory array of heterosexual imperatives and homosexual possibilities. The fact that women athletes disrupted a critical domain of male power and privilege made sport a strategic site for shoring up existing gender and sexual hierarchies. The image of the mannish lesbian confirmed both the masculinity of sport and its association with female deviance. Lesbian athletes could not publicly claim their identity without risking expulsion, ostracism, and loss of athletic activities and social networks that had become crucial to their lives. Effectively silenced, their image was conveyed to the dominant culture primarily as a negative stereotype in which the mannish lesbian athlete represented the unfeminine "other," the line beyond which "normal" women must not cross.

The paradox of women's sport history is that the mannish athlete was not only a figure of homophobic discourse but also a human actor engaged in sexual innovation and struggle. Lesbian athletes used the social and psychic space of sport to create a collective culture and affirmative identity. The pride, pleasure, companionship, and dignity lesbians found in the athletic world helped them survive in a hostile society. The challenge posed by their collective existence and their creative reconstruction of womanhood formed a precondition for more overt, political challenges to lesbian oppression which have occurred largely outside the realm of sport.

Notes

I would like to thank Birgitte Soland, Maureen Honish, Kath Weston, George Chauncey, Jr., and Nan Enstad for their criticisms, encouragement, and editorial advice on earlier versions of this essay.

1. Fred Wittner, "Shall the Ladies Join Us?" *Literary Digest* 117 (19 May 1934): 43.

2. Jim Murray, on impressions of Didrikson as a young woman, from 1970s' column in *Austin American Statesman* (n.d.), Zaharias scrapbook, Barker Texas History Center (hereafter, BTHC), University of Texas, Austin; Arsenio Hall Show, 1988.

3. "Fastest Women in the World," *Ebony* 10 (June 1955): 28.

4. Among the works that do consider the issue of homosexuality are Helen Lenskyj, *Out of Bounds: Women, Sport, and Sexuality* (Toronto: Women's Press, 1986); Yvonne Zipter, *Diamonds Are a Dyke's Best Friend* (Ithaca, N.Y.: Firebrand Books, 1988); Roberta Bennett, "Sexual Labeling as Social Control: Some Political Effects of Being Female in the Gym," *Perspectives* (Fresno, Calif.: Western Society for Physical Education of College Women) 4 (1982): 40–50. On the relationship between male homosexuality and sport, see Brian Pronger, *The Arena of Masculinity: Sport, Homosexuality, and the Meaning of Sex* (New York: St. Martin's Press, 1990).

5. There is a large literature on sport as a male preserve. See J. A. Mangan and Roberta J. Park, eds., *From "Fair Sex" to Feminism: Sport and the Socialization of Women in the Industrial and Post-Industrial Eras* (London: Frank Cass, 1987); Donald J. Mrozek, *Sport and the American Mentality, 1880–1910* (Knoxville: University of Tennessee Press, 1983); Michael S. Kimmel, "The Contemporary 'Crisis' of Masculinity in Historical Perspective," in *The Making of Masculinities: The New Men's Studies*, ed. Harry Brod (Boston: Allen & Unwin, 1987), 137–53; and Eric Dunning, "Sport as a Male Preserve: Notes on the Social Sources of Masculine Identity and Its Transformation," in *Quest for Excitement: Sport and Leisure in the Civilizing Process*, ed. Eric Dunning and Norbert Elias (New York: Basil Blackwell, 1986), 267–83.

6. 1904–5 Scrapbooks of Anne Maude Butner, Butner Papers, University of Minnesota Archives, Minneapolis.

7. Violet W. Mange, "Field Hockey for Women," *Harper's Bazaar* 44 (April 1910): 246; Anna de Koven, "The Athletic Woman," *Good Housekeeping* 55 (August 1912): 150.

8. On the philosophy and policies of women physical educators and their conflict with male sport promoters, see Ellen W. Gerber, "The Controlled Development of Collegiate Sport for Women, 1923–1936," *Journal of Sport History* 2 (Spring 1975): 1–28; Cindy L. Himes, "The Female Athlete in American Society, 1860–1940" (Ph.D. diss., University of Pennsylvania, 1986), chaps. 2–4; and Joan Hult, "The Governance of Athletics for Girls and Women," *Research Quarterly for Exercise and Sport* (April 1985): 64–77.

9. Dudley A. Sargent, "Are Athletics Making Girls Masculine?" *Ladies Home Journal* 29

(March 1913): 71–73; William Inglis, "Exercise for Girls" *Harper's Bazaar* 44 (March 1910): 183; J. Parmley Paret, "Basket-Ball for Young Women," ibid. 33 (October 1900): 1567.

10. See, for example, Bernard MacFadden, "Athletics for Women Will Help Save the Nation," *Amateur Athlete* 4 (February–July 1929): 7; Fred Steers, "Spirit," ibid. (October 1932): 7.

11. On eroticism and early-twentieth-century popular culture, see Kathy Peiss, *Cheap Amusements: Working Women and Leisure in Turn-of-the-Century New York* (Philadelphia: Temple University Press, 1986); Lewis Erenberg, *Steppin' Out: New York Nightlife and the Transformation of American Culture, 1890–1930* (Westport, Conn.: Greenwood Press, 1981); Estelle Freedman and John D'Emilio, *Intimate Matters: A History of Sexuality in America* (New York: Harper & Row, 1988), chaps. 10–12.

12. On Black physical education, see Ruth Arnett, "Girls Need Physical Education," *Chicago Defender*, 10 Dec. 1921; Amelia Roberts, letter to *Chicago Defender*, 12 Mar. 1927, sec. 2, p. 7; Elizabeth Dunham, "Physical Education for Women at Hampton Institute," *Southern Workman* 53 (April 1924): 167; and A. W. Ellis, "The Status of Health and Physical Education for Women in Negro Colleges and Universities," *Journal of Negro Education* 8 (January 1939): 58–63.

13. In his 1883 article, "Case of Sexual Perversion," P. M. Wise described the "peculiar girlhood" of a lesbian who had "preferred masculine sports and labor, had an aversion to attentions from young men and sought the society of her own sex" (*Alienist and Neurologist* 4 [1883]): 88. Sexologist Havelock Ellis commented as well that among lesbians "there is often some capacity for athletics." See Havelock Ellis, *Sexual Inversion*, vol. 2 of *Studies in the Psychology of Sex*, 3d rev. ed. (Philadelphia: F. A. Davis, 1915), 250; Wise and Ellis, quoted in George Chauncey, Jr., "From Sexual Inversion to Homosexuality: Medicine and the Changing Conceptualization of Female Deviance," in *Passion and Power: Sexuality in History*, ed. Kathy Peiss and Christina Simmons (Philadelphia: Temple University Press, 1989), 90, 91. Chauncey argues that sexologists were in the process of separating gender inversion from lesbianism, but his evidence indicates that the phenomena remained linked even as they became more differentiated.

14. George Nathan, "Once There Was a Princess," *American Mercury* 19 (February 1930): 242.

15. A. Moats, "He Hasn't a Chance," *Ladies Home Journal* 51 (December 1934): 12.

16. This is an extremely brief and simplified summary of an extensive literature. For a good synthesis, see Freedman and D'Emilio, chaps. 8–10. On antifeminism and the lesbian threat, see Christina Simmons, "Modern Sexuality and the Myth of Victorian Repression," in *Passion and Power*, 157–77.

17. William Marston, "How Can a Woman Do It?" *Redbook*, September 1933, 60.

18. *Gopher* Yearbook (1937), University of Minnesota Archives.

19. Gertrude Mooney, "The Benefits and Dangers of Athletics for the High School Girl," 1937, Department of Physical Training for Women Records (Health Ed. folder), box 3R251, BTHC; Alice Allene Sefton, "Must Women in Sports Look Beautiful?" *Journal of Health and Physical Education* 8 (October 1937): 481.

20. Wittner, 42; and Ada T. Sackett, "Beauty Survives Sport," *Literary Digest* 117 (19 May 1934): 43.

21. John D'Emilio, *Sexual Politics, Sexual Communities: The Making of a Homosexual Minority in the United States, 1940–1970* (Chicago: University of Chicago Press, 1983), 9–53; Freedman and D'Emilio, chap. 12; and Alan Bérubé, *Coming Out under Fire: The History of Gay Men and Women in World War Two* (New York: Free Press, 1990).

22. On the relation between postwar gender dynamics and studies of the "masculine"' lesbian, see Donna Penn, "The Meanings of Lesbianism in Post-War America," *Gender and History* 3 (Summer 1991): 190–203. On postwar gender anxieties and social science, see Wini Breines, "The 1950s: Gender and Some Social Science," *Sociological Inquiry* 56 (Winter 1986): 69–92.

23. *Gopher* Yearbook (1952), 257, University of Minnesota Archives.

24. *Texan*, 10 May 1956, from the *Texan* scrapbook, box 3R212, Department of Physical

Training for Women Records, BTHC. Although the term "gay" as a reference to homosexuals occurred only sporadically in the mass media before the 1960s, it was in use as a slang term among some homosexual men and lesbians as early as the 1920s and quite commonly by the 1940s.

25. John Kord Lagemann, "Red Heads You Kill Me!" *Collier's* 119 (8 Feb. 1947): 64.

26. Paul Gallico, *Houston Post*, 22 Mar. 1960; Pete Martin, "Babe Didrikson Takes Off Her Mask," *Saturday Evening Post*, 20 Sept. 1947; 26–27; *Life*, 23 June 1947; 90; and Roxy Andersen, "Fashions in Feminine Sport," *Amateur Athlete*, March 1945, 39.

27. William B. Furlong, "Venus Wasn't a Shotputter," *New York Times Magazine*, 29 Aug. 1960, 14.

28. This ideology has been discussed by many scholars of African American women. See, for example, Paula Giddings, *When and Where I Enter: The Impact of Black Women on Race and Sex in America* (New York: William & Morrow, 1984), chaps. 1, 2, 4; Patricia Hill Collins, *Black Feminist Thought: Knowledge, Consciousness, and the Politics of Empowerment* (Boston: Unwin Hyman, 1990), chaps. 4, 8; Hazel V. Carby, *Reconstructing Womanhood: The Emergence of the Afro-American Woman Novelist* (New York: Oxford University Press, 1987).

29. Elizabeth Lunbeck notes a similar pattern in her discussion of medical theories of the "hypersexual" white female. Because psychiatrists assumed that Black women were naturally "oversexed," when defining the medical condition of hypersexuality, they included only young white working-class women whose sexual ardor struck physicians and social workers as unnaturally excessive. See her, " 'A New Generation of Women': Progressive Psychiatrists and the Hypersexual Female," *Feminist Studies* 13 (Fall 1987): 513–43.

30. Alice Coachman Davis and Lula Hymes Glenn, interviews with the author, Tuskegee, Alabama, 7 May 1992; Leila Perry Glover, interview with the author, Atlanta, Georgia, 8 May 1992.

31. Gloria Wilson (pseudonym), interview with the author, 11 May 1988.

32. *Baltimore Afro-American*, Magazine Section, 29 June 1957; 1.

33. "Fastest Women in the World," 28, 32; *Detroit News*, 31 July 1962, sec. 6, p. 1.

34. On the "female apologetic," see Patricia Del Rey, "The Apologetic and Women in Sport," in *Women and Sport*, ed. Carole Oglesby (Philadelphia: Lea & Febiger, 1978), 107–11.

35. National Amateur Athletic Federation-Women's Division, Newsletter, no. 79 (1 June 1938), from Department of Women's Physical Education, University of Wisconsin Archives.

36. Mildred A. Schaeffer, "Desirable Objectives in Post-war Physical Education," *Journal of Health and Physical Education* 16 (October 1945): 446–47.

37. Physical Education Director, Official Reports, Kristin Powell's collected materials on Radcliffe Athletics, Radcliffe College Archives, acc. no. R87.

38. "Coeducational Classes," *Journal of Health, Physical Education, and Recreation* 26 (February 1955): 18. For curricular changes, I examined physical education records at the universities of Wisconsin, Texas, and Minnesota, Radcliffe College, Smith College, Tennessee State University, and Hampton University.

39. Dudley Ashton, "Recruiting Future Teachers," *Journal of Health, Physical Education, and Recreation* 28 (October 1957): 49.

40. The 1949–50 Physical Training Staff Handbook at the University of Texas stated (p. 16), "Legs should be kept shaved." Box 3R213 of Department of Physical Training for Women Records, BTHC. Restrictions on hair and dress are spelled out in the staff minutes and physical education handbooks for majors at the universities of Wisconsin, Texas, and Minnesota.

41. Roxy Andersen, "Statistical Survey of Former Women Athletes," *Amateur Athlete*, September 1954, 10–11.

42. All-American Girls Baseball League (AAGBL) Records, on microfilm at Pennsylvania State University Libraries; and "Next to Marriage, We'll Take Golf," *Saturday Evening Post*, 23 Jan. 1954, 92.

43. AAGBL 1951 Constitution, AAGBL Records.

44. Morris Markey, "Hey Ma, You're Out!" undated publication reproduced in the 1951 Records of the AAGBL; and "Feminine Sluggers," *People and Places* 8, no. 12 (1952), reproduced in 1952 AAGBL Records.

45. AAGBL 1951 Constitution, AAGBL Records. On physical education rules, see Ashton, 49; and records from universities of Texas, Wisconsin, and Minnesota.

46. The sample included forty-two women, ranging in age from their forties to their seventies, who had played a variety of sports in a range of athletic settings in the West, Midwest, Southeast, and Northeast. The majority were white women from urban working-class and rural backgrounds. Researching lesbian experience, which has been silenced, suppressed, and made invisible, raises many methodological problems. Because the fear of discussing such a sensitive topic made finding openly lesbian narrators extremely difficult, I had to rely on supporting evidence from women who did not claim to be lesbians (although observation and indirect comments led me to believe that many of the narrators are or have been lesbian-identified but chose not to reveal it to a relative stranger in the interview setting). Except when I knew in advance that the narrator was willing to discuss her lesbian experience, I raised the subject by asking about lesbian stereotypes in sport. From there, many narrators went on to tell me what they knew about actual lesbianism as well as stereotypes in sport.

47. On softball, see Zipter. Lillian Faderman also mentions the popularity of lesbian softball teams in the 1950s; see *Odd Girls and Twilight Lovers: A History of Lesbian Life in Twentieth-Century America* (New York: Columbia University Press, 1991), 154, 161–62.

48. Ann Maguire, interview with the author, Boston, 18 Feb. 1988.

49. Loraine Sumner, interview with the author, West Roxbury, Massachusetts, 18 Feb. 1988.

50. Nora Cross (pseudonym), interview with the author, 20 May 1988; Dorothy Ferguson Key, interview with the author, Rockford, Illinois, 19 Dec. 1988.

51. Wilson interview.

52. Lisa Ben, interview in Jonathan Ned Katz, *Gay / Lesbian Almanac* (New York: Harper & Row, 1983), 619.

53. Barbara Grier, quoted in Zipter, 48.

54. Sumner interview.

55. Anonymous. In a few cases I have left quotes unattributed when I believed they might involve more self-disclosure than the narrator intended.

56. Jessie Steinkuhler, interview with the author, Douglas, Nebraska, 10 Oct. 1987.

57. The concept of lesbian masculinity was so deeply entrenched that when asked to explain the lesbian-athlete stereotype narrators uniformly reported that the association between sport and lesbianism derived from the masculine reputation of sport, but none continued the line of thought by stating explicitly that people also thought lesbians were masculine. The masculinity of lesbians was the social "fact" that did not even have to be mentioned for the explanation to make sense.

58. Key interview.

59. Anonymous.

60. Audrey Goldberg Hull, interview with the author, Santa Cruz, California, 18 Nov. 1988.

61. Josephine D'Angelo, interview with the author, Chicago, 21 Dec. 1988.

62. On lesbian culture, see Madeline Davis and Elizabeth Lapovsky Kennedy, "The Reproduction of Butch-Fem Roles," in *Passion and Power*, 241–56, and "Oral History and the Study of Sexuality in the Lesbian Community: Buffalo, New York, 1940–1960," *Feminist Studies* 12 (Spring 1986): 7–26; Joan Nestle, "Butch-Fem Relationships: Sexual Courage in the 1950s" in Joan Nestle, *A Restricted Country* (Ithaca, N.Y.: Firebrand Books, 1987), 100–109; and D'Emilio, chaps. 2–3.

63. Steinkuhler interview.

64. Sumner interview.

65. The notion of gay subculture turning stigmatized qualities into valued attributes is discussed by Joseph P. Goodwin in *More Man Than You'll Ever Be! Gay Folklore and Acculturation in Middle America* (Bloomington: Indiana University Press, 1989), 62.

66. D'Angelo interview.

67. Sumner interview.

68. Although theorists rightly question the existence of an "authentic," "unified," or "coherent" self, athletes' testimony suggests that although the notion of "self" and individual identity might be a product of particular historical conditions and ideologies, to people living within that context a sense of authentic self is both real and necessary. Women athletes drew upon the cultural resources they found within sport and female athletic networks to search for and find a sense of authenticity and coherence in their lives.

69. Anonymous.

70. Sumner and Hull interviews.

4

Creating G.I. Jane

The Regulation of Sexuality and Sexual Behavior in the Women's Army Corps during World War II

Leisa D. Meyer

SEVERAL YEARS AFTER World War II ended, a journalist summed up the difficulties the Women's Army Corps encountered in recruiting women by observing:

> Of the problems that the WAC has, the greatest one is the problem of morals . . . of convincing mothers, fathers, brothers, Congressmen, servicemen and junior officers that women really can be military without being camp followers or without being converted into rough, tough gals who can cuss out the chow as well as any dogface. . . . [1]

The sexual stereotypes of servicewomen as "camp followers" or "mannish women," prostitutes or lesbians, had a long history both in the construction of notions of femaleness in general and in the relationship of "woman" and "soldier" in particular. Historically, women had been most visibly associated with the military as prostitutes and crossdressers.[2] The challenge before women and men who wanted to promote "women" as "soldiers" during World War II was how to create a new category which proclaimed female soldiers as both sexually respectable and feminine. The response of Oveta Culp Hobby, the Women's Army Corps director, to this challenge was to characterize female soldiers as chaste and asexual; such a presentation would not threaten conventional sexual norms. Clashing public perceptions of servicewomen and internal strugles within the U.S. Army over the proper portrayal and treatment of military women were the crucibles in which this new category was created. Such

Feminist Studies 18, no. 3 (Fall 1992). © 1992 by Feminist Studies, Inc.

struggles profoundly shaped the daily lives of women in the Women's Army Auxiliary Corps (WAAC) and the Women's Army Corps (WAC)[3] and framed the notorious lesbian witchhunts of the mid- to late-forties.

This article focuses on the regulation and expression of women's sexuality within the army during World War II. I will examine the debates between female and male military leaders over the most appropriate methods of controlling female soldiers' sexual behavior and the actions and responses of army women themselves to the varied and often conflicting rulings emanating from WAAC / WAC Headquarters and the War Department. Framed by public concern with the possibilities of both the sexual independence and sexual victimization of servicewomen, the interactions between and among these groups illuminate the ongoing tension between the mutually exclusive, gendered categories "woman" and "soldier."

The entrance of some women into the army paralleled the movement of other women into nontraditional jobs in the civilian labor force as the need for full utilization of all resources during World War II brought large numbers of white, married women into the labor force for the first time and created opportunities for many women and people of color in jobs historically denied them.[4] Women's service in the armed forces was especially threatening, however, because of the military's function as the ultimate test of "masculinity."

The definition of the military as a masculine institution and the definition of a soldier as a "man with a gun who engages in combat" both excluded women. Moreover, military service had historically been the obligation of men during wartime, and the presence of female soldiers in the army suggested that women were abdicating their responsibilities within the home to usurp men's duty of protecting and defending their homes and country.[5] Thus, the establishment of the WAAC in May 1942, marking women's formal entrance into this preeminently masculine domain, generated heated public debate. It heightened the fears already generated by the entry of massive numbers of women in the civilian labor force and by the less restrictive sexual mores of a wartime environment.

Public fears of the possible consequences of women's independence were often manifested in concerns with women's economic independence as the war accelerated the shift to city living and provided millions of young people with increased opportunities for economic autonomy and social freedom.[6] Such changes had historically triggered fears of declining standards of morality and disintegrating gender and racial boundaries.[7] Historian Elaine Tyler May has argued that in the forties the anxieties generated by these changes focused on female sexuality as a "dangerous force . . . on the loose" and featured calls for women, especially those engaged in more "masculine" pursuits, to maintain their "femininity" in order to offset this danger. In particular, May has demonstrated that public concerns over the potential increase in heterosexual promiscuity among women were generated by the belief that women's right to "behave like a man" by joining the work force or the military meant also their "right to misbehave as he does," especially sexually.[8]

The dangers inherent in women's loss of "femininity" were inscribed not only in public fears of increasing promiscuity but also in the specter of female homosexuality. As John D'Emilio has observed, the theories of Freud, Ellis, and Krafft-Ebbing all linked "proper sexual development" to conventional definitions of "femininity" and "masculinity" and described women's deviations from prescribed "feminine" gender norms as one possible sign of female homosexuality.[9] In addition, although contemporary psychiatric wisdom was moving away from connections between "mannishness" in women and homosexuality, prevailing popular attitudes still linked the two.

In a culture increasingly anxious about women's sexuality in general, and homosexuality in particular, the formation of the WAAC, a women-only environment within an otherwise wholly male institution, sparked a storm of public speculation as to the potential breakdown of heterosexual norms and sexual morality which might result. Not surprisingly, these concerns focused on the potentially "masculinizing" effect the army might have on women and especially on the disruptive influence the WAAC would have on sexual standards. Public fears were articulated in numerous editorials and stories in newspapers and journals, as well as in thousands of letters to the War Department and the newly formed WAAC Headquarters in Washington, D.C.[10] These anxieties were expressed in accusations of heterosexual promiscuity and lesbianism and concerns over women's lack of protection within the military. Among other allegations, the public expressed fear that, in forming the WAAC, the military was trying to create an organized cadre of prostitutes to service male GI's.[11]

The potentially "masculinizing" effect of the military on women was not only in women's taking on male characteristics, appearance, and power but also in women adopting a more aggressive, independent, and "masculine" sexuality. Many civilians as well as some elements of the mainstream media characterized Waacs as sexual actors who engaged in the same type of promiscuity, drunkenness, and sexual adventure condoned in male GI's. Although explicit references to female homosexuality in the WAAC were seldom made in the mainstream press, reports of rumors submitted to WAAC Headquarters by recruiting officers in the field demonstrated that public concern with lesbianism was also pervasive.[12] As WAC historian Mattie Treadwell notes, there was a "public impression that a women's corps would be the ideal breeding ground for [homosexuality]." She attributes this view to the "mistaken" popular belief that "any woman who was masculine in appearance or dress" was a homosexual.[13] In a postwar interview Col. Oveta Culp Hobby, WAAC / WAC director from 1942 to 1945, elaborated on this, remarking: "Just as a startled public was once sure that women's suffrage would make women unwomanly, so the thought of 'women soldiers' caused some people to assume that WAC units would inevitably be hotbeds of perversion."[14] Thus, "masculinization" implied both women's potential power over men and their sexual independence from them, a threat to gender and sexual norms. "Promiscuous" heterosexual women were presumably independent from and uncontrolled by particular men, and "mannish" women were presumably independent of all men.

The sexual stereotypes of the female soldier as "loose" or "mannish" were seen both as inherent in women's military service *and* as a product of the particular kinds of women believed to be most likely to enter the WAAC. In other words, the army either attracted women who were already "sexually deviant," or the experience of military life would make them that way. In addition, the corollary to concerns with women's sexual agency were discussions of army women as potential sexual victims. Integral to this contention were questions of who would protect women inside the military. Removed from the control of their families, what would the state's control of servicewomen mean?

The army's response to this negative publicity was orchestrated by Col. Hobby.[15] She organized this response around the need to assure an anxious public that servicewomen had not lost their "femininity." Hobby's definition of "femininity" was rooted in the Victorian linkage between sexual respectability and female passionlessness. As a result she characterized the woman soldier as chaste, asexual, and essentially middle-class. For example, in cooperation with the War Department she arranged public statements by a number of religious leaders who assured all concerned that the army was a safe and moral environment for young women, and further, that women who joined the WAAC / WAC were of the highest moral character and from "good family backgrounds."[16] She characterized the WAAC / WAC as acting *in loco parentis*, as a guardian of young women's welfare and morals.[17] And to demonstrate that the WAAC / WAC attracted "better-quality" women, Hobby emphasized the greater educational requirements mandated for women compared with their male counterparts, illustrated by the high ratio of women with college degrees. Thus, in countering allegations that to join the WAAC / WAC meant to "lower one's self,"[18] army propaganda reflected and supported contemporary definitions of respectability which explicitly connected class status and sexual morality.[19]

These pronouncements on sexual respectability coincided with other army public relations campaigns aimed at defusing public concerns with homosexuality. In these efforts, attempts to limit the visibility of lesbians in the women's corps were linked with the implicit encouragement of heterosexuality. In responding to fears that the military would make women "mannish" or would provide a haven for women who were "naturally" that way, for instance, some army propaganda highlighted the femininity of WAAC / WAC recruits and stressed their sexual attractiveness to men. These articles assured an anxious public that "soldiering hasn't transformed these Wacs into Amazons—far from it. They have retained their femininity."[20] Presenting women in civilian life in the period as sexually attractive to men did not necessarily imply that they were sexually available. However, public hostility toward women's entrance into the military and conjecture over the army's "real need" for Waacs / Wacs frequently focused on the potential for women's sexual exploitation and/or agency within the army. The army's policy of portraying servicewomen as feminine and sexually attractive to men worked to both contest the image of the female soldier as a "mannish" woman, or lesbian, *and* to reinforce the public characterizations of Waacs / Wacs as heterosexuallly available. Hobby's efforts to control the effects of these campaigns was to emphasize that Waacs / Wacs remained passionless and chaste while in the military and that their sexual behavior in the military was, and should be, profoundly different from that of men in the same institution.

The framework created by Hobby and disseminated in military propaganda efforts was occasionally undercut by the conflicting responses to the question of whether Waacs / Wacs should be treated and utilized as "soldiers" or as "women." On several occasions the male army hierarchy, much to Hobby's dismay, attempted to treat the regulation and control of women's sexuality and sexual behavior in the same manner as that of male soldiers. The army's approach to the issue of sexual regulation and control for men stressed health and combat readiness among troops, not morality. In fact, the army expected and encouraged heterosexual activity among male soldiers and controlled male sexuality with regulations prohibiting sodomy and addressing the prevention and treatment of venereal disease, as well as more informal mechanisms upholding prohibitions on interracial relationships.[21] The male military hierarchy's desire for uniformity collided with the female WAAC director's firm belief in different moral standards for women and her insistence that this difference be reflected in army regulations. This struggle was clearly represented in the army's battle to fight the spread of venereal disease within its ranks.

Hobby believed the army's venereal disease program for men, premised on the assumption of heterosexual activity, would seriously damage the reputation of the corps if applied to women and would undermine her efforts to present Waacs as sexless, not sexual. Her strategy of moral suasion clashed with the U.S. surgeon general's efforts to institute a system of chemical prophylaxis in the women's corps. The surgeon general's plan for control of venereal disease in the WAAC included a full course of instruction in sex education and the distribution of condoms in slot machines placed in latrines so that even "modest" servicewomen might have access to them. This program was completely rejected by Hobby. She argued that even proposing such measures placed civilian and military acceptance of the WAAC in jeopardy.[22] She pointed to public fears of women's military service and accusations of immorality already present as evidence that the course proposed by the surgeon general would result in catastrophic damage to the reputation of the WAAC and seriously hamper her efforts to recruit women to the corps.

Her concern was not with venereal disease per se, but rather with creating an aura of respectability around the WAAC. Her victory in this struggle resulted in the development of a social hygiene pamphlet and course which stressed the "high standards" of moral conduct (i.e., chastity) necessary for members of the corps and the potential damage one woman could do through her misbehavior or immoral conduct. The pamphlet, distributed to all WAAC officers, discussed venereal disease only in reference to the "frightful effects" of the disease on women and children, the difficulties in detection and treatment, and the ineffectiveness of all prophylactic methods for women. Hobby supported combining this policy with the maintenance of strict enlistment standards. She believed that if the corps accepted only "high types of women," no control measures would be necessary.[23]

In stressing the class status of enrollees and the high standards of sexual morality expected of servicewomen, Hobby's response to the issue of venereal disease control in the WAAC was an attempt to place military women back within the bounds of propriety and respectability that had historically afforded a certain kind of protection for white middle-class and upper-class women. Although her goals were to build and repair the reputation of the WAAC, as well as to protect individual women from potential sexual exploitation, her methods—withholding information and highlighting the dangers of heterosexual activity for women—served to institutionalize differential expectations and consequences for the behavior of female and male GI's. Waacs, for example, could be discharged for "illicit sexual activity," but such behavior was expected and often encouraged in male soldiers.[24] Thus, Hobby's policies firmly reinforced the sexual double standard.

Hobby's fears of the adverse public reaction that might result from the distribution of prophylactics information and equipment to Waacs were confirmed by the slander campaign against the WAAC / WAC which started in mid-1943 and continued through early 1944.[25] This "whispering campaign" began with the publication of a nationally syndicated article which reported that in a secret agreement between the War Department and the WAAC, contraceptives would be issued to all women in the army.[26] This piece provoked a storm of public outcry and marked the resurgence of accusations of widespread sexual immorality in the women's corps.

Subsequent army investigations showed that most rumors about the WAAC / WAC originated with male servicemen and officers.[27] Telling "slanderous" stories about the WAAC / WAC was one expression of the resentment men felt at women's entrance into a previously male-only preserve. These attitudes also indicated the confusion present on the command level and among rank-and-file enlisted personnel as to the purpose and function of a women's corps. Was the mission of the women's corps a military one or was the WAAC created to help "improve male morale"? Was a servicewoman's primary function as a soldier, supporting her comrades in arms, or as a woman boosting sagging male spirits and providing feminine companionship for the lonely? A number of servicemen answered these questions by writing home advising girlfriends and family members against joining the women's corps, both because of the "bad reputation" of its members and the belief of some GI's that the WAAC was created solely to "serve" male soldiers sexually.[28]

Public fears that the only "real uses" the army had for women were sexual were exacerbated by male officers who claimed that the most important function of the WAAC / WAC was not the soldierly duties it performed but the positive impact the women had on the "morale" of male soldies.[29] Although "morale boosting" did not necessarily imply prostitution or sexual service, the two were often linked in the public consciousness. For example, one army investigator reported that in Kansas City, Kansas, it was believed that "Waacs were issued condoms and enrolled solely for the soldier's entertainment, serving as 'morale builders' for the men and nothing more."[30] Hobby worked to eliminate all references to Waacs / Wacs being used for "morale purposes," believing that these bolstered public concerns with heterosexual immorality in the corps.[31]

In addition, the occasional use of WAAC / WAC units to control male sexuality seemed to confirm suspicions that the role the army envisioned for women was sexual. For example, African American WAAC / WAC units were in general stationed only at posts where there were Black male soldiers present. In part this was a product of the army's policy of segregating its troops by race. However, white officers, particularly at southern posts, also explicitly referred to the "beneficial" presence of African American WAAC / WAC units as a way to insure that Black male troops would not form liaisons with white women in the surrounding communities. Thus, in this instance, African American WAAC / WAC units were used by the army as a means of upholding and supporting prohibitions on interracial relationships.[32] Similarly, in December 1944, Field Marshall Sir Bernard L. Montgomery proposed using white, American WAC and British Auxiliary Territorial Service units in the Allied occupation of Germany to curb the fraternization of male GI's in the U.S. and British armies with enemy (German) women, especially prostitutes. Field Marshall Montgomery's proposal was made public in a number of articles and editorials and harshly criticized by WAC Headquarters, as well as by Wacs stationed overseas in the European theater of operations.[33] It is clear from these examples that military policy and practice were sometimes contradictory.

This situation was made more complicated by the fact that Waacs / Wacs and male soldiers regularly dated and socialized. This was particularly true in overseas theaters of war where military women were often the only U.S. women in the area. The only army regulations dealing with the social interaction of female and male military personnel were long-standing rules against fraternization between officers and enlisted personnel. Again the question arose of whether Waacs / Wacs should be treated like all other soldiers or if allowances should be made for female/male interactions across the caste lines established by the military. No clear answer to this query developed during World War II. In practice, the regulations concerning the socializing of male officers and female enlisted personnel and vice versa varied from post to post and over different theaters. Many Waacs / Wacs were extremely vocal in their resentment of what they perceived as army policies dictating whom they should not date.[34] When fraternization policies were enforced between women and men, it was usually the Waac / Wac who was punished, not the male soldier or officer, if discovered in violation of these regulations.[35] This practice made it clear that it was women's responsibility to say "no" to these encounters and reinforced the sexual double standard which excused men's heterosexual activity and punished that of women.

Informal policies addressing issues of whether male soldiers and officers should be allowed in WAAC / WAC barracks and dayrooms (recreational and reading rooms) were usally set by the ranking WAAC / WAC officer or the theater commander in overseas areas and varied enormously. The emphasis was on keeping such interactions local and controlled; thus, although no formal regulations were present, WAAC / WAC Headquarters recommended that women bring their soldier dates to the dayrooms and recreational facilities provided on army posts. Hobby believed that this would allow for informal supervision and chaperonage, as well as decrease the opportunities for sexual relations between female and male GI's.[36]

The army's negotation between anxieties about assertive female sexuality, whether heterosexual or homosexual, and the realities of servicewomen's sexual vulnerability to abuse by male GI's and officers can be seen by examining the army's efforts to control the sexuality of servicewomen in the Southwest Pacific Area. Upon arrival in Port Moresby, New Guinea, in May 1944, Wacs found their lives unexpectedly restricted. The theater headquarters directed that in view of the great number of white male troops in the area, "some of whom allegedly had not seen a nurse or other white woman in 18 months,"[37] Wacs should be locked within their barbed wire compound at all times except when escorted by armed guards to work or to approved group recreation. No leaves, passes, or one-couple dates were allowed at any time. Many Wacs found these restrictions unbearable and patronizing and complained that they were being treated as criminals and children. The mounting complaints from women at WAC Head-quarters and rumors of plummeting morale moved Hobby to protest to the War Department and ask for a discontinuation of what many Wacs referred to as the "concentration camp system." The War Department responded that it was in no position to protest command policies, especially because the theater authorities insisted that the system was required "to prevent rape of Wacs by Negro troops in New Guinea."[38] Societal stereotypes of African American men, in particular, as rapists, and of male sexuality, in general, as dangerous for women, were used to defend the extremely restrictive policies of the military toward Wacs in the Southwest Pacific Area. In this situation the army stepped in as the surrogate male protector defending white military women's honor and virtue by creating a repressive environment designed to insure a maximum of "protection" and supervision.

One consequence of the controls placed on women's heterosexual activities in the Southwest Pacific Area was a series of rumors in late 1944 claiming wide-spread homosexuality among Wacs in New Guinea. The concerns originated in letters of complaint from several Wacs stationed there who asserted that restric-tive theater policies created an ideal habitat for some women to express and ex-plore their "abnormal sexual tendencies." The War Department and Hobby sent a WAC officer to the theater to investigate the rumors.[39] The report issued by Lt. Col. Mary Agnes Brown, the WAC staff director, noted that although homo-sexuality was certainly not widespread, several incidences of such behavior had occurred. Lieutenant Colonel Brown felt that the situation was accentuated by the rigid camp security system to which Wacs were subjected. She suggested increasing Wacs' opportunities for recreation "with a view of maintaining the normal relationships between men and women that exist at home and avoid the creation of abnormal conditions which otherwise are bound to arise."[40] When faced with a choice of protecting women from men or "protecting" them from lesbian relationships which might occur in a sex-segregated and restricted com-pound, Lieutenant Colonel Brown's recommendation was to protect service-women from the possibility of homosexuality.

The more repressive framework created by Hobby to control women's sexu-ality in the face of public antagonism was also challenged by women, both heterosexual and lesbian, who asserted their autonomy and right to find their own means of sexual expression within the authoritarian structure of the army. Indeed, heterosexual women sometimes manipulated fears of homosexuality in the women's corps to expand their own opportunities for heterosexual activity. They accused female officers who enforced army regulations against fraternization of male and female officers and enlisted personnel of being "antimale" and discouraging "normal" heterosexual interactions. For example, in February 1944, Capt. Delores Smith[41] was ordered to report for duty as the commanding officer of the Army-Air Forces WAC Detachment at Fort Worth, Texas. As a new commanding officer, Captain Smith sought the help and advice of her officer staff in familiarizing herself with the company and environment. Receiving little support from her officers, she turned for advice to the ranking enlisted woman, Sgt. Norma Crandall. Shortly after her arrival, Smith reprimanded several of her company officers for allowing enlisted men to frequent the WAC barracks and mess hall. In addition, she cautioned these officers on their fraternization with male enlisted personnel. Two weeks later these officers brought charges of homosexuality against Captain Smith. They cited her restrictions on female/male interactions on post, her "dislike" of socializing with servicemen, and her "close association" with the enlisted woman, Sergeant Crandall, as evidence of her "abnormal tendencies." Despite the lack of concrete documentation to support these accusations, Hobby and the Board of Inquiry felt that to allow Captain Smith to continue as a WAC officer would only damage the reputation of the corps, and she was forced to resign from service.[42]

The WAC officers at Fort Worth were angered by what they perceived as the imposition of unfair restrictions on their social lives by Captain Smith. They responded by invoking homophobic anxieties. In doing so they simultaneously defended their right to choose how and with whom they would socialize and reinforced social taboos and army proscriptions against lesbianism. The "lesbian threat" thus became a language of protest to force authorities to broaden their heterosexual privilege.

Lesbian servicewomen, like their heterosexual counterparts, also tried to create their own space within the WAC. In these efforts army lesbians were affected by the contradiction between official proscriptions of homosexuality and the WAC's informal policies on female homosexuality, which were quite lenient. For example, in literature distributed to WAC officer candidates, potential corps leaders were instructed to expect some degree of homosexuality within their commands. They were cautioned:

Homosexuality is of interest to you as WAC officers, only so far as its manifestations undermine the efficiency of the individuals concerned and the stability of the group. You, as officers, will find it necessary to keep the problem in the back of your mind, not indulging in witch hunting or speculating, and yet not overlooking the problem because it is a difficult one to handle. Above all, you must approach the problem with an attitude of fairness and tolerance to assure that no one is accused unjustly. If there is any likelihood of doubt, it is better to be generous in your outlook, and to assume that everyone is innocent until definitely proved otherwise....

Army regulations providing for the undesirable discharge of homosexuals were rarely used against lesbians in the WAC, and WAC officers were warned to consider this action only in the most extreme of situations. Hobby felt that such proceedings would only result in more intensive public scrutiny and disapproval of the women's corps. Instead, it was suggested that WAC officers use more informal methods of control. These included shifting personnel and room assignments, transferring individuals to different posts, and as was exemplified in New Guinea, insuring that corps members were provided with "opportunities for wholesome and natural companionship with men." Another recommended method for dealing with homosexuality was to encourage a woman with "homosexual tendencies" to substitute "hero worship" of a WAC officer for active participation in homosexual relations. WAC policies stated:

> If she is deserving of the admiration of those under her command, the officer may be enabled, by the strength of her influence, to bring out in the woman who had previously exhibited homosexual tendencies, a definite type of leadership which can then be guided into normal fields of expression, making her a valued member of the Corps.... [43]

In addition, on several posts informal WAC policy prohibited women from dancing in couples in public and cautioned against the adoption of "mannish" hairstyles. WAC leaders were concerned primarily with the image of the corps, and Hobby felt that the adverse publicity generated by intense screening procedures, investigations, and court-martials of lesbians within the WAC could only hurt the corps. Thus, as historian Allan Bérubé has noted in his work on gay GI's during World War II, the expanding antihomosexual apparatus of the military was focused much more closely on regulating and screening for male homosexuals than for their female counterparts. [44]

Within these parameters, lesbians within the WAC developed their own culture and methods of identifying one another, although the risks of discovery and exposure remained. The court-martial of T. Sgt. Julie Farrell, stationed at an army school in Richmond, Kentucky, provides an interesting example of this developing culture and its limits. Although she was given an undesirable discharge because of "unsuitability for military service," Technical Sergeant Farrell's court-martial focused on her alleged homosexuality. According to the testimony of Lt. Rosemary O'Riley, Farrell approached her one evening, depressed at what she felt were the army's efforts to make her "suppress her individuality," including criticisms and reprimands for her "mannish hairstyle" and "masculine behavior." Receiving a sympathetic response, Farrell went on to ask the lieutenant if she understood "double talk" and if she had ever been to San Francisco. It is clear that these questions were used by Farrell to determine if it was safe to discuss issues of homosexuality with O'Riley. When the lieutenant answered in the affirmative to her queries, Farrell went on to speak more explicitly of the "natural desires" of women which the military attempted to suppress. She ended with what Lieutenant O'Riley later termed as a "humiliating suggestion." Farrell was surprised by O'Riley's insistence that she had "no interest in such things" and remarked, "Well, when you first came on this campus we thought that maybe you were one of us in the way you walked."[45]

As this example illustrates, mannerisms and coded language were a few of the ways in which lesbians identified one another. It is also clear from O'Riley's testimony that Farrell, a woman exhibiting more "masculine" mannerisms and traits, was more visible as a lesbian. In part, this seems to confirm Bérubé's arguments that "butch" servicewomen, because of their greater fit with popular lesbian stereotypes, were more likely to be targeted as female homosexuals in discharge proceedings.[46] However, lesbians, unlike their gay male counterparts, violated prescribed gender norms simply as women entering the male military. The presence of "butch" women in the WAC subverted Hobby's efforts to frame the women's corps as a "feminine" entity. Thus, "butch" women, because they refused to work at proving their femininity, were suspect.[47]

Lieutenant O'Riley's reports of Farrell's comments and behavior resulted in a court-martial proceeding against Technical Sergeant Farrell. In the course of this proceeding it was argued that in addition to this latest breach of military regulations, Farrell had already been the subject of "malicious gossip and rumor."[48] Most damaging, however, were love letters between Farrell and a WAAC officer, Lieutenant Pines, that were entered as evidence. The tender and explicit discussions of the women's relationship contained within these letters were crucial to the decision of the board to dismiss Farrell from service. Lieutenant Pines avoided prosecution by claiming that the interactions described in the letters occurred only in the imagination of Farrell. Pines covered herself by asserting that she had kept the letters because of her own suspicions of Farrell. Thus, in saving herself, Pines sealed the fate of her lover.[49]

Despite the opportunities for creating and sustaining a lesbian identity or relationship within the WAAC/WAC, the process was also fraught with danger and uncertainty. Army policies provided a space in which female homosexuals could exist, recognize one another, and develop their own culture. Yet this existence was an extremely precarious one, framed by army regulations which also provided for the undesirable discharge of homosexuals, female and male. These regulations could be invoked at any time and were widely used in purges of lesbians from the military in the immediate postwar years, purges that were in part the result of the army's decreasing need for women's labor.[50] In these efforts the army utilized the techniques illustrated in Julie Farrell's court-martial, enabling some women to protect themselves by accusing others of lesbianism. In addition, some lesbians used heterosexual privilege and respectability to obscure their sexual identity by getting married or becoming pregnant in order to leave the army and protect themselves and their lovers. Pat Bond, a lesbian ex-Wac who married a gay GI to avoid prosecution, described one of these purges at a base in Japan: "Every day you came up for a court-martial against one of your friends. They turned us against each other. . . . The only way I could figure out to save my lover was to get out. If I had been there, they could have gotten us both because other women would have testified against us."[51]

The tensions between agency and victimization illustrated here are characteristic of women's participation within the U.S. Army during World War II. Hobby's attempts to portray Wacs as sexless and protected in response to accusations of heterosexual promiscuity were undercut by the need also to present Wacs as feminine and sexually attractive to men to ease fears that the military would attract or produce "mannish women" and lesbians. In addition, the army's occasional utilization of WAC units to control male sexuality seemed to confirm the belief that women's role within the military was sexual. Within this confusing and fluctuating environment, and in negotiation with army regulations and public opinion, Wacs tried to define their own sexuality and make their own sexual choices. Their actions sometimes challenged and other times reinforced entrenched gender and sexual ideologies and were crucial to the development of a role for women within the military. The process of creating a category of "female soldier" was defined by these interactions between Wacs, the army hierarchy (which was often divided along gender lines), and public opinion. The reformulation and reconstruction of gender and sexual norms involved in this process did not end with the war but is still going on today. Women's service continues to be circumscribed by debates over the contradictory concepts of "woman" and "soldier," and servicewomen continue to grapple with the sexual images of dyke and whore framing their participation.

Notes

Many of the arguments contained within this article were in part the product of dialogues with my colleagues in the Graduate Program of Women's History at the University of Wisconsin, especially Laura McEnaney, Andrea Friedman, and Jennifer Frost. I would also like to acknowledge the suggestions and advice I have received from Linda Gordon, Jeanne Boydston, and especially Allan Bérubé, whose thoughtful comments on my original paper given at the Berkshire Women's History Conference in the summer of 1989, were crucial to the final form of this article. Last, I wish to thank my friend and partner Maureen Fitzgerald for her unwavering support throughout this process.

1. Nona Brown, "The Army Finds Woman Has a Place," *New York Times Magazine*, 26 Dec. 1948, 14.

2. Leisa D. Meyer, "Image v. Reality: Public Perceptions of Women in the Women's Army Corps, 1942-1943" (Paper presented at the Social Science History Association Conference, Washington, D.C., fall 1989).

3. The Women's Army Auxiliary Corps (WAAC) was formed on May 14, 1942, by congressional legislation. It was transformed into the Women's Army Corps (WAC) on Oct. 1, 1943. This change marked the end of women's status as "auxiliaries" and the beginning of their official role as soldiers *in* the military proper. For the purposes of this paper I use the acronym "WAAC" and "WAC" depending on when the events I am discussing take place, and "WAAC/WAC" when arguments I am making are applicable to both groups. When referring to women in the service, I use Waac/Wac.

4. There has been a great deal of historical research on women's participation in the civilian labor force during World War II. The major debate among these historians is whether to characterize World War II as a period of temporary or permanent change in women's position in society. Although William Chafe, in his work *The American Woman: Her Changing Social, Economic, and Political Roles, 1920-1970* (New York: Oxford University Press, 1972), saw World War II as a watershed, accelerating the movement of women, especially married women, into the labor force, there has been general agreement among later historians that various forces worked against the retention of the most progressive changes adopted to encourage women's entry into nontraditional fields. Karen Anderson's *Wartime Women: Sex Roles, Family Relations, and the Status of Women during World War II* (Westport, Conn.: Greenwood Press, 1981), along with Susan Hartman's *The Homefront and Beyond: American Women in the 1940s* (Boston: Twayne Publishers, 1982), D'Ann Campbell's *Women at War with America: Private Lives in a Patriotic Era* (New York: Oxford University Press, 1984), and Ruth Milkman's *Gender at Work: The Dynamics of Job Segregation during World War II* (Urbana: Illinois University Press, 1987), acknowledge that the war was in some ways a turning point for U.S. women. They agree that wartime mobilization swept aside the traditional sexual division of labor, and women entered "men's" jobs in basic industry on a massive scale. Yet, they also assert that during the postwar period, women were forced back into traditional female occupations or out of the labor market completely. The work of Maureen Honey, in *Creating Rosie the Riveter: Class, Gender, and Propaganda during World War II* (Amherst: University of Massachusetts Press, 1984), and Leila Rupp, in *Mobilizing Women for War: German and American Propaganda, 1939-1945* (Princeton: Princeton University Press, 1978), on the use of propaganda in the mobilization of women workers is also extremely helpful.

For a specific discussion of African American women's role in the labor force during the war, see Paula Giddings, *When and Where I Enter: The Impact of Black Women on Race and Sex in America* (New York: Bantam Books, 1984), chap. 14, pp. 231-60; Alice Kessler-Harris, *Out to*

Work: A History of Wage-Earning Women in the United States (New York: Oxford University Press, 1982), chap. 10, pp. 273–99; Gerda Lerner, *The Majority Finds Its Past: Placing Women in History* (New York: Oxford University Press, 1979), chap. 5, pp. 63–82.

5. This issue was actually the subject of heated debate surrounding the WAAC bill in Congress. One particularly vehement opponent of women's presence in the army protested:

> I think it is a reflection upon the courageous manhood of the country to pass a law inviting women to join the armed forces in order to win a battle. Take the women into the armed service, who then will do the cooking, the washing, the mending, the humble homey tasks to which every woman has devoted herself? Think of the humiliation. What has become of the manhood of America?

Cited in Mattie Treadwell, *The United States Army in World War II: The Women's Army Corps* (Washington, D.C.: U.S. Army Office of the Chief of Military History, 1953), 25. See also the *Congressional Record*, vol. 88, no. 55 in File: "Congressional Record," located at National Archives and Records Administration (hereafter cited as NARA) in Washington, D.C., Box 217, Series (S)55, Record Group (RG)165.

6. John D'Emilio and Estelle Freedman, *Intimate Matters: A History of Sexuality in America* (New York: Harper & Row, 1988), 260, 288–89. See also John Costello, *Love, Sex, and War: Changing Values, 1939–1945* (London: Williams Collins Sons & Co., 1985); and Allan Bérubé, *Coming Out under Fire: The History of Gay Men and Women in World War II* (New York: Free Press, 1990), 6. See also Elaine Tyler May, *Homeward Bound: American Families in the Cold War Era* (New York: Basic Books, 1988), 69.

7. Kathy Peiss, " 'Charity Girls' and City Pleasures: Historical Notes on Working-Class Sexuality, 1880–1920," in *Passion and Power: Sexuality in History,* ed. Kathy Peiss and Christina Simmons, with Robert A. Padgug (Philadelphia: Temple University Press, 1989).

8. May, 69–71.

9. John D'Emilio, *Sexual Politics, Sexual Communities: The Making of a Homosexual Minority in the United States, 1940–1970* (Chicago: University of Chicago Press, 1983), 16–17. See also D'Emilio and Freedman, 193–94.

10. The African American press did not address the issue of women's military service in the same way as the white mainstream media did. Within their editorials, gender stereotyping still occurred and fears of the possible problems that might arise from the creation of a women's corps were expressed. However, they were not raised as accusations but rather as concerns and were more veiled. Most criticisms of the military addressed by the African American press were directed at its Jim Crow policies and included anger over the assignments of African American soldiers, female and male, to menial tasks and duties. For examples of this see *Philadelphia Afro-American* (March–December 1943), in particular Charles Howard's regular column, "At Home and Abroad with the WAAC"; *The Crisis* (February 1943); *The Opportunity*, 1943–45; File: "Scrapbook," *Headlines and Pictures: A Monthly Negro News Review*, Box 2, S54, RG165, NARA; "Turn Down Negro Wacs for Overseas Service," *Chicago Defender* (December 1943); and excerpts from the *Ohio News* (December 1943); Dovey Johnson Roundtree Papers, Bethune National Archives for Black Women's History, Washington, D.C.

11. There are numerous examples of these fears expressed in the media, letters to the War Department and WAAC Headquarters, letters written by female and male soldiers intercepted by post censors, and reports of army investigations into these rumors. Specific cites will be given throughout this paper; most come from the following groups of records: NARA, RG165, S54, WAC Decimal File, 1942–46; RG165, S55, WAC Historical Background Information Files, 1942–49; Oveta Culp Hobby Papers, Library of Congress, Washington, D.C.; WAC Publicity and Newspaper Files, WAC Museum, Anniston, Alabama. For example, see 9 June 1943 letter to Mrs. Gold (mother of a Waac) and 11 Aug. 1943 letter from Cpl. Badgett to Cpl. Helen Stroude

and 2 Dec. 1943 letter from 1st Lt. Roland to Sgt. Ray Coley caught by Base Censor, File: "Rumors," Box 192, S55, RG165, NARA.

12. "Reports on Rumors," Headquarters, Minneapolis Recruiting District, Minneapolis, Minnesota; 3 July 1943, Harrisburg (Pennsylvania) Armed Forces Recruiting and Induction District, 1st Officer Lovella M. Jones, Assistant Waacs Recruiting Officer; File: "Rumors," Box 192, S55, RG165; See also "Reports on Rumors," Fifth Service Command, Fort Hayes, Columbus, Ohio, 10 July 1943, 1st Officer Helen Y. Hedekin to Col. Oveta Culp Hobby; Box 92, S54, RG165, NARA. For examples of mainstream media coverage, see "Waac Whispers," and "Waac Rumors," *Newsweek*, 14 June 1943, 34–35, and 21 June 1943, 46.

13. Treadwell, 625.

14. Col. Oveta Culp Hobby, interview by Joan Younger of the *Ladies Home Journal*, File: "*Ladies Home Journal*, Article on WAC, 1952," Box 9, Oveta Culp Hobby Papers.

15. Hobby's approach to her role as WAAC director was influenced by her membership in a broader network of elites, white women who gained positions within the state in the 1930s. The power wielded by these women was based on a philosophy of women's and men's difference and the belief that women had a special role to play in society. See Susan Ware, *Beyond Suffrage: Women in the New Deal* (Cambridge: Harvard University Press, 1981), 14; Nancy F. Cott, *The Grounding of Modern Feminism* (New Haven: Yale University Press, 1987); and Kathryn Kish Sklar, "Hull House in the 1890s: A Community of Women Reformers," in *Unequal Sisters: A Multicultural Reader in U.S. Women's History*, ed. Ellen Carol Dubois and Vicki L. Ruiz (New York: Routledge, 1990), 109–22.

16. 3 June 1943 speech by Msgr. Michael J. Ready, General Secretary, National Catholic Welfare Conference, Box 1, S54, RG165, NARA; June 1943 press release by church leaders following their visit to WAAC Training Centers at Fort Des Moines (Iowa) and Fort Oglethorpe (Georgia), Box 21, S54, RG165, NARA.

17. For an example of this, see 19 July 1943 letter from Mrs. Ceil Howard (Waac mother) to Hobby, Box 90, S54, RG165, NARA. See also File: National Civilian Advisory Council Forum, Box 191, S55, RG165, NARA.

18. "Summary of Reports on Rumors," Seventh Service Command, File: "Rumors," Box 192, S55, RG165, NARA.

19. Kathy Peiss and Christina Simmons, "Passion and Power: An Introduction" (3–13), and Kathy Peiss, " 'Charity Girls' and City Pleasures" (57–65) in *Passion and Power*.

20. Ernest O. Houser, "Those Wonderful GI Janes," *Saturday Evening Post* 217, (9 Sept. 1944): 20–26, 60, 63. For other examples of articles dealing specifically with the issue of "mannish women" and lesbianism, see "War Women" (Racine, Wis.) *Journal-Times* (21 July 1942) File: Newspaper Clippings, WAAC, Box 8, Oveta Culp Hobby Papers; Jack Kefoed, *Miami, Florida, News* (20 May 1942), Box 9, RG319, Center of Military History MSS File, Mattie Treadwell's Background Files, NARA.

21. Bérubé, 2. Bérubé's book also includes a unique and important discussion of the changes in the way the military dealt with homosexuality occurring during World War II. He demonstrates how the professions of psychiatry and neuropsychiatry influenced the military to move from policies punishing a particular sexual act, sodomy, to policies addressing a personality type defined as homosexual.

For a more general discussion of the relationship between the military and venereal disease, see Allan Brandt's *No Magic Bullet: A History of Venereal Disease in America since 1880* (New York: Oxford University Press, 1985). See also D'Emilio and Freedman, chap. 9 and File: Articles, Box 1; File: Joint Army and Navy Disciplinary Control Board, Social Protection Division, Box 5; File: Magazines, Box 7, all in S37 and File: 849 (June 1945), Box 1; File: 849.1 (1944), Box 4, all in S38; all in RG215, Records of the Office of Community War Service, Social Protection Division 1941–46, NARA. The Records of the Office of Community War Service, Social Protection Division, NARA, contain a great deal of information on the development of military policies on prevention of venereal disease among male troops and the treatment of infected soldiers. These records also address military policy on the issue of interracial liaisons formed by African American troops.

22. 17 July 1942 letter to Hobby from Comdr. E. H. Cushing, U.S. Naval Reserve, Division of Medical Science re: The Conference Group called by the Surgeon General's Office; 27 July 1942 memo for Director WAAC from Lt. Col. Harold Tasker, "Report of the Conference on Prevention of VD in Female Personnel of Armed Forces"; 13 Aug. 1942 memo for Hobby from Emily Newell Blair, Chief Women's Interest Section, Planning and Liaison Branch, War Department; 18 May 1943 memo to Hobby from Surgeon General, Box 145, S54, RG165, NARA. See also Treadwell, 615–16.

23. War Department Pamphlet 35-1, "Sex Hygiene Course for the Women's Army Corps" (May 1945), 12–19, Box 145, S54, RG165, NARA. See also Treadwell 616–19.

24. For a discussion of the development of policies on discharging Waacs/Wacs for "morals offenses," see Treadwell, 498–500. See also WAAC Regulations (Tentative) 1942, Sec. V; Army Regulations 615-630, 615-368, and 615-369.

25. Correspondence between the WAAC and the Syracuse Rumor Clinic and letters from Daytona Beach (Florida) residents concerning the WAAC Training Center there, May 1943 through August 1943, Box 13, S54, RG165, NARA. See also File: 250.1, Box 48, S54, RG165, NARA. This slander or rumor campaign was widely documented, and several historians have commented on the problems it created for military women. See D'Ann Campbell, chap. 1; Ruth Roach Pierson, *"They're Still Women After All": The Second World War and Canadian Womanhood* (Toronto: McClelland & Stewart, 1986), chap. 5; Treadwell, 32, 231–46.

26. John O'Donnell, "Capitol Staff," *Washington Times-Herald,* 9 June 1943.

27. Summary of Reports on Rumors, Seventh Service Command; 9 June 1943 letter to Mrs. Gold (mother of a Waac) from Hobby; 11 June 1943 letter to Comdr. Neil B. Wolcott from Mr. John Warren; 10 July 1943 letter to Mrs. Miriam J. Cohen from Hobby on behalf of Mrs. Roosevelt based on army press release dated 1 July 1943; File: "Rumors," Box 192, S55, RG165, NARA. For examples of how these rumors were articulated in the press, see "Waac Whispers" and "Waac Rumors," *Newsweek,* 14 June 1943, 34–35 and 21 June 1943, 46.

28. For examples of this type of commentary on the part of male GI's and officers see, 3 Feb. 1944 letter to Hobby from Ruth Clellan, File: 095, Box 17, S54, RG165, NARA; 7 Feb. 1945 letter to War Department from Miss Elizabeth King, File: K, Box 19, S54, RG165, NARA; 17 Jan. 1945 letter to WAC Headquarters from Lee Robinson, Box 20, S54, RG165, NARA; 2 May 1944 letter to Hobby from Alfred E. Puls, and 9 Aug. 1944 letter to Hobby from a concerned ex-Wac, File: P, Box 21, S54, RG165, NARA; "Report from Confidential Files of Colonel Scott Bailey, Chief Base Censor of Allied Forces, HQ," Box 57, S54, RG165, NARA.

29. These types of statements were widespread. One example is: "WACs in the European Division, ATC, June 1944–August 1945, Historical Record Report," 108, File: "Wacs in the European Division, ATC [Air Transport Command]," June 1944–August 1945, Box 308.04-1 (31 Jan. 1945), 308.072 (June 1944–August 1945), Maxwell Air Force Base, Historical Research Center, Montgomery, Alabama.

30. Report of Rumors from Seventh Service Command, Army Service Forces, Col. Jacob J. Gerhardt, Director Personnel Division, 1st Officer Mary S. Bell, WAAC Staff Director Reporting, 9 July 1943, File: "Rumors," Box 192, S55, RG165, NARA.

31. Treadwell, 48.

32. 3 Aug. 1942 memo to General Somervell from Brig. Gen. W. B. Smith, File: 320.0 75th and 76th Post Headquarters Companies (18 Aug. 1942) (1) Sec. 1, Box 79, S54, RG165, NARA; 30 June 1943, Colored Requisitions, Box 43, S54, RG165, NARA; 5 Jan. 1943 memo to Colonel Catron re: Negro WAAC Companies for duty with 92d Division, File: Activation of Post Headquarters Companies and Photographic Lab Companies, Aerial 320.2 1-1-43 (1) Sec. 2, Box 74, S54, RG165, NARA. See also Report of AAFTC [Army Air Force Tactical Center], Sioux Falls, South Dakota, on status of requisitions for colored Waacs, July 1943, File: "Assignment and Classification," Box 190, S55, RG165, NARA.

33. James McDonald, "Sending of Women to Germany Urged," *New York Times*, 5 Dec. 1944; "WACS, ATS [Auxiliary Territorial Service] Plenty Angry at New 'Role,' " 8 Dec. 1944; 16 Dec. 1944 letter to Hobby from Miss Gertrude M. Puelicher, National Federation of Press Women; 26 Dec. 1944 letter to Miss Puelicher from Lt. Col. Jessie Rice, Executive Officer, WAC, Box 14, S54, RG165, NARA.

34. For examples of this resentment being expressed and reported by WAC officers see, 8 Jan. 1944 memo to Lt. Patricia Lee, Editorial Officer, WAC Director, from Maj. Helen Woods, WAC Staff Director, File: 095, Box 17, S54, RG165, NARA; 3 June 1943, Southwest Pacific Area 320.2 (4-17-43) E memo to Maj. Gen. E. S. Hughes, Deputy Theater Commander, NATO, from Col. T. B. Catron, Military Advisor, Box 94, S54, RG165, NARA.

35. Treadwell, 446–47.

36. Ibid., 520–22. See also Joanne J. Meyerowitz, *Women Adrift: Independent Wage Earners in Chicago, 1880–1930* (Chicago: University of Chicago Press, 1988), chap. 4, for discussion of similar situations involving organizations like the Young Women's Christian Association which invoked parental authority, often acting as "surrogate families," in their provisions of services to working-class women.

37. Treadwell, 421–25.

38. There were both Black and white troops stationed in New Guinea at the time of the Wacs' arrival. The army's reasons for barricading women shifted as, at first, a general warning about white male troops was issued and later, in response to Hobby's pressure, a more specific warning about "Negro troops" was issued. 22 Dec. 1944 letter to Representative Cravens from Lt. Col. Jessie Rice, Executive Officer, WAC, File: C 201, Box 25, S54, RG165, NARA; WDWAC 314.7 Military Histories, Historical Data and Notes on Southwest Pacific Area WACS, Box 58, S54, RG165, NARA; WDWAC 333.2 August 1945, List of Complaints on Conditions in Southwest Pacific Area and Corrective Action Taken (Summary), File: 333, Boc 95, S54, RG165, NARA. See also Treadwell, 421–24, 450.

39. 1 Oct. 1944 letter from Pvt. Ruth Ricci to friend in the United States (intercepted by post censor); 12 Oct. 1944 letter to Hobby from Lt. Col. Elizabeth Strayhorn re: Private Ricci's Accusations of Widespread Homosexuality; 28 Oct. 1944, Report of Conditions for Wacs in New Guinea, File: 330, Box 89, S54, RG165, NARA.

40. 23 Oct. 1944 memo to Lt. Col. Brown from Maj. Gen. Frink re: List of Recommendations Made by Brown for Southwest Pacific Area; 24 Nov. 1944 memo to Colonel Coursey from Lieutenant Colonel Brown, File: 330, Box 89, S54, RG165, NARA.

41. All names used within the case studies that follow are pseudonyms, except for the WAAC/WAC Director, Colonel Hobby.

42. 20 Mar. 1944 letter to Hobby from Captain Smith's mother; 28 Mar. and 31 Mar. 1944, transcribed phone conversations between Colonel Hobby and Colonel Morrisette, Judge Advocate General's Office, concerning this situation; 17 Oct. 1944, WDGAP 201—"Report on Relief of WAC Officer from Active Duty," File: "Data, WAAC Officers," Box 201, S55, RG165, NARA.

43. War Department Pamphlet 35-1, p. 25, 26.

44. Bérubé 59–61; chaps. 1, 2.

45. 22 July 1943, Report of Proceedings of a Board of Officers in the Case of Tech. 4th Grade Julie Farrell, WAAC, WAAC Branch No. 6, AAS, Richmond, Kentucky, Testimony of Tech. 4th Grade Julie Farrell and Lt. Rosemary O'Riley, 3d Officer, WAAC, File: P, Box 29, S54, RG165, NARA.

46. Bérubé, 54–57, 170, 203.

47. For a discussion of this point in reference to gay men and lesbians in sports, see Nancy Boutilier, "Playing Games: Gender and Sexuality in the Sports World," *Outlook*, no. 14 (Fall 1991): 74–76.

48. Testimony of Lt. Linda Daniels, 2d Officer, WAAC, File: P, Box 29, S54, RG165, NARA.

49. Testimony of T4g. Farrell, Lt. Madden, 2d Officer, WAAC, and Lt. Pines, 2d Officer, WAAC, File: P, Box 29, S54, RG165, NARA.

50. "Tapioca Tapestry," in *Long Time Passing: Lives of Older Lesbians*, ed. Mary Adelman (Boston: Alyson Publications, 1986). For a discussion of the impact of these purges particularly for gay men and the "legacy" of the war for gays and lesbians, see Bérubé, 213–15, 217, and chap. 10. I believe these purges of lesbians similar to those of gay men were primarily motivated by the demobilization of the armed forces and the need to cut personnel. This pattern is no different today than it was fifty years ago, as homosexuality is tolerated when the military needs personnel, and then gays and lesbians are purged when the need no longer exists.

51. Adelman, 166.

5

When Virginia Looked at Vita, What Did She See; or, Lesbian : Feminist : Woman—What's the Differ(e/a)nce?

Elizabeth Meese

I am reduced to a thing that wants Virginia.
—Vita Sackville-West, *Letters of Vita Sackville-West to Virginia Woolf*

I lie in bed making up stories about you.
—Virginia Woolf to Vita Sackville-West, *Letters of Virginia Woolf*

I don't know if love's a feeling. Sometimes I think it's a matter of seeing. Seeing you.
—Marguerite Duras, *Emily L.*

"LESBIAN" AND "WOMAN" interest me most when "Feminism" occupies the site of the conjunction, the colon as copula that seeks to balance the terms, to strike relationships between them which do not necessarily exist. I always write about the lesbian : the woman as though she were a feminist, as if she (all three of us) occupied the same body. This improper way of speaking disturbs me as a way of defining the lesbian body, as flesh or word. I suspect that impropriety marks every instance of speaking or writing about the lesbian, just as it does the body, the woman. In regard to this problematic of sexual identity and definition, Stephen Heath observes:

> We exist as individuals in relation to and in the relations of language, the systems of meaning and representation in which, precisely, we find ourselves—try to imagine the question of who you are and any answer outside of language, outside of those systems. Sexual relations are relations through language, not to a given other sex; the body is not a direct imme-

Feminist Studies 18, no. 1 (Spring 1992). © 1992 by Feminist Studies, Inc.

diacy, it is tressed, marked out, intrinsically involved with meanings. Of course, we can shake our heads, appeal to the fact that *we know* the direct experience of the body, two bodies in love, making love. Yet "direct experience," "the body" and so on are themselves specific constructions, specific notions; the appeal to which is never natural but always part of a particular system.[1]

What does this mean about my lover's body? That I will never have "it," approximating my lover's beauty only imperfectly in letters. But one thing I know: we are dangerous. Imperfections in the letter demand caution. The slip and slide of the signifying chain requires the lover's vigilance just as compellingly as her mouth and hands attend to her beloved when she makes love to her.

Letters are ill-suited to the body, to the "natural." As the Biographer in *Orlando* explains, taking the teenage writer's text as a subject:

> He [Orlando] was describing, as all young poets are for ever describing, nature, and in order to match the shade of green precisely he looked (and here he showed more audacity than most) at the thing itself, which happened to be a laurel bush growing beneath the window. After that, of course, he could write no more. Green in nature is one thing, green in literature another. Nature and letters seem to have a natural antipathy; bring them together and they tear each other to pieces.[2]

In the modern, anti-romantic frame, the "liter-al" and the "letter-al" (differ[e/a]nce) are at war with one another. The belief in language's capacity to stand in for its subject, or to render the object a subject, is shattered but not forgotten.

With respect to knowing and speaking the body, Rodolphe Gasché comments:

> Of the body—the body proper—we can speak only improperly. So it will not only be necessary to talk about it in metaphors, but also to develop the discourse *of* the body, by a process of substitution, as a chain of figures amongst others. Wishing to speak of the body, we can therefore only speak of quite other things, to the point where we might ask ourselves if the body does not consist precisely in those other things, in that grouping of initially heterogeneous elements. In which case the body would be dependent on a certain confusion, because it is always more or less than a body properly speaking.[3]

There is no properly spoken body, no body properly speaking; it being always "more" or "less." We speak it improperly as an always imperfect translation, a bad match of flesh and word, but also as a violation of the law, its spirit if not its letter, identity and language.

The body is a "sum(mary)" of the words accumulated to articulate it, more or less; Gasché continues, "the sum of the body is the result of a selection, of an elimination (subtraction) of many things. The only things selected to go into the sum(ma) are of the sort that can be summarised in one's own sum."[4] But according to some, this body is never a sum, never whole, always a hole; or, every textual body is an imperfect body. In this sense, the lesbian (like the feminist, the woman, and the text) has an improper body that fails according to language's phallic measure. By all rights, man's textual, that is, his "liter-al" body is similarly deficient or inadequate, but the (w)hole of woman's body is doubly marked.[5]

"Difference"/"Differance"—e/a—what's the differ(e/a)nce? A letter here, a letter there. When a woman chooses not to measure up, she can be a lesbian and sometimes a feminist. She posts a letter, "L," to those who care to read it. Every lesbian : woman might be one.

Dear L—

Although these words appear and will reappear, remember that they were written in your name, just as Virginia and Vita wrote to one another.

Dear V—

Do you believe that desire is more interesting than consummation? And so we must become experts of deferral. Deferral—was it you or I who determined that?
V.

An agony inhabits deferred desire, the pain and excitement of letters writing tracks never finished word upon word: Can there be a meaning without consummation? But what ambiguity is there   in the way my tongue traces   ever so slowly   gently the tip just meeting the surface of you   fold by fold around whorl to whorl I follow the subtle turns of your ear wanting to take it all in at once seeking   the dark of your certain   desiring places   mysteries just at the point where inner and outer meet, writing my way down your body letter after letter one formless ecstatic sound following another toward places we have not met before, that I only imagine we will discover, there first and there again. We wait always for the next time which will be the first time. Still, because not still at all, I know you understand just how these words feel on/in your body. Love,
L

How to know you is the mystery I engage as your lover. It is installed at the heart of the lover's task, never finished, compelling vision and voice, moving tongue and hands.

"But could I ever know her?" —Virginia on Vita

Virginia Woolf's *Orlando: A Biography* (1928) has been called "the longest and most charming love letter in literature."[6] I like that. The lesbian love letter is a genre that I am inventing as I write.[7] Woolf dedicates her book "To V. Sackville-West." Her "dedication" to Vita precedes the text, an exergue, a going forth that suggests something before the letter of the text, that presents itself as an answer to Vita's letters, especially *Seducers in Ecuador* (1924),[8] a study in the curiosity of vision, love letters, property, and tradition, dedicated to Virginia four years earlier. It is another letter in the series of letters that constitutes their relationship, their *"epistolarium* of love."[9] Something re-presents itself in these exchanges, where Mitchell A. Leaska's "virgin, shy, schoolgirlish" (really) Virginia so seductively engages Vita, "a grenadier, hard, handsome, manly."[10] An affection that the text as gift stands (in) for. Like true gifts, the text is something uncalled for, unexpected. A surprise of love. Love: a gift of what one does not have. (Vita to Virginia: "I wish, in a way, that we could put the clock back a year. I should like to startle you again—even though I didn't know then that you were startled.") Or, as Virginia describes their sexual intimacy, "The night you were snared, that winter, at Long Barn" [18 December 1925]. Through the agency of the letter, Virginia : Vita constitutes herself as subject, and startles her lover by desire's request that the lover make the asker a subject not an object: "I try to invent you for myself, but find I really have only 2 twigs and 3 straws to do it with. I can get the sensation of seeing you—hair, lips, colour, height, even, now and then, the eyes and hands, but I find you going off, to walk in the garden, to play tennis, to dig, to sit smoking and talking, and then I can't invent a thing you say."[11] In other words, they take each other and themselves, through the lover/other, as subjects of desire, but also as objects, the beloved of the speaker/lover.[12] As Nicole Brossard puts it, "a lesbian is . . . the centre of a captivating *image* which any woman can claim for herself."[13] Through the letter, Woolf stakes out her claim.

Orlando begins with the qualified certainty of Orlando's sex as male: "He—for there could be no doubt of his sex, though the fashion of the time did something to disguise it—was in the act of slicing at the head of a Moor which swung from the rafters." But "his" clothing poses an element of confusion. Freud reads sex "literally," through the clothing, which, for him, reveals the certainty of one's sexual position. Woolf's narrator-Biographer, however, reads from another position, the "unscientific" one of "riot and confusion of the passions and emotions" where, for the speaker and the character, the sex and "nature" of others is not quite clear: "Ransack the language as he might, words failed him. . . . For in all she [Sasha, his beloved] said, however open she seemed and voluptuous, there was something hidden; in all she did, however daring, there was something concealed."[14]

In a sense, critical interest in androgyny in Woolf's work prepares us for and distracts us from as it disguises her lesbian interests—a diversionary tactic she deploys. Rachel Blau DuPlessis describes Woolf's circumstances as follows: "*Orlando* is released into a space not only beyond narrative conventions but also beyond sexual norms. Lesbianism is the unspoken contraband desire that marriage liberates and that itself frees writing. The love of women appears with some circumspection, intermingled with the androgynous, ambisexual marriage and the doubled gender identities of Orlando."[15] Makiko Minow-Pinkney, Maria DiBattista, and Francette Pacteau also shed light on the question. Minow-Pinkney regards the sex change in *Orlando* as a fantasy concerning "the transgression of boundaries as a play with the limit, as a play of difference," enacting "alteration not resolution" or a Hegelian synthesis of the either/or to the static reification of "both."[16] Orlando swings from pole to pole "as if she belonged to neither [sex]; and indeed, for the time being she seemed to vacillate; she was man; she was woman; she knew the secrets, shared the weaknesses of each. It was a most bewildering and whirligig state of mind to be in."[17] The differences between the sexes elude specification in "pure" (as opposed to relational) terms, a phenomenon Woolf's text enacts as it moves through epochs and sexes: "It is a matter of where the dividing line is, and its location varies historically and socially. Any definition only has meaning in relation to a specific sociohistorical context, since there is no innate bond between signifier and signified." As such, then, the transgressions androgyny enacts, Minow-Pinkney maintains, "can only be presented in metonymical displacements, a sliding of one form into another."[18] These slips and slides, the hide and seek of how sexual identity can be represented, remain in motion, but the slide of "one form into another" depends upon preexisting types.

DiBattista views androgyny similarly, as "a double triumph. It overwhelms those stubborn, basically artificial divisions between men and women and thus discovers the basis of a legitimate social order governed by the law of equal association. And it also liberates the mind of women from the most enduring form of cultural and biological tyranny—the tyranny of sex!"[19] Androgyny is a way out of the either/or trap through substitution of a both/and relationship. Arguing along similar lines, DuPlessis sees the "Orlando figure" as "both A and not-A, a logical contradiction, but a narratable prototype of constant heterogeneity."[20]

According to DiBattista, the ruse of the "objective biographer" permits Woolf to "hide . . . the radical subjectivity and indeterminism that invariably attends the treatment of sex in social and political life and in fiction itself. Sex is not a fact, but a space in the psychic life, a hole or lapsus in identity onto which are projected the imagoes, archetypes, or stereotypes comprehended in terms male and female."[21] Pacteau presents a more complex, labile view of androgyny. It is and is not, because it vexes representation: "Androgyny can be said to belong to the domain of the imaginary, where desire is unobstructed; gender identity to that of the symbolic, the Law. . . . "[22]

Probably there are some things that desire doesn't know, some limits and circumstances that it does not recognize. It only finds itself, and that, sometimes obscurely, in the lover. How, then, can I know her?

> Dear L,
>
>   I have been waiting for your call, a reward for waiting. Just a sound is worth my attention. Such a small thing. But then we both know how it makes all the difference, begins to spin out the matrix of difference and meaning we live in. I am always so intent on hearing your voice, more lovely than Satie, etching tracks on the surface of memory like the tips of my fingers trying to memorize the smooth skin on your hand, your arms and back, to remember precisely the viscosity of fluid you when we make love. Fine calibrations of measure and degree, surface and interior distance. Ways of trying to know you/me/what it is we see in one another.
>   Love,
>   L

Starting again. The lesbian question is this: when Virginia looks at Vita, what does she see? What happens when a woman thinks of woman "in what is called 'that way' "?[23] It is the question Rachel Bowlby as a feminist reader of Woolf fails to ask. Or that Mitchell Leaska answers in too literal and limited a way: "In the early months Virginia saw Vita as supple, savage, and patrician. To Vita, Virginia was the 'gentle genius'—lovely, idolized, and remote."[24] This answer begs the question, saying nothing about attraction and affection between women, about lesbian relationship. Is the question—what does one "see" in the other?—too personal, too speculative (from *specere*, to look at)? Another improper embodiment for the serious critical inquirer who would prefer not to look?

This is the difference between Bowlby, the feminist critic, who can write a chapter about *Orlando* without mentioning the word *lesbian*, and me. Or Nigel

Nicolson who avoids the word in his affectionate "liberal"-minded description of *Orlando:*

> The effect of Vita on Virginia is all contained in *Orlando*, the longest and most charming love letter in literature, in which she explores Vita, weaves her in and out of the centuries, tosses her from one sex to the other, plays with her, dresses her in furs, lace and emeralds, teases her, flirts with her, drops a veil of mist around her, and ends by photographing her in the mud at Long Barn, with dogs, awaiting Virginia's arrival next day.[25]

I say it matters when a critic avoids (a form of suppression) the word *lesbian*; as long as the word matters, makes a social, political, or artistic difference, it matters when *lesbian* is not spoken.

These critics also differ substantially from Sherron E. Knopp's more probing and explicit treatment of lesbianism in her essay, " 'If I Saw You Would You Kiss Me?': Sapphism and the Subversiveness of Virginia Woolf's *Orlando*"—an exploration in which Knopp, while refusing, unlike Blanche Wiesen Cook, to specify her relationship to their relationship, installs the lesbian subject at the center of her argument, as she claims, "Yet the extent to which Vita and Virginia did love each other—profoundly and, in every sense of the words, erotically and sexually (the frequency or infrequency with which they went to bed is irrelevant)—is something that continues to be resisted, denied, ignored, qualified out of significance, or simply unrecognized, even by the feminist revolution that enshrined Virginia as its saint."[26] The lesbian critic, "reading as a lesbian critic," reading "in *that* way," searches for something else and finds it, there in the sometimes silent language of the look between those two women, the space between words, the awesome passion of their engagement, even when they are (only) writing. Asking this improper question marks the lesbian scene or angle of vision, brings it into being. Virginia chooses to look and sees. (Virginia to Vita: "and Vita is a dear old rough coated sheep dog: or alternatively, hung with grapes, pink with pearls, lustrous, candle lit.")[27] This lesbian gaze is incompatible with Joanne Trautmann's desexualizing view of Virginia and Vita as cloistered nuns, a figure that is meant (before such explosive works as *The Three Marias* and *Lesbian Nuns: Breaking Silence*)[28] to undercut the sensuality and eroticism of their lives and texts:

> Part of both women's solitude, as discussed before, was an almost fierce sexlessness, or more accurately, a narcissistic sexuality, a state of contemplating themselves and their own feminine sensibilities, which at these times substituted in intensity for the erotic. In this solitude no man could

get at them for a while. Both Vita and Virginia had this and other qualities
of the cloistered nun.[29]

The critical assortment of faulty or incomplete deductions and simple analogies
produces the barren, imprisoned reading its figures lead us to make, as it runs
counter to the playful eroticism that marks these modern love letters as lesbian.

When Virginia looked at Vita, did she see Orlando/*Orlando*? What did she
want? In 1928 she wrote to Vita, demanding her love through the imperative
"first" choice:

> Love Virginia (imperative)
> Love Virginia (absolute)
> Love? Virginia? (interrogative)
> Mine was the 1st.

Did she discover, in this looking, a projection of indirection and inflection, a
going and a return, or, in other words (her—Virginia's/Vita's?) "style"? In the
process of writing *Orlando*, Virginia writes to Vita: "Shall I come Saturday for
the night?—seems the only chance. Let me know. . . . Should you say, if I rang
you up to ask, that you were fond of me? If I saw you would you kiss me? If I
were in bed would you—I'm rather excited about Orlando tonight: have been
lying by the fire and making up the last chapter." Orlando/Vita (who signs her
name so, and to whom Virginia addresses other "love" letters), and *Orlando*, that
novel inventing and commemorating Vita, excite Virginia. Are they separable?
What's the differ(e/a)nce: Vita and Orlando, "Orlando" and Orlando or *Orlando*?
As she completes her novel, Virginia is not certain: "The question now is, will
my feelings for you be changed? I've lived in you all these months—coming out,
what are you really like? Do you exist? Have I made you up?"[30]

Orlando/*Orlando* performs a trajectory of desire as it constructs and propels
itself toward its desiderata, or as Louise DeSalvo puts it, *Orlando* is "a book in
which [Virginia] would possess Vita utterly."[31] But as Orlando's Biographer
notes, the meditation on love, that "first question," yields an unending meta-
phorics rather than the certainty of conclusion: "And as the first question had
not been settled—What is Love?—back it would come at the least provocation
or none, and hustle Books or Metaphors or What one lives for into the margins,
there to wait till they saw their chance to rush into the field again." Line by line,
desire marks out a future, or as the Biographer tells us three times on a page,
"Life and a lover."[32] Concerning this mysterious trajectory, Jacques Lacan writes:
"What counts is not that the other sees where I am, but that [s]he sees where I
am going, that is to say, quite precisely, that [s]he sees where I am not. In every
analysis of the intersubjective relation, what is essential is not what is there,

what is seen. What structures it is what is not there."[33] This is true and not true, isn't it? Perhaps true only to the extent that we *are* interested in the "intersubjective relation" as Virginia pursues the volcanic Vesuvius, Vita.[34] We want to see what she sees, to know how she wants to be seen. We also want to see what she cannot see, the "what is not there" of desire as she writes it.

> Dear "Orlando"—
>
> I reread all your letters today for signs of how, then, you knew that I would later stand in front of you displaying my passion, that I will later still, though you already know it and knew it then, make love to you in words and ways you will forget only with great difficulty and after a long time. What wisdom is it that lets you write a future for me—seeing me where I was not yet, as I look at you now—that even I had not read for me and was powerless to invent. This must be the way that desire through its persistent longing makes what we will become for one another, as in the deferred space of love, a future consummation first imagines and then writes itself as it waits for us to take ourselves down full length, length to length, our bodies finally side by side one on the other and again, searching for the points, compelling the intersection where two are not two any longer, subject and object indistinct, as with my eyes closed I cannot tell my pleasure from yours, and begin to feel that certain ecstasy we become in one another.
> Love,
> V.

Pacteau argues that "fantasy, rooted in the absence of an object, is contingent upon a distance; that between viewer and viewed, where the unconscious comes to rest, along which look and psyche travel."[35] The complex intersection of observer and observed—in an intricate fabric of desire, in an erotics of engazement—recalls Roland Barthes's exploration of the ecstasy of the gaze, as the object pierces the subject in an ecstatic confusion of activity and passivity. Jane Gallop explains: "Ecstasy etymologically derives from the Greek *ekstasis*, from ex-, 'out,' plus *histanai*, 'to place.' Thus, it means something like 'placed out.' Ecstasy is when you are no longer within your own frame: some sort of going outside takes place."[36] Barthes calls this excessive ecstatic pleasure *jouissance*; Orlando/the Biographer/Virginia sums it up in "Ecstasy! . . . Ecstasy!"; "Laughter, Laughter!"; "Life, Life, Life!"[37]—the Latin translation of which, Leaska points out, becomes, "Vita, Vita, Vita!"[38] the lover's signature.

   "I try to invent you for myself." —Virginia on Vita

"For myself." "You" for "me." That there is an "I" and a "you" has great import. As Peggy Kamuf explains, "If there is to be a coming together in a convention of meaning, 'I' and 'you' cannot be subsumed into only an 'I.' By itself, in other words, 'I' makes no sense. There is no meaning, no contract without the more-than-one of an 'I/you' articulated by their difference."[39] Vita writes from Tehe-ran that she wants a picture of Virginia and asks if her own has turned up: "It is a torment not being able to visualize when one wants to. I can visualize you as a matter of fact surprisingly well,—but always as you stood on your door-step that last evening, when the lamps were lit and the trees misty, and I drove away."[40] Virginia saw in Vita the spectacular image of herself, of Virginia the lesbian lover. She invents the lesbian woman who loves women, who might love her, whom she might love. Through speculation, surmise, and even imagina-tion, Woolf, like Orlando's Biographer, attempts "to elucidate a secret that has puzzled historians for a hundred years": to fill in the "hole in the manuscript [record of Orlando's life] big enough to put your finger through."[41] She invents herself as she writes the other, or as Linda S. Kauffman puts it in her probing work on epistolarity and desire, "Since every letter to the beloved is also a self-address, . . . the heroine's project—aided by her reading and her writing—also involves self-creation, self-invention."[42] Through the Biographer and Vita, Woolf constructs herself as a lesbian of letters at the same time that she gives us the lesbian in letters. But who *is* "she"?

Dear V—
   You invite perceptual study:
   Parallax, n. [Gr. *parallaxis*, from *parallas sein*, to vary, to decline or wander; *para*, beyond, and *allassein*, to change.]
      1. the apparent change in the position of an object resulting from the change in the direction or position from which it is viewed.

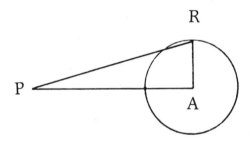

      2. the amount or angular degree of such change; specifically, in as-tronomy, the apparent difference in the position of a heavenly body

with reference to some point on the surface of the earth and some other point, as the center of the earth (*diurnal, of geocentric, parallax*) or a point on the sun (*annual,* or *heliocentric, parallax*): the parallax of an object may be used in determining its distance from the observer.

—*Webster's New World Dictionary*

What is the parallax of you, the graceful angle we compose of you me surface and center, seen in this way, a bright star that suddenly changes direction in the night sky, a new sun I gradually alter myself to see. Was it you who moved or I, standing now in a shy ecstasy (mine and yours) at the door as you come up the walk, your head turned eyes slightly angled toward me waiting through the distance between years the night the morning hours slowly assembling themselves with diurnal regularity toward such an orderly vision, like the way my words ultimately compose themselves on the page, toward the feel of you.
Love,
L

The parallax distance is a function of the view, the coursing of desire, the elaboration of fantasy. Pacteau explains the figure of the androgyne in similar terms:

The androgyne dwells in a distance. The androgynous figure has to do with *seduction*, that which comes before undressing, seeing, touching. It can only exist in the shadow area of an image; once unveiled, once we throw a light on it, it becomes a woman or man, and I (myself) resume my position on the side of the female. The perfect symmetry of the figure of the androgyne positions the viewer at the convergence of the feminine and the masculine where "s/he" oscillates. The androgyne is excessive in its transgression of the boundaries of gender identity; however, this threat of superabundance, of overflowing, is safely contained within the frame of the feminine and the masculine.

The androgyne, as a gap, an excess, resembles the lesbian, but without community, without the sociopolitics of identity and the history of movement and struggle, and still caught within the oppositional categories of gender. The androgyne, as such, then, is the "first figure," but s/he is a figure in motion, the "origin" that never was, only to be re-figured or given over to the either/or. The androgyne, as/when represented, according to Pacteau, shows up

as an attempt to objectify desire, to reduce into one *still* image a process, is in itself contrary to the dynamics of the fantasy that produces it.... Representation of the androgynous "in between" is an impossibility. Perhaps it is because of the image's overwhelming concern with the "body" as the site of all truth. The "body" as an entity, as an end in itself, cannot contain the excess of the androgynous fantasy.[43]

Letters, like all texts, but love letters in particular as a signed pledge from me to you, leave "the door open for all sorts of improprieties and expropriations"; as Kamuf explains, there "is no guarantee that [s/]he [the signer] feels what [s/]he expresses or expresses what [s/]he feels."[44] (Vita to Virginia: "Do you ever mean what you say, or say what you mean? or do you just enjoy baffling the people who try to creep a little nearer?")[45]

Through Orlando/*Orlando*, Virginia becomes (most like) Vita; she imagines her as a lover, her love affair. When she began the book, she wrote to Vita,

> Yesterday morning I was in despair. . . . I couldn't screw a word from me; and at last dropped my head in my hands: dipped my pen in the ink, and wrote these words, as if automatically, on a clean sheet: Orlando: A Biography. No sooner had I done this than my body was flooded with rapture and my brain with ideas. I wrote rapidly till 12. . . . But listen; suppose Orlando turns out to be Vita; and its [*sic*] all about you and the lusts of your flesh and the lure of your mind (heart you have none, who go gallivanting down the lanes with [Mary] Campbell) . . . Shall you mind? Say yes, or No: . . . "[46]

On these grounds, Françoise Defromont argues that *Orlando* is a public exposé of Vita's affections and infidelities, and Virginia's jealousy which she displaces through writing.[47] Similarly, Knopp describes the novel as both "public proclamation" and private exploration: "Far from being a way to create distance in the relationship, *Orlando* was a way to heighten intimacy—not a substitute for physical lovemaking but an extension of it."[48] A love affair of the letter.

We could say that Virginia saw herself and not herself, herself as she wished to be-come (that is, a woman like the Vita she saw), herself as she wished Vita to see her (a woman Vita could love), and Vita as Virginia wished her to be, the one who puts Virginia on the "first rung of her ladder." Virginia sees, first and foremost, a lesbian, and invests in Vita, through the character of Orlando, the history of women "like" her—five hundred years of lesbianism, or four hundred years of English tradition—one of Woolf's most striking realizations, and the very awareness that produces (itself) in the curious construction of Orlando, larger than life, longer than life, all of life.

Vita responds that the experience of *Orlando* gives a new meaning to narcissism: "you have invented a new form of Narcissism,—I confess,—I am in love with Orlando—this is a complication I had not foreseen."[49] Virginia/Orlando/Vita. Desire, according to Lacan, is always triangulated, but I see Vir-

ginia/Vita—Orlando/Virginia/Vita—Virginia/Leonard; Vita—Virginia/Vio-
let/Rosamund—Harold. Father : mother/lover/daughter.

Vita's image returns her to herself. But it is Virginia's narcissism as well—
an autoerotic gesture (loving one's self enough to create a lover), a self-engen-
dering move (becoming lesbian, beloved and beloved), a creation of one's (and
one's self as) lover and love object,[50] a brilliant circuitry. A "writer's holiday,"
"an escapade,"[51] Orlando/*Orlando* is a love affair.

"intimate letters" —Virginia to Vita (*Letters*, 3: 117)

In writing *Orlando*, Virginia Woolf set out to make an intimate story very public,
or perhaps it was to make a public story very intimately her own. She wrote in
her diary on October 22, 1927: "I am writing *Orlando* half in a mock style very
clear and plain, so that people will understand every word. But the balance between truth & fantasy must be careful."[52] As Defromont contends in *Virginia
Woolf, Vers la maison de lumière*, Woolf's texts explore the relation between life,
writing, and libidinal energy, "between talent and femininity, emotion and art."
Flush, the biography of Elizabeth Barrett Browning's spaniel, most pointedly
displays this investigation. Woolf struggles between the poles of intellect and
instinct, the differ(e/a)nce constitutive of *jouissance* in both instances.[53]

In *Signature Pieces: On the Institution of Authorship*, Peggy Kamuf suggests a
way of describing the relationship between Virginia and her lover Vita and the
text or letter/character of Orlando, or *Orlando*. Kamuf writes provocatively that
the signature is

> an always divisible limit within the difference between writer and work,
> "life" and "letters." Signature articulates the one with the other, the one
> *in* the other: it both divides and joins. It is this double-jointedness of sig-
> natures that will be lost to any discourse that continues to posit an essen-
> tial exteriority of subjects to the texts they sign.[54]

Thus the problematic of lesbian : writing is inscribed in what Defromont describes as the "or/and, *Or/l/and/o*,"[55] the passage from one sex to the other, one
writing function to the next. *Orlando* is a play on words, on/in the letter. The
signature "is the mark of an articulation at the border between life and letters,
body and language. An articulation both joins and divides; it joins and divides
identity with/from difference. A difference from itself, within itself, articulates
the signature on the text it signs." It joins and divides "the historically singular
subject to which it refers (or seems to refer) and the formal generality of language."[56]

Desire writes the absence at its heart, a lack, as Lacan puts it, "beyond anything which can represent it. It is only ever represented as a reflection on a
veil,"[57] the shadowy hand on a fine sheet of paper or the faint tracks on the

sheets after rising, inscribing the love letter. Will I be able to read it? The Biographer cautions us that "the most poetic is precisely that which cannot be written down. For which reasons we leave a great blank here, which must be taken to indicate that the space is filled to repletion."[58] How do I see what Virginia sees? How do I see her seeing Vita? In a sense, "the Biographer" tells me how to imagine Virginia looking at Vita, a gap and an overflow. And my lover and I (re)enact the scene.

> Dear L—
>   It is you startled I see in the near distance eyes opened and my fluid love for you begins to move, the shudders of desire wash over me, lap on lap. Orlando sees the woman s/he loves and thinks of names—melon, pineapple, olive tree, emerald, the clear-eyed fox startled as it crosses the snow. These names the senses supply to construct their desire in the lover, to approximate "the green flame [that] seems hidden in the emerald, or the sun prisoned in a hill."[59]
> What names do I have for that desiring lover whose dark eyes are haunted with me, who is surprised by the love we make together, whose surprise takes me by surprise, leads me to invent something more. Invention—the events, the feelings, the names for the words that fail to speak what is hidden, concealed in the ways we move in one another, how much we want it in the space of deferral, whether we are together or apart.
> This letter locates us side by side, puts us here in the same place, even though I know you are away, that I must wait for your return as I construct my desire in memory of your body. It must be the lover's work to write love letters, character after character, arranging the white spaces and the dark shapes, forms of silence and sound, presence and absence, hour after hour, with the same careful attention she pays to her lover's body, as she waits for her to come back so she can put this letter aside and lead her to the bedroom, take off her clothes, arrange her gently but ever so quickly on the bed and continue together with a violent tenderness to compose their love in gestures and sounds that have no easy names, shapes that come to us from a place beyond memory.
> Love,
> L

Like Woolf, who first places Chloe and Olivia in the laboratory, and then sees their differences (from one another, two women who are not waiting for men but for each other, an economy of difference not lack, not sameness; and their sufficiency, not waiting for a man to fulfill them, to fill them up, to plug up the w/hole so the body can be summed up).[60] She sees their secret, hers and mine, or at least the possibility of a future for them. In Vita, she sees herself loving Vita; she sees lesbian : woman. Her lesbian feminist readers see it too, and some feminist readers can learn to recognize the figure as well. Virginia writes to Vita about a woman who sent her a letter: "A woman writes that she has to stop and kiss the page when she reads O.—Your race I imagine. The percentage of Lesbians is rising in the States, all because of you."[61] More writing : more lesbians.

Dear Vita and Virginia,

How can I read your letters without, above all, wanting to write? Years of correspondence, circulating affection and longing make me desire more letters. I don't want them to end or to stop, so I continue (y)our correspondence.

Dear V, Your sheepdog puts her muzzle on her paws and waits at the door. Will you pet her when you arrive? Will you remember the feel of her fur and discover new ways to startle her? Love, V.

Dear V and V, I feel an absence when I write one without the other. Even the letter V—one side an obverse mirroring of the other, only connected at that precise swelling point. There must be a name for this effect—V. In any case, it reads like a lesbian effect; a lesbian can claim it as her own. (Y)ours is, after all, "a captivating image."

VVVVVVVVVVVVVVVVVVVVV

Taking flight,

Love,

L

Notes

1. Stephen Heath, *The Sexual Fix* (London and Basingstoke: Macmillan Press, 1982), 154.

2. Virginia Woolf, *Orlando: A Biography* (Harcourt Brace Jovanovich, 1956), 17. Originally published in 1928.

3. Rodolphe Gasché, "*Ecce Homo* or the Written Body," *Oxford Literary Review* 7 (1985): 3.

4. Ibid., 11.

5. In "The Match in the Crocus: Representations of Lesbian Sexuality," in *Discontented Discourses: Feminism/Textual Intervention/Psychoanalysis*, ed. Marleen S. Barr and Richard Feldstein (Urbana and Chicago: University of Illinois Press, 1989), 100–116, Judith Roof observes that "the representation of the lesbian is an open site for the play of sexual difference in its relationship to the perception and representation of sexuality. Conscious of a kind of phallic preeminence, women writers are faced with the difficulty of representing perceptions unaccounted for in a phallic economy in terms of that economy" (p. 109).

6. Nigel Nicolson, *Portrait of a Marriage* (New York: Athenaeum, 1973), 218.

7. I am indebted to previous lesbian and feminist scholarship on Woolf and desire: Louise DeSalvo, "Lighting the Cave: The Relationship between Vita Sackville-West and Virginia Woolf," *Signs* 8 (Winter 1982): 195–214; Sonya Rudikoff, "How Many Lovers Had Virginia

Woolf?" *Hudson Review* 32 (Winter 1979): 54–66; Joanne Trautmann, *The Jessamy Brides: The Friendship of Virginia Woolf and V. Sackville-West* (University Park: Pennsylvania State University Press, 1973); and especially Sherron E. Knopp, " 'If I Saw You Would You Kiss Me?': Sapphism and the Subversiveness of Virginia Woolf's *Orlando*," *PMLA* 103 (January 1988): 24–34. Also see Jane Marcus, *Virginia Woolf and the Languages of Patriarchy* (Bloomington and Indianapolis: Indiana University Press, 1987); and Linda S. Kauffman, *Discourses of Desire: Gender, Genre, and Epistolary Fiction* (Ithaca and London: Cornell University Press, 1986).

  8. Vita Sackville-West, *"Seducers in Ecuador"* and *"The Heir"* (London: Virago Press, 1987).

  9. Mitchell A. Leaska, Introduction, *The Letters of Vita Sackville-West to Virginia Woolf*, ed. Louise DeSalvo and Mitchell A. Leaska (New York: William Morrow, 1985), 27. For discussions of Woolf's "letters," see Leaska's introduction to *The Letters of Vita Sackville-West to Virginia Woolf*; and Catharine Stimpson's "The Female Sociograph: The Theater of Virginia Woolf's Letters" in *The Female Autograph*, ed. Domna Stanton and Jeanine Parisier Plottel (New York: New York Literary Forum, 1984), 193–203.

  10. Victoria Glendinning, *Vita: A Life of V. Sackville-West* (New York: Knopf, 1983), 128.

  11. DeSalvo and Leaska, eds., *Letters of Vita Sackville-West to Virginia Woolf*, 151, 301; and *The Letters of Virginia Woolf*, ed. Nigel Nicolson and Joanne Trautmann (New York and London: Harcourt Brace Jovanovich, 1977), 3 (1923–1928): 204–13.

  12. E. Ann Kaplan, "Is the Gaze Male?" in *Powers of Desire: The Politics of Sexuality*, ed. Ann Snitow, Christine Stansell, and Sharon Thompson (New York: Monthly Review Press, 1983): 309–27, turns the common assumption that the gaze *is* male into a problematics deserving of investigation. She asserts that in lesbian fantasies women occupy both the dominated and dominating positions and that "dominance-submission patterns are apparently a crucial part of both male and female sexuality as constructed in western capitalism." She maintains that while "the gaze is not necessarily male, to own and activate the gaze, given our language and the structure of the unconscious, is to be in the masculine position" (pp. 317, 318, 319).

  13. Nicole Brossard, *The Aerial Letter*, trans. Marlene Wildeman (Toronto: Women's Press, 1988), 121.

  14. Woolf, *Orlando*, 13, 16, 47.

  15. Rachel Blau DuPlessis, *Writing beyond the Ending: Narrative Strategies of Twentieth-Century Women Writers* (Bloomington: Indiana University Press, 1985), 63.

  16. Makiko Minow-Pinkney, *Virginia Woolf and the Problem of the Subject* (Brighton, England: Harvester Press, 1987), 122, 131.

  17. Woolf, *Orlando*, 158.

  18. Minow-Pinkney, 130, 131.

  19. Maria DiBattista, *Virginia Woolf's Major Novels: The Fables of Anon* (New Haven: Yale University Press, 1980), 19.

  20. DuPlessis, 63.

  21. DiBattista, 118.

  22. Francette Pacteau, "The Impossible Referent: Representations of the Androgyne," in *Formations of Fantasy*, ed. Victor Burgin, James Donald, and Cora Kaplan (London and New York: Methuen, 1986), 3.

  23. Nicolson, 29.

  24. Rachel Bowlby, *Virginia Woolf: Feminist Destinations* (Oxford: Blackwell, 1988); Trautmann, 3; DeSalvo and Leaska, eds., *Letters of Vita Sackville-West to Virginia Woolf*, 11.

  25. Nicolson, 218.

  26. Knopp, 24. See also Blanche Wiesen Cook, " 'Women Alone Stir My Imagination': Lesbianism and Cultural Tradition," *Signs* 4 (Summer 1979): 718–39.

  27. DeSalvo and Leaska, eds., *Letters of Vita Sackville-West to Virginia Woolf*, 79.

  28. Maria Barreno, Maria Teresa Horta, Maria Velho da Costa, *The Three Marias: New Portuguese Letters*, trans. Helen R. Lane (New York: Bantam, 1976); and *Lesbian Nuns: Breaking Silence*, ed. Rosemary Curb and Nancy Manahan (Tallahassee: Naiad Press, 1985).

29. Trautmann, 32.

30. Nicolson, ed., *Letters of Virginia Woolf*, 3: 446; DeSalvo and Leaska, eds., *Letters of Vita Sackville-West to Virginia Woolf*, 246, 264.

31. DeSalvo, 204.

32. Woolf, *Orlando*, 100, 185.

33. Jacques Lacan, *The Seminar of Jacques Lacan*, ed. Jacques Alain Miller, *Book 1: Freud's Papers on Technique, 1953–1954*, trans. John Forrester (New York and London: W.W. Norton, 1988), 224.

34. Glendinning, 124.

35. Pacteau, 77–78.

36. Jane Gallop, *Thinking through the Body* (New York: Columbia University Press, 1988), 15.

37. Woolf, *Orlando*, 287, 271, 270.

38. Leaska, 46.

39. Peggy Kamuf, *Signature Pieces: On the Institution of Authorship* (Ithaca and London: Cornell University Press, 1988), 53.

40. DeSalvo and Leaska, eds., *Letters of Vita Sackville-West to Virginia Woolf*, 112.

41. Woolf, *Orlando*, 119.

42. Kauffman, 25.

43. Pacteau, 78–79, 81.

44. Kamuf, 25.

45. DeSalvo and Leaska, eds., *Letters of Vita Sackville-West to Virginia Woolf*, 52.

46. Ibid., 237.

47. Françoise Defromont, *Virginia Woolf: Vers la maison de lumière* (Paris: éditions des femmes, 1985), 185.

48. Knopp, 27.

49. DeSalvo and Leaska, eds., *Letters of Vita Sackville-West to Virginia Woolf*, 289.

50. On the question of narcissism, see Jacqueline Rose, *Sexuality in the Field of Vision* (London: Verso, 1986): 167–83.

51. Virginia Woolf, *A Writer's Diary*, ed. Leonard Woolf (New York: Harcourt Brace Jovanovich, 1953), 117–18, 124.

52. Virginia Woolf, *The Diary of Virginia Woolf*, ed. Anne Olivier Bell and Andrew McNeillie (New York: Harcourt, 1980), 3 (1925–1930): 162.

53. Defromont, 171, 61–62, 137.

54. Kamuf, viii.

55. Defromont, 209.

56. Kamuf, 39–40, 41.

57. Jacques Lacan, *The Seminar of Jacques Lacan, Book 2: The Ego in Freud's Theory and in the Technique of Psychoanalysis, 1954–1955*, trans. Sylvana Tomaselli (New York and London: W.W. Norton, 1988), 223.

58. Woolf, *Orlando*, 253.

59. Ibid., 37, 47.

60. Jane Marcus (136–87) traces the repressed lesbian narrative of Woolf's relation to other lesbian writers.

61. DeSalvo and Leaska, eds., *Letters of Vita Sackville-West to Virginia Woolf*, 318.

6

Imitations of Marriage

Crossdressed Couples in Contemporary Lesbian Fiction

Anne Herrmann

Women who adopt the male standpoint are passing, epistemologically
speaking.
—Catharine MacKinnon, "Feminism, Marxism, Method, and the State"

Feminism is nothing but the operation of a woman who aspires to be like a man.
—Jacques Derrida, *Spurs*

RECENT THEORIZING ABOUT lesbian and gay subjectivity has relied on two
dominant paradigms: the epistemological and the performative. The epistemological focuses on questions of knowing and asks with hesitation, how
does one know if one is gay? It deconstructs the relation between ignorance and
knowledge by relying on the construction of what Eve Kosofsky Sedgwick in
Epistemology of the Closet calls an "open secret" (homosexuality exists, but I don't
know any homosexuals) policed by "homosexual panic" (what if someone
thinks I'm gay?). The performative, theorized primarily by Judith Butler in *Gender Trouble*, questions identity as a source of knowledge and states bluntly: gender is drag. It constructs gender as something one does rather than something
one is. To perform one's gender is to produce the effect of "woman" or "man"
as real, an effect mistaken for a cause when "woman" and "man" are understood to be the origin not the result of compulsory heterosexuality.

The "epistemology of the closet," as formulated by Sedgwick in the context
of male homosexuality, explains the position of both genders inasmuch as

Feminist Studies 18, no. 3 (Fall 1992). © 1992 by Feminist Studies, Inc.

women also feel compelled to conceal their sexual identity by "passing" as straight; yet inasmuch as the lesbian is already of an inferior gender status and not a legally prohibited subject (laws against homosexuality foreground the male homosexual), "homosexual panic" describes the ontology of only one sex, the masculine. On the other hand, the performative also constructs both genders, but insofar as mimicry and masquerade have been theorized by feminist scholars as feminine,[1] how does one know when a "femme" is not the same as a "queen" is not the same as a "bottom" is not the same as a straight woman with false consciousness?

Thus, the epistemological and the performative should not be conceived of as contradictory but rather as mutually informing paradigms. Sedgwick suggests that " 'closetedness' itself is a performance initiated as such by the speech act of a silence."[2] "Coming out of the closet" involves no simple revelation of a knowledge through the reversal of that speech act. One could come out in silence, by lipsynching in drag; one could be "outed" by someone else's speech act. One could also—given homosexuality's construction as "open secret"—know that one is gay, be acknowledged as gay, but never put that knowledge into shared speech. In "Imitation and Gender Insubordination" Judith Butler argues that *"outness can only produce a new opacity; and the closet produces the promise of a disclosure that can, by definition, never come."*[3] The meaning of "I am a lesbian" as performative act contains an epistemological uncertainty, because the meaning of that act is both out of the control of the "I" and marked by the specificity of only a single individual. Here an understanding of the performative focuses not on whether the knowledge is "out" but on how its meaning can never be contained.

The narrative of the "closet" is the "coming out" story: the lesbian or gay subject discloses an identity in the form of an ontology (I was always gay) through a speech act that can never happen just once. At the same time, gender as performative becomes most obvious through crossdressing; clothes put into question the ontological status of the body as the signifier of a "true" gender. What "coming out" and crossdressing have in common is the revelation of something that was always known: in the first case an "essential" sexuality that is not heterosexual; in the second case a "true" sex underneath the clothes. But the relation between these two knowledges needs further exploration, because the revelation of a "true sex" is precisely to ensure the compulsoriness of heterosexuality.

Because Sedgwick's theory focuses almost exclusively on male homosexuality and Butler's on the destabilizing of all gender identities, neither has sufficient explanatory power for addressing popular lesbian fictions with crossdressing plots. How can an "essential" lesbian sexuality reveal itself when one of the women crossdresses, performing an "untrue" or masculine sex? Combining the "coming out" story with the literal "performance of sex," these fictions construct the "open secret" as "marriage," an arrangement that produces not "homosexual panic" but the possibility of an eroticized lesbian subject. This subjectivity requires the couple to ensure a stable lesbian identity, one that relies on the butch provisionally (to make it sexual), but a butch who remains incomplete without the femme (otherwise she or the couple might mistake her for a man).[4] The semblance of a "heterosexual marriage" does not enable the recognition of something that was always known (gayness) but the possibility of making known the unrecognizable (lesbian sexuality). At the same time the "imitation" of that which is all too familiar (heterosexual marriage), denaturalizes the roles and emphasizes the sex beneath the gender—the sameness and thus the subversion of sexual difference. The fear, then, is not that the "marriage" will be discovered, thereby unmasking the lesbian subject but, rather, that the roleplaying will reintroduce heterosexual hierarchies into a same-sex, that is, egalitarian couple.

Three works of fiction published in the last twenty-three years by and for lesbian readers—Isabel Miller's *Patience and Sarah* (1969), Jeannine Allard's *Légende: The Story of Philippa and Aurélie* (1984), and Shelley Smith's *The Pearls* (1987)—confront the performative aspect of gender roles through the knowledge that "marriage" enables two women to live openly as a couple while keeping secret their status as lesbian subjects. All three novels negotiate between the silence about same-sex relations that are policed by homophobia in a world of compulsory heterosexuality and the "truthfulness" about gender required by partners within a lesbian "marriage." In these novels, monogamous female "marriages"—historically constructed in terms of the pastoral retreat and passionlessness made legendary by the many rewritings of the story of the Ladies of Llangollen[5]—offset the stereotype of a "pastoral retreat" with a carefully articulated "passion" enabled by the illusion of a "masculine" subject. The "masculine" subject simultaneously eroticizes the lesbian relationship, by allowing it to be coded as sexual, and hides the eroticization of the same-sex couple through the semblance of a publicly sanctioned heterosexual "marriage." The necessity of crossdressing (as a form of physical protection in *Patience and Sarah*, as a form of legal protection in *Légende*, and as a form of professional advancement in *The Pearls*) also allows for a reading of these stories within a historical chronology that ranges from making a lesbian domestic arrangement possible outside of pathology and prohibition to making possible same-sex desire apart from a politicized lesbian feminism.

Although the three texts appear to replicate each other in the use of a crossdressing plot and in an appropriation of the naturalized relationship of wife and husband, they map out three different moments in the construction of a contemporary lesbian subject. Rather than invoking the conventional heterosexual romance plot involving a woman who needs to learn to read the man as he who has always loved her, the lesbian couple must come to accept "the man" as a necessary deception in order to make possible the "natural" love between two women. Although the "masculine" as male identification denaturalizes the lesbian couple, the "butch" comes by her role "naturally": she is raised as the son necessary for agricultural labor; she wants to be a man in order to go to sea; she accepts a dangerous mission that will further her career. Although in *Patience and Sarah* the lesbian subject seeks her gendered complement to produce an egalitarian couple, in *Légende* the role playing is contrasted to the more desirable coupling of two androgynous subjects, and in *The Pearls* the gendered couple refuses a butch-femme public construction of erotic attachment. Each plot closes with a discarding of the male costume in order to return to "natural" subject positions and the recuperation of an egalitarian ideal; thus, all three novels seem to negate the subversive potential of gender as performance.

At the same time these narrative structures foreground the butch not because she makes sex visible but because she signifies the deception necessary to allow the sexualized relationship to "pass" as a marriage. Although the plots establish crossdressing as an epistemological fraud, they also represent it as a performative act. In *Patience and Sarah* passing signifies the imitation of a man, in *Légende*, a masquerade necessary for survival, and in *The Pearls*, a form of role-playing required by the job. "Passing" as male, in contrast to playing the role of the butch, necessarily raises epistemological questions that focus less on how one knows one is gay than on how to circulate that knowledge as ignorance, how to "lie" in order to preserve the "truth" of same-sex desire, how to recognize that desire given its reliance on deception. The lesbian romance plot moves away from the categories of the "real" woman and a "natural" same-sex relationship by relying on a system of sexual signs—butch-femme roles as the sign of an eroticized and public lesbian subculture as well as a gay male culture in its production of a greater familiarity with the currency of artifice. Both *Patience and Sarah* and *The Pearls* rely on a gay male figure to initiate the butch into deception, one which subverts the equation of the natural with the feminine by including variations on the "feminized" man. Once crossdressing has been accepted as disguise, it allows the lesbian couple to feign a "marriage" that enables the representability of a female romance as both same-sexed and sexual.

Patience and Sarah
Famous companion lovers from the Large Country (First Continent, Steam Age). They lived on a farm that they built west of the Green Mountain

State. They worked in polyculture and did a little breeding. Sarah was a
woodcutter and Patience a painter. She painted in particular the episode
of the destruction of Gomorrha.

—Monique Wittig and Sande Zeig,
Lesbian Peoples: Material for a Dictionary

Isabel Miller's *Patience and Sarah* (1969)—read by Catharine Stimpson as an exception to "the bristling contempt for sexual role-playing"[6] in lesbian fiction and by Bonnie Zimmerman as a misread butch-femme couple because "the more significant difference between them is class"[7]—represents the ur-text of current lesbian fictions and those employing crossdressing plots. Originally printed privately by Alma Routsong in 1969 under the title *A Place for Us*, the novel was reissued by McGraw-Hill in 1973 under the pseudonym "Isabel Miller." Miller retells the story of Mary Ann Willson, a primitive painter in New York State in the early nineteenth century, who had a "romantic attachment" to a "farmerette" companion, Miss Brundidge.[8] Sarah, a farmer's daughter raised as a son, and Patience, a painter provided for by her father's will, live on neighboring farms in Connecticut until they set up house together on an isolated homestead in Greene County, New York. Sarah only crossdresses in Patience's absence, initially setting out alone in men's clothes because the failure to keep their love a secret has led to Patience's loss of faith in its survival and thus to her renunciation of it. Although the experience of crossdressing teaches Sarah the art of deception, it is an art she must learn to renounce if she is to enter a "marriage" with Patience as a "natural" act. Neither an exception to the lesbian feminist rejection of butch-femme roles nor "more" about class difference than about sexuality, the novel negotiates the contradiction between femininity as a middle-class construct and an iconography of the lesbian feminist as "butch."

Deception in *Patience and Sarah* is initially disconnected from literal cross-dressing. Shortly after Sarah first encounters Patience she confesses to her sister, Rachel "I found my mate,"[9] to which Rachel responds, "I used to worry about you. That no man would have you. I never thought to worry you'd think you *was* a man." Sarah replies, "I'm not. I'm a woman that's found my mate" (p. 37). Rachel, who betrays her sister by passing this information on to their father—partly out of rivalry and partly out of a sense of the relationship's "unnaturalness"—confuses object choice with ontology. In refusing to recognize her sister's difference, she sees the solution to this confusion in simply renouncing the truth as a lie. Sarah is encouraged to engage in deception as something that comes "naturally" to women from a sister whose potentially incestuous affection must be coded as rivalrous.

Patience, whose affection must be differentiated from Rachel's, responds with a different sense of betrayal to Sarah's finding "a mate": "I'd say, 'Betrayed! Betrayed!' and think of myself as like Jesus and Sarah as Judas, and then, more moderately, as Peter. Foolish and impetuous and weak, like Peter" (p. 44). Patience realizes she could be accused of even greater betrayal because she seeks to deny her desire: " 'No, I never loved her, no I never kissed her, no I'm not her mate' " (p. 45). Deception is distinguished from feminine deviousness when Patience is unable to follow the advice Rachel gave Sarah that she confess not to have known that mate could mean either "partner" or "wife": "You just say it was all a lie, what you said before" (p. 48), Rachel suggests to Sarah. If what Sarah really wants is a partner with whom to go west, then she must disavow her desire for a "wife" by disclaiming her affection and by claiming that all she wanted was Patience's money. For either lesbian in Miller's novel to love and then renounce that love is a greater betrayal than never to have named it at all.

Patience betrays Sarah by not following her on the journey west, not because there is another man but because she can't be one, thereby conflating identification with desire.

> And I felt, I think for the first time, a rage against men. Not because they
> could say, 'I'm going,' and go. Not because they could go to college and
> become lawyers or preachers while women could be only drudge or or-
> nament but nothing between. Not because they could be parents at no cost
> to their bodies. But because when they love a woman they may be with
> her, and all society will protect their possession of her. (P. 51)

The iconography of the lesbian as butch allows Patience, the femme, to identify as a butch by adopting a feminist ideology; while Sarah cuts her hair, changes her name, and leaves her role as oldest son to another sister. She promises her father not to tell anyone that she is a girl, even as this would facilitate rather than obviate a same-sex object choice. But this deception proves to be as dangerous as the initial honesty, because boys traveling alone are no less vulnerable than women, and Sarah is now at the mercy not of her father's physical violence but another man's sexual advances. En route she encounters Daniel Peel, a Yankee peddler and former parson, who sells books in New England every summer from a "little blue house on red wheels," leaving his wife and children in New York City. Peel becomes the "good" father, serving as mentor to "Sam," teaching him to read as well as decipher things that aren't written: "I assure you that men have loved and embraced each other since the beginning of time" (p. 80). Although same-sex relations among men has a history based on a tradition of reading "signs," the signs available to women can only be misread as an appro-

priation from the other gender. That this is "a common natural thing" nevertheless makes any relation between Peel and "Sam" unnatural not as the relation between two men but as the relation between a butch lesbian and a gay
man.

The most important lesson Sarah learns from Peel is how to lie about their
encounter so as to reinitiate her visits with Patience, now that lying no longer
is coded in terms of cross-gender identification. On her return home she convinces Rachel that she has developed an affection for the parson, thereby allowing her sister to invent an elaborate tale about how, trapped in the "lie of being
a boy," she was unable to express her love and was eventually forced to abandon
her lover. Sarah learns deception from a gay man who regularly deceives his
wife, and marriage is the deceit that allows him to follow his "natural" desires.
The tale that Peel tells his family about "Sam" is equally untrue, because it hides
the fact that Sarah was forced into revealing her "true sex" due to his sexual
interest; he tells his daughter that once, when her father couldn't find his shav-
ing kit he asked "Sam" if he had it, if he had seen it, if he could borrow his. At
that point "he" had to admit that he had none because he was a girl. Sarah uses
an illicit heterosexual affair to legitimate a lesbian one, while Peel desexualizes
the moment of discovery of Sarah's "true" sex to conceal his own homosexuality.

The lies necessary to keep silent about gay relations within a straight world
must nevertheless be discarded between partners once they enter into a "marriage." As "the husband," Sarah is concerned about where to homestead once
she and Patience leave Connecticut. Having heard that land is still available in
Greene County, which is much closer than they had expected to settle, Sarah
invents a story about having an uncle there in order to legitimate her decision.
Having learned from her father that it is the prerogative of the husband to tell
the wife where to follow, Sarah nevertheless is made uncomfortable by her lie,
so much so that guilt causes her to confess. Although the deceptive tales of Peel
are likened to the theater, Sarah's lie to Patience is placed in metonymic relation
to entertainments such as the flea circus and other "natural curiosities": when
wires hold on the other head of the two-headed calf, theatrical illusion has
turned to "cheat." Equally, although a sexual double standard remains in the
realm of "illusion" and thus acceptable for men, the hierarchy produced by gender roles between women becomes equated with fraud.

While traveling as two women alone, Patience insists that Sarah adopt the
role not of a boy but of a lady. If, as Patience suspects, "it may be that one must
be male, or owned by one, not to be their natural victim" (p. 138), the only other
option is to "denaturalize" oneself by becoming asexual, that is, middle-class.
By making Sarah follow the edict: "Don't see, don't hear, don't blush" (p. 141),

Patience puts herself in the role of the "man," not by crossdressing but by asserting her class superiority in the form of a gender consciousness. Although Patience hesitates to "improve" Sarah because she wants her to remain the same (that is, different from herself and thus complementary), that difference should be indifferent to the social differences of gender and class, which are seen by Patience as "denaturalizing." The only legitimate differences are individual ones, even as these are already coded in terms of Sarah being raised as a boy and Patience being provided for by a will. By avoiding the subject positions of both male and middle-class, Sarah is left with none at all, temporarily positioned as blind, deaf, and speechless, a final eradication of the masculine through the subjectlessness of femininity. In the final scene Sarah builds the bed on their homestead and Patience paints the picture to hang above it, thus reinforcing the division of labor that began in gender and class differences even as the sartorial signifiers of those differences have been discarded. The elimination of a gendered iconography produces the classless (middle-class) ideal of "marriage" as a complementary distribution of labor signifying an egalitarian sexual relationship.

Jeannine Allard's *Légende: The Story of Philippa and Aurélie*, published by Alyson Press in 1984, is based on a tale passed down orally of two women who lived as a married couple on the coast of Brittany in the middle of the nineteenth century. Deception takes the form of crossdressing itself, because Britanny is described as fiercely nationalist, xenophobic, and staunchly Catholic, a society so traditional that an official marriage between two members of the same sex would have led to punishment by death. Philippa becomes Philip because she always wanted to go to sea. She is also an orphan who crossdresses to protect herself against the male violence that ended her mother's life on the docks. Like Sarah, she seeks to emulate her absent father who was English, and like Sarah she acquires a "good" father, a former lover of her mother's who cuts her hair and lands her first job as a deckhand.

When Philippa is washed on shore after a shipwreck she is discovered by Aurélie who, unlike Philippa, is rural, pagan, and an adoptive mother. She has always identified with her own mother, a witch whose visions and visits to the menhirs (ancient rock formations) were passed on to her daughter. Aurélie becomes a mother by adopting the daughter of her deceased sister, in contrast to Philippa, also a motherless daughter, who seeks mothering from an aristocratic nun while growing up in the convent. On the one hand, they share an initial female love object in the form of a "good" or "natural" mother. On the other hand, their distinction lies with the difference between Aurélie's secret, which belongs to her gods and can only be deciphered by a visionary, and Philippa's lie, which will at some point be discovered as betrayal. Although a full-fledged member of the world of men, Philippa feels locked out of the world she belongs to "naturally": "I was the foreigner, a man, who cannot share women's talk. Once or twice I thought of telling the truth about myself, but thought better of it. Lies are hard to admit to."[10] Here the lies are not difficult to fabricate but difficult to confess. What originally seemed acceptable in order to enter a world of men as a form of protection against it is no longer acceptable in a world that has been divested of them. Aurélie thinks she has fallen in love with a "boy," someone who doesn't exist: "She loved Philippe Chardonnais, the cabin boy; she never dreamed I was deceiving her. If she had, she would surely hate me" (p. 78). Crossdressing does not facilitate a "sentimental journey and education" as in *Patience and Sarah* but, rather, perpetuates the deception associated with the male sphere.

Philippa returns to the city and realizes that living a mistaken vocation is worse than revealing the deception and that marriage is as legitimate a way to serve God as becoming a nun. She rejoins Aurélie and the two of them feign a "marriage" in the public square, although they still do not share their secret with Mimi, the adopted daughter. Mimi's knowledge takes the form of an "open secret," because the lie which had by then become a secret reveals itself as never having been one, because she had always known her "father's" true sex. When Philippa dies at sea and Aurélie subsequently takes her own life, Mimi's secret is "openly" memorialized by a statue, commissioned from Paris and built to commemorate Aurélie's self-sacrificial love: "It represented a man dressed in fishing gear, with his arm around a woman's shoulders; she had a shawl tightly pulled about her, and her eyes saw only the waves beyond" (p. 123). This spectacle reveals itself as fraud when once again a rivalrous woman, this time Marie—a lifelong friend of Aurélie's—betrays the couple by destroying the statue. Feeling betrayed herself when she discovers the love letters between her deceased daughter and Mimi, she commits the violent act of an "unnatural" mother.

Mimi's retelling of the tale as framing narrator provides the subtext to the romance plot, accusing the parental narrative of participating in unnecessary deceptions that make the "marriage" tragic and inevitably anachronistic. The daughters Mimi and Adèle who appear as "naturalized" sisters present a lesbian feminist alternative to the role playing required by the officially sanctioned couple: "There was never any mystery about Adèle: we didn't need to go through the nonsense and struggles that Aurélie and Philippa had. We knew from the start that we loved each other, and it was simple, and good. Never questioned, never challenged" (p. 79). But Mimi and Adèle's story also lacks a plot, just as Sarah in the role of a lady lacks a subjectivity. The parental story is as much a tale of struggle and conflict—symbolized by the rose that signifies both "beauty and pain"—as it is a story of failure; at the same time it is a narrative that tries to subsume contradictions ("there was trust in the anger," "there was intimacy even in pain" [p. 97]) by relying on a "naturalized" epistemology that confuses paradox with metaphor. Aurélie's discovery of poetry provides the synthesis necessary to mediate between her silences and Philippa's absences, because poetry "trapped one's heart into admitting that which it had already known," namely, that "we are all the same" (p. 104). But, like Patience and Sarah, Philippa and Aurélie are not the same, signified by the distinction between "husband" (Philippa who doesn't know whether she is woman or man) and "wife" (Aurélie who feels trapped in her gender role but has no access to Patience's lesbian feminism). "Sameness" of biological sex is constructed as an epistemological truth that denies the contradictions produced by the narrative, subsuming them under the poetic rather than the performative. Sartorial differences are not discarded but demolished, not because they are anachronistic but because they are "unnatural," like certain mothers, some of whom play the role of "fathers" and others who seek revenge on their daughters. In this novel the "marriage" serves as a warning to the daughter who rejects the "openness" of the secret in favor of not having any secrets at all.

The Pearls, published by Naiad Press in 1987 and written by Shelley Smith— a pseudonym for two authors who previously collaborated on *Horizon of the Heart*—provides an example of a generic shift to the increasingly popular genre of the lesbian detective story.[11] Two straight CIA agents, Bunny and Harriet, agree to "pass" as wife and husband in order to investigate the suspicious activities of a career diplomat on the Caribbean island nation of Los Pagos. Harriet becomes "Harry" as a way of attracting and thereby eliciting information from Maria Hosado, wife of the island's dictator. "Harry" and Bunny, who gradually fall in love with each other, return to the United States as a couple—neither crossdressed nor "out"—having left their secret safely with Maria. "Postfeminist" in its politics, the only realm of unequal power relations remains that of male-dominated professions where women are impeded by the glass ceiling. Crossdressing does not conceal a same-sex love; it does not even assume that women are "natural" allies. Harriet Pearl and Bunny Silver are partners in an intelligence agency where for fourteen years they have been passed up for promotion because their boss would rather not hire any women at all. Harriet is a divorcée who never wanted to be a housewife and has put all her libidinal energy into her career, and Bunny is a middle-aged Barbie doll who feigns helplessness in order to sleep with the men at work. The hypersexual professional is coupled with the asexual career woman as a means of determining whether "passing" as wife and husband will lead to their promotion or resignation; the question becomes not whether they can pull off their roles as Midwest matron and devoted husband but whether they will take the role playing too far.

That crossdressing is a form of role playing and not a means to discovering or hiding one's "true nature" is emphasized in the very first scene. Mel, the best in New York for "show business cosmetology and makeup," transforms Harriet into Harry in his beauty salon, ostensibly for a role in a Broadway show. This is followed by a shopping spree to the most exclusive Madison Avenue boutiques, where expense is irrelevant because the costumes must fit the partners' cover as the Pearls, a Cleveland couple who made their money in industry and are now trying to enter New York society. Unlike the other two novels, in which the couples feel a strong sense of being the first and only ones of their "type," Harriet and Bunny are able to follow the examples of both Hollywood—specifically *Queen Christina*—and gay men. As opposed to the uniforms straight men wear, "most gay men . . . dressed with imagination and flair, and Harriet vowed, that was the way she would dress."[12] On the one hand, Harriet must retain the subtle distinction between "pretty boy" and "fag" in order to become the object of desire for Maria. On the other hand, once dressed for her new part, Harry becomes the object of attraction to both women and gay men, thereby positioning Bunny not just as fellow professional but as potential rival. The relationship of "partner" begins to take on as ambiguous a meaning as Sarah's "mate."

What further distinguishes this plot from the others is the relationship between Harriet and her mirror image. If women and gay men share an attraction for men, then Harriet's desire is mediated by an attraction to her own mirror image in the form of "Harry": "Harriet was becoming a distant relative for Harry while at the same time, Harry was becoming Harriet's ideal man. When she looked at herself in the mirror each morning, she was no longer sure of whom she was seeing. She felt a gradual merging of two people" (p. 26). This merging represents an androgynous subject position whereby one gender is signified by the body and the other by clothes, but it is also clearly a (hetero)sexual fantasy. For Bunny this fantasy puts into question the status of her object choice in terms of both the romance plot and her sexual orientation: "Thoughts raced through her mind. Who am I failing for anyway? Harry Pearl—who doesn't really exist? Or Harriet? If it's Harriet, what in the hell does that mean? But it's as if Harriet just isn't here. If she isn't, then *who* is Harry?" (p. 64). Ontological questions are raised not in terms of fraud but in terms of the performative nature of gender. Is the viewer to privilege the "true sex" (Harriet) or the role (Harry), and to what extent is gender simply the "effect" of a role produced in the mirror? Subjectivities (or cover stories) depend on the illusion or misrecognition of a cohesive identity, but confusion over object choice is the point of this plot.

When the Pearls arrive in the Caribbean, Harry is nicknamed "Mr. USA" by Maria, whose dying husband prepares to marry her off to his best friend even as she formulates her own plans to govern the island as a woman alone. Maria represents the femme fatale who uses femininity as a means to an end, her "warrior's face" to trick men and her dyed blond hair as a symbol to her people, "for the time when I will come to represent the lioness of democracy on this island" (p. 119). Although her entrusted female servant warns her that the Pearls are frauds, only when Harry is wounded while attempting to intercept the gun-running plot which solves the mystery does Maria unmask "her Prince Charming." Once all the men have been killed, there is a new Maria, one who has returned to "nature," as "natural" ruler: "She wore no makeup and her skin glowed with freshness" (p. 169). She now also shares in rather than is the dupe of the couple's secret, their promotion, and their future life together. This triangulation of female desire is no longer based on a feeling of envy whereby one woman exposes the other two but rather on solidarity, a shared desire to wrest power from men now that women have entered their sphere.

As in the other two novels, questions of sexuality remain confined to the atemporality of the "pastoral," in this case the island paradise. Lesbianism remains a private secret lurking in the heart of any woman, even one who is not woman-identified. What distinguishes this novel is the construction of lesbianism not as something "already known" but ready to be discovered through role playing. Dressing becomes a form of consumption reserved for gay men with large disposable incomes, and "third world" islands as tourist attractions enlarge the notion of "sameness" to include the "natives" who are really just like the "first world" tourists.

In *The Pearls* gay men have the money to pay for or produce illusion by engaging in activities coded as "feminine" without encountering the gender oppression faced by biological women who contend with overt discrimination on the job. Gay men replace women in those jobs—hairdressing and retail sales— that women have abandoned in order to enter male-dominated professions. Gender serves to mask sexuality as a political category by appropriating the "epistemology of the closet" for those women with the most at stake in the workplace. In contrast, gay men find employment in the "glamour industry" that feeds directly into a gay male subculture.

This construction of the gay male subject allows for a lesbian appropriation of performance as a vehicle of pleasure by circumventing the ontological construction of the "woman-identified woman" through role playing. No longer does gay male performance imply a sexual double standard that produces marital infidelity, as it did in the case of Daniel Peel. Rather, it eroticizes the relation between professional female "partners," avoiding the public sexual signals of butch-femme roles that would jeopardize an already precarious professional status. Butch-femme roles are now appropriated for professional advancement, not for entrance into a sexual subculture. The "open secret" has become, in the end, doubly performative: the "marriage" is only a "cover story," not the cover for a "coming out" but the "closet" for a class-based "lesbian panic."

Chronologically, these three novels move from needing masculine dress for physical protection (women and men are different, making women vulnerable) to not needing it because same-sex love should pass unnoticed (lesbian and gay couples are the same as straight couples) to using it to find the lesbian in any straight woman (masculine dress eroticizes). In *Patience and Sarah* and *Légende* the lesbian feminist subject is positioned in relation to the violence of compulsory heterosexuality as a feminist issue, thereby constructing the lesbian subject position as political choice.[13] In *The Pearls* the agenda becomes a liberal feminist one inasmuch as the advancement of women in the professions is the political issue motivating the plot. The model for sexual identity, however, shifts from the lesbian butch to that of the gay man.

Patience and Sarah and *Légende* are both historical fictions, relying on the past to provide the pastoral setting which will invoke the "timelessness" of such relationships now constructed as "natural" even if provisionally dependent on the "unnatural" gender hierarchy imposed by the feigned "marriage." *The Pearls*, in contrast, appropriates the formulaic genre of detective fiction to present gender roles themselves as the mystery and sexual identities as something one can safely return to the closet with the clothes. In both cases popular genres enable the treatment of lesbian subject matter by making the "marriage" inevitable or by making it overtly a game. Unlike *The Well of Loneliness*, the "original" popular lesbian novel, the butch in these texts does not abandon the femme to a better butch, that is, a real man, by feigning infidelity. Instead, she discards the clothes that signify the role in order to avoid not the pathology of inversion but, rather, a politically incorrect lesbianism.

Notes

1. The most interesting work on mimicry and masquerade has been done by Carole-Anne Tyler. See especially "The Feminine Look," in *Theory between the Disciplines: Authority/Vision/Politics*, ed. Martin Kreisworth and Mark A. Cheetham (Ann Arbor: University of Michigan Press, 1990), 191–212.

2. Eve Kosofsky Sedgwick, *Epistemology of the Closet* (Berkeley: University of California Press, 1990), 3.

3. Judith Butler, "Imitation and Gender Insubordination," in *Inside/Out: Lesbian Theories, Gay Theories*, ed. Diana Fuss (New York: Routledge, 1991), 16.

4. Sue-Ellen Case briefly mentions that "the butch-femme couple inhabit a subject position together." See her "Toward a Butch-Femme Aesthetic," in *Making a Spectacle: Feminist Essays on Contemporary Women's Theatre*, ed. Lynda Hart (Ann Arbor: University of Michigan Press, 1989), 283.

5. For the most popular accounts, see Elizabeth Mavor, *The Ladies of Llangollen* (Harmondsworth, England: Penguin, 1971), and *A Year with the Ladies of Llangollen* (Harmondsworth, England: Penguin, 1984). For rewritings, see Mary Gordon, *Chase of the Wild Goose* (London: Hogarth, 1936; rpt., New York: Arno, 1975); Colette, *The Pure and the Impure*, trans. Herma Birffault (New York: Farrar, Straus & Giroux, 1967); and Doris Grumbach, *The Ladies* (New York: Fawcett Crest, 1984).

6. Catharine Stimpson, "Zero-Degree Deviancy: The Lesbian Novel in English," *Critical Inquiry* 8 (Winter 1981): 376.

7. Bonnie Zimmerman, *The Safe Sea of Women: Lesbian Fiction, 1969–1989* (Boston: Beacon, 1990), 114.

8. See Alma Routsong, "Writing and Publishing *Patience and Sarah*," in *Gay American History: Lesbians and Gay Men in the U.S.A.*, ed. Jonathan Katz (New York: Harper & Row, 1976), 433–43.

9. Isabel Miller, *Patience and Sarah* (New York: Fawcett Crest, 1969), 36. All references are to this edition; subsequent citations appear in parentheses in the text.

10. Jeannine Allard, *Légende: The Story of Philippa and Aurélie* (Boston: Alyson, 1984), 77. All references are to this edition; subsequent citations appear in parentheses in the text.

11. For an example of a popular lesbian novel that uses crossdressing (as well as transsexualism) in the genre of detective fiction, see Barbara Wilson's *Gaudí Afternoon* (Seattle: Seal Press, 1990).

12. Shelley Smith, *The Pearls* (Tallahassee: Naiad, 1987), 18. All references are to this edition; subsequent citations appear in parentheses in the text.

13. See Katie King, "The Situation of Lesbianism as Feminism's Magical Sign: Contests for Meaning and the U.S. Women's Movement, 1968–1972," *Communication* 9 (Fall 1985): 65–91.

Intermission

THE PHOTOGRAPHS REPRODUCED here from the British anthology *Stolen Glances* playfully foreground the contradictions of homosexuality in a heterosexual world. These images include the superimposition of an obviously "butch" woman onto well-known movie stars or advertising images, drawing attention to the artificiality of popular heterosexual romance. Others evoke the playful world of dress-up, echoing the costume parties of the wealthy lesbians of early twentieth-century Paris. Still others confront the autobiographical or denaturalize a romantic garden. But all insist upon making visible the determinedly invisible—lesbian desire. The insistent destabilizing of familiar situations and figures highlights the extraordinary degree to which public images exclude the lesbian. The vampiric lesbian of Hollywood is replaced by the prankish montage; the realistic by the fantastic; the visual by a bricolage of words, images, and historical references. The pictures speak to lesbians, but also by their defiant anti-realism, they refuse any totalizing position that speaks for lesbians.

Tee A. Corinne creates richly layered photomontages of female genitalia which embrace a romanticism in regard to women's bodies that confirms a sense that so-called romantic friendships in the past may have been more embodied than we have previously accepted. She makes public what is hidden—what women themselves never see, indeed, are taught never to look at—and shows the kaleidoscopic beauty inherent in a forbidden sensuality. She has given a visual language to lesbian fantasies by avoiding a reductive literalism that often plagues efforts to imagine a specifically lesbian art.

Jill Posener, from "Dirty Girls' Guide to London," 1987.

"Lesbian sex in public places; Writing slogans on the wall; Abseiling through the House of Lords; ACT-UP shouting down the U.S. Health Minister at an AIDS conference in San Francisco; All these are on a continuum; If we don't take public spaces nobody will hear us" (Jill Posener).

7

Stolen Glances

Lesbians Take Photographs

Introduction by Tessa Boffin and Jean Fraser

[Stolen Glances: Lesbians Take Photographs *represents the work of a group of diverse lesbian photographers and writers. Here,* Feminist Studies *presents edited excerpts from the introduction by editors Tessa Boffin and Jean Fraser and an edited selection from some of the book's photo-essays. An accompanying exhibition of a small selection of the book's photographic work has toured Britain and North America. Anyone interested in renting the exhibit may obtain further details from either Cambridge Darkroom, England (0223-350725) or the Visual Studies Workshop, Rochester, New York (716-442-8676). —editors]*

IN THE SUMMER of 1988, while sitting in a car on Walworth Road in London, we conceived the idea for this book about lesbian representation by lesbian photographers and writers. Lesbians and gay men in the United Kingdom were fresh from the struggle against Section 28 of the Local Government Act, disappointed that we had not succeeded in preventing it from being passed into law, yet exhilarated by the increased sense of lesbian and gay community that those struggles had engendered. We were aware of the irony that, despite its attempts to repress us, Section 28 had given us more visibility in the mainstream media than ever before. We wanted our work to be visible too. We had seen exciting photographic work by lesbians both here and in North America, and we knew there must be more, but this work existed in isolated contexts; we wanted to make it accessible to a wider audience of lesbians and the "independent" photography sector. We also knew that there were many parallels between the United States and the United Kingdom in relation to right-wing promotion of traditional family values, repression of diversity, and a growing climate of censorship. Section 28 legislates against "the promotion of homosexuality"; we felt

Feminist Studies 18, no. 3 (Fall 1992). © 1991 by Tessa Boffin and Jean Fraser

that promotion was precisely what was needed. To the embryonic idea of a book, we added an exhibition.

Our imagination was caught by the inventiveness of lesbian photographers who had "stolen" and inverted the meanings of mainstream, heterosexual imagery. We therefore set out to produce a book that addressed the representation of lesbianism and lesbian identities in this way. Lesbianism exists in a complex relation to many other identities; concerns of sexuality intersect with those of race, class, and the body, and our contributors discuss these issues. When we set out to select contributions, rather than attempting to naturalize a "lesbian aesthetic," we looked for work that concentrated on constructed, staged, or self-consciously manipulated imagery which might mirror the socially constructed nature of sexuality. We have not included much documentary work as the realism of documentary has often been used ideologically to reinforce notions of naturalness. We do not want this book to claim a natural status for lesbianism but rather to celebrate that there is no natural sexuality at all.

Defining Lesbian Photography

There is no easy way to define a lesbian photograph. It is unclear whether its status depends on the photographer, the subject matter depicted, the audience of the photograph, or the context in which it appears. And it is open to discussion whether an image has to satisfy all these categories or only one of them. For instance, although biographical research on the lives of lesbian photographers of the past can effectively reveal previously suppressed personal details, such material is both rare and potentially reductive. It just isn't possible to transpose to our predecessors late-twentieth-century definitions of what it means to be a lesbian. Contemporary image makers, theoreticians, and curators who do not want to conflate the sexuality of the photographer on one side of the lens with its representation on the other have therefore to distinguish clearly between at least four different kinds of work produced by lesbians.

First, there are photographs, usually documentary, which frequently appear in family albums or in the lesbian or gay press. Then there are images in mainstream, predominantly heterosexual, photographic galleries and journals whose lesbian producers still cling to a modernist commitment to a purity of visual image, which transcends sexuality, language, culture, and politics. A third body of work is defined in relation to a lesbian essence, its producers maintaining that it emits a "lesbian aura," aesthetic, or sensibility. This, we feel, presents problems in that a lesbian sensibility seeks to privilege a particular use of photography as essentially lesbian, instead of seeing photography as a medium with subversive potential for everyone.

Fourth, there are those photographers who deal overtly with lesbian issues; in the main they do not assume that their sexuality could ever in itself be the defining factor for their work or that content, or the style they deploy, could ever be essentially lesbian. What they do share is an interest in subversive strategies of representation and a skepticism about the reflective nature of the photograph. It is mainly work in this fourth category that we have sought to include here; we believe this work holds the greatest potential for a progressive and transgressive lesbian and gay photographic practice. A politics of resistance can never be solely the product of lesbian experience, or of a "lesbian aesthetic," because clearly no such unity or cohesiveness exists.

Hysterical Morals

This book is emerging into a climate characterized by increasing homophobia, racism and censorship, and fierce promotion by the moral Right of "family" values. And if state regulation and surveillance in both the United States and the United Kingdom were not enough, there is no shortage of moral attitude from within sections of the women's movement and the lesbian community. *Quim*, a United Kingdom-produced magazine of lesbian erotica, and the 1990 U.S. *On Our Backs* calendar were censored from feminist and lesbian and gay bookshops in the United Kingdom, one of which had only recently fought a major Customs and Excise seizure of its stock.

In the United States in 1984, the Feminists against Censorship Taskforce formed following the introduction by Catharine MacKinnon and Andrea Dworkin of the Minneapolis Ordinance, which permitted women to take civil action against anyone producing or distributing pornography on the grounds that they had been harmed by its images of their sexuality. In Britain, Feminists against Censorship formed in 1989 in reaction to the attempts by Dworkin-inspired groups, such as the Campaign against Pornography and the Campaign against Pornography and Censorship, to establish a feminist orthodoxy in favor of antipornography legislation. As observed:

> Suddenly the feminist movement that once fought for freedom and sexual self-determination is advocating giving power over our lives to the judges and the police; suddenly what it says about our freedom and our sexual desires sounds like the ravings of the Right. Suddenly feminism is about censorship rather than about opening possibilities.[1]

The collusion of antipornography feminists with right-wing organizations has serious implications for lesbians and gay men, whose own images are likely to be the first casualties of any censorship legislation. Carole Vance has pointed out how minority communities need affirmative images of themselves within the public arena:

> People deprived of images become demoralized and isolated, and they become increasingly vulnerable to attacks on their private expressions of nonconformity, which are inevitable once sources of public solidarity and resistance have been eliminated.[2]

This underlines the crucial importance of a diversity of representation for the lesbian and gay communities. Rather than seeing this book as the quintessential handbook of lesbian photography, we hope it will be a useful contribution to the ongoing struggle to keep our selves and our images visible to the outside world and to each other. We hope that it will engage with contemporary debates on the politics of representation and that it will motivate further image production in gallery exhibitions, books, and public spaces.

Notes

1. *Ask Yourself: Do You Really Want More Censorship?* Feminists against Censorship pamphlet, 1989. See also Gillian Rodgerson and Linda Semple, "Who Watches the Watchwomen?" in *Feminist Review*, no. 36 (Autumn 1990): 19–28.

2. Carole S. Vance, "The War on Culture" in *Art in America* 77 (September 1989): 39–43.

Tessa Boffin, from "The Knight's Move," 1990.

"We need to resurrect and honour the concept of role models which was so important to the early gay movement . . ." (John Preston).

"Yet we need to acknowledge that the stakes are remarkably high because of the relative paucity of lesbian imagery. There are so few representations and so many unfulfilled desires. The burdens imposed by this scarcity of representation can, however, be overcome if we go beyond our impoverished archives to create new icons. One way we can move forward is by embracing our idealized fantasy figures, by placing ourselves into the great heterosexual narratives of courtly and romantic love: by making 'The Knight's Move'" (Tessa Boffin).

Tessa Boffin, from "The Knight's Move," 1990.

Somewhere in a cemetery
Down a dark pathway
Underneath a stone angel
I stumble across your
   photographs
Where is my knight
My knave
My angel
My casanova
My lady-in-waiting?
I could hardly find you
In my history books
But now in this scene
You all come together.

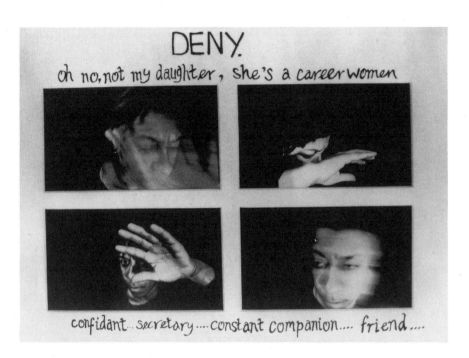

Ingrid Pollard, from "Deny: Imagine: Attack."

Deborah Bright, untitled from the series "Dream Girls," 1989.

"The impulse for a lesbian photomonteur (menteur) to paste (not suture, please) her constructed butch-girl self-image into conventional heterosexual narrative stills from old Hollywood movies requires no elaborate explanations" (Deborah Bright).

Jacqui Duckworth from "Coming Out Twice."

"She experiences the unreality of everyday things made strange. Does she imagine the flea which crawls out of the fur cup and saucer and hops with great vitality beyond her reach?" (Jacqui Duckworth).

8

On Sexual Art

Tee A. Corinne

Artist's Statement: On Sexual Art

SOMETIMES I THINK I have the wrong kind of personality to be making art out of sexual imagery. I don't like confrontation, don't like negative public commotion. Nonetheless, since 1974 I have been actively involved with labia imagery and with images of women making love with other women or with themselves.

It started before 1974, maybe as early as 1950 when I was seven and looked, using a mirror, at my body between my legs. It was confusing. I was shocked, somehow, at the formlessness of what I saw. What did I expect? I don't know. I didn't look again until I was twenty-seven. By that time I had a bachelor's and a master's degree in art. I had drawn and sculpted men's genitals. But women's? No.

One day I took it into my head to draw my own. I did several renderings which I hid so that my husband wouldn't see them. I didn't think he would approve. Later I tore them into small pieces. That was the winter of 1970–71.

By mid-1973 I had separated from my husband and was exploring options for women in San Francisco. I went to a workshop sponsored by the Esalen Institute. I chose it because it had the words "lesbian" and "feminism" in its title. We sat on the floor in a circle. At some point in the evening, paper and pencils were passed around and we were asked to draw, from memory, women's external sexual organs. Mine was the most detailed drawing. I admitted I'd done drawings before and destroyed them. A book was passed around, opened to a glossy reproduction of "Female Genitalia." I didn't look long, not nearly as long as I wanted.

I knew that the things we don't have names for, or images of, are the ones we label crazy and bad. I believed that reclaiming labial imagery was a route to

Feminist Studies 19, no. 2 (Summer 1993). © 1993 by Feminist Studies, Inc.

claiming personal power for women. Using soft pencils, I did drawings of every woman who would let me, then I used tracing paper to translate them into easy-to-reproduce ink drawings. I made copies on card stock and sold them through local women's bookstores. I learned there was a market for these images. Women really liked them, liked to hang them on their walls, and give them as gifts.

By November 1975, I had turned the drawings into a coloring book called *The Cunt Coloring Book*. No other name seemed really to fit, although the word "cunt" was not one with which I was particularly comfortable. The alliteration, though, was nice. I also liked the idea of combining a street term for genitalia with a coloring book, because both are ways that, as children, we get to know the world.

By the end of 1975 I knew that I wanted to make my life with women and was willing to claim the word "lesbian." I wanted to find ways to use my art to clarify and make sense out of this new life and culture into which I was moving. I started taking photos of women kissing, hugging, touching each other's bodies in intimate ways.

I also started taking photos of women's genitals. What excited me about the pictures I was making was the portrayal of grace and beauty, coupled with the tang of traversing forbidden territory.

It has been said of my work that it is essentializing: reducing women to our biological manifestation. Those voices do not understand the radicalism of turning the lights on in secret, darkened places and making that enlightening into a public record. I understand what I am doing as contributing to a kind of sanity, a witnessing, an affirmation of the fleshy side of lesbianism with more than a whiff of the transcendent. That is, when I'm successful.

I have been accused of romanticizing lovemaking between women, of leaving out the times one kicked one's lover, accidentally, in the head while turning over. It's true. Lesbians have often been portrayed negatively. And I decided that it was not my inclination to do this. In making my audience what Barbara Grier has called the "Garden Variety Lesbian," I turned away from the theorists who defined cutting-edge work as necessarily deconstructionist or sadomasochistic.

Dreamy. My work participates in a mythologizing dream: sex as a way of knowledge and a route to power. I am almost fifty and think that I am close to being finished with sexual imagery. My body and my life are taking me different places. Yet I have thought this before and changed my mind. Why? Because no one else was making the images I wanted to see. Perhaps, though, this is part of what moves an artist; the visual dream, that with work, can be manifest and shared.

Yantra #41, from *Yantras of Womanlove*, 1982.

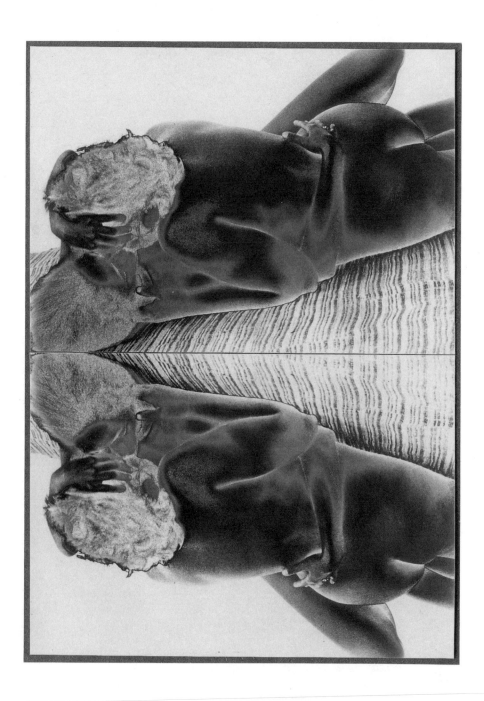

Yantra #35, from *Yantras of Womanlove,* 1982.

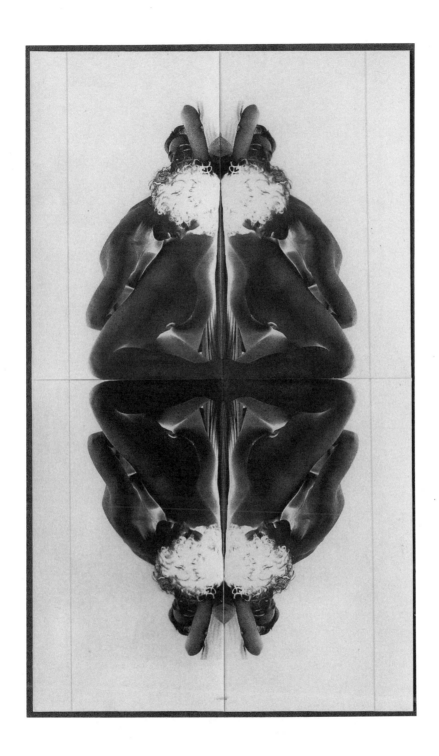

Yantra #52, from *Yantras of Womanlove,* 1982.

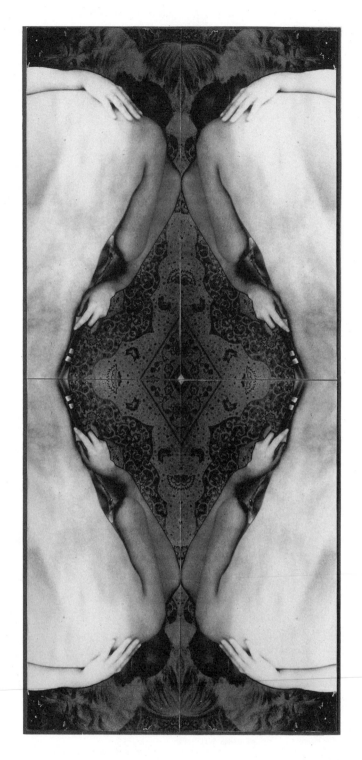

Yantra #38, from *Yantras of Womanlove,* 1982.

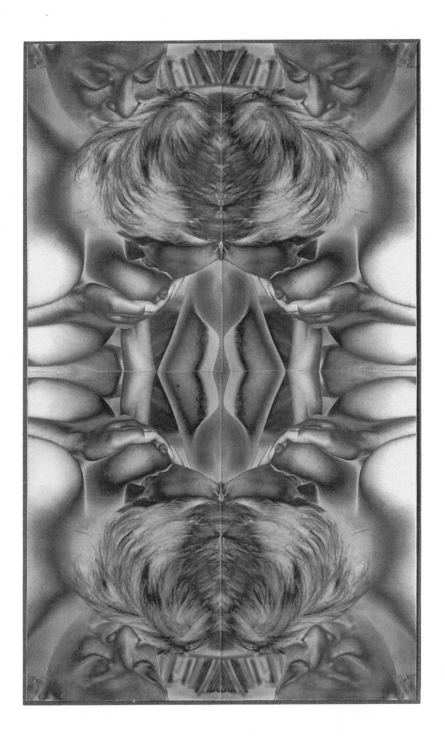

Yantra #48, from *Yantras of Womanlove,* 1982.

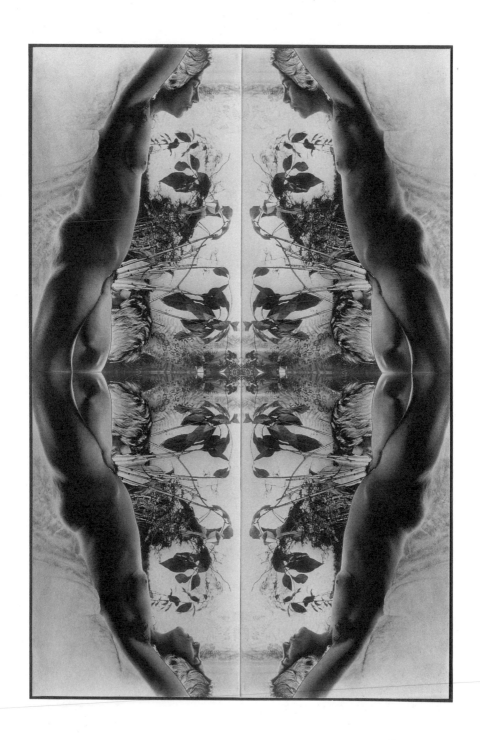

Yantra #22, from *Yantras of Womanlove,* 1982.

PART II

Affirmations

THE ESSAYS IN this section focus on definitions, rather than discoveries, but here too the personal and the scholarly mingle, indicating the powerful imaginative hold searching for our foremothers has had on lesbian studies during its short lifetime. In this section the essays explicitly or implicitly address the political importance of claiming a lesbian identity, a point frequently raised in part I. The recuperation of women-centered lives, work, and politics also involves a reappraisal of definitions—what and how is a lesbian? However unstable the lesbian subject may appear, these essays all affirm her existence, but the authors do not agree with each other on the taxonomy, position, or history of this troubling figure.

Elizabeth Wilson's intervention argues powerfully for the irreducible irrationality of forbidden desires, in contrast to any theorizing about the social structuring of desire. It is a powerful personal reminder of the difficulties of definitions and the necessity for affirmations. But Heather Findlay's witty analysis of the "dildo wars" of recent history makes clear how fragile an affirmation of lesbian sexual practices can be. Loving a woman who wears and uses a dildo—a forbidden fantasy for many lesbians—seems to bring into question not only the definition of lesbian sexual practices, but also what a lesbian is.

Makeda Silvera's essay insists on the importance of affirming her Afro-Caribbean lesbian identity, in conflict with both her grandmother, who finds her sexual choice is "a white people ting," and the Afro-Caribbean activists of her Toronto community who prioritize race over sexual preference. Implicit in this position, she argues, is the sense that a black lesbian loses her cultural identity because of her sexual identity. In opposition to this political position, she reconstructs a culturally complicated Caribbean past that confirms an unspoken history of black lesbian desire.

In contrast, Karen V. Hansen discusses a loving correspondence between two freeborn African-American women at the mid-nineteenth century. She carefully unravels the ways in which their community accepted their intense, erotic friendship, as well as the economic constraints they faced as independent black women. The thematics of romantic love, so pervasive in literature of the nineteenth century, gave meaning to their love for each other. As evidence of self-conscious sexual relations between women, these letters, reveling in "bosom sex," are an important addition to the sparse documentation of women's sexual customs in the past, when silence was customary. Two Hartford, Connecticut, women confirm Silvera's belief in a silenced lesbian past.

For Calhoun, it is a question of the cultural marginality of the lesbian within feminist discourse that is so troubling, rather than the cultural denial faced by Silvera. Calhoun describes what she calls the "closeting of lesbians under 'difference,' " whereby heterosexism is simply added to racism and classism as evils to be fought by feminists. She goes on to argue for the instability of lesbian representation; for her the lesbian remains conceivable only as a category outside the sex/gender categories of woman/man. She returns to the third sex of the late-nineteenth-century sexologists as the most appropriate signifier for the lesbian, even at the risk of repudiating feminism.

The concluding essay in this section returns to an examination of the past two hundred years, documenting the continuities of lesbian history. In opposition to those who have defined the sexually active lesbian as a product of late-nineteenth- and early twentieth-century sexologists, I analyze the several competing definitions of women who desired women, showing how they coexisted, even when they contradicted each other. I conclude that women who loved women, and were sexually active, have existed, and been openly discussed, for at least two hundred years. In addition, I analyze the weaknesses of basing lesbian history on an identity model and point out the impossibility of retrieving lesbians only through their self-identification or through a generalized sense of the homoerotic. Both definitions have been conceptualized so as to leave little room for women who might behave differently at different times.

9

Forbidden Love

Elizabeth Wilson

Love hurts
Love scars
Love wounds
And mars
Any heart not tough
Nor strong enough
To take a lot of pain. . . .
—The Everley Brothers, circa 1960.

THE LESBIAN IS an inhabitant of the great cities, first glimpsed by Baudelaire in Paris, "capital of the nineteenth century."[1] A new kind of woman emerges from the restless anonymity of the crowds, aloof from the sullen aimless excitement of the thousands that drift along the pavements and surge through the squares, a figure whose mystery and danger is that she is alone. The lesbian stands outside family, yet is not simply a worker. Her sexuality necessarily defines her. That is enough to make her lurid. She is a mirror image of the prostitute.

This at least was the prevailing romantic, literary image of the lesbian in the late nineteenth and early twentieth centuries, and one that lesbians themselves seem to have accepted. Later the lesbian is defined in Radclyffe Hall's *The Well of Loneliness*, as innately and therefore tragically masculine, a member of the "third sex." The erotic love that Radclyffe Hall's heroine, Steven, feels for each of her lovers is of an "invert" for a "womanly woman." She constructs a romantically, narcissistically masculine being about whom there nevertheless remains a haunting ambiguity. The dissonance between Steven's woman's body, no matter how thin-flanked and boyish, and her male personality, creates an aura of the impossible. She is one of the haunted, tormented, and damned who transcend the degradation which is itself their glory.

Feminist Studies 10, no. 2 (Summer 1984). © by Feminist Studies, Inc.

Steven embodies the masculinity attributed to lesbians—a masculinity that contributes to a sense of their danger and power, but which is also open to ridicule and caricature. This claim to masculinity can be dramatized, the stigmata transformed into the hallmarks of a doomed and *therefore* fascinating personality. In this second guise, the lesbian resembles the archetypal Romantic movement hero, the doomed rebel, often an artist, often sexually ambiguous, of whom Byron, who was really the first modern pop star, is the classic example. This image is different from the first, which tried simply to be manly, for it lays claim to heroism and to a place above the crowd. It can also degenerate into the sometimes vulgar decadence of Aubrey Beardsley, Oscar Wilde, and other *fin de siècle* dandies, who, Ellen Moers suggests, *spoilt* their dandyism by being overtly homosexual instead of glacially beyond sexuality.[2]

This lesbian's dandyism is androgyny. Colette, who had a six-year liaison with a woman of this kind, writes insightfully—although perhaps also rather maliciously—about the strangeness and possibly the humorlessness of the androgynous poseur. "The seduction emanating from a person of uncertain or dissimulated sex is powerful. . . . Anxious and veiled, never exposed to the light of day, the androgynous creature wanders, wonders and implores in a whisper. . . . There especially remains for the androgyne the right, even the obligation, never to be happy. . . . It trails irrevocably among us its seraphic suffering, its glimmering tears. . . . She is the person who has no counterpart anywhere."[3] Djuna Barnes also tried to analyze the attraction. "What is this love we have for the invert, boy or girl? It was they who were spoken of in every romance that we ever read. The girl lost, what is she but the Prince found? The Prince on the white horse that we have always been seeking . . . in the girl it is the prince, and in the boy it is the girl that makes a prince a prince—and not a man. They go far back in our lost distance where what we never had stands waiting. . . . They are our answer to what our grandmothers were told love was . . . the living lie of our centuries."[4] These women writers, who at various times loved women, accepted an understanding of lesbianism that saw the homoerotic as going against the grain of biological sex, yet as still biologically determined. In this they followed sexologists such as Havelock Ellis,[5] for whom "lesbianism" and "femininity" would have been contradictions in terms.

I shall try to chart how this changed, and how, although it constitutes an advance from biologically defined notions of lesbianism, a different set of problems confronts us when we examine contemporary feminist assumptions about lesbianism and lesbian eroticism. Among other things, I shall discuss romanticism as an unexamined and neglected experience by feminists.

My approach is subjective and personal. My own experience may be un-

usual in that, as a lesbian "before the movement," I feel that feminism has ultimately distanced me from, rather than intensified my commitment to, lesbianism. This is more than just a peculiar quirk of personal fate however, for it re-
lates to the way in which the contemporary movement has understood what it
means for women to love women.

In the 1950s the homosexual reform movements in Britain tried to create a
more sensible, normalizing image of the lesbian. Lesbians themselves seemed
at this time to be divided between those who still saw their condition as innate,
and those who accepted a more psychological view that homosexuality is the
result of childhood experiences. In practice there tended to be, in England at
any rate, a distinction between the adoption of "butch" and "femme" roles
among working-class lesbians, and an egalitarian insistence among middle-
class lesbians, that they were really just like everyone else. Then came the 1960s,
a period during which the "permissive society" and the "swinging scene" emphasized androgyny rather than sexual difference. Many lesbians and mate homosexuals found this atmosphere more congenial than a heavy emphasis on
roles that began to seem old-fashioned and "naff."[6] Yet this new androgyny dif-
fered from the old. Its imagery was resolutely bright; it was pretty rather than
darkly damned.

It was not until the late sixties that lesbians and gay men began seriously
to question the relationship of sexual proclivities to gender roles. Later still, with
the publication of the work of Jeffrey Weeks[7] and others, it came as a revelation
for gay men that the "homosexual identity" had existed in Western societies for
only about two hundred years. There had been homosexual acts in almost all
societies, but only in relatively few were there individuals who came to be described as homosexuals, a "master" identity that defined all aspects of their lives
and behavior, not just what they did in bed.

The construction of the lesbian identity appeared to be of even more recent
origin, not gaining widespread recognition, in Britain at least, until *The Well of
Loneliness* was prosecuted and banned in 1928.[8] So it is not surprising that lesbians, emerging at the same time with a conscious identity, had, during these
years, accepted the sexologists' definition of their "condition" as biologically determined and clinical, one to which masculinity was the key.

The 1970s saw a break with this tradition and a definitive move away from
any lingering idea of the lesbian as a member of the "third sex." For feminists,
a lesbian was now first and foremost a *woman*; and lesbianism became a major
theme of the women's movement. The movement itself had grown out of the
"sexual liberation" of the 1960s. The whole New Left had taken as central to its

project the disruption of repressed sexuality, and this implied a vision of sexuality as energy. Sexual liberation was to be the nuclear fission of radicalism, and would rocket us into a stratosphere of intensity and power. The women's movement took over this view, and similarly assumed it to be revolutionary. Feminism gave it a new twist, however, for women began to understand how their subordination was enacted in the power relationships that heterosexual love so often created and served to perpetuate.[9] They assumed that the key to women's liberation lay in an understanding of the construction of gender and sexuality. But if heterosexuality was the foundation of female subordination, then for some women lesbian sexuality came to be seen as an immediate source of liberation. Many women felt that a relationship with a man involved the collapse of their own identity, and it was to get away from this internalized sense of inferiority that some turned to other women with whom alone an equal relationship seemed possible.

But lesbianism in this context no longer involved the adoption of roles and dandyism was far from their aspirations. On the contrary, lesbianism now came to seem the escape route from the socially constructed gender roles imposed in a particularly rigid way on women. Paradoxically, the role-playing falsity of gender was, according to this scenario, the mark of heterosexuality, while lesbianism by contrast became the arena for the flowering of real womanhood.

Lesbianism in the early seventies was seen, then, as a *solution* to heterosexuality.[10] I can remember many meetings at which women spoke of their hopes that lesbian relationships would be free of jealousy, possessiveness, and romantic obsessions. Yet even at the time there was for me, and many others, something obscurely unsatisfactory about the terms of the debate. Feminists described a Manichaean struggle between the hell of wrong desires and the heaven of a love devoid of pain. They spoke of their right to orgasm and the thralldom of being in love. Often, to talk about sexuality was to talk not about sex at all, but about relationships, about life-styles, about emotions. The word "sexuality" went wider, in any case, than sex: "sex" referred to acts and the engagement in practices; "sexuality" was about identity and gender, about masculine and feminine, about desire, fantasy, and the whole construction of the self. Feminists also took over, unquestioned from established revolutionary movements and from the New Left, a moralism about the meaning of sexual behavior in relation to politics, even if the moralism had rather different imperatives from stereotypic "socialist morality." Monogamy, possessiveness, and jealousy were still taboo, as was romantic love with its aura of repression and exaggeration, its displacement of sexuality into hysterical, obsessive feelings.

Lesbian sexuality assumed a special importance because, if sex *was* the deepest and most potent of all forms of personal communication, then that communication between two women took on a privileged and special role. In a sense, lesbianism became simply the transcendent moment of sisterhood. Moreover, lesbianism was seen as a fundamental political challenge to male domination. And, in a society in which both the familial and the nonkin female networks that had once supported women were breaking down, lesbianism might provide a new and powerful replacement.

Not until the mid-seventies, in Britain at least, did some feminists begin to question the idea that our sexuality expresses the core and center of our being. They began to suggest that, far from being revolutionary, this essentialism acts as a central ideological support to modern capitalist societies: the culture we oppose itself accepts sexual passion and sexual relationships as the key to selfhood. British feminists used psychoanalytic theory to challenge the view that all women needed to do was "let it all hang out," unlock their sexuality from patriarchal suppression, and allow "it" to flower. Juliet Mitchell[11] and others used psychoanalysis to argue that there is no pregiven "it" of sexual energy, and that sexuality is largely a social construct. The work of Lacan questioned the very notion of stable sexual identity.[12] For the Lacanians, the sexual self is at best a fragile thing, wobbling on the border between the conscious "personality" and the formless depths of the unconscious; for the very notion of sexual *identity* becomes to this way of thinking a kind of ideology, almost an example of false consciousness.

Michel Foucault has been more interested in the social organization of sexuality and in "sexual discourses" than in the individual.[13] But his challenge to the view that sexuality is coherent and unitary, his belief—to put it perhaps rather simplistically—that sex *is* about practices rather than conditions, has led to a conscious rejection by some feminists and gay men of the very notion of an identity organized around homoeroticism.

From a radically different perspective, other feminists have rejected lesbian identity in favor of a seamless conception of womanhood. The most extreme and best known statement of this position is by Adrienne Rich.

I mean the term *lesbian continuum* to include a range . . . of woman-identified experience; not simply the fact that a woman has had or consciously desired genital experience with another woman. If we expand it to embrace many more forms of primary intensity between and among women, including the sharing of a rich inner life, the bonding against male tyranny, the giving and receiving of practical and political support . . . we begin to grasp breadths of female history and psychology which have lain out of reach as a consequence of limited, mostly clinical, definitions of "lesbianism."[14]

And Lillian Faderman has elucidated a history of romantic friendships between women that claims to rescue these from the "clinical" definitions of lesbianism created by the hated nineteenth-century medical men.[15]

One criticism leveled against this, the lesbian feminist perspective, is that it desexualizes lesbianism. It has also been seen as "reductionist" in denying the specificity and difference of the diverse experience of women.[16] I share these criticisms, yet I have always felt that intellectual disagreement was not enough to account for my deeply felt hostility to lesbian feminism, my anger at what I have felt to be its sentimentality and simplistic blurring of a complex reality.

A difference in life experience gave lesbianism for me a different meaning. I too rejected "clinical" definitions of the lesbian, but I did still see the homosexual as positively deviant, a rebel against the oppressive society of the 1950s. I adopted the identity as some sort of protection against the fifties' marriage and the "feminine mystique." It served that purpose, but for that very reason— because it set me apart—I never did experience it as an identification with other women. Rich has written: "The passion of debating ideas with women was an erotic passion for me, and the risking of self with women that was necessary in order to win some truth out of the lies of the past was also erotic."[17] Not for me, and perhaps I have missed out. I don't know, but I certainly never longed for "the power of woman-bonding." That suggested something too maternal, too suffocating; I always wanted my lover to be *other*, not like me. I did not want to be bathed, drowned in the great tide of womanliness.

Yet how sour and mean it seemed that the truth of my experience contradicted the great feminist imperative of Affirmation. But it did. The more strongly feminists insisted upon the magnificence of women, the more that love between them, erotic and emotional, was elevated into the highest moment of political consciousness, the more doubtful I became, the more alienated I felt. For a long time this confused me, and I tried not to think about it. It could not be talked about. I did not understand it.

For after all, I had entered the 1970s on a high. I became part of the meteoric glare of London Gay Liberation. At the time we experienced it as an explosion of energy that blew apart the permissive sixties. The demonstrations were impromptu street theatre, the politics were the politics of outrage. We dramatized our oppression and in so doing converted subordination into a weapon of attack. Politics was a new kind of good time. We wrenched an optimism and vitality from the menace of the future. We were the urban guerillas of the ideological war. We were the froth on the nightmare of capitalism, riding the breakers of revolution. It seems hysteric, strident now, but at the time I experienced more intensely than ever before, or since, my *identity* as lesbian. This wasn't about sexual practices at all, it was about the assumption of a deviant identity, an identity that ran counter to every notion of womanhood, yet wasn't "mannish" either.

My whole involvement with feminism has been something of a morning after this first intoxication. This was inevitable since it involved a much fuller acknowledgment of myself as a woman in a male society, as a woman—ironically—who could desire men as well as women: it was an acknowledgment of many complexities and uncertainties that had been conveniently censored out by my particular "lesbian identity."

Yet there was always a lack, an absence somewhere, in my engagement with feminism; at some level I could never identify with the feminist ideal woman— affirmative, woman-loving, positive, strong. A sense of unease grew slowly more pervasive about the sort of person I as a feminist was supposed to be. I'm not talking about media caricatures, but what I perceived as feminist assumptions. In all sorts of ways I retreated: into work, into a relationship that itself became a kind of mask. But I could not ward off the unease, and eventually it became a suppressed depression, which crystallized, rather oddly, around the issue of lesbian sadomasochism. This, and butch-femme roles, have not achieved as much importance in Britain as they seem to have done in North America, but the Sex Issue of *Heresies* was nonetheless widely read and greeted with acclaim by many British women. It was also sold under the counter in at least one London feminist bookshop, because other women so deeply disapproved.

Why did it all leave me cold? So far as I was concerned it might as well have been the General Motors catalog. Was there then something wrong with me? What *did* I want? It was depressing to feel so unmoved, because this role-playing, "deviant" lesbian sexuality has been the only clearly spelled-out alternative to "woman bonding," and it seems to be an attempt to put outlawry and sex very much back into lesbianism.

It also seemed however to carry with it its own romanticism about deviant identity. And when I thought about romanticism I grasped the fact that that *did* have an erotic charge for me. Operatic, star-crossed, forbidden loves were the silent movie backdrop to my sexual forays. My secret life was peopled with Fatal Strangers, vampiric seducers, Idealized violators. Nothing so crude as flagellation or bondage, no silly sex games or dressing up for me; rather the refined thrill of psychic pain, the "real thing" of rows, reconciliations, parting, absence—thrills, tragedy, and drama.

Feminists have dismissed romanticism, yet it has a psychic reality that can't simply be banished. The magic of dominance and submission is written into romance as it is written into pornography; romance *is* actually a sort of pornography of the feelings, in which emotions replace sexual parts, yet may be just as fetishized.

The themes of romance are compulsion and denial. In romantic fantasy, feelings are not entered into freely, they are stronger than oneself; the lover draws one on, yet ultimately denies. When, and if, the moment of final consummation comes, it has to be the end of the story because—or so Freud suggested—sexual gratification destroys the compulsion. New forms of affection, or indeed thralldom, may ensue, but these are distinct from the original romantic longing. Domestic life, after all, is designed (however unsuccessfully) to maximize emotional security, while danger is the essence of romantic love. The romantic hero (or heroine) is "mad, bad and dangerous to know" as Caroline Lamb said of Byron. Byron's own poems, like the gothic novels of his period, typically rely on the theme of the abducted heroine, victim in the toils of a tormented tormentor.

Why do such fantasies have the power to compel? Is it that the danger of romantic love acts as a drug or a form of escapism in industrial mass society? Is it that we must have our dreams since life in the typing pool or on the assembly line is so monotonous? But even if we were to accept such a tidy fit between fantasy and economy, it would not explain the content of our dreams.

Romance—again like some genres of pornography—approximates to a kind of Grail legend in resembling the journey of the questing individual in search of enlightenment. For a woman particularly, so long at least as the "taboo of virginity" is powerful, romantic passion can be felt as a transformation, and the first night of passion as a chasm between her former and her future life. In a long chapter in *The Second Sex*[18] Simone de Beauvoir demonstrated with many examples from diaries, memoirs, autobiographies, and novels the importance and significance of this moment, even when the reality is sadly unlike the myth. Sex then becomes a *rite de passage* and, as such, a kind of rebirth. This may partly explain its association—within the romantic tradition at least—with death.

Like so many other features of modern life, romantic love can be seen as a secularization of spiritual impulses that once expressed themselves in mysticism, ritual, and magic. We cannot return to former beliefs, but the insufficiency of nineteenth- and twentieth-century scientism and hyper-rationalism has led rather to a secular irrationalism. Our culture *is* spiritually impoverished, and we therefore have all sorts of emotional impulses and needs that lack real nourishment. Astrology and encounter groups can hardly satisfy these needs.

Freud was a great debunker of romantic love: "Sexual overestimation is the origin of the peculiar state of being in love, a state suggestive of a neurotic compulsion."[19] On the other hand, Freud saw desire as incapable of being fulfilled and indeed as compelling precisely because of the obstacles in its way. "An obstacle is required in order to heighten libido; and where natural resistances to satisfaction have not been sufficient men have at all times erected conventional ones so as to be able to enjoy love."[20] Since Freud perceived erotic love as rooted in the infant's love of its parental figures, which in turn grows, according to him, out of the satisfaction of the baby's bodily needs (ultimately the need for survival), he viewed the state of being in love as a development from narcissism. The individual in love abandons narcissism, but seeks indirect satisfaction for it by projecting it onto the idealized love object, thereby in a sense reappropriating the love of self.

Adult love, for Freud, was always to some extent a reenactment of the grandiose and unattainable aspirations of the infant. Romantic passion is really, therefore, a longing for the impossible, representing, like so much else in Freud, the wish to escape the confines of reality and return to a former state of pleasure and happiness untinged by compromise.

In this respect, Freud might himself be seen as a part of the very romantic tradition he at one level challenged. The themes of his work are the tragic themes of opera, novel, and film: renunciation, loss, and the suppression of the erotic. Passion is intense because it is forbidden. Such an idea is anathema to modern feminism, built as it is on the belief that female sexuality should be unleashed and no longer taboo.

Thus to identify romanticism as something too important to be merely willed away by the power of positive thinking is to state a problem, not a solution. To state that romanticism has been important to me psychologically is not to "come out" as a romantic. It is inadequate merely to justify romanticism; in the same way that the previous rejection of it was an inadequate response and just as there is insufficiency in the testimony—however heroic and difficult it may have been—of these feminists who have "come out" as sadomasochists. We also must pursue the whole issue of the social construction of sexual identity and sexual desire: how we become masculine or feminine; why our desires and fantasies are as they are. Simply to affirm a "right" to be sadomasochistic on civil liberties grounds is to beg the question of why, for each of us, our longings tend to get channeled into a particular narrow and highly specific range. The justifications for sadomasochism have never seriously tried to answer that million orgasm question. Probably just as many women—feminists—have romantic as have masochistic fantasies (and perhaps the two are inextricably linked). Yet it has remained a stifled discourse within the women's movement, the still shameful secret when so many others have been brazenly revealed. To romanticize one's own identity is merely one way of trying to stabilize the fluctuating subjectivity at which Lacan makes us look. To romanticize desire is, perhaps, to try to stabilize the tide of time that rocks the boat of eternal love and fidelity.

For me, lesbianism was not simply about desires and practices, but was also about my *self*. My involvement in my own lesbian identity was itself romantic, and I can see now that the romance is over. The possibility of being a *femme damnée*, a Baudelairean lesbian, disappeared when the women's movement came along, and I was left caught between two—for me—impossibilities. On one side was the "lesbian continuum" and woman bonding, on the other the fetishistic specificity of key codes, leather, and colored handkerchiefs. Romanticism was no magical third way. I do believe, though, that it is far more pervasive than we realize, an attitude to life so deeply woven into our culture that it permeates even radical ideologies—even sadomasochist outlawry and woman bonding are ultimately romanticizations.

Psychoanalysis is in one sense a negative process. It challenges us to confront the dark side of ourselves, the negative, the fearful, the destructive. Like the romantic tradition of which it is itself a part, it acknowledges that passion is contradictory, that eroticism is more than a celebratory hedonism, and that part of its cutting edge may be when it is touched with fear of loss and set against the vista of its own impermanence.

Yet psychoanalysis as a theory, although fascinating and suggestive, cannot be *the* theory for feminists. It has its own silences. It has failed to give a convincing account of lesbianism, and none of the contemporary feminists that has used it has seriously attempted to give lesbianism more than a marginal place. Psychoanalysis is itself to some extent romantic as a process and as a method of self-exploration, with its imagery of quest and hoped-for salvation, its tactic of enlightenment by metaphor. On the other hand, its "negative" aspect is a potential positive; the process is the unpicking of what has gone wrong rather than the affirmation of what always has to be so brightly right—and this may be more supportive in its acknowledgment of failure and disappointment than the feminist ideology of the strong woman. Of course we need strength; but that strength must be built on a recognition and understanding of our vulnerabilities rather than on a censoring out of all unacceptable feelings.

I recognize that my experience runs counter not only to the admissible feminist reality, but also to the experienced reality of many women who discovered lesbian eroticism, if not identity, as a result of their involvement in feminism. Yet whatever my own experience, the haunting image of the lesbian remains. The lesbian was once the woman who stood alone, unprotected by men, in a refusal of male domination that was profoundly challenging. As Lillian Faderman herself acknowledges, nineteenth-century women's romantic friendships as such did not challenge patriarchy. Baudelaire's woman of the metropolis did. She was part of the disorder of great cities, of the underworld, the underground, the unconscious. Because no man protected her, she herself took on "male" qualities. She still demands from us a response to what we always thought of—and often rejected—as masculine. She still stands as a metaphor of this "dark side": of the glamour of masculinity in both women and men; of the ambiguities of passion; of the excitement of danger.

This may itself sound romantic, but it isn't just romanticism. Woman bonding and the lesbian continuum enfold us in a sense of strength and support—the positive political contribution of this perspective has been to suggest a basis for women's collective power. However, it specifically evades a threat that the outlaw lesbian compels us to confront. Far from securing gender and womanliness, she destabilizes female and male; for with homosexuality gender runs amok. Both a woman and a homosexual, she elicits a special horror, for in a homophobic society we are all homophobic at heart.

Psychoanalysis is not an answer. It is a method. It can help us ask useful questions. Above all, like homosexuality, it questions the construction of gender, and it is therefore actually rather surprising that the feminists who have explored and developed psychoanalytic theory have paid so little attention to homosexuality. For to insist on lesbianism as a challenge to stereotypes of gender is ultimately more political than the political importance so far given to it in practice by feminists. To see lesbianism as love for women is to widen it too far; it tends to return women to biology without even achieving unity, since most women don't identify as lesbians. To narrow it down to consensual sexual acts and as nothing else but the exploration of new sensuality won't do either. Both neglect the real reason that homosexuality remains taboo: it challenges the very "rock" on which society is built.

In what is currently regarded as the best and most comprehensive British textbook on pregnancy the following passage occurs: "The intensely feminine female ought to be the ideal human reproductive machine and such a person will usually attract and also be attracted to the masculine type of male, so that by a process of natural selection at a biological level the ideal reproductive female is mated with the ideal reproductive male. . . . From a purely biological aspect the masculine type of female and the effeminate type of male are not good vehicles for reproduction and the procreation of the human race."[21] No matter what we in our progressive ghettos may imagine, the ideological battle over gender is far from won. We must continue to insist on the complexity of sexuality and sexual identity. The discussion and exploration of lesbianism and what it means must continue. The lesbian still challenges reductive and conformist beliefs about what it means to be human. Feminists still need her often lonely courage.

Notes

1. Walter Benjamin, *Charles Baudelaire: A Lyric Poet in the Era of High Capitalism*, trans. Harry Zohn (London: New Left Books, 1973).

2. Ellen Moers, *The Dandy: Brummell to Beerbohm* (London: Secker & Warburg, 1960).

3. Colette, *The Pure and the Impure*, trans. Herma Briffault (Harmondsworth, Middlesex: Penguin, 1980). Originally published as *Ces Plaisirs* in 1932.

4. Djuna Barnes, *Nightwood* (London: Faber & Faber, 1963), 194.

5. Henry Havelock Ellis, *Sexual Inversion* (London: Wilson & Macmillan, 1897), and *Studies in the Psychology of Sex* (New York: Random House, 1936). Originally published in 1905–10.

6. Homosexual slang for "unstylish," lacking in chic or front.

7. Jeffrey Weeks, *Coming Out: Homosexual Politics in Britain from the Nineteenth-Century to the Present* (London: Quartet, 1977); Mary McIntosh in "The Homosexual Role," *Social Problems* 16 (Fall 1968): 182–92, was the first to discuss this. Alan Bray, *Homosexuality in Renaissance England* (London: Gay Men's Press, 1982), places the differentiation of the homosexual role rather earlier than either Weeks or McIntosh.

8. Sonja Ruehl, "Inverts and Experts: Radclyffe Hall and the Lesbian Identity," in *Feminism, Culture, and Politics*, ed. Rosalind Brunt and Caroline Rowan, (London: Lawrence & Wishart, 1982).

9. See Sue O'Sullivan, "Passionate Beginnings: Ideological Politics, 1969–72," Special Issue on Sexuality, *Feminist Review*, no. 11 (1982): 70–86, for an account of the early years of the contemporary British women's liberation movement.

10. See Alix Kates Shulman, "Sex and Power: Sexual Bases of Radical Feminism," in *Women: Sex and Sexuality*, ed. Catharine R. Stimpson and Ethel Spector Person (Chicago: University of Chicago Press, 1980), 21–35.

11. Juliet Mitchell, *Psychoanalysis and Feminism* (London: Allen Lane, 1974).

12. See Mitchell; also Jacques Lacan and the Ecole Freudienne, *Feminine Sexuality*, ed. Juliet Mitchell and Jacqueline Rose (London: Macmillan, 1982); see also *m/f*, nos. 1–9, 1978–83.

13. Michel Foucault, *The History of Sexuality* (Harmondsworth, Middlesex: Penguin, 1980).

14. Adrienne Rich, "Compulsory Heterosexuality and Lesbian Existence," in *Women: Sex and Sexuality*, 79–80.

15. Lillian Faderman, *Surpassing the Love of Men: Romantic Friendship and Love between Women from the Renaissance to the Present* (London: Junction Books, 1981).

16. See Bonnie Zimmerman, "What Has Never Been: An Overview of Lesbian Literary Criticism," *Feminist Studies* 7 (Autumn 1981): 451–75.

17. Adrienne Rich, "Split at the Root," in *Fathers: Reflections by Daughters*, ed. Ursula Owen (London: Virago, 1983).

18. Simone de Beauvoir, *The Second Sex*, trans. H. M. Parshley (London: Jonathan Cape, 1953), pt. 4, chap. 14.

19. Sigmund Freud, "On Narcissism: An Introduction," *Collected Papers*, vol. 4 (London: Hogarth Press and the Institute of Psychoanalysis, 1948). Originally published in 1915.

20. Sigmund Freud, "On the Universal Tendency to Debasement in the Sphere of Love," *On Sexuality* (Harmondsworth, Middlesex: Penguin, 1977). Originally published in 1912.

21. Gordon Bourne, *Pregnancy* (London: Cassell, 1972), 27.

10

Freud's "Fetishism" and the Lesbian Dildo Debates

Heather Findlay

From the pages of lesbian porn magazines to the meetings of the Modern Language Association, a highly organized discourse has developed around a rather unlikely object: the dildo. No other sex toy has generated the quantity or quality of discussion among mostly urban, middle-class, white lesbians than the dildo.[1] What interests me about this discourse is that a number of subcultural products (advertisements, erotic fiction, the sex toys themselves) have consistently drawn from a set of familiar conventions, thus constituting a kind of shared fantasy about lesbian dildo use. Like all fantasy, this one no doubt occludes more than it reveals about the reality of lesbian desire, whatever that may be. My focus, however, is on what the French might call the *mise-en-scène* of a particular dildo fantasy and its relation to the issues raised in Freud's 1927 essay on fetishism.[2] By analyzing the dildo in conjunction with Freud's text, I hope to shed light not only on the dildo debates and the feminist "sex wars" of which they are a part but also on the (perhaps paradoxical) relevance to lesbians of the psychoanalytic theory of fetishism, a "perversion" which Freud—as a number of his feminist readers have discussed in some detail[3]—claims to be exclusively male. My aim is not simply to apply psychoanalysis to lesbian sexuality but also to do what is in a sense more difficult: to reread Freud from the perspective of lesbian theory and practice and to unravel those points at which his text may be as "symptomatic" as the behavior it attempts to describe.

The Dildo Wars

To date, discourse among lesbians over the dildo has been marked by a debate divided roughly into two camps. On the one hand, some lesbians have debunked the dildo and its notorious cousin the strap-on, calling them "male-

Feminist Studies 18, no. 3 (Fall 1992). © 1992 by Feminist Studies, Inc.

identified." The most colorful, if noncanonical, spokeswomen for this position have been published in the "Letters" column of the lesbian pornographic magazine *On Our Backs*. These letters are written in protest of the fact that, as Colleen Lamos puts it, "The dildo is clearly a matter of intense interest and a focus of fetishistic desire for the readers" and publishers of the magazine.[4] For example, Daralee and Nancy, two self-described "outrageous and oversexed S/M dykes" from Birmingham, Alabama, confess that they are nonetheless puzzled about the current lesbian romance with the dildo.

> What's the deal with women "portraying" themselves as equipped with penises? We can't figure out how this could be erotic to a woman-identified-woman. If they want a dick, why are they with a woman wearing a dildo and not a man? Don't misunderstand us; we're heavily into penetration . . . but this whole life-like dildo market is baffling to us.[5]

The authors' distaste for dildos, especially "lifelike" ones, is based on the conviction that a dildo represents a penis and is therefore incompatible with "woman-identified" sexuality. In fact, the letter's reference to women-identified-women situates it within a larger, radical feminist critique of sex,[6] including (as an editor at *off our backs* put it) "games that rely on paraphernalia [and] roles."[7] Ironically enough for our kinky Birmingham correspondents, the critique of the dildo has developed in tandem with radical feminist attacks on butch-femme and sadomasochism such as Sheila Jeffreys's, which hold that both practices reproduce a "heteropatriarchy" based on masculine and feminine sex roles.[8]

On the other hand, some lesbians have argued that dildos do not represent penises; rather, they are sex toys that have an authentic place in the history of lesbian subculture. This argument can be detected in Joan Nestle's writings on butch-femme sexuality[9] or, more explicitly, in the columns of self-made lesbian sexologist Susie Bright, a.k.a. Susie Sexpert. "The facts about dildos," she assures us, "aren't as controversial as their famous resemblance to the infamous 'penis' and all that *it* represents." In an attempt to downplay the "political, social, and emotional connotations of dildos," Bright writes that "a dildo can be a succulent squash, or a tender mold of silicon. Technically, it is any device you use for the pleasure of vaginal or anal penetration. . . . Penises can only be compared to dildos in the sense that they take up space.[10] As a mere "device," a sex toy that can be vegetable or mineral, a dildo has only a remote, sheerly ontological relationship to the penis: like it, the dildo exists, it "takes up space" in the vagina or anus. In sum, as part of their challenge to what they see as the repressive sexual politics of radical feminism, Bright and other "prosex" feminists have defended the dildo by downplaying its referentiality, by denying that the dildo represents a penis.

Among other things, we might accuse the antidildo camp of having an unsophisticated understanding of representation. Daralee and Nancy's letter, for example, assumes that a dildo not only represents but is also the same thing as "a dick." This assumption announces itself in the quotation marks Daralee and Nancy put around "portraying"; by doubting the difference a representation can make, the authors affirm that wearing a dildo is, quite literally, equipping oneself with a penis.[11] To Bright's credit, her comments shift the burden of suspicion from the representation to the thing represented: if the lesbians from Birmingham put "portraying" in quotation marks, Bright quotes and italicizes "the infamous 'penis' and all *it* represents," thereby referring to the organ itself as if it were somebody else's peculiar idea—as if, in other words, it were already a signifier. Bright may, however, fall prey to her own brand of literalism: is it possible for a dildo to stand, as it were, only for itself? In the face of "this whole life-like dildo market" so baffling to the Birmingham lesbians—or, for that matter, the popularity of huge Black dildos so troubling to *Black Lace* editor Alycee J. Lane[12]—is it possible to insist that dildos are strictly nonrepresentational, that they are not (to quote Lane) the "location" of both sexual and racial "terror and desire"?

Enter Freud With Fetish

Putting these questions aside for the moment, I would like to point out that, regardless of the speakers' feelings about psychoanalysis, the dildo debate may be said to revolve around the question of whether the dildo is a fetish in Freud's definition of the term. At the beginning of "Fetishism," Freud tells a parable about how the fetish reveals itself to be a penis replacement. According to the story, fetishism is the little boy's response to the castration anxiety he experiences upon first seeing his mother's genitals.

> What happened, therefore, was that the boy refused to take cognizance of the fact of his having perceived that a woman does not possess a penis. No, that could not be true: for if a woman had been castrated, then his own possession of a penis was in danger; and against that there rose in rebellion the portion of his narcissism which Nature has, as a precaution, attached to that particular organ.

Freud gives his story a happy ending, at least for the boy: "To put it more plainly: the fetish is a substitute for the woman's (the mother's) penis that the little boy once believed in and—for reasons familiar to us—does not want to give up."[13] Because the fetish represents a penis, Freud argues, it allows the subject to maintain, despite evidence to the contrary, that castration is not a danger. In fact, it allows him to maintain that castration has not happened at all. I will go on to say more about this passage, but for the moment we should note that the question of whether the dildo is a penis replacement lies at the very heart of the debate I summarized above. Critics of the dildo claim that it is a penis replacement, and its proponents claim that it is not. The debate over dildo use, in other words, is a debate about the politics of fetishism.

This may seem surprising, considering that Freud's theory of fetishism seems inhospitable to lesbian experience, so exclusive is its phallo- and heterocentrism. The most glaring example of this is Freud's generic fetishist himself, who is a straight man.[14] Moreover, dildos may not be fetish objects, technically speaking. In the fetishism essay, Freud explains that fetishes, due to unconscious censorship, most often take their form from whatever the little boy sees *just before* he witnesses the spectacle of his mother's castration: fur and velvet symbolize the mother's pubic hair, undergarments "crystalize the moment of undressing," and so on. Fetishistic desire exemplifies how (if I may refer to the oft-quoted formula) the unconscious is like a language: the fetishist finds himself representing his love object by means of contiguous associations, that is, by metonymy. Thus, to the extent that fetishes most often refer indirectly to the penis (that is, they tend not to be obvious phallic symbols) dildos may not be "true" fetishes. Freud's essay, in fact, does not discuss them at all.

Nevertheless, recent representations of dildos in lesbian publications conform, in many ways, to Freud's paradigm. Take, for example, this advertisement for Scorpio dildo products (fig. 1), which runs regularly in various pornographic magazines, including *On Our Backs*. The advertisement bases itself on a comparison between, and potential substitution of, a dildo and the penis, or "Nature itself," according to the euphemistic language of the ad. By foregrounding the "naturalistic" dildo which looks like a penis, and contrasting it to the "nonnaturalistic" one in the background, the ad makes it clear that dildos supplement nature—indeed, they are *more* natural than nature itself—and that the natural object in question is the penis. The very terms of the ad repeat what we already find in Freud. In both cases, nature is the name for an archaic state of plenitude and satisfaction, and the penis stands as persuasive evidence of the subject's citizenship in this state. "Nature," we will remember from Freud's essay, has providentially "attached" to this organ a good measure of the boy's narcissism—so much so that nature, the organ, and narcissism seem linked indissolubly in a kind of pact. The ad also points to the very mechanism of fetishism as a form of substitution and representation: the mirror placed beneath the fore-

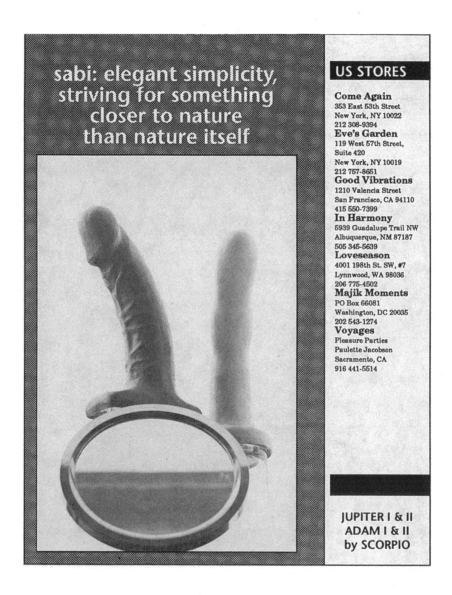

Scorpio Products "Sabi" advertisement.

grounded dildo suggests that the fetish works precisely because it represents something else. Because the mirror tilts toward the reader, the ad further thematizes the role of fetishistic representation in the production and maintenance of an imaginary "I," an ego whose narcissistic whole is authenticated or (quite literally in this case) crowned by the phallus-fetish.

More often than not, dildo ads will deny that dildos are penis substitutes. One ad from Eve's Garden, a feminist sex boutique in New York, ends with this terse message to anyone who might be wondering: "Finally, we should add that we don't think of dildos as imitation penises"; they are "sexual accessories, not substitutes." Upon reading this kind of disclaimer, we may wonder if perhaps the lady doth protest too much. In the end, lesbians with uncooperative sexual tastes still market and purchase politically incorrect dildos which are shaped like penises and named after mythological patriarchs, as in the "Adam I" or the "Jupiter II." Even the conventions of English usage undermine the ad's nonsensical explanation, "We've designed [our dildos] to be factually and aesthetically pleasing." If dildos do not owe their allure to the fact that they represent penises, then how are they "factually pleasing"? For that matter, who ever says that anything is "factually pleasing"? In sum, dildo ads may cause us to conclude with Elizabeth A. Grosz that, in the case of lesbianism, "it may be possible to suggest some connection" between women and fetishism after all[15] and that the maleness of fetishism is determined more by one's subject position than by biological gender.

Yet we might want to pay close attention to this recurrent anxiety—peculiar to lesbian dildo fetishism—over conflating a representation (a dildo) with reality (a penis). For one thing, this anxiety is totally absent in gay male fetishism, where dildos (and their purveyors) strive overtly to replicate penises, even particular penises, like porn star Jeff Stryker's. The makers of the Jeff Stryker model guarantee that their dildos are cast in a mold taken directly from Stryker's erect member. Exact replication, even a kind of indexical representation, is celebrated among gay men—perhaps all too uncritically. Lesbians, on the other hand, have marketed a series of dildos which, in an obvious attempt to break the association between a piece of silicon and a penis, are shaped like dolphins, ears of corn, and even the Goddess. This urge to steer away from realism stems from the fact that these feminist dildo suppliers and their customers are suspicious of conflating a representation with reality, especially in the case of a phallus. One of the most important and repeated gestures of feminist critique has been to show how patriarchy asserts itself by making precisely this conflation, by collapsing the difference between a symbol and a real body organ.[16] In this light, being penetrated by the Goddess amounts to a defiant response to the patriarchal law that symbols of pleasure and potency always refer back to, or be somehow proper to, men's bodies. Like good Lacanians, these feminists are busily and happily disarticulating the phallus from the penis.

The Cunt We Wish Did Not Exist

But the problem of substitution is not the only issue in lesbian dildo use; nor is it the only function of the fetish for Freud. In his essay, Freud specifies further that the fetish is a representation not of just any "chance penis" but of the *mother's* penis, the penis that the boy child once imagines his mother to have had but then discovers unhappily that she has lost. Faced with the "fact" of his mother's castration, and thus the possibility of his own, the little boy replaces this image with a fetish which "remains as a token of triumph over the threat of castration and a protection against it."[17] At first glance, lesbian dildo fetishism seems to have nothing to do with mothers, castrated or not. But in Freud's account, the fetish does not refer to a real woman; it represents an imaginary, phallic one. In light of this, is not Joan Nestle's bedildoed lover in her short story, "My Woman Poppa,"[18] the fetishist's primal love object, the phallic woman the little boy imagines his mother to be? A more dramatic example may be a sequence from Fatale Video's pornographic collection *Clips*.[19] In this episode, set in a ranch house-style living room complete with a sonorous television, a recliner, and copies of the *Wall Street Journal*, a very femme Fanny kneels in front of her shirtless butch lover Kenny and watches as Kenny unzips her pants to reveal her pinkish-brown, "realistic" dildo. Is Fanny not taking pleasure in the fetishistic fantasy of a woman with breasts *and* a penis? Because Fanny is in the position of the spectator, is our gaze on the scene fetishistic as well? Indeed, Fanny and the spectator rehearse Freud's formula for fetishism: despite evidence to the contrary, she insists (as we also do?) upon the fantasy that the penis is (still) there.

Fetishism occurs as well on the level of the video's narrative. After Kenny unzips her pants, Fanny takes her to the couch. Although the camera centers on Fanny as she sucks Kenny's dildo, we are also shown that Fanny is stimulating her lover's clitoris by rubbing her crotch with her shoulder. As she brings Kenny to orgasm, even though we know that the pleasure is clitoral, for the sake of the fantasy we believe it is phallic. In terms of recent reformulations of Freud's theory of fetishism, pleasure in this sequence conforms to Slavoj Žižek's version of fetishistic logic: she knows very well what she is doing, but she is doing it anyway.[20]

As an aside, we might also raise the issue of the dildo harness, which is sometimes the object of as much fetishistic attention as the toy it is designed to hold. Indeed, the harness may approximate the classical Freudian fetish more closely than the dildo, precisely because, as I suggest above, the fetish usually refers metonymically, rather then metaphorically, to the mother's missing penis. For the sake of testing Freud's paradigm we might say that the harness, which few lesbian fetishists ever imagine being made out of anything but the blackest of black leather, gains its allure from the fact that it is—like a woman's crotch—fleshy and dark. Even more significant may be the gaping hole at the front. Inserting and removing a dildo from this hole rehearses, in a literal manner, the traumatic primal experience of Freud's little fetishist: now she has it, now she doesn't.

Yet this function of the fetish, its use as a protective device against the mother's castration, is its most troubling one. How much do lesbians have in common with Freud's little fetishist, who believes in the "fact" that his mother—and thus all women—are lacking what he possesses, if only precariously? This question is a pressing one because, as a consequence of his belief in women's castration, the fetishist is deeply misogynist. He understands sexual difference simply in terms of women's deficiency. More concretely, Freud insists that after the fetishist represses the terrifying scenario of his mother's lack, "an aversion, which is never lacking in any fetishist, to the real female genitals remains a *stigma indelebile* of the repression which has taken place."[21] In the case of lesbian dildo fetishism, if lesbians take up the position of Freud's straight, male fetishist, how much is their pleasure accompanied by this aversion—which is supposedly never absent in any fetishist—to women and their bodies?

As light as the kind of butch-femme play in "My Woman Poppa" or *Clips* may seem, more than one lesbian has suffered from the darker undercurrents of fetishistic desire. In an article entitled "Sex, Lies, and Penetration: A Butch Finally 'Fesses Up," Jan Brown details what for her is the painful by-product of butch-femme roleplaying and of the dildo that constitutes its fetishistic center. "We butches," she writes,

> have a horror of the pity fuck. We cannot face the charity of the mercy orgasm or the thought of contempt in our partner's eyes when we have allowed them to convince us that they really do want to touch us, take us, that they really do want to reach behind our dick and into the cunt we both wish did not exist.[22]

Brown's account reverses the usual subject/object relation and suggests that a subtle objectification is at work not of the feminine but of the masculine partner in butch-femme play. What Brown refers to sneeringly as "the sacred myth of the stone butch," a myth held in place by her holy fetish object, turns out to be a defensive construct that both partners use to veil a lack, "the cunt we both wish did not exist."

If, for Brown, the dildo allows lesbians to circumvent the question of the cunt, some feminists of color are concerned that it serves a similar function vis-à-vis racial difference. Alycee J. Lane, for example, writes that a friend once accused her of having "race issues" because she owns a dildo which, as Lane explains, is "six inches, rubbery, cheap and *mauve*." Lane defends her anatomically incorrect dildo in the tradition of "prosex" feminism: "a dildo is a dildo, not a dick. . . . The only thing that mattered, really, was the way my g-spot got worked." Yet Lane remains unsatisfied with this explanation, especially after a trip to her local sex shop reveals that "flesh-colored" dildos are actually cream-colored ("What does it *mean*," she ponders, "when white hegemony extends to the production of dildos?") and that brown dildos are hard to get because, as the cashier explains, "They sell rather quickly, you know." She is directed to another bin. "I turned and looked. They were not dildos; they were *monstrosities*. Twenty-four inches and thick as my arm. 'Big Black Dick' said the wrapper. . . . I looked around for some 'Big White Dick' or even 'Big Flesh Colored Dick.' No luck. And I seriously doubt that *they* were in high demand." Lane's experience changes her mind about the referentiality of the dildo. "Race," she concludes, "permeates American culture. A sex toy easily becomes the location for racial terror and desire, because sex itself is that location."[23]

In precisely what way, however, does a monstrous black dildo function as a signifier of racial terror and desire? When Freud claims that, in the heterosexual encounter, the fetishist's toy allows him to circumvent castration (the fetish "endows women with the attribute which makes them acceptable as sexual objects"),[24] he suggests that the fetish alleviates the fact that (to cite Jacques Lacan's dictum) there is no relation between the sexes. Similarly, it seems that the black dildo fetish can "make acceptable" a specifically racial lack—the lack, that is, under white hegemony of a relation between the races. As in the case of Freud's fetishist and his "woman," the big black dildo allows whites to carry on a relation with Blacks which is, in reality, no relation at all. If sex *itself* is the location of racial terror and desire, we might say that the more general (and apparently lucrative) sexual fantasy of Black superpotency—a fantasy that Jackie Goldsby accuses lesbians of sharing[25]—is another, powerful cultural fetish that allows us to circumvent the Real of racial disintegration. Behind the big black dick, in other words, is the race we wish did not exist.

The Chance Penis

I am not suggesting that all lesbian fetishism ends in this kind of aversion. Even if we go back to Freud and reread, we see that the fetishistic perspective may not be monolithic. Freud's fetishist, in fact, is guilty of some rather reckless logic, and his triumph over women's castration is not as quick and easy as it may appear. Here, in full, is the passage I have already quoted:

> When now I announce that the fetish is a substitute for the penis, I shall certainly create disappointment; so I hasten to add that it is not a substitute for any chance penis, but for a particular and quite special penis that had been extremely important in early childhood but had later been lost. . . . What happened, therefore, was that the boy refused to take cognizance of the fact of his having perceived that a woman does not possess a penis. No, that could not be true: for if a woman had been castrated, then his own possession of a penis was in danger. . . .

First off, I am struck by the sense of urgency in Freud's rhetoric, produced perhaps by his identification with the frightened little boy. This identification is rendered most obvious when Freud speaks for the little boy and ventriloquizes his response to seeing his mother's genitals: "No, that could not be true: for if a woman had been castrated . . . ," and so on. Indeed, Freud "hastens" to erect a completed theoretical framework in the place of a lack, the "disappointment" he fears he will "certainly create" in his reader, in the same way that the little boy erects a fetish in the place of his mother's supposed castration. Emphasizing the uncanny way in which his theory doubles that of the little boy's, Freud hastens to complete it by adding, as we know, the notion of the mother's lack.

Because both Freud and his exemplary boy are in such a rush to posit the mother's castration, we might wonder if, contrary to Freud's insistence, the penis in question *may be* a "chance penis." In other words, perhaps it is not necessarily the mother's and perhaps somebody or something else might trigger the first blow to the child's narcissism. Actually, Freud describes rather circuitously the consequences of the little fetishist's sight of his mother's genitals: "what happened, therefore, was that the boy refused to take cognizance of the fact of his having perceived that a woman does not possess a penis." At this crucial moment, Freud does not write that the fetishist represses the fact of women's castration but, rather, "the fact of his having perceived" that women are castrated. The idea of women's lack, in other words, is *already* part of the boy's defensive reaction.

If everyone were not hastening to erect defenses around whatever it is we fear to lose, perhaps we might pause to consider that, in a different context, such a loss might be perceived or represented as something other than women's "fault." For example, in the context of a developed lesbian subculture, might the butch figure represent a different sort of lack, such as the absence of men like fathers and male lovers? And is it possible to imagine this lack as something other than deficiency, as something other than what my mother had in mind when she pleaded with me to "try more men"? Ideally, we might reenvision this lack as cultural difference in all its complexity. In Freud's account, this is exactly what the classic fetishistic perspective fails to do when, in its simplicity, it reduces difference to an economy of the same (to cite Jacques Derrida's formula). Faced with the alterity of the mother's body, the little boy interprets it in terms of his own body: like him, she either has or does not have a penis.

I would like to suggest a third position in the debate on lesbian dildos. If, in answer to the question of whether dildos represent penises, one camp says "yes" and the other says "no," perhaps a third position might be "yes, but. . . ." This kind of affirmation/negation is, as Sarah Kofman reminds us, the logic of fetishism itself as an "undecidable compromise."[26] In her reading of the fetishism essay, Kofman points out that Freud's subjects choose fetishes which, in the final analysis, both deny *and* affirm women's castration. For example, in the case of his patient who enjoys cutting women's hair, Freud discovers that the fetish "contains within itself the two mutually incompatible assertions: 'the woman has still got a penis' and 'my father has castrated the woman.' "[27] This undecidable compromise is also, I believe, what Fatale's video *Clips* performs, and the way that it does it is through parody: the goofy background music, the stereotypical middle-class living room, Kenny's beer drinking, even Fanny's virginal white lingerie. Through the duplicitous strategy of parody, the video audaciously inserts lesbianism into a context which still refers lovingly to the standard components of bourgeois heterosexuality—this is, after all, a video produced and consumed primarily by lesbians from more or less nuclear, middle-class families. The representation of Kenny's dildo is also inflected through parody; the video pokes fun at the association between dildo and penis, and at the same time it acknowledges and exploits its erotic power. If, as Judith Butler has proposed, such "parodic redeployment[s] of power" may have a specifically political value for lesbians,[28] we might add that parody is also a fundamentally fetishistic strategy. The makers of *Clips*, for example, know very well that what they are doing is phallocentric but, with a subversive laugh, they are doing it anyway.

Postscript: The Safer Sex Fetish

One of the most interesting aspects of the gay response to AIDS—one that sets it apart from all other communities' responses to the epidemic—has been the invention of a whole new category of fetish objects: the safer sex fetish. In order to make safer sex erotic, AIDS activists have made great efforts to turn condoms, dental dams, and rubber gloves into sex toys. Phone sex and—as we can see in some ads for 1-900 lines—phones themselves have become fetishized *qua* safer sex. These ads capitalize on the familiar fetishistic association by veiling the model's groin and stringing a cord out of his fly, thus representing phones as penis substitutes. As for lesbians, the fact that they are leaping lustfully on to the bandwagon is evidenced by the fact that a company in San Francisco called Stormy Leather now sells harnesses (black, of course) that hold dental dams in place over the vagina.

Whereas Freud discusses fetishism as the psychic process of an individual, the work of AIDS activists—safer sex workshops, condom ads, porn films and literature that foreground fetish objects as safer sex—provides us with examples of fetishism as a *cultural* labor. Because some genital sex is now threatening because it can transmit HIV, AIDS activists have begun to carry out consciously what Freud's fetishist does unconsciously, that is, to sexualize an object in the place of real genitals. In the case of condoms, the idea is to swerve the sexual drive away from direct genital contact and on to an object used to cover the penis. Take, for example, the condom ad created by the Gay Men's Health Crisis (fig. 2). The ad doesn't just tell you that a condom in your pocket is your friend because it can prevent AIDS. It tells the viewer that a condom in your pocket is sexy. It tells you that a condom can be a fetish, especially for a man like this one who has already fetishized his entire appearance by working out at the gym and wearing skin-tight clothing. The sexual allure of this poster hinges on the way that it eroticizes nearly everything about the man's body except his penis; in fact, the poster tantalizingly veils the man's "lack" (i.e., his asshole) by displacing it and representing it as the suggestive little circle of the rubber in his back pocket.

It would be incorrect, actually, to speak of this cultural labor as fully conscious. Like the psychic process Freud describes, the making of the safer sex fetish is marked by its own brand of repression or at least a kind of motivated forgetting. AIDS activists have incorporated this necessary forgetfulness into the design of the typical safer sex workshop: the purpose of going to one is to worry about AIDS during the workshop, and then—armed with your fetish—to forget about it during sex itself. Once again, we see the "refusal to take cognizance" at the heart of Freud's definition of the fetish.

In the case of the safer sex fetish, the threat to be repressed is not the threat of castration but the fear of contracting a terrible and probably fatal disease. Admittedly, some AIDS educational campaigns *exploit* castration fears in order to frighten people away from prostitutes and promiscuity.[29] I don't think this has been the case in the lesbian and gay response to AIDS. Queers in the age of AIDS have shunned these kinds of scare tactics, not only because they result in overt misogyny but also because members of groups like ACT UP have dedicated themselves personally and politically to the sanctity of sexual pleasure.

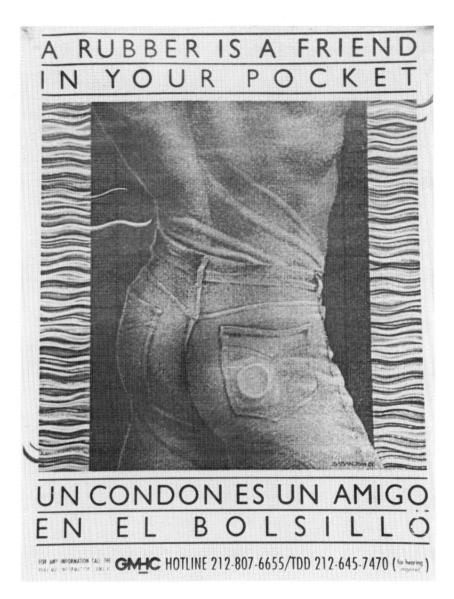

"A Rubber Is a Friend in Your Pocket." Ad created by
Gay Men's Health Crisis. Illustration by Michael
Sabanosh. Photograph by Paisley Currah.

And the fetish, it seems, is an efficient, safe, and satisfying vehicle for it. In fact, Freud opens his essay by marveling at how happy fetishists are with their toys. He writes that these well-adjusted perverts never come to analysis because they want to be cured of their fetish.

> There is no need to expect that these people came to analysis on account of their fetish. For though no doubt a fetish is recognized by its adherents as an abnormality, it is seldom felt by them as the symptom of an ailment accompanied by suffering. Usually they are quite satisfied with it, or even praise the way in which it eases their erotic life.[30]

In this passage, Freud seems impressed with the fetish object's accessibility, versatility, and capacity for gratification. Rather than focusing on the fear and anxiety which goes into the making of a fetish, AIDS activists have taken advantage of these, its more delightful, characteristics—all for the sake of pleasure and survival.

Notes

1. See Colleen Lamos's excellent essay on pornographic representations of the dildo, "*On Our Backs*: Taking on the Phallus" (unpublished manuscript of a talk delivered at the Annual Convention of the Modern Language Association, San Francisco, 28 Dec. 1991), forthcoming in *The Lesbian Postmodern* (Columbia University Press). In general, a number of papers at the 1991 Annual Lesbian and Gay Studies Conference, including my essay and the panel entitled "Flaunting the Phallus" in which it appeared, attest to the curious increase of scholarly interest in lesbianism and the phallus, epitomized perhaps by Judith Butler's "The Lesbian Phallus and the Morphological Imaginary" (*differences* 4 [Spring 1992]: 133–71). Recent interventions by women of color in the dildo debate include Jackie Goldsby's "What It Means to Be Colored Me," *Outlook* 9 (Summer 1990): 15; and Alycee J. Lane's editorial on dildos, "What's *Race* Got to Do with It?" in the Black lesbian pornographic magazine *Black Lace* (Summer 1991): 21.

2. Sigmund Freud, "Fetishism," in *The Standard Edition of the Complete Psychological Works of Sigmund Freud*, ed. James Strachey, 24 vols. (London: Hogarth, 1964), 21: 153–61. All further references to Freud are from this volume. For an excellent summary of French psychoanalysis's emphasis on the "syntax" of fantasy, see Elizabeth Cowie, "Fantasia," in *The Woman in Question*, ed. Parveen Adams and Elizabeth Cowie (Cambridge: Massachusetts Institute of Technology Press, 1990), 149–96.

3. Several of his feminist readers have discussed Freud's exclusion of women from fetishism. See Naomi Schor, "Female Fetishism: The Case of George Sand," in *The Female Body in Western Culture: Contemporary Perspectives*, ed. Susan Suleiman (Cambridge: Harvard University Press, 1985), 363–72; and Elizabeth A. Grosz's "Lesbian Fetishism?" *differences* 3 (Summer 1991): 39–54.

4. Lamos, 3.

5. Daralee and Nancy, "Letters" column *On Our Backs* (Winter 1989): 5.

6. See Anne Koedt et al., eds., *Radical Feminism* (New York: Quadrangle, 1973). Daralee and Nancy's "women-identified-women" is a catchphrase, of course, originating in part from the Radicalesbian manifesto, "The Woman-Identified Woman," reprinted in *Radical Feminism*, 240–45. For a recent discussion of the radical feminist critique of sexuality, see Alice Echols's *Daring to Be Bad: Radical Feminism in America, 1967–1975* (Minneapolis: University of Minnesota Press, 1989).

7. See Fran Moira's review of a panel at the 1982 Barnard sexuality conference, "lesbian sex mafia (l s/m) speak out," *off our backs* 12 (June 1982): 24.

8. Sheila Jeffreys, "Butch and Femme: Now and Then," in *Not a Passing Phase: Reclaiming Lesbians in History, 1840–1985*, ed. Lesbian History Group (London: Women's Press, 1989), 178.

9. See, for example, "The Fem Question" in *Pleasure and Danger: Exploring Female Sexuality*, ed. Carole S. Vance (London: Pandora, 1989), 233; and Joan Nestle's "My Woman Poppa" in *The Persistent Desire: A Femme-Butch Reader*, ed. Joan Nestle (Boston: Alyson, 1992), 348–51.

10. Susie Bright, *Susie Sexpert's Lesbian Sex World* (Pittsburgh: Cleis Press, 1990), 19.

11. Similarly, radical feminist attacks on butch-femme can be accused of failing to distinguish between gender stereotyping and "gender performance" in Judith Butler's sense of the term (see Judith Butler, *Gender Trouble: Feminism and the Subversion of Identity* [New York: Routledge, 1989], 137–39); that is, between butch-femme as a duplication of masculine/feminine sex roles, and butch-femme as a performative, "erotic statement" (Joan Nestle, *A Restricted Country* [Ithaca: Firebrand Books, 1986], 100).

12. Lane, 21.

13. Freud, 153, 152–53.

14. He is, at least, not a homosexual. Fetishism, according to Freud, "saves the fetishist from being a homosexual by endowing women with the attribute which makes them acceptable as sexual objects" (154). In other words, the fetish object displaces the sight of the horrifying female sex organ and thus "saves" the subject from having to seek sex with other men. Interestingly, Freud pauses at this moment to admit he remains puzzled as to why a "great majority" of men are heterosexual, considering the fact that "probably no male human being is spared the fright of castration at the female genital." See also 155.

15. Grosz, 51.

16. See, for example, Jane Gallop's writings on the penis/phallus distinction, in particular her chapter, "Beyond the Phallus," in *Thinking through the Body* (New York: Columbia, 1988), 119–33.

17. Freud, 154.

18. Nestle, "My Woman Poppa," 348–50.

19. "When Fanny Liquidates Kenny's Stocks," in *Clips*, dir. Nan Kinney and Debi Sundahl, Fatale Video (1988).

20. See Slavoj Žižek, *The Sublime Object of Ideology* (London: Verso, 1989), 28–33.

21. Freud, 154.

22. Jan Brown, "Sex, Lies, and Penetration: A Butch Finally 'Fesses Up," *Outlook* 7 (Winter 1990): 34; reprinted in Nestle, *A Persistent Desire*, 410–15.

23. Lane, 21.

24. Freud, 154.

25. See Jackie Goldsby's critique of Susie Bright's video presentation, "All Girl Action: A History of Lesbian Erotica" (1990). Responding in part to Bright's defense of Russ Meyer's *Vixen*, which portrays a white woman getting "ram[med]" by a Black woman with a "larger-than-life white dildo," Goldsby concludes that "as Bright's lecture presented it, lesbian eroticism—its icons, its narratives, its ideologies—is white" (15).

26. Sarah Kofman, *The Enigma of Woman: Woman in Freud's Writings*, trans. Catherine Porter (Ithaca: Cornell University Press, 1985), 88.

27. Freud, 157.

28. Butler, 124.

29. See, for example, J. D. Crowe's cartoon with the caption "DEATH FOR SALE," portraying four street prostitutes with A-I-D-S spelled over their heads (reprinted in Sander L. Gilman, "AIDS and Syphilis: The Iconography of a Disease," *October*, no. 43 [Winter 1987]: 106).

30. Freud, 152.

11

Man Royals and Sodomites

Some Thoughts on the Invisibility of Afro-Caribbean Lesbians

Makeda Silvera

I WILL BEGIN with some personal images and voices about woman loving. These have provided a ground for my search for cultural reflections of my identity as a Black woman artist within the Afro-Caribbean community of Toronto. Although I focus here on my own experience (specifically, Jamaican), I am aware of similarities with the experience of other Third World women of color whose history and culture has been subjected to colonization and imperialism.

I spent the first thirteen years of my life in Jamaica among strong women. My great-grandmother, my grandmother, and grand-aunts were major influences in my life. There are also men whom I remember with fondness—my grandmother's "man friend" G., my Uncle Bertie, his friend Paul, Mr. Minott, Uncle B., and Uncle Freddy. And there were men like Mr. Eden who terrified me because of stories about his "walking" fingers and his liking for girls under age fourteen.

I lived in a four-bedroom house with my grandmother, Uncle Bertie, and two female tenants. On the same piece of land, my grandmother had other tenants, mostly women and lots and lots of children. The big veranda of our house played a vital role in the social life of this community. It was on that veranda that I received my first education on "Black women's strength"—not only from their strength but also from the daily humiliations they bore at work and in relationships. European experience coined the term "feminism," but the term "Black women's strength" reaches beyond Eurocentric definitions to describe what is the cultural continuity of my own struggles.

The veranda. My grandmother sat on the veranda in the evenings after all

Feminist Studies 18, no. 3 (Fall 1992). © 1992 by Makeda Silvera

the chores were done to read the newspaper. People—mostly women—gathered there to discuss "life." Life covered every conceivable topic—economic, local, political, social, and sexual: the high price of salt-fish, the scarcity of flour, the nice piece of yellow yam bought at Coronation market, Mr. Lam, the shopkeeper who was taking "liberty" with Miss Inez, the fights women had with their menfolk, work, suspicions of Miss Iris and Punsie carrying on something between them, the cost of school books. . . .

My grandmother usually had lots of advice to pass on to the women on the veranda, all grounded in the Bible. Granny believed in Jesus, in good and evil, and in repentance. She was also a practical and sociable woman. Her faith didn't interfere with her perception of what it meant to be a poor Black woman; neither did it interfere with our Friday night visits to my Aunt Marie's bar. I remember sitting outside on the piazza with my grandmother, two grand-aunts, and three or four of their women friends. I liked their flashy smiles and I was fascinated by their independence, ease, and their laughter. I loved their names—Cherry Rose, Blossom, Jonesie, Poinsietta, Ivory, Pearl, Iris, Bloom, Dahlia, Babes. Whenever the conversation came around to some "big 'oman talk"—who was sleeping with whom or whose daughter just got "fallen"—I was sent off to get a glass of water for an adult, or a bottle of Kola champagne. Every Friday night I drank as much as half a dozen bottles of Kola champagne, but I still managed to hear snippets of words, tail ends of conversations about women together.

In Jamaica, the words used to describe many of these women would be "Man Royal" and/or "Sodomite." Dread words. So dread that women dare not use these words to name themselves. They were names given to women by men to describe aspects of our lives that men neither understood nor approved.

I heard "sodomite" whispered a lot during my primary-school years; and tales of women secretly having sex, joining at the genitals, and being taken to the hospital to be "cut" apart were told in the schoolyard. Invariably, one of the women would die. Every five to ten years the same story would surface. At times, it would even be published in the newspapers. Such stories always generated much talking and speculation from "Bwoy dem kinda gal naasti sah!" to some wise old woman saying, "But dis caan happen, after two shutpan caan join"—meaning identical objects cannot go into the other. The act of loving someone of the same sex was sinful, abnormal—something to hide. Even today, it isn't unusual or uncommon to be asked, "So how do two 'omen do it? . . . What unoo use for a penis? . . . Who is the man and who is the 'oman?" It's inconceivable that women can have intimate relationships that are whole, that are not lacking because of the absence of a man. It's assumed that women in such relationships must be imitating men.

The word "sodomite" derives from the Old Testament. Its common use to describe lesbians (or any strong independent woman) is peculiar to Jamaica—a culture historically and strongly grounded in the Bible. Although Christian values have dominated the world, their effect in slave colonies is particular. Our foreparents gained access to literacy through the Bible when they were being indoctrinated by missionaries. It provided powerful and ancient stories of strength, endurance, and hope which reflected their own fight against oppression. This book has been so powerful that it continues to bind our lives with its racism and misogyny. Thus, the importance the Bible plays in Afro-Caribbean culture must be recognized in order to understand the historical and political context for the invisibility of lesbians. The wrath of God "rained down burning sulphur on Sodom and Gomorrah" (Genesis 19:23). How could a Caribbean woman claim the name?

When, thousands of miles away and fifteen years after my school days, my grandmother was confronted with my love for a woman, her reaction was determined by her Christian faith and by this dread word "sodomite"—its meaning, its implication, its history.

And when, Bible in hand, my grandmother responded to my love by sitting me down, at the age of twenty-seven, to quote Genesis, it was within the context of this tradition, this politic. When she pointed out that "this was a white people ting," or "a ting only people with mixed blood was involved in" (to explain or include my love with a woman of mixed blood), it was a strong denial of many ordinary Black working-class women she knew.

It was finally through my conversations with my grandmother, my mother, and my mother's friend five years later that I began to realize the scope of this denial which was intended to dissuade and protect me. She knew too well that any woman who took a woman lover was attempting to walk on fire—entering a "no man's land." I began to see how commonplace the act of loving women really was, particularly in working-class communities. I realized, too, just how heavily shame and silence weighed down this act.

A conversation with a friend of my mother:

Well, when I was growing up we didn't hear much 'bout woman and woman. They weren't "suspect." There was much more talk about "batty man businesses" when I was a teenager in the 1950s.

I remember one story about a man who was "suspect" and that every night when he was coming home, a group of guys use to lay wait for him and stone him so viciously that he had to run for his life. Dem time, he was safe only in the day.

Now with women, nobody really suspected. I grew up in the country and I grew up seeing women holding hands, hugging-up, sleeping together in one bed and there was no question. Some of this was based purely on emotional friendship, but I also knew of cases where the women were dealing, but no one really suspected. Close people around knew, but not everyone. It wasn't a thing that you would go out and broadcast. It would be something just between the two people.

Also one important thing is that the women who were involved carried on with life just the same; no big political statements were made. These women still went to church, still got baptized, still went on pilgrimage, and I am thinking about one particular woman name Aunt Vie, a very strong woman, strong-willed and everything; they use to call her "man royal" behind her back, but no one ever dare to meddle with her.

Things are different now in Jamaica. Now all you have to do is not respond to a man's call to you and dem call you sodomite or lesbian. I guess it was different back then forty years ago because it was harder for anybody to really conceive of two women sleeping together and being sexual. But I do remember when you were "suspect," people would talk about you. You were definitely classed as "different," "not normal," a bit of a "crazy." But women never really got stoned like the men.

What I remember is that if you were a single woman alone or two single women living together and a few people suspected this . . . and when I say a few people I mean like a few guys, sometimes other crimes were committed against the women. Some very violent; some very subtle. Battery was common, especially in Kingston. A group of men would suspect a woman or have it out for her because she was a "sodomite" or because she act "man royal" and so the men would organize and gang rape whichever woman was "suspect." Sometimes it was reported in the newspapers; other times it wasn't—but when you live in a little community, you don't need a newspaper to tell what's going on. You know by word of mouth and those stories were frequent. Sometimes you also knew the men who did the battery.

Other subtle forms of this was "scorning" the women. Meaning that you didn't eat anything from them, especially a cooked meal. It was almost as if those accused of being "man royal" or "sodomite" could contaminate.

A conversation with my grandmother:

I am only telling you this so that you can understand that this is not a profession to be proud of and to get involved in. Everybody should be curious and I know you born with that, ever since you growing up as a child and I can't fight against that, because that is how everybody get to know what's in the world. I am only telling you this because when you were a teenager, you always say you want to experience everything and make up your mind on your own. You didn't like people telling you what was wrong and right. That always use to scare me.

Experience is good, yes. But it have to be balanced; you have to know when you have too much experience in one area. I am telling you this because I think you have enough experience in this to decide now to go back to the normal way. You have two children. Do you want them to grow up knowing this is the life you taken? But this is for you to decide. . . .

Yes, there was a lot of women involved with women in Jamaica. I knew a lot of them when I was growing up in the country in the 1920s. I didn't really associate with them. Mind you, I was not rude to them. My mother wouldn't stand for any rudeness from any of her children to adults.

I remember a woman we use to call Miss Bibi. She lived next to us—her husband was a fisherman, I think he drowned before I was born. She had a little wooden house that back onto the sea, the same as our house. She was quiet, always reading. That I remember about her because she use to go to the little public library at least four days out of the week. And she could talk. Anything you wanted to know, just ask Miss Bibi and she could tell you. She was mulatto woman, but poor. Anytime I had any school work that I didn't understand, I use to ask her. The one thing I remember though, we wasn't allowed in her house by my mother, so I use to talk to her outside, but she didn't seem to mind that. Some people use to think she was mad because she spent so much time alone. But I didn't think that because anything she help me with, I got a good mark on it in school.

She was colorful in her own way, but quiet, always alone, except when her friend come and visit her once a year for two weeks. Them times I didn't see Miss Bibi much because my mother told me I couldn't go and visit her. Sometimes I would see her in the market exchanging and bartering fresh fish for vegetables and fruits. I use to see her friend, too. She was a jet Black woman, always her hair tied in bright colored cloth, and she always had on big gold earrings. People use to say she lived on the other side of the Island with her husband and children and she came to Port Maria once a year to visit Miss Bibi.

My mother and father were great storytellers and I learnt that from them, but is from Miss Bibi that I think I learnt to love reading so much as a child. It wasn't until I move to Kingston that I notice other women like Miss Bibi. . . .

Let me tell you about Jones. Do you remember her? Well she was the woman who lived the next yard over from us. She is the one who really turn me against people like that and why I fear so much for you to be involved in this ting. She was very loud. Very show-off. Always dressed in pants and man-shirt that she borrowed from her husband. Sometimes she use to invite me over to her house, but I didn't go. She always had her hair in a bob haircut, always barefoot and tending to her garden and her fruit trees. She tried to get me involved in that kind of life, but I said no. At the time I remember I needed some money to borrow and she lent me, later she told me I didn't have to pay her back, but to come over to her house and see the thing she had that was sweeter than what any man could offer me. I told her no and eventually paid her back the money.

We still continued to talk. It was hard not to like Jonesie—that's what everybody called her. She was open and easy to talk to. But still there was a fear in me about her. To me it seem like she was in a dead end with nowhere to go. I don't want that for you.

I left my grandmother's house that day feeling anger and sadness for Miss Jones—maybe for myself, who knows? I was feeling boxed in. I had said nothing. I'd only listened quietly.

In bed that night, I thought about Miss Jones. I cried for her (for me) silently. I remembered her, a mannish-looking Indian woman, with flashy gold teeth, a Craven A cigarette always between them. She was always nice to me as a child. She had the sweetest, juiciest Julie, Bombay, and East Indian mangoes on the street. She always gave me mangoes over the fence. I remember the dogs in her yard and the sign on her gate. "Beware of bad dogs." I never went into her house, although I was always curious.

I vaguely remember her pants and shirts, although I never thought anything of them until my grandmother pointed them out. Neither did I recall that dreaded word being used to describe her, although everyone on the street knew about her.

A conversation with my mother:

Yes, I remember Miss Jones. She smoke a lot, drank a lot. In fact, she was an alcoholic. When I was in my teens she use to come over to our house—always on the veranda. I can't remember her sitting down—seems she was always standing up, smoking, drinking, and reminiscing. She constantly talked about the past, about her life. And it was always women: young women she knew when she was a young woman, the fun they had together and how good she could make love to a woman. She would say to whoever was listening on the veranda, "Dem girls I use to have sex with was shapely. You shoulda know me when I was younger, pretty, and shapely just like the 'oman dem I use to have as my 'oman."

People use to tease her on the street, but not about being a lesbian or calling her sodomite. People use to tease her when she was drunk, because she would leave the rumshop and stagger down the avenue to her house.

I remember the women she use to carry home, usually in the daytime. A lot of women from downtown, higglers and fish-women. She use to boast about knowing all kinds of women from Coronation market and her familiarity with them. She had a husband who lived with her and that served her as her greatest protection against other men taking steps with her. Not that anybody could easily take advantage of Miss Jones; she could stand up for herself. But having a husband did help. He was a very quiet, insular man. He didn't talk to anyone on the street. He had no friends so it wasn't easy for anyone to come up to him and gossip about his wife.

No one could go to her house without being invited, but I wouldn't say she was a private person. She was a loner. She went to the rumshops alone, she drank alone, she staggered home alone. The only time I ever saw her with somebody were the times when she went off to the Coronation market or some other place downtown to find a woman and bring her home. The only times I remember her engaging in conversation with anybody was when she came over on the veranda to talk about her women and what they did in bed. That was all she let out about herself. There was nothing about how she was feeling, whether she was sad or depressed, lonely, happy. Nothing. She seemed to cover up all of that with her loudness and her vulgarness and her constant threat—which was all it was—to beat up anybody who troubled her or teased her when she was coming home from the rumshop.

Now Cherry Rose—do you remember her? She was a good friend of Aunt Marie and of Mama's. She was also a sodomite. She was loud too, but different from Miss Jones. She was much more outgoing. She was a barmaid and had lots of friends—both men and women. She also had the kind of personality that attracted people—very vivacious, always laughing, talking, and touching. She didn't have any children, but Gem did.

Do you remember Miss Gem? Well, she had children and she was also a barmaid. She also had lots of friends. She also had a man friend name Mickey, but that didn't matter because some women had their men and still had women they carried on with. The men usually didn't know what was going on, and seeing as these men just come and go and usually on their own time, they weren't around every day and night.

Miss Pearl was another one that was in that kind of thing. She was a dressmaker; she use to sew really good. Where Gem was light complexion, she was a very black Black woman with deep dimples. Where Gem was a bit plump, Pearl was slim, but with big breasts and a big bottom. They were both pretty women.

I don't remember hearing that word sodomite a lot about them. It was whispered sometimes behind their backs but never in front of them. And they were so alive and talkative that people were always around them.

The one woman I almost forgot was Miss Opal, a very quiet woman. She use to be friends with Miss Olive and was always out of her bar sitting down. I can't remember much about her except she didn't drink like Miss Jones and she wasn't vulgar. She was soft-spoken, a half-Chinese woman. Her mother was born in Hong Kong and her father was a Black man. She could really bake. She use to supply shops with cakes and other pastries.

So there were many of those kind of women around. But it wasn't broadcast.

I remembered them. Not as lesbians or sodomites or man royals, but as women that I liked. Women whom I admired. Strong women, some colorful, some quiet.

I loved Cherry Rose's style. I loved her loudness, the way she challenged men in arguments, the bold way she laughed in their faces, the jingle of her gold bracelets. Her colorful and stylish way of dressing. She was full of wit; words came alive in her mouth.

Miss Gem: I remember her big double iron bed. That was where Paula and Lorraine (her daughters, my own age) and I spent a whole week together when we had chicken pox. My grandmother took me there to stay for the company. It was fun. Miss Gem lived right above her bar and so at any time we could look through the window and on to the piazza and street which was bursting with energy and life. She was a very warm woman, patient and caring. Every day she would make soup for us and tell us stories. Later on in the evening she would bring us Kola champagne.

Miss Pearl sewed dresses for me. She hardly ever used her tape measure—she could just take one look at you and make you a dress fit for a queen. What is she doing now, I asked myself? And Miss Opal, with her calm and quiet, where is she—still baking?

What stories could these lesbians have told us? I, an Afro-Caribbean woman living in Canada, come with this baggage—their silenced stories. My grandmother and mother know the truth, but silence still surrounds us. The truth remains a secret to the rest of the family and friends, and I must decide whether to continue to sew this cloth of denial or break free, creating and becoming the artist that I am, bringing alive the voices and images of Cherry Rose, Miss Gem, Miss Jones, Opal, Pearl, and others. . . .

There is more at risk for us than for white women. Through three hundred years of history we have carried memories and the scars of racism and violence with us. We are the sisters, daughters, mothers of a people enslaved by colonialists and imperialists.

Under slavery, production and reproduction were inextricably linked. Reproduction served not only to increase the labor force of slave owners but also, by "domesticating" the enslaved, facilitated the process of social control. Simultaneously, the enslaved responded to dehumanizing conditions by focusing on those aspects of life in which they could express their own desires. Sex was an area in which to articulate one's humanity but, because it was tied to attempts "to define oneself as human," gender roles, as well as the act of sex, became badges of status. To be male was to be the stud, the procreator; to be female was to be fecund, and one's femininity was measured by the ability to attract and hold a man and to bear children. In this way, slavery and the postemancipated colonial order defined the structures of patriarchy and heterosexuality as necessary for social mobility and acceptance.

Socioeconomic conditions and the quest for a better life has seen steady migration from Jamaica and the rest of the Caribbean to the United States, Britain, and Canada. Upon my arrival, I became part of the "visible minorities," encompassing Blacks, Asians, and Native North Americans in Canada. I live with a legacy of continued racism and prejudice. We confront this daily, both as individuals and as organized political groups. Yet for those of us who are lesbians, there is another struggle: the struggle for acceptance and positive self-definition within our own communities. Too often, we have had to sacrifice our love for women in political meetings that have been dominated by the "we are the world" attitude of heterosexual ideology. We have had to hide too often that part of our identity which contributes profoundly to make up the whole.

Many lesbians have worked, like me, in the struggles of Black people since the 1960s. We have been on marches every time one of us gets murdered by the police. We have been at sit-ins and vigils. We have flyered, postered; we have cooked and baked for the struggle. We have tended to the youths. And we have all at one time or another given support to men in our community, all the time painfully holding on to, obscuring, our secret lives. When we do walk out of the closet (or are thrown out), the "ideologues" of the Black communities say "Yes, she was a radical sistren but, I don't know what happened; she just went the wrong way." What is implicit in this is that one cannot be a lesbian and continue to do political work and, not surprisingly, it follows that a Black lesbian/artist cannot create using the art forms of our culture. For example, when a heterosexual male friend came to my house, I put on a dub poetry tape. He asked, "Are you sure that sistren is a lesbian?"

"Why?" I ask.

"Because this poem sound wicked; it have lots of rhythm; it sounds cultural."

Another time, another man commented on my work, "That book you wrote on domestic workers is really a fine piece of work. I didn't know you were that informed about the economic politics of the Caribbean and Canada." What are we to assume from this? That Afro-Caribbean lesbians have no Caribbean culture? That they lose their community politics when they sleep with women? Or that Afro-Caribbean culture is a heterosexual commodity?

The presence of an "out" Afro-Caribbean lesbian in our community is dealt with by suspicion and fear from both men and our heterosexual Black sisters. It brings into question the assumption of heterosexuality as the only "normal" way. It forces them to acknowledge something that has always been covered up. It forces them to look at women differently and brings into question the traditional Black female role. Negative responses from our heterosexual Black sisters, although more painful, are, to a certain extent, understandable because we have no race privilege and very, very few of us have class privilege. The one privilege within our group is heterosexual. We have all suffered at the hands of this racist system at one time or another and to many heterosexual Black women it is inconceivable, almost frightening, that one could turn her back on credibility in our community and the society at large by being lesbian. These women are also afraid that they will be labeled "lesbian" by association. It is that fear, that homophobia, which keeps Black women isolated.

The Toronto Black community has not dealt with sexism. It has not been pushed to do so. Neither has it given a thought to its heterosexism. In 1988, my grandmother's fear is very real, very alive. One takes a chance when one writes about being an Afro-Caribbean lesbian. There is the fear that one might not live to write more. There is the danger of being physically "disciplined" for speaking as a woman-identified woman.

And what of our white lesbian sisters and their community? They have learned well from the civil rights movement about organizing, and with race and some class privilege, they have built a predominantly white lesbian (and gay) movement—a precondition for a significant body of work by a writer or artist. They have demanded and received recognition from politicians (no matter how little). But this recognition has not been extended to Third World lesbians of color—neither from politicians nor from white lesbian (and gay) organizations. The white lesbian organizations/groups have barely (some not at all) begun to deal with or acknowledge their own racism, prejudice, and biases—all learned from a system which feeds on their ignorance and grows stronger from its institutionalized racism. Too often white women focus only on their oppression as lesbians, ignoring the more complex oppression of nonwhite women who are also lesbians. We remain outsiders in these groups, without images or political voices that echo our own. We know too clearly that, as nonwhite lesbians in this country, we are politically and socially at the very bottom of the heap. Denial of such differences robs us of true visibility. We must identify and define these differences and challenge the movements and groups that are not accessible to nonwhites—challenge groups that are not accountable.

But where does this leave us as Afro-Caribbean lesbians, as part of this "visible minority" community? As Afro-Caribbean women we are still at the stage where we have to imagine and discover our existence, past and present. As lesbians, we are even more marginalized, less visible. The absence of a national Black lesbian and gay movement through which to begin to name ourselves is disheartening. We have no political organization to support us and through which we could demand respect from our communities. We need such an organization to represent our interests, both in coalition building with other lesbian/gay organizations, and in the struggles which shape our future—through which we hope to transform the social, political, and economic systems of oppression as they affect all peoples.

Although not yet on a large scale, lesbians and gays of Caribbean descent are beginning to seek each other out—are slowly organizing. Younger lesbians and gays of color are beginning to challenge and force their parents and the Black community to deal with their sexuality. They have formed groups, "Zami for Black and Caribbean Gays and Lesbians" and "Lesbians of Color," to name two.

The need to make connections with other Caribbean and Third World people of color who are lesbian and gay is urgent. This is where we can begin to build that other half of our community, to create wholeness through our art. This is where we will find the support and strength to struggle, to share our histories and to record these histories in books, documentaries, film, sound, and art. We will create a rhythm that is uniquely ours—proud, powerful, and gay. Being invisible no longer. Naming ourselves, and taking our space within the larger history of Afro-Caribbean peoples. A dream to be realized, a dream to act upon.

12

"No *Kisses* Is Like Youres"

An Erotic Friendship between Two African-American Women during the Mid-Nineteenth Century

Karen V. Hansen

ADDIE BROWN, a free-born African-American domestic worker, wrote letters before, during, and immediately after the Civil War to her 'only dear and loving friend', Rebecca Primus, an African-American school teacher. In May, 1861, in characteristically vivid prose, Addie wrote to Rebecca: 'Your most af-fec[tionate] letter to me was like a peices of meat to hungere wolfe'.[1] Addie and Rebecca's letters tell the story of a passionate relationship that endured nine years of intermittent separation, the ebb and flow of their romantic love, and male suitors attempting to woo each of them. Theirs was not a secretive liaison. It was highly visible and deeply enmeshed in the domestic networks of Hart-ford's African-American community.

Because Rebecca preserved a cache of letters, the resonant voices of these two remarkable yet ordinary women fill a silence about free-born African-American women of the nineteenth century.[2] Addie and Rebecca spoke their minds and hearts to each other, not intending their words to be published. They worked hard and loved fiercely. Through their friendship they provided a safe space, as Patricia Hill Collins labels it, to voice confidently their point of view and reaffirm their self-conceptions.[3]

The correspondence between Rebecca and Addie fills a gap in the literature about African-American women in the nineteenth century.[4] This flourishing scholarship has creatively drawn from the limited available evidence to explore women's activism in the abolitionist movement, the church, the club movement,

© Blackwell Publishers Ltd. 1995, 108 Cowley Road, Oxford OX4 1JF, UK and 238 Main Street, Cambridge MA 02142, USA. *Gender & History* 7, no. 2 (August 1995).

the struggle for Black men's suffrage, anti-lynching campaigns, and everyday acts of rebellion.[5] However, primarily because of the dearth of primary sources written by ordinary women, historical analysis has focused largely on organizations and on women in positions of leadership. As a result, intimate friendships between women have remained a relatively unexplored area. The historical and literary writing about Black women in the nineteenth century places Addie and Rebecca in an over-arching context, but their letters alone forge new ground in documenting friendships and everyday life in the North. Moreover, like the Black women abolitionists studied by Shirley Yee, Addie and Rebecca were 'not passive victims of oppression, but active participants in efforts to help their families and communities and to secure racial equality'.[6] As agents of their own livelihoods, they created networks of support and exchange, sought and found employment, indulged in a passionate friendship with each other, and battled racism in the urban North.

Approximately 120 of Addie Brown's letters to Rebecca Primus and fifty of Rebecca's letters to her family, written between 1859 and 1869, have been preserved (see Appendix A). Addie's almost illegible handwriting, poor grammar, and cryptic references make her letters difficult to decipher. At the same time, there is a magic to her letters, a rhythm to her speech, a forthrightness about her feelings, and a drama to her emotional turmoil that immediately captivates the reader. Because Rebecca's direct replies to Addie are missing, it is necessary to infer Rebecca's reactions and perspective.[7] Rebecca's responses can be gauged and partially reconstructed from the conversational way that Addie writes. In a typical letter, Addie laments their separation, reports local gossip, and searches for affirmation of mutual love. She then turns to the questions posed in Rebecca's last letter. Rebecca's letters to her family paint a fuller portrait of her. Her correspondence illustrates her eloquence and grace, and reveals her dedication to her vocation and to the improvement of conditions for African Americans. Evidence of Addie's importance to Rebecca lies in the fact that it was Rebecca who preserved Addie's letters for sixty-two years.

The letters of Rebecca Primus and Addie Brown also prompt us to reinterpret the sexuality of women's friendships. In conducting studies of white middle-class women, Carroll Smith-Rosenberg, Nancy Cott and Lillian Faderman have found that close bonds between women in the nineteenth century often became passionate and sometimes erotic.[8] My research on friendship between working-class white women finds a similar romantic attachment amongst women who otherwise rejected middle-class notions of womanhood.[9] This literature on romantic friendship has sparked a scholarly debate about the degree to which women's affection for one another simply expressed the romantic discourse dominant in the nineteenth century, reflected a unique women's culture, or revealed a lesbian sexual practice. It has also generated controversy regarding the degree to which society unproblematically accepted the intense emotional relationships between women.[10] Collectively these studies challenge contemporary readers to reconsider sexual categories such as homosexuality and heterosexuality, and to appreciate the fluidity of boundaries in nineteenth-century sexuality. Addie Brown and Rebecca Primus push us further to reanalyze the literature on romantic friendship.

After more fully introducing Rebecca Primus and Addie Brown, I organize this article around two moments in the correspondence that proved major turning points in my interpretation of their relationship. The first, an explicit discussion of a sexual encounter between Addie and a white woman, prompted me to re-evaluate the degree to which Addie and Rebecca's relationship transcended literary conventions and entered the carnal world. The second, a chronicle of a heated debate between Addie, Rebecca's mother and a disapproving neighbor, uncovers the competing perceptions of, and responses to, Addie and Rebecca's relationship. Addie and Rebecca's attachment—complete with romance and eroticism—unfolded within an elaborate network of neighbors, friends and kin, and was ultimately circumscribed by a predominantly heterosexual culture.

At first glance, Addie and Rebecca seem an unlikely pair, and precisely how they met remains a mystery. Rebecca was born in 1836 to a family who had resided in Connecticut for several generations. Her father, Holdridge Primus, worked as a clerk in a grocery store for forty-seven years and her mother, Mehitable Primus, was self-employed as a dress-maker, a highly skilled position.[11] The Primuses owned their home at 20 Wadsworth Street in Hartford. In 1850, the household claimed $1,200 worth of real estate, far exceeding the average wealth of free Blacks in the North.[12]

Mehitable Primus, along with other Christian worshipers, rejected the segregation of local white churches and founded the Talcott Street Congregational Church in 1833. Within the Black community, the church reigned supreme as a central place for gathering, educating and organizing. The Talcott Street Church was also known as the 'First Colored Church' and the 'Fifth Congregational'. The other Black church in Hartford was the Methodist Episcopal-Zion's Church, founded in 1836. Both churches sponsored fairs, festivals, concerts and political forums throughout the 1860s. The Reverend Dr. James W. C. Pennington, an eminent abolitionist, served as the Talcott Street Church's pastor from 1840 to 1845. The church also organized successfully to improve public education available to African-American children, which its pastor described in 1846 as 'exceedingly irregular, deficient, and onerous'.[13] In response, the School Society of Hartford raised taxes better to equip the 'African schools', although educational facilities remained inadequate compared to white schools.[14] For over sixty years, Mehitable Primus actively participated in the congregation and in its numerous secular events.

Rebecca, the eldest of four children, obtained a high school education and became a highly respected teacher.[15] Her Christianity, her 'missionary spirit', and her determination to improve the conditions of freed slaves motivated her to venture southward after the Civil War (see Appendix B for a table of residences). In this act alone, she was daring. She described herself as liking speed—'fast driving and quick movements in any body or any thing'.[16] At the same time, she was sensible and proud of her capacities as a wage earner. From her family and community she inspired respect, admiration, and awe. Addie described her as 'a fastidious young lady'.[17] Conferring respectability in the Black community often reflected a class consciousness and defied white society's opinions to the contrary.[18]

Rebecca's conception of respectable womanhood did not prompt her to shrink from confrontation or political commitment. Through the sponsorship of Hartford's newly established Freedmen's Aid Society, she went South in the fall of 1865 to establish a school for ex-slaves.[19] In Royal Oak, Maryland, Rebecca taught seventy-five day and evening students of various ages. Rebecca's letters reveal her enduring commitment to improving the condition of African Americans as she raised money from her Hartford community to construct a school house in Maryland, and worked relentlessly to persuade local citizens as well. In 1867, she wrote: 'Their invariable plea is we're all poor, just out of bondage, and times are hard with us &c. My reply is, very true, nevertheless, we must have a school house'.[20] Rebecca worked in Maryland for four years, and the local community named the school the Primus Institute in her honor.

Rebecca wrote home from Maryland about verbal harassment, physical abuse, and threats to the lives of teachers from the North who acted as moral crusaders in a racially stratified and deeply hostile political and social environment. With great dignity, Rebecca bravely set a high standard of treatment: 'These white people want all the respect shown them by the col^d people. I give what I rec. & no more'.[21]

Maltreatment by whites was not unique to the South, however. The North maintained segregationist laws and customs as well, and even within radical abolitionist circles, African Americans had to fight for equal treatment. Connecticut, Rebecca's home state, had abolished slavery by 1800, but permitted out-of-state slaveholders unlimited transit with their slaves until 1837.[22] Although several New England states gave free Black men the right to vote, in Connecticut they remained disfranchised until 1869, when the fifteenth amendment to the US Constitution granted suffrage to Black men.[23] With the passage of the Fugitive Slave Act in 1850, the US nationally rendered any person of color—born free or not—vulnerable to slave catchers from the South.[24] For Rebecca and the free Black community, neither equal access to public facilities nor the right to personal dignity came without a struggle.

Addie Brown, an orphan five years Rebecca's junior, was eighteen when her correspondence to Rebecca begins. She remains invisible in nineteenth-century government documents. Addie lamented the fact that she had to make her way in the world without the support of family ties.[25] Rebecca's relative abundance of kin and education contrasted sharply with Addie's dearth. Nonetheless, Addie's buoyant and charismatic personality finds a voice in her vivid but functional writing style, an unmistakable divergence from Rebecca's more circumspect, polished eloquence. She combined passion, earnestness, and sensuality, all the while sustaining a commentary on the moral appropriateness of people's behavior, and avidly reading novels. A tall woman with great force of personality, Addie characterized herself as 'singular', an adjective she used to describe women whom she found contentious. Addie judged others quickly and harshly for moral transgressions or for disagreeing with her.

Black women found few jobs open to them outside of laundry and domestic service, and Addie Brown was no exception.[26] Hartford's prosperity in the 1860s did not guarantee economic security to free Blacks, for they were excluded from factory jobs and most of the skilled trades.[27] Addie made a living alternately as a seamstress (a low-skilled and poorly paid position), a domestic servant, a worker in a dye factory, an assistant cook, and, shortly before she died at the age of twenty-nine, a teamster (a driver of a team of horses). She recognized the limits of her narrow horizons: 'You say don't allow myself to indulge in glumy forebodings for the future. How can I help it? I can't get any work. I have no money, and I stand to live out to service long at the time. That all I can aspire in this place'.[28] Like most domestic servants in the nineteenth-century US, Addie changed jobs and shifted households repeatedly. In fact, she moved at least eight times between 1859 and 1868.[29] She strove to maintain her status as a seamstress and to avoid the even more punishing work that many of her peers were forced to take: 'I went to see Mrs. Manings. She looks just the same, up to eyes in washing. I hope I will never have to take in washing for my livelyhood'.[30] Addie regarded laundry, a grueling chore largely relegated to poor African-American women, as an employment of last resort.

Despite her dire economic situation, Addie was unafraid of employers who overstepped their bounds. Speaking of the small-minded, autocratic supervisor at a white household where she worked, Addie wrote: 'I don't like her. You know how I am with any one I don't like'.[31] Addie felt even more intolerant of racism and segregation at white churches. In 1867, while working at Miss Porter's School in Farmington, Connecticut, she attended church only once. After regularly attending the Talcott Street Church in Hartford, she had no patience for white segregationists who maintained separate seating for African Americans, and so refused to attend church while in Farmington.

Addie worried about her right to love Rebecca because Rebecca was older, more educated, and obviously of a higher status within the Black community. She explored the disparities in her and Rebecca's status by discussing a novel she had recently read, which in her mind exemplified the dilemmas within her relationship with Rebecca. *Women's Friendships*, published in 1850 by Grace Aguilar, tells a tale of friendship between the aristocratic Lady Ida and the naive, middle-class Florence Leslie. Aguilar conveys the honor of a passionate attachment between white women and illustrates the power of true friendship to change their lives.[32] The disparity in class status between Lady Ida and Florence precipitates a crisis when Lady Ida marries into the upper echelons of English society at the same time that a series of misfortunes leave Florence penniless, fatherless, and doubtful about the respectability of her parentage. Addie found the book captivating in part because in her estimation, the protagonists' relationship mirrored her own with Rebecca. In an enthusiastic letter, Addie confided that Florence loved Lady Ida as 'I do you'.[33] Yet the book's message must have been disturbing. 'Friendship demands equality of station, true affections devoid of selfishness', Addie wrote to Rebecca.[34] Identifying with Florence, Addie speculated about the fate of mixed-class relationships: 'I fear this warm attachment must end in disappointment, fully as I can sympathize in its present happiness'. In the novel, the crisis resolves when Florence discovers she was born of nobility after all. Her restored station assures her income, status, and a future husband; and equally importantly, it places her on secure ground for continuing her friendship with Lady Ida. How Addie viewed this resolution relative to her own life she did not reveal, but in relaying her interpretation of the book to Rebecca, she struggled with her own insecurity about their class difference.

Rather than simply a romantic outpouring of sentiment, the passion between Addie and Rebecca that suffuses the letters expressed a selfconsciously sexual relationship. Although they left no evidence of genital contact, their friendship included passion, kisses and what I call 'bosom sex', and competed with their heterosexual relationships. My interpretation of the sensuality of their relationship takes on greater meaning in the context of what is known about women's friendships in the nineteenth century. Since the historical scholarship is largely based on the experiences of white middle-class women, there are obvious limitations. Regardless, the literature frames the physical intimacy between women as part of a sexual continuum, with fluid boundaries between heterosexuality and homosexuality.[35] Writing at great distances, white women, working-class and middle-class, both single and married, professed their great love for each other. These liaisons included physical expressions such as kissing, hugging, and sharing a bed, but were not considered improper or sexual, either by the women themselves or by their communities. They were presumed not to involve genital contact and frequently occurred in the context of heterosexual marriage.[36]

No comparable body of evidence exists for Black women in the nineteenth century. Historians and literary critics have turned to African-American fiction to try to construct what might have happened in relationships between women and in everyday life. The significance of Addie and Rebecca's correspondence is thus twofold. One, it is the only collection of writings by Black women who were not related, not abolitionists, and not famous that documents an intimate relationship. Two, it differs from the white women's correspondence in many ways, most importantly, in that it documents an explicitly erotic—as distinct from romantic—friendship.[37]

Embedded in an extensive network of social and economic relationships, Addie and Rebecca embraced friendship and sisterhood, yet surpassed both. They pronounced the language of friendship inadequate to their situation: 'I need never name the tie which exist between us. Friendships, this term is not applicable to you. And you even say that you are not worthy of it. Call it any thing else'.[38] Although Addie protested when Rebecca deemed herself unworthy of the high office of friend, she nevertheless celebrated the honorable nature of friendship. Four years later she declared, 'You have been more to me then a *friend* or *sister*'.[39] Both Rebecca and Addie realized that the language of friendship, even when fused with the language of kinship, proved inadequate for capturing the complexity of their relationship. Their struggle with language is endemic both to the study of friendship and to friendship itself.

Intense amorous feeling permeates the correspondence between Addie and Rebecca in the early 1860s. Predating the late nineteenth-century novels by African-American women, but thematically anticipating them, Addie's letters use the language of romance and love.[40] While imagining a rendezvous of their souls, Addie fantasized, 'Methink my *Dearest Sister* I am near the, breathing the same air with your arm gently drawn around me, my head reclining on your noble breast in perfect confidence and love'.[41] These declarations of love follow patterns observed within US society as a whole. In her study of nineteenth-century romantic love, Karen Lystra points out that private life provided an arena of 'personal unmasking and freedom from etiquette' where lovers freely disclosed their innermost feelings.[42] In a similar vein, Addie unself-consciously poured out her ardor in the language of romantic love. She relayed the advice offered by her employer in New York City, whom she called 'Mother':

Dear Rebecca, it's just three weeks yesterday since I've been home. I've not call on any one yet. Mother ask me if I don't want to and see some of my friends. I told her *no I did not*, never, while I am away from you. You are my only companion and [it] if I deprive of your society I don't wish no one else.[43]

She brooded when apart from Rebecca. In the tradition of great undying love in the nineteenth century, Addie suffered through their separations:

Darling I will try and express my feelings when I see you better. O it's useless for I can't. Rebecca, when I bid you good by it's seem to me that my very heart broke. I have felt wretched ever since. Sometime I feel that I could not live one hour to another. My Darling Friend I shall never be happy again unless I am near you eather here on earth or in heaven. Since you have left me I want nothing. O Rebecca, why can't I be with you? Will I never have that pleasure? Don't tell me no, for I must.[44]

Letter-writing consoled her little: 'Do not be surprise to hear from me again. I am *heart sick* to see you once more'.[45] Rebecca tried to console Addie: 'you say absence strengens friendship and our love will not grow cold. Mine will never. I will always love you and you only'.[46]

One key exchange that shaped my interpretation of Addie and Rebecca's relationship occurred in the autumn of 1867. In her letter, Addie revealed a sexual practice that for me threw startling new light on their then eight-year-old friendship. She wrote reassuring Rebecca that she did not suffer from loneliness at Miss Porter's School where she worked as an assistant cook: 'The girls are very friendly towards me. I am eather in they room or they in mine, every night out ten and sometime past. One of them wants to sleep with me. Perhaps I will give my consent some of these nights. I am not very fond of whit[ie] I can assure you'.[47] Although nineteenth-century custom encouraged sharing a bed, the sexual innuendo did not escape Rebecca's notice. When she wrote back inquiring about Addie's new bed partner, Addie replied quickly:

If you think that is my bosom that captivated the girl that made her want to sleep with me, she got sadly disappointed injoying it, for I had my back towards all night and my night dress *was* butten up so she could not get

to my bosom. I shall try to keep your f[avored] one always for you. Should
in my excitement forget, you will partdon me *I know*.[48]

In this most explicit passage, Addie reveals a sexual practice whose particulars
she assumed Rebecca would understand. Sleeping with a woman involved providing access to her breasts. By preventing this fondling, Addie disappointed her bed partner. Addie articulated what some historians of women
have long suspected, that the passion expressed by nineteenth-century
women was not solely cerebral. However, in the absence of comparable explicitness in the letters of white women, scholars have had to imagine the
details. Without this interchange, Addie's correspondence more closely parallels the letters of white middle-class women. With the interchange complete with sexual innuendo, it provides graphic evidence of the erotic
dimension of the relationship.

For two reasons, we can surmise that 'bosom sex' was part of Addie's
relationship with Rebecca as well. First, Rebecca reacted jealously. She worried that Addie might forsake their exclusive relationship when she learned
of other women's sexual interest in Addie. Addie recognized that in the heat
of a passionate moment she might abandon reason and fail to observe Rebecca's sacred privileges. Two weeks later, Addie responded somewhat de-
fensively to Rebecca's deeper probe of the incident:

I thought I told you about the girl sleeping with me whether I injoyed
it or not. I can't say that I injoyed it very much. I don't care about her
sleeping with me again. I don't know what kind of an excitement I refer
to now. I pesume I know at the time. I can't recalled.[49]

Thereafter Addie changed the subject and it did not resurface in the subsequent letters.

Second, we can assume that 'bosom sex' was part of Addie and Rebecca's
relationship because the exchange revealed that Addie and Rebecca shared
assumptions about what could happen between sleeping partners. Had Rebecca lacked knowledge about Addie's night-time practices, she would not
have responded jealously. She knew Addie 'injoyed' her sexuality, and was
perhaps prone to getting carried away in a moment of passion. Addie
flaunted her power over Rebecca, evidenced in her arrogant retort: 'Should
in my excitement forget, you will partdon me *I know*'. Indisputably, Addie
and Rebecca had a romantic friendship, one common to nineteenth-century
womanhood. However, they also indulged in an erotic sensuality.

In her letters, Addie expressed her longing for Rebecca by evoking the image of Rebecca's bosom. Writing from Hartford in the autumn of 1860, Addie addressed a note to her 'cherish friend':

> O my Dear Dear Rebecca when you press me to your dear bosom O how happy I was. Last night I gave any thing if I could only layed my poor aching head on your *bosom*. O Dear how soon will it be I can be able to do so? . . . It is very gloomy here. If I was only near you now. I rather have my head on your lap then pencil the few lines to you . . . Addie
>
> P. S. except a sweet kiss. I will imprint on here so look good.[50]

The imagery of breasts evokes notions of comfort, nurturing and maternity as well as female sexuality. In an 1861 letter, Addie wrote:

> How I have wanted to see you. If I only could have rested my head on your bosom for a moments give vent to my feeling. I have been sad. I am so ful some time that I could take a knife and cut my heart out, perhaps then I feel better. If I could be with you daily, I know that I would be happy. Well, that can't be.[51]

'Bosom talk' appears everywhere in the correspondence.

In her other letters, Addie often spoke of exchanging caresses, kisses, and hugs, and of sharing a bed. In one 1859 letter, Addie prefers the memory of Rebecca's kisses to those offered by Mr. Games, the Black man who headed the household where she worked as a domestic servant: 'How I did miss you last night. I did not have anyone to hug me up and to kiss. Rebbeca, don't you think I am very foolish? I don't want anyone to kiss me now. I turn Mr. Games away this morning. No *kisses* is like youres'.[52] Sensuality figured centrally in Addie's satisfaction with Rebecca. 'I wish I was going to be [imbraced] you loving arms to night. How happy I would be. Well, I guess the time will soon arrises when I will have that most exquisit pleasure so doing'.[53]

Addie repeatedly compared her feelings toward Rebecca to those between women and men.

> You are the first girl that I ever *love* so and you are the *last* one. Dear Rebeca, do not say anything against me *loving* you so, for I mean just what I say. O Rebbeca, it seem I can see you now, casting those loving eyes at me. If you was a man, what would things come to? They would after come to something very quick. What do you think the matter? Don't laugh at me. I not exactly crazy yet.[54]

The echoes of a marital vow appear in an 1860 letter: 'Yours for ever, untill death parts us'.[55] In 1865 Addie delighted in the fantasy of a marriage to Rebecca:

'What a pleasure it would be to me to address you *My Husband*'.[56] Addie found the prospect of loving someone else—male or female—with the same intensity virtually unfathomable. All evidence indicates that Rebecca reciprocated Addie's love with the same fervent passion:

> Rebecca, my Darling, you can't imagine what pleasure I take in perusing those notes. Its send such a thrilling sensation through me, particular were you say, "I do indeed love you with my whole heart." My Dear you say I am entirely ignorant of the depth of your love. Not quite my persuous Darling. I am little wise of it. I can't help being so to see how much you do for me daily.[57]

Anxiety and conflict accompanied infatuation in Rebecca and Addie's romantic friendship, as they did for other friends and lovers in the nineteenth century. Romantic 'love brought anxiety in its wake', along with numerous other emotions such as sympathy, longing, joy, pain, jealousy and sadness.[58] Both Addie and Rebecca felt the plague of insecurity at different points in their relationship. In 1862, at the height of their proclamations of love, they agonized over their tumultuous emotional journey. That September, Addie implied that they had just reconciled after reaching the brink of estrangement. Addie had perceived an alteration in Rebecca's attachment to her: 'Dearest Sister, I hope you feeling will never again change towards me. To think I was on edge of loseing your *purest* love. O how my heart leap for joy when I think I have regain it, as strong as it was before, perhaps stronger'.[59] Three days later she wrote: 'I feel sad to night for I don't think you have got over the feeling you had towards me when you bid me good night. It seem cold and would not even kiss me. That something you have never done yet'.[60] Rebecca, in turn, felt vulnerable to Addie's moods and uncertain about how to interpret them. Addie replied:

> Sweat Sister, I have peruse your note again. It make the six time. I cannot perceive why you thought thus I was indefferent towards you that A. M. My Darling, I did not feel so, although I felt sad that morning. I awoke before you. I imprint several kisses upon your lips and gave you a fond imbrace. While I was in that position a shade of sadness stole over me and it has not been remove yet.[61]

Addie eventually smoothed over the hurt feelings by going through the ritual of reassuring her beloved.[62]

The tenor of their bond shifted perceptibly over the nine years of Addie's correspondence. Their relationship changed as Rebecca and Addie grew older and were intermittently separated. Their passion erupted in 1860, and flourished and peaked in 1862 through outpourings of the heart and conflicted misunderstandings about commitment. Beginning in 1863 the correspondence virtually evaporates for two-and-a-half years, presumably because they were both living in Hartford. When their correspondence resumes in the fall of 1865, after Rebecca went South to teach, the letters tone down and reflect a deeper, more mature relationship. While their love did not abate, their infatuation did. Addie continued to refer to Rebecca as her beloved and cherished sister. At the same time, she began addressing her letters to her 'adopted sister', indicating a decline in emotional intensity, although rooted more stably in kinship. When Addie talked about Mr. Joseph Tines, her new suitor, she made it clear that she did love him, but not *passionately*. Passion was the hallmark of her love for Rebecca. And when separated, Addie missed Rebecca no less intensely. In 1866 she wrote: 'Dear Sister how my very soul yearn for you for the past few days and even brought tears to my eyes, but it was all in vain'.[63]

The level of explicit eroticism and passion in the letters declined, but did not disappear. In January, 1866, Addie wrote: 'Dearest friend & only Sister, I will never doubt your *love* for me again. You say you put my picture under your pillow. I wish I had the pleasure laying along side of you'.[64] Addie's references to Rebecca's bosom consistently alluded to their emotional intimacy and shared confidence but referred less often to their sensual love. In May, 1866, Addie wrote, 'My Dear & Adopted Sister, I truly wish that I could exchange pen and paper for a seat by your side and my head reclining on your soft bosom and having a pleasure chit chat with thee'.[65] Bosoms became more exclusively a symbol of safety, intimacy, and unconditional love. A more dramatic shift in tone occurred after the summer of 1866. Addie's letters got shorter in 1867 and became much more matter of fact, with little if any emotional embellishment. Nonetheless, the jealous exchange over Addie's sleeping partner took place in the winter of 1867. Throughout the nine years of Addie's correspondence, despite these transformations in the relationship, Rebecca figured as the centerpiece to Addie's emotional well-being.

The intense romantic friendship between Addie Brown and Rebecca Primus was recognized, facilitated, and sanctioned by their kin and friends within the African-American community, but not without some ambivalence. Another turning point in my interpretation of their friendship underscores this point. An incidence Addie recounted in January, 1866, reveals the multiple perceptions of Addie and Rebecca's relationship. Shortly after Rebecca went South for the first time, Addie visited the Primus household and found that the family had recently received a letter from Rebecca, which Bell Primus, Rebecca's sister, offered to show her. A neighbor, Mr. James, came in when she handed over the letter and provocatively inquired if it was a 'gentleman letter'. Fully aware the letter was from Rebecca, he may have thought the letter was written to Addie. Regardless, he intentionally implied that the letter was romantic, one properly written by a gentleman to a lady. His question suggested that the relationship between Addie and Rebecca was one most appropriate between a man and a woman, not two women. Mrs. Primus came to Addie's defense, Addie reported in her letter to Rebecca:

> She said I thought as much of you if you was a gentleman. She also said if either one of us was a gent we would marry. I was quite surprise at the remark. Mr. James & I had quite a little arguement. He says when I find some one to *love* I will throw you over the shoulder. I told him, 'never'.[66]

Addie inserted a line above the text: 'I have unshaken confidence in your love. I do sincerely believe'. Mr. James's insinuation that the right man would prompt the two women to abandon their love for each other offended Addie. Mrs. Primus's understanding of the commitment Addie and Rebecca made to one another and her willingness to defend the association caught Addie off guard, although it pleased her greatly.

She continued her story: 'You mother also agreed with me. What do you think of that? He has no idea that someone is now paying there [respects? addresses? distresses?] to me'.[67] Addie indignantly responded to Mr. James's implication that she showered her love on Rebecca only because no men were interested in her. In fact, she did have male suitors; Joseph Tines, a worker on a steam ship, was courting her. Regardless, subsequent correspondence reveals that having a beau did not prevent her from ardently loving Rebecca and pledging a commitment first and foremost to her.[68]

This episode reveals the acceptance and support the Primus kin gave to Addie and Rebecca, but also suggests that, at least in the eyes of Mr. James, Rebecca and Addie's relationship crossed previously observed but unspoken boundaries. Their community and kin recognized their mutual attachment as unusually powerful, yet they actively facilitated and fortified the relationship. What permitted, indeed encouraged, the relationship to flourish?

African Americans in the Northeast lived mainly in the major cities; nevertheless they were a small group. In Hartford, the state capital, African Americans composed 2.4 per cent of the population in 1860. On the day she first traveled to Baltimore, Maryland, Rebecca Primus commented, 'I guess I have already seen almost as many colored people as there are in the whole of Hartford'.[69] An important New England city on the Connecticut River, one of the major transportation and industrial arteries of the Northeast, Hartford was also a literary center, home to Mark Twain, the famous Beecher family, and the Black essayist and poet, Ann Plato, among others.

Like many African-American communities in the North, Hartford had flourishing systems of exchange; people shared food, loaned money, traded goods and services, ran errands, and conducted business with one another.[70] Addie and Rebecca fully participated in these networks. Their communities overlapped, although they were not identical. In the web of the Primus family network, Mehitable Primus cared for Addie through several illnesses and regularly found her employment; Rebecca loaned 'a large portion' of one of her pay checks to her boarding housekeepers, Mr. & Mrs. Thomas; and Rebecca and Addie borrowed money from each other.[71] Virtually every letter sent between them carried greetings and wishes for good health sent by neighbors and friends. The conveyances reveal that the members of the domestic networks were aware of Addie and Rebecca's constant communication and their commitment to each other. In turn, Addie and Rebecca both gossiped about people's health, their whereabouts, premarital pregnancies, and foiled courtships. Rebecca and Addie's immersion in these webs of relations signifies that the Black community in Hartford accepted them as full-fledged members.

In the African-American tradition, Addie and Rebecca claimed each other as sisters, expecting unconditional and enduring support. From slave ships to Southern plantations to free communities in the North, Americans of African heritage have created 'fictive kin' to supplement biological ties and to establish systems of socio-economic exchange.[72] Rebecca invited Addie to address her as sister in the spring of 1862. Addie responded:

> My dearest here is [nise] question. You ask a favor and that is this, too *call* you my *sister*. And then you ask me if it will be agreeable. O My Darling, Darling, you know it would. It has been my wish for sometime I dare not [voice]. My Dear I cannot find words to express my feeling to you.[73]

Fully embracing Rebecca as her sister/partner, Addie signed several letters, 'Addie Brown Primus'.

In the process of accepting Rebecca as kin, Addie also adopted the Primus kin network. After a visit in 1859, Addie wrote, 'I was treated so rich by all the family . . . you Dear Ma, there is no one like her if you was to [search] all over United States'.[74] Mehitable Primus advised Addie, found her employment, and shared Rebecca's letters with her. Her daughters, Rebecca's sisters Henrietta and Bell, similarly drew Addie into their orbit. Although Addie did not address Mehitable Primus in kin terms, she regarded her as a pillar of her domestic network.

Addie did use kin terms to refer to Rebecca's maternal aunt, Emily Sands. At several points during the 1860s, she lived with Aunt Emily, her husband Raphael, a Portuguese immigrant, and their young daughter, Sarah, in their house a few doors from the Primuses on Wadsworth Street. Both the Sands helped Addie find employment and in 1867, Addie became Raphael's assistant in the kitchen of Miss Porter's School in Farmington, Connecticut. Over time, Addie became more reserved in her relationship with Aunt Emily:

> I do think Aunt Emily is a singular woman. . . . I have made up my mind not to be so confiding to her as I have been. In future I am going to be just like her. Dear Sister, I don't think that Aunt Emily think as much of me as she once did although I don't know that I have done anything to lessen her love for me.[75]

The emotional limits she placed on her relationships did not temper the importance of the Primus/Sands judgments about her or their inclusion of her in the network.

Rebecca's kin embraced Addie in all of her 'singularity' and sensuality. Deeply involved in kin dynamics, Addie helped to mediate Rebecca's relations with her family. In the fall of 1862, Addie strongly urged Rebecca not to leave home.[76] The person most likely to suffer would have been Rebecca's mother, whom Addie wanted to protect. (However, because of her own interest in Rebecca's proximity, this intervention cannot be seen as completely selfless.) Later, after Rebecca had moved to Maryland, Addie told her of Henrietta Primus's conflicted feelings about her. In the wake of Rebecca's successes, Henrietta felt undereducated and insufficiently accomplished, and turned to Addie for comfort.

Henrietta Primus, who worked as a domestic servant and occasionally as a seamstress, regularly appears in Addie's letters over the years. At various times she shared work or a bed with Addie. Addie treated Henrietta with the same intensity as her other friends, occasionally getting angry with her and then forgiving her. Bell Primus, the youngest child, also sustained a friendship with Addie. They had a falling out when Addie thought that a suitor, Mr. Aldridge, negatively influenced Bell. Addie reported that Mr. Aldridge was rumored to be married with two children. Rebecca tried to make amends between the two women, reminding Addie of her own culpability. Addie gave in when Bell visited her carrying two little cakes: 'I was quite please. It remind me of old times'.[77]

Addie created conflict in her relationships with men in the Primus network. The exception was Rebecca's father, Holdridge Primus, who rarely surfaces in Addie's letters. However, Addie's relationship with Rebecca's only brother, Nelson Primus, a prominent portrait painter based in Boston, prompted conflict with Rebecca. In 1862, Addie pleaded with Rebecca not to be angry at her for flirting with Nelson:

> I shall not be as friendly with your brother as I have been. I know you
> don't like it and I also understand another member of the family don't like
> it. You know I like your family very much and sometime like to be in there
> society very much. But for the future I will treat him as I would any other
> young man acquaintance.[78]

Thereafter Nelson only rarely appears in Addie's letters. As with Nelson,
Addie's flirtatiousness with Thomas Sands, Rebecca's cousin, eventually led to
what Addie characterized as misperceptions about the nature of the relationship and her intentions. In 1867, Bell Sands, Thomas's wife, began circulating
rumors insinuating that Thomas and Addie were romantically involved.
Henrietta warned Addie that her engagement with Joseph Tines would be
threatened if her fiance learned about the letters that they exchanged. Interestingly, the suggestion of romantic interest in two of the men in the Primus family
network—Nelson Primus and cousin Thomas Sands—proved troublesome,
whereas with a woman it did not. That said, Thomas Sands was married, which
put his flirtation in a different category. (Addie denied improper involvement.)
However, Addie's intense attachment to Rebecca did not provoke the same res-
ervations. Perhaps the family viewed her relations with Rebecca as transitional,
a stage during young adulthood that would not interfere with eventual heterosexual marriage. While her relationships with women were sometimes contentious, they were always more important. Addie terminated her relations with
men in the network in order to sustain those with the women.

Within this constellation of relatives, friends and coworkers, Addie and
Rebecca openly discussed their mutual relationship and commiserated over
their separation. While living in New York City, Addie disclosed to her co-
worker, Aunt Chatty, that she had visited the Primus household. She began cry-
ing because she could not bear her separation from Rebecca. 'I wish that I was
going to sleep in your fond arms to night. How happy I would be. Aunt Chatty
& I having been talking about you. Did your ears burn? For we spend nearly
two hours talking. How I did wish that you was hear'.[79]

Although they appeared to harbor no misgivings about the passion the
women felt for each other, Addie and Rebecca's kin tried to assist them in negotiating their relationships with men. While supporting the friendship, they
warned that it should not interfere with male-female courtship. In their admo-
nitions to Addie about her open proclamations of devotion to Rebecca, they acknowledged the depth and strength of her feelings. For instance, Rebecca's
Aunt Emily cautioned Addie that she would be wise not to tell her Hartford
beau, Joseph Tines, that she loved Rebecca better than anyone. Addie wrote to
Rebecca:

> How I have miss you. I have lost all; no more pleasure for me now. Aunt Emily ask me last eve if I was going to carry that [sober] face until you return. She also said if Mr. T[ines] was to see me, think that I care more for you then I did for him. I told, I did love you more then I ever would him. She said I better not tell him so. It would be the truth and most else.[80]

Addie's avowed preference for Rebecca, like her argument with Mr. James, reveals that the community knew about the primacy of these two women's attachment to each other. At the same time, their ties were not regarded as exclusive, but rather as compatible with social obligations and heterosexual partnership, as long as they finessed the situation skillfully.

Consistent with this attitude, for both Addie and Rebecca, involvement with each other did not preclude relationships with men. Addie admitted to her attraction to men. However, her devotion to Rebecca created obstacles for those men drawn to her. Addie's admirers quickly learned that they had to vie with her love for Rebecca. Despite Aunt Emily's advice, Addie measured all other affections against this standard of unconditional and ardent love. In Addie's eyes, no one else could even approach this pinnacle of devotion. Addie relayed the news of a proposal from a sailor, Mr. Lee, in 1862: 'He said it will not be long before he will return and make me his wife. He said that he has met with gr[at] many ladies since he is be gone but none compare with his sweat Addie. He says his love is stronger than ever'. A reassuring line quickly followed: 'Dear Rebecca, I never shall love any person as I do you'.[81] While relaying her news, she simultaneously confided and tried to provoke jealousy in her beloved. In another letter that month, Addie relayed a conversation with Mr. Lee, probably in part to assuage Rebecca's feelings of insecurity and in part to speak truthfully. 'I want to tell you what I done. The evening before he went, he ask me if I love you better then I did him. I told him, yes, I did'.[82] That fall, Addie again juxtaposed her feelings for Mr. Lee with those for Rebecca: 'Dear Sister, I like him much better then I did. He has truly been kind to me. *But he never be to me as you are*'.[83] The competition over attention and affection moved perilously into the physical realm as well:

> Dear Rebecca I don't know what Mr. Lee will think. I would not let him kiss me for nearly two weeks. . . . he said in his note that I owed him great many kisses, so I thought I would let him know. I told him I did not like his kisses. I don't know how he will feel about it. I thought I might as well tell him as to think it, don't you think so, my only and Dearest Sister?[84]

After Addie moved to Hartford from New York City in 1862, Mr. Lee receded in importance, but Addie's attempts to foster competition continued. However, as

Addie and Rebecca's relationship changed, so too did the way Addie talked about her suitor. In 1865, she made sure that Rebecca met Mr. Joseph Tines, a man whose employment on a steam ship, the *Granite State*, brought him regularly up the Connecticut River through Hartford. When Rebecca left for Maryland, Mr. Tines 'says I must not worry to much, best of friends must part. How can I help it, for all is gone? No one feel as I do about you and nev[er] will'.[85] However, Rebecca remained Addie's primary love object: 'I had the pleasure of seeing Mr. Tines twice last week . . . I shall miss him very much. If you was here I should not care very much. He seems to be rather doubtful of my *love* for him. I do love him but not passinately and never will'.[86] After 1865, Addie seemed less interested in pitting her loves against one another. While she continued to compare her feelings and commitments, her comparisons no longer held the same taunting edge.

Although we do not have her letters to Addie, it appears that Rebecca did not cultivate rivalry in the same way. Once she reported home from Maryland about her numerous male visitors. Henrietta passed the information on to Addie. Addie closed the gossip loop by teasing Rebecca: 'H[enrietta] was saying you will be sending word that you intend to marry, having so many gent calling. I shall have to think so myself'.[87] Three years later, Addie heard it rumored that Rebecca was considering marriage: 'I realy think I should be little surprise to hear you thoghts of marrying too. Well, you will have a nerve'.[88] That said, Addie expressed explicit jealousy only after dreaming about Rebecca in the arms of another woman: 'I also dreampt of you t[oo] night. One night I was standing and seeing you carases anther lady and not me. How bad I did feel'.[89]

Addie approached marriage in the practical way she approached her work rather than the romantic way she thought about friendship. Assessing her situation as a single woman without kin, engaged in a low-wage occupation, she pragmatically weighed the economic and social advantages of potential marriage against the dangerous prospect of a bad relationship or difficult childbirth. Marriage seemed a risky venture that promised little and guaranteed less: 'I guess no ones know what triall that married people has to goes through, not only triall but how they have to suffer'.[90] Childbirth in particular loomed as foreboding. The right to marry legally, when viewed in the context of a slave society, was a long-sought centerpiece to family legitimacy and stability. That said, marriage did not offer African Americans the same advantages it did European Americans. As Dorothy Sterling puts it, 'Although white women usually retired from the labor market after marriage, most blacks were obliged to keep on working to augment their husbands' earnings'.[91] Still, Addie concluded: 'Dear Rebecca, if I should ever see a good chance I will take it, for I'm tired roving around this unfriendly world'.[92] At the age of twenty, Addie wearied of the struggle to make her own way in the world and saw marriage as a solution—a way to forge a partnership and to establish a secure home base.

A life with Rebecca seemed remote and unlikely. Female-headed households were more common in Black communities than in white communities, especially in urban areas. Because of a higher mortality rate for Black men and more job opportunities for women, many cities, such as Boston and Providence in the North and Charleston and Washington, D.C., in the South, had more women than men.[93] This meant that 'the decision not to marry was unconventional', according to James Oliver Horton, 'but it offered one means of reconciling the conflicting responsibilities placed on black women'. Thus, 'unmarried women were not common, but neither were they unique'.[94] The Black community's reaction to two romantically involved women setting up a household together is a subject virtually untouched in historiography. In 1861 Addie wrote from New York City:

> I want to ask you one question. That is, will you not look at my marrying in a different light then you do? Look at this my Darling, I'm here with Mother, perhaps see you about three time in a year. I'm sometimes happy, more time unhappy. I will get my money regular for two or three week and then iregular. What would you rather see me do, have one that truly *love* me that would give me a happy home, and or give him up and remain in this home, or part of me? Rebecca, if I could live with you or even be with you some parts of the day, I would never marry.[95]

This response to Rebecca indicates that Rebecca opposed Addie's thoughts of marriage, but also resisted her suggestion to live together. Both women realized that marriage posed a threat to their relationship. Five years later, after Addie agreed to marry Mr. Tines, she had second thoughts. She postponed the wedding several times. Even when a firm date was arranged, she felt ambivalent. 'I very serious thoughts and make me feel unhappy at times. I often wonder if every [ones] feels as I do'.[96] As if fulfilling a prophecy, Addie's correspondence to Rebecca abruptly halts near the time of her wedding. She moved to Philadelphia to live with the Tines family, and died of tuberculosis two years later at the age of twenty-nine.[97]

Although we do not have a comparable account of Rebecca's courtship, we have a few facts with which to work. Rebecca taught in Royal Oak, Maryland, until June of 1869 when the Hartford Freedmen's Aid Society dissolved and called its teachers home. Upon returning, she accepted a position as the Assistant Superintendent of the Sabbath School at the Talcott Street Congregational Church. In 1872, Charles H. Thomas, Rebecca's former landlord in Maryland

and a recent widower, moved north to Hartford, presumably to pursue Rebecca, and lived temporarily with the Primus family. An ex-slave who had purchased his own freedom, he was an established horse trainer and sawmill engineer when Rebecca met him in 1865, and was deeply involved in Maryland's Reconstruction politics. He actively helped to facilitate the building of Rebecca's schoolhouse and served on the school committee. Charles cut an imposing figure. With a 'very large frame' (he weighed 199 pounds), he 'carried a cane and wore gold bowed glasses and was noticed by whoever saw him'.[98] The one preserved letter he wrote to Rebecca's mother indicates he was well educated and conducted himself formally and graciously.

As with thousands of other skilled Black artisans from the South who migrated north, Charles found primarily menial jobs in Connecticut, working first as a janitor and later as a gardener. In 1885 and 1886 Charles worked as the door keeper of the Connecticut State Senate. After he and Rebecca married in 1872, they settled near Rebecca's parents, but Rebecca's life was not easy. Charles suffered a severe head injury in an accident in the late 1880s, and was mentally incompetent and destitute for the last several years of his life. After he died in 1891, Rebecca returned home to live with her mother on Wadsworth Street. There she resided until her mother died in 1899. At that point Rebecca moved to a boarding house, where she lived until 1932 when she met her death at the age of 95.

Eventually, both Addie and Rebecca married men. Addie felt attracted to men as well as women, she enjoyed their attentions, and liked to boast of her allure to both sexes. While she remained ambivalent about her relationships with men, she recognized the economic advantages of heterosexual marriage, however marginal. At the same time, because Black men had few occupational opportunities, received low wages, and faced periodic unemployment, married women regularly had to work. Marriage did not promise a life free of labor or from the threat of destitution. Yet African-American working women who did not marry suffered economic hardships throughout their lives. In the mid-nineteenth-century United States, women engaged in wage labor had to struggle to eke out an independent livelihood. Although some women lived with female kin because they did not marry or because their husbands died or deserted them, most women did not have the option of choosing a female partnership over heterosexual marriage. Addie knew that ultimately she would have to find a husband, for economic reasons at the very least.

Addie and Rebecca forged a fierce, enduring bond with each other despite their difference in age, family security, education, class status, and personality. They respected and valued themselves and each other in a culture that denigrated Black women. Their mutuality helped to stave off the crippling effects of

racial and gender oppression. The surviving correspondence began in 1859, revealing an intense infatuation fraught with insecurities. The nature of their relationship shifted over time, and while their passion may have waxed and
waned, their commitment to one another did not. Addie identified Rebecca as a
sister; she was her family, her best friend, her beloved, one who offered unconditional love, attention, affection, help, advice and comfort. Rebecca, in turn, relied on Addie for help with her personal affairs, adoration, passionate love, and
sensuality.

The domestic networks of the African-American community in Hartford
strengthened the two young women's connection by embracing them as individuals and as a couple, by intertwining their work and social lives, and by accepting their offerings to the community. They understood Addie and Rebecca's
relationship as analogous to a heterosexual partnership, an honorable commitment based on mutual attachment. As long as this commitment did not completely usurp relationships with men, the community did accept Addie and
Rebecca falling in love, prioritizing their friendship, and becoming sisters.
However, the community and culture did not endorse their consideration of a
life-long partnership that excluded men.

When I initially began reading the Primus Family collection, I was struck
with the similarities between Rebecca and Addie's relationship and the romantic friendships among white working-class and middle-class women of the
same period. The correspondence jubilantly celebrated the relationship and
drew from the flowery language of romantic love so prevalent in the nineteenth
century. With erotic overtones, it referred to physical moments of intimacy. Like
the white women's relationships, this relationship flourished in the context of
a predominantly heterosexual society. Addie and Rebecca enjoyed the widespread acceptance of female friendship in nineteenth-century America, and
adapted the conventional language of romantic love to express their attachment.
Although Addie and Rebecca circulated primarily in the Black community, they
also participated in and were influenced by the dominant white culture. By her
profound identification with a white British aristocrat, Addie made it clear that
her own imagination did not observe strict color or class lines.

Despite its similarities to the well-documented ties between white women
of the period, Rebecca and Addie's relationship is distinctive. Addie's correspondence, her outpourings of the heart, and her sassy commentary on friend
and foe more vividly convey a personality and world view than any I have read
or heard of during my seven years of research on these issues. Her passion for
Rebecca was more intent and focused than that expressed by any of the white
working-class women whose letters and diaries I have read. Unfortunately, no
comparable documents by or about Black women are known to exist, so we cannot say how Addie and Rebecca's relationship compares to other same-gender

friendships in Black communities of the time. However, because of their extraordinary quality and nature, the letters remain a treasure trove, with numerous discoveries to be made and interpretations to be developed.

Addie and Rebecca's relationship poses important contrasts to the existing literature on white women. Unlike the white middle-class women's friendships, Addie and Rebecca's relationship was not cultivated and nurtured in a separate women's world. It was part and parcel of the Black community and domestic networks that included women and men. Moreover, as Black women, Addie and Rebecca were subject to racial harassment and to employment and wage discrimination. Their opportunities were few and resources scarce. Although legally free, as Black women they did not have access to even the limited citizenship of white women. They began writing when four million Blacks were enslaved. A civil war divided the nation over, among other things, the status of Black Americans. In the face of wrenching debates that disputed the humanity of African Americans and a ravaging war over whether they could be owned as private property, Addie and Rebecca lived with great dignity, bravely commanding respect from the furthest reaches of their communities.

My interpretation of Addie's spiritual and emotional attachment to Rebecca was transformed when Addie spoke of 'bosom sex'. This action convinced me of the robust sexuality Addie and Rebecca shared. They were more than romantic friends; they were erotic sister/friends. Prior to the letter describing 'bosom sex', the numerous references to 'bosoms' in their letters aroused no suspicion that they coded a sexual custom. References to 'bosoms' pervade the letters of white working women of the same period. 'Bosom' in the late twentieth-century US connotes a nestling intimacy and a desexualized maternal comfort. Discovering that Addie exposed her bare breasts to a bed partner exponentially expanded the possible meanings of 'bosom'.

We can interpret the practice of 'bosom sex' in many ways; I suggest three. One alternative is that Addie and Rebecca were not romantic friends, but rather lesbian lovers for whom 'bosom sex' was part of their sexuality. In agreement with others studying nineteenth-century sexuality, I find it inappropriate to label the relationship as lesbian. This term was not part of mid-nineteenth-century parlance and not part of the culture's consciousness. I am persuaded by John D'Emilio's argument that 'lesbian' signifies an identity unique to twentieth-century industrial capitalism.[99] A second possibility is that only Addie, Rebecca, and their coterie of lover/friends practiced 'bosom sex', making it a feature of one small sub-culture. A third interpretation is that many or most romantic friends engaged in 'bosom sex'. Although scholarship has not yet unearthed explicit evidence, it is possible that women's silence about it reflects either its taken-for-granted nature or the customary sexual silence of the time. The casual references to bosoms throughout the letters of romantic friends could be further evidence of its commonality. The practice may have been viewed as natural, pleasurable, and an appropriate means of expressing affection for or attraction to another woman.

While other interpretations are possible, I think it is virtually certain that Addie, her white friend from Miss Porter's School, and Rebecca were not the only practitioners of 'bosom sex'. The case of Addie and Rebecca challenges the assumption in the literature on white women's romantic friendships that such relationships were socially acceptable because of their marked difference from heterosexual relationships. While Addie and Rebecca's family and friends did not endorse a same-gender partnership that excluded marriage, they accepted these women's partnership as similar to a heterosexual one. Perhaps white women's friendships were not accepted merely because they were presumed to be platonic. Understanding sexual relationships between women in the nineteenth century will always be a challenge, because of the centrality of texts as historical evidence, their unspoken assumptions, and their multiplicity of meanings. Assessing the pervasiveness of 'bosom sex' necessitates re-examining the extant evidence with new eyes and continuing to search for more documents by both Black and white women.

Although heterosexual imperative prevailed, it did so within a context that simultaneously affirmed the validity of Addie and Rebecca's love. The African-American community in Hartford seemed to embrace Addie and Rebecca and accept their passionate relationship, with no hint of discord until Mr. James disdainfully tagged Rebecca's missive as a 'gentleman's letter'. In contrast to Rebecca's mother, he found passion between women improper and ephemeral. Mrs. Primus defended the relationship as honorable and the women's attachment to each other as morally impeccable. Addie and Mrs. Primus recognized the cultural conventions of friendship versus courtship, but insisted on negotiating their alternative interpretation with Mr. James: if Rebecca were a man, Addie would marry her; she was not, so Addie was destined to marry someone else.

Only when Addie and Rebecca's attachment threatened to interfere with relations with men did people worry. When Addie pitted her love for Rebecca against the affections of her male suitors, Aunt Emily advised her to reconsider her action. What others found problematic about Addie and Rebecca's relationship was not their passionate love for one another, but the possibility that it would hinder or replace heterosexual marriage. They loved each other with an intensity that Addie pledged no man would disrupt. Yet in the end, a man did interfere. When Addie married, her correspondence stopped, she moved away, and shortly thereafter, she died. It was only then, a few years later, that Rebecca also married.

This first attempt at piecing together the puzzle of Addie and Rebecca's relationship is necessarily provocative and incomplete. By virtue of my selective focus on friendship and sexuality, and given the depth and richness of the letters themselves, whole areas of Addie and Rebecca's lives, mapped in episodic, but informative ways in the text, warrant further examination—their work, their political views, their community life, and their activism. I encourage others to grapple with the complexities of the relationship and to explore the multifaceted Black and white communities which Addie and Rebecca inhabited and so eloquently described. Because of the extraordinary quality of their letters and what they document about daily lives and passions in a free Black community in the North during the 1860s, these remarkable women deserve further study.

Notes

For Eva, a compassionate sister, friend and teacher. Many thanks to my friends and colleagues who read earlier versions of this article and pushed me to take risks: Paula Aymer, Carol Brown, Andrew Bundy, Nancy Cott, Dwight Davis, Alice Friedman, Anita Garey, Farrah Griffin, Arlie Hochschild, Jacqueline Jones, Cameron Macdonald, Afie Murray, Susan Ostrander, Jennifer Pierce, Jo Anne Preston, Shulamit Reinharz, Susan Sibbet, Dorothy Sterling, Andrea Walsh, and Marcia Yudkin. I appreciate the extensive comments of Sarah Deutsch and the anonymous reviewers for *Gender & History*, and I am especially grateful for the discerning eye of Grey Osterud, who read more drafts than I counted and helped improve the article at every stage.

1. Addie Brown to Rebecca Primus, 24 May 1861. The correspondence cited in this article is part of the Primus Family Papers collection at the Connecticut Historical Society in Hartford. All primary documents are quoted with the spelling and underlining as they appear in the original. The punctuation and capitalization have been modernized to attempt to communicate the meaning intended by the author. Brackets frame my educated guesses for words that were not decipherable.

2. Evelyn Brooks Higginbotham laments the 'sounds of silence' that emanate from a largely unrecorded history in 'Beyond the sound of silence: Afro-American women in history', *Gender & History*, 1 (1989), p. 50. In the process of searching for documents by and about working-class women, my research assistant, Cameron Macdonald, found the letters at the Connecticut Historical Society. The only article written about the Primus Family Papers dismisses the relationship between Addie and Rebecca in one sentence: 'Most of the letters are interesting despite the fact that the earlier ones reflected the thoughts of a rather sentimental and immature person'; David O. White, 'Addie Brown's Hartford', *Connecticut Historical Society Bulletin*, 41 (1976), p. 58. Ironically, the historical moment at which White wrote simultaneously gave birth to the work of Carroll Smith-Rosenberg and Nancy Cott, who re-interpreted such 'immature' relationships and 'sentimental' attachments by posing new questions about sexuality and its meaning in women's lives. Upon reading the correspondence, I felt challenged to interpret the letters from a feminist perspective, and to make the collection known to scholars of Black women's history.

3. Patricia Hill Collins asserts the importance of capturing lost African-American women's voices as women defined the self and supported each other to fight multiple oppres-

sions. *Black Feminist Thought: Knowledge, consciousness, and the politics of empowerment* (Unwin Hyman, Boston, 1990).

4. Only a small body of evidence exists documenting the lives of African-American women in the nineteenth century. It primarily takes the form of novels, ex-slave narratives, and organizational documents, and includes a few scattered letters and diaries, mostly of activists and more privileged women. See, for examples of interpretations of these documents, Joanne M. Braxton, *Black Women Writing Autobiography: A tradition within a tradition* (Temple University Press, Philadelphia, 1989); Hazel V. Carby, *Reconstructing Womanhood: The emergence of the Afro-American woman novelist* (Oxford University Press, New York, 1987); Angela Y. Davis, *Women, Race, and Class* (Vintage, New York, 1981); Paula Giddings, *When and Where I Enter: The impact of Black women on race and sex in America* (Bantam, New York, 1984); Evelyn Brooks Higginbotham, *Righteous Discontent: The women's movement in the Black Baptist Church, 1880–1920* (Harvard University Press, Cambridge, 1993); Darlene Clark Hine (ed.) *Black Women in United States History: From colonial times to the present*, 8 vols (Carlson Publishing, Brooklyn, N.Y., 1990); Jacqueline Jones, *Labor of Love, Labor of Sorrow: Black women, work, and the family from slavery to the present* (Basic Books, New York, 1985). There have also been extensive efforts to locate and reprint both published and unpublished sources written by Black women in the nineteenth century. See, for example, William L. Andrews, *Sisters of the Spirit: Three Black women's autobiographies of the nineteenth century* (Indiana University Press, Bloomington, 1986); Marilyn Richardson (ed.) *Maria W. Stewart: America's first Black woman political writer* (Indiana University Press, Bloomington, 1987); Dorothy Sterling (ed.) *We Are Your Sisters: Black women in the nineteenth century* (W. W. Norton, New York, 1984); and The Schomburg Library of Nineteenth-Century Black Women Writers series, edited by Henry Louis Gates, Jr., and published by Oxford University Press.

5. Giddings, *When and Where I Enter*; Higginbotham, *Righteous Discontent*; and Shirley J. Yee, *Black Women Abolitionists: A study in activism, 1828–1860* (University of Tennessee Press, Knoxville, 1992).

6. Yee, *Black Women Abolitionists*, p. 41. The literature on Black women's sexuality focuses historically on the early twentieth century, especially the Harlem Renaissance. While it contributes to understanding variation in sexual practice, the two eras are so different that comparison illuminates little.

7. Addie reports a day in October 1866 when she went to Rebecca's Aunt Emily's house, and picked up her box of letters from Rebecca. This is presumably how they were separated from other correspondence and eventually got lost. (Addie Brown to Rebecca Primus, 1 October 1866) A smaller collection of letters from Rebecca's brother, Nelson Primus, to his family also remain. Nelson's letters and Addie's letters both abruptly halt in 1868, while Rebecca's letters to her parents continue until 1869.

8. Carroll Smith-Rosenberg, 'The Female World of Love and Ritual', *Disorderly Conduct: Visions of gender in Victorian America* (Oxford University Press, New York, 1985), pp. 53–76; Nancy Cott, *The Bonds of Womanhood: Woman's 'sphere' in New England, 1780–1835* (Yale University Press, New Haven, 1977); and Lillian Faderman, *Surpassing the Love of Men: Romantic friendship and love between women from the Renaissance to the present* (William Morrow, New York, 1981).

9. Karen V. Hansen, *A Very Social Time: Crafting community in antebellum New England* (University of California Press, Berkeley and Los Angeles, 1994), ch. 3.

10. For a cogent analysis of the literature to date on the history of lesbian sexuality, see Martha Vicinus, ' "They Wonder to Which Sex I Belong": The historical roots of the modern Lesbian identity', *Feminist Studies*, 18 (1992), pp. 467–97. Also see Lisa Moore, "Something More Tender Still than Friendship": Romantic friendship in early-nineteenth-century England', *Feminist Studies*, 18 (1992), pp. 499–520; reprinted in this work, p. 21.

11. Joan M. Jensen, 'Needlework as Art, Craft, and Livelihood before 1900', in *A Needle, A Bobbin, A Strike: Women needleworkers in America*, ed. Joan M. Jensen and Sue Davidson (Temple University Press, Philadelphia, 1984), pp. 1–19.

12. As a point of comparison, only *one half of one percent* of free blacks in Boston owned property and the average value of their real estate was $3,223. Leonard P. Curry, *The Free Black in Urban America, 1800–1850* (University of Chicago Press, Chicago, 1981), p. 39. Figures from Providence, Rhode Island, reveal a range of $30 to $5,500 worth of property for those Blacks owning property; the median in 1860 was $900. Robert J. Cottrol, *The Afro-Yankees: Providence's Black community in the antebellum era* (Greenwood Press, Westport, Connecticut, 1982), p. 121. The Primus household property is comparable to working-class white households in 1850; see Hansen, *A Very Social Time*. However, Holdridge and Mehitable Primus had limited ability to pass along their wealth and status to the next generation. To put things in perspective, Rebecca had but one woolen dress that she wore during her winters in Maryland. She rejoiced when spring arrived and she could finally wear a calico dress and wash her dirty woolen one. Rebecca's class status is difficult to assess. The members of her family had different resources and occupations. While her parents both worked at stable jobs and her brother became a portrait painter, her sisters largely performed domestic service and needlework. Compared to her sisters, Rebecca was successful, educated, and upwardly mobile while a young woman. But her status changed over her life course. For a while she was a teacher with a missionary spirit. Later on she married a man with a very respectable job. However, Rebecca's status fell when her husband suffered an injury and was no longer able to work. Documents describe him as 'destitute' when he died. Rebecca lived as a widow for forty-one years thereafter. Darlene Clark Hine exhorts us to locate our historical subjects firmly within a class matrix if we are to understand the interrelationships of race and gender in 'Black women's history, white women's history: The juncture of race and class', *Journal of Women's History*, 4 (1992), p. 127.

13. Kenny J. Williams, 'Introduction', to *Essays; Including Biographies and Miscellaneous Pieces, in Prose and Poetry* by Ann Plato (1841; reprint Oxford University Press, New York, 1988). Carter G. Woodson, *The Education of the Negro Prior to 1861* (Arno Press, New York, 1968), p. 318.

14. Hartford did not officially desegregate the public school system until 1868. David O. White, 'Hartford's African Schools, 1830–1868', *Connecticut Historical Society Bulletin*, 39 (1974), p. 53.

15. Rebecca did not teach in the Hartford Public schools, at least according to the available school reports. She perhaps taught in one of the local private schools for African-American children. There is a debate among scholars about the class status of school teaching, given that white teachers were low-paid, wrestled with difficult working conditions, and often rotated between factory work and the classroom. Jo Anne Preston, *Teaching Becomes Women's Work. The transformation of job structures, gender identity, and women's aspirations in nineteenth-century New England* (unpublished manuscript, 1995). In the Black community, teachers were paid even less, yet there was a premium placed on education. During the nineteenth century, especially in the North, very few occupations were open to Blacks, so positions that required some education—such as ministering and teaching—assumed professional status. See James Oliver Horton and Lois E. Horton, *Black Bostonians: Family life and community struggle in the antebellum North* (Holmes and Meier, New York, 1979), p. 129.

16. Rebecca Primus to Parents & Sister, 8 December 1867.

17. Addie Brown to Rebecca Primus, 28 October 1866. Rebecca's uncle, Raphael Sands, concurred with Addie: 'Mr. Sands was speaking of you this A. M. You are the *best one* out of all the family and you was a lady'. Addie Brown to Rebecca Primus, 5 May 1867. At no point does anyone refer to Addie as a lady.

18. According to Paula Giddings, 'for Black women, *acculturation* was translated as their ability to be "ladies"—a burden of proof that carried an inherent class consciousness'; *When and Where I Enter*, p. 49, emphasis in original. Yee makes the point that appeals to 'respectable' or 'genteel' Blacks reflected 'a sort of class consciousness within the free black community'; *Black Women Abolitionists*, p. 54. Linda M. Perkins's survey of Black women's activism in the pre-Civil War period notes that 'educational, civic and religious organizations in the north bore the word "ladies" in the titles, clearly indicating their perceptions of self', in spite of white

society's opinion to the contrary; 'The Impact of the "Cult of True Womanhood" on the Education of Black Women', in *Black Women in American History*, ed. Darlene Clark Hine (Carlson, Brooklyn, N.Y., 1990), vol. 3, p. 1067. Higginbotham discusses the importance of respectability in upward mobility in *Righteous Discontent*, ch. 7. Also see Claudia Tate, *Domestic Allegories of Political Desire: The Black heroine's text at the turn of the century* (Oxford University Press, New York, 1992).

19. Women constituted 65–85 per cent of teachers in schools for freed slaves during the first five years of Reconstruction. Robert Charles Morris, *Reading, 'Riting, and Reconstruction: The education of freedmen in the South, 1861–1870* (University of Chicago Press, Chicago, 1981), p. 58. By 1867, African Americans made up 'a full third of the teaching force, and the number was rising steadily as rural districts and plantations gave them preference "even when inferior in qualifications" '; Morris, p. 85. Also see Jacqueline Jones, *Soldiers of Light and Love: Northern teachers and Georgia Blacks, 1865–1873* (University of North Carolina Press, Chapel Hill, 1980). Rebecca earned $19 per month in 1865, and her wage rose to $30 per month by the time she left Maryland in June 1869. The three other teachers sponsored by the Hartford Freedmen's Aid Society were white and received higher wages. According to Jones, such racial discrepancies were a common practice.

20. Rebecca Primus to Parents & Sister, 2 February 1867. Admittedly, Rebecca wrote home to an audience, not just her family. She referred to her correspondence as her 'home weeklie', and occasional comments make clear that she knew her family shared the news with neighbors, friends, and members of the Freedmen's Aid Society.

21. Rebecca Primus to Parents & Sister, 23 February 1867.

22. Paul Finkelman, *An Imperfect Union: Slavery, federalism, and comity* (University of North Carolina Press, Chapel Hill, 1981), p. 80. Connecticut passed abolition acts in 1784 and 1797. However, legislation contained grandfather clauses which enabled slaveholders to maintain ownership of young slaves. Leon F. Litwack, *North of Slavery: The Negro in the free states, 1790–1860* (University of Chicago Press, Chicago, 1961), p. 3, footnote 1.

23. Property-holding free blacks actually had the vote until 1820 when it was rescinded. It was reinstated in 1869 by an act of Congress. Litwack, *North of Slavery*, p. 75. Even then, some claim that had the public voted on Black suffrage it would not have passed. William C. Fowler, *The Historical Status of the Negro in Connecticut* (Walker, Evans & Cogswell, Charleston, S. C., 1901). Presentation to the New Haven Colony Historical Society, p. 41.

24. Peter P. Hinks, " 'Frequently Plunged into Slavery": Free Blacks and kidnapping in antebellum Boston', *Historical Journal of Massachusetts*, 20 (1992), pp. 16–31.

25. Addie did have a brother, Ally. I have not been able to unearth any information about him, even his full name.

26. Giddings, *When and Where I Enter*, p. 48. See also Perkins, 'The impact of the "cult of true womanhood" ', pp. 1065–76.

27. As historian Curry puts it, 'Discrimination in employment was extreme in the northern cities; segregation in churches was well-nigh universal; and Blacks were segregated in the public schools of every city from which they were not excluded'; *The Free Black in Urban America*, p. 90.

28. Addie Brown to Rebecca Primus, 16 January 1866.

29. See, for example, Faye E. Dudden, *Serving Women: Household service in nineteenth-century America* (Wesleyan University Press, Middletown, Connecticut, 1983), and David M. Katzman, *Seven Days a Week: Women and domestic service in industrializing America* (Oxford University Press, New York, 1978).

30. Addie Brown to Rebecca Primus, 3 June 1866.

31. Addie Brown to Rebecca Primus, 1 April 1866.

32. Grace Aguilar writes: 'A girl who stands alone, without acting or feeling friendship, is generally a cold unamiable being, so wrapt in self as to have no room for any person else, except, perhaps, a love, whom she only seeks and values, as offering his devotion to that same

idol, self'. According to Aguilar (and to Addie), while there are many parallels between friendship and heterosexual love, friendship does not require the same kind of self-abnegation or bending of one's will to a dominant other. And because friendship is pure and selfless (while heterosexual love is selfish), it is transcendent, elevated, and raises both friends' character to noble heights. *Woman's Friendship; A story of domestic life* (New York, 1850), p. 42.

33. Addie to Rebecca, 30 January 1862.

34. Addie to Rebecca, 30 January 1862.

35. Smith-Rosenberg, 'Female World of Love and Ritual'. Alternatively, Adrienne Rich posits a lesbian continuum upon which all women of all times and places fall; 'Compulsory Heterosexuality and Lesbian Existence', *Signs*, 5 (1980), pp. 631–60.

36. Faderman, *Surpassing the Love of Men*, p. 16.

37. I do not mean to suggest that it represents correspondence typical of all African-American women. I do not intend to generalize from the experiences of Rebecca Primus and Addie Brown. Nor do I mean that the explicit sexuality can be attributed to racial differences. Some white women's correspondence might be interpreted as erotic. This correspondence documents only one case, a case which can be better understood by placing it in the context of both Black and white women's history.

38. Addie to Rebecca, 23 February 1862.

39. Addie to Rebecca, 10 April 1866, emphasis in original.

40. Tate, *Domestic Allegories of Political Desire*.

41. Addie to Rebecca, 30 March 1862, emphasis in original.

42. Karen Lystra, *Searching the Heart: Women, men, and romantic love in nineteenth-century America* (Oxford University Press, New York, 1989), p. 38.

43. Addie to Rebecca, 4 June 1861, emphasis in original.

44. Addie to Rebecca, 3 November 1861.

45. Addie to Rebecca, 16 February 1860, emphasis in original.

46. Addie to Rebecca, 16 November 1865. Of course, the letters document a wrenching separation. The trauma of loneliness and longing for each other's company undoubtedly heightened their passion and desire. We have no way of knowing whether or not their behavior or their language changed when they were together.

47. Addie to Rebecca, 27 October 1867.

48. Addie to Rebecca, 24 November 1867, emphasis in original.

49. Addie to Rebecca, 8 December 1867.

50. Addie to Rebecca, 17 November 1860, emphasis in original.

51. Addie to Rebecca, 13 April 1861.

52. Addie to Rebecca, 30 August 1859, emphasis in original.

53. Addie to Rebecca, 25 June 1861.

54. Addie to Rebecca, 30 August 1859, emphasis in original.

55. Addie to Rebecca, 17 November 1860.

56. Addie to Rebecca, 16 November 1865, emphasis in original.

57. Addie to Rebecca, 18 September 1862.

58. Lystra, *Searching the Heart*, pp. 51 and 46.

59. Addie to Rebecca, 18 September 1862, emphasis in original.

60. Addie to Rebecca, 21 September 1862.

61. Addie to Rebecca, 11 September 1862.

62. Lystra refers to the rituals of insecurity and reassurance as endemic to romantic attachment and important in determining the limits of commitment and the depth of feeling; *Searching the Heart*, p. 41.

63. Addie to Rebecca, 16 January 1866.

64. Addie to Rebecca, 21 January 1866, emphasis in original.

65. Addie to Rebecca, 20 May 1866.

66. Addie to Rebecca, 21 January 1866, emphasis in original. It is possible that Mr. James

was attracted to one of the women and that was part of what prompted his provocation. This is merely speculation, however.

67. Addie to Rebecca, 21 January 1866.

68. The correspondence from Addie abruptly stops in 1868. It is possible that Mr. James was right, and that once Addie or Rebecca married, they would cease to be as important to each other. It is also possible that they argued over Addie's marriage and subsequently halted their correspondence. Equally possible is that subsequent letters were lost or destroyed. Given the intensity of passion and sensuality expressed in the surviving letters, this would not surprise me; a twentieth-century reader might have felt compelled to edit for sexual content. Since Nelson Primus's letters also stop in 1868, I think it is most likely that the letters were originally saved and later lost.

69. Rebecca Primus to Parents and Sister, 8 November 1865.

70. Yee, *Black Women Abolitionists*, p. 12.

71. Rebecca Primus to Parents and Sister, March 1868; Addie to Rebecca, 1 October 1866. Addie also lent money to other people. For example, when Mrs. Johnson approached her for a dollar, Addie wrote that she 'thought of her mother, Miss Freeman, so I lend it to her'. Addie to Rebecca, 8 March 1867. She was, however, sometimes reluctant. She had to go and collect the two dollars she loaned her friend Jennie. 'I have promise I shall never lend her money again'. 16 December 1866.

72. Jones, *Labor of Love, Labor of Sorrow*. In her 1974 study of an urban African-American community on welfare, Carol B. Stack found extensive interdependence and cooperation between people not biologically related. 'When friends more than adequately share the exchange of goods and services, they are called kinsmen. When friends live up to one another's expectations, their social relations are conducted as kin.' *All Our Kin: Strategies for survival in a Black community* (Harper and Row, New York, 1974), p. 58.

73. Addie to Rebecca, March 1862, emphasis in original. It is interesting that Addie wanted to go for kin earlier, and although she occasionally referred to Rebecca as 'sister', she waited until Rebecca asked her to celebrate a kin status. Perhaps this is one way that class differences played themselves out in the relationship.

74. Addie to Rebecca, 30 August 1859.

75. Addie to Rebecca, 14 May 1866.

76. Addie to Rebecca, 26 October 1862.

77. Addie to Rebecca, 29 April 1866.

78. Addie to Rebecca, 21 September 1862.

79. Addie to Rebecca, 23 February 1862.

80. Addie to Rebecca, 8 November 1865.

81. Addie to Rebecca, 5 March 1862.

82. Addie to Rebecca, March 1862.

83. Addie to Rebecca, 29 October 1862, emphasis in original.

84. Addie to Rebecca, 5 December 1862.

85. Addie to Rebecca, 8 November 1865.

86. Addie to Rebecca, 28 October 1866, emphasis in original.

87. Addie to Rebecca, 8 November 1865.

88. Addie to Rebecca, 19 January 1868. No hint of marriage appears in Rebecca's correspondence to her family.

89. Addie to Rebecca, 21 January 1866.

90. Addie to Rebecca, 14 November 1861.

91. Sterling (ed.) *We Are Your Sisters*, p. 92.

92. Addie to Rebecca, 24 May 1861.

93. Curry, *The Free Black in Urban America*, p. 253. Also see Jones, *Labor of Love, Labor of Sorrow*.

94. James Oliver Horton, *Free People of Color Inside the African American community* (Smithsonian Institution Press, Washington, D.C., 1993), pp. 114 and 115.

95. Addie to Rebecca, 23 February 1862, emphasis in original.

96. Addie to Rebecca, 19 January 1868.

97. Death certificate No. 13613, for "Annie Tines" of 256 Vanderveer Street, Philadelphia. City Archives, Philadelphia, Pennsylvania.

98. Obituary, *Hartford Courant*, 3 August 1891. Rebecca did not record his height. She herself weighed 118 pounds, although we do not know how tall she was.

99. John D'Emilio, 'Capitalism and Gay Identity', in *The Powers of Desire: The politics of sexuality*, ed. Ann Snitow, Christine Stansell, and Sharon Thompson (Monthly Review Press, New York, 1983), pp. 100–16.

Appendix A
EXTANT LETTERS FROM ADDIE BROWN AND REBECCA PRIMUS

Year	Addie to Rebecca	Rebecca to Addie	Rebecca to Primus Family
1859	2	—	—
1860	4	—	—
1861	18	—	—
1862	16	—	—
1863	—	—	—
1864	—	—	—
1865	5	—	2
1866	36	—	12
1867	33	—	22
1868	6	—	11
1869	—	—	4
Total	120	—	51

Appendix B
KNOWN RESIDENCES OF REBECCA PRIMUS AND ADDIE BROWN

	REBECCA PRIMUS	ADDIE BROWN
1859	Hartford, CT	Waterbury, CT
1860	Hartford, CT	Waterbury, CT
		Hartford, CT
1861	Hartford, CT	New York, NY
1862	Hartford, CT	New York, NY
		Hartford, CT
1863		
1864		
1865	Royal Oak, MD	Hartford, CT
	Hartford, CT	
1866	Royal Oak, MD	Hartford, CT
	Hartford, CT	
1867	Royal Oak, MD	Hartford, CT
	Hartford, CT	Farmington, CT
1868	Royal Oak, MD	Farmington, CT
	Hartford, CT	[Philadelphia, PA]
1869	Royal Oak, MD	Philadelphia, PA
	Hartford, CT	
1870	Hartford, CT	Philadelphia, PA

13

The Gender Closet

Lesbian Disappearance under the Sign "Women"

Cheshire Calhoun

"Looking at women's studies from my Lesbian perspective and with my
Lesbian feminist sensibility, what I see is that women's studies is
heterosexual. The predominance of heterosexual perspectives, values,
commitments, thought and vision is usually so complete and ubiquitous that
it cannot be perceived, for lack of contrast."

—Marilyn Frye

"When Monique Wittig said at the Modern Languages Association Conference several
years ago, 'I am not a woman, I am a Lesbian,' there was a gasp from the audience,
but the statement made sense to me. Of course I am a woman, but I belong to another
geography as well, and the two worlds are complicated and unique."

—Joan Nestle

"[I]t is first necessary to bring the lesbian subject out of the closet of feminist history."
—Sue-Ellen Case

CAN ONE THEORIZE about lesbians within a feminist frame? If one simply assumes that because lesbians are women they can of course be theorized
within feminism, then neither the "whether" nor the "how" of doing this theorizing can be problematized. One need not work out what it is in the feminist
frame and what it is about lesbians that enables the former to be applied to the
latter. I am not sanguine about a "yes" answer to my question. For me, feminist
theorizing about lesbians *is* a problem.

Feminist Studies 21, no. 1 (Spring 1995). © 1995 by Feminist Studies, Inc.

Consider: Outside of literature whose specific topic is lesbianism, lesbians do not make an appearance in feminist writing except via an occasional linguistic bow in their direction executed through the words "lesbian," "sexual orientation," or "sexualities." Race and class do not similarly remain systematically in the ghostly closet of referring terms. In 1994, one might truthfully repeat Sue-Ellen Case's 1988 caustic observation about

> the catechism of "working-class-women-of-color" feminist theorists feel impelled to invoke at the outset of their research. What's wrong with this picture? It does not include the lesbian position. In fact, the isolation of the social dynamics of race and class successfully relegates sexual preference to an attendant position, so that even if the lesbian were to appear, she would be as a bridesmaid and never the bride.[1]

The problem is not just the lesbian's bridesmaid status. Her complete absence from the wedding may also go unnoticed.[2]

It is of course possible that the feminist frame *is* fully adequate to representing lesbians but, for various reasons, simply has not been adequately deployed to that end; thus, the problem is simply one of unrealized potential. But—and it is this "but" that I intend to explore—it is also possible that the feminist frame itself operates in various ways to closet lesbians.

This may seem unlikely. The turn in feminism to an anti-essentialist, difference-sensitive frame promises to open whatever doors may formerly have been closed against lesbian inclusion. It is as a caution against automatic confidence in the power of this feminist frame to represent lesbian difference that I intend this essay. In the first part, I probe the constructed concept of difference, examining both what difference has come to mean and the kind of sociopolitical analysis that enables the representation of difference. I argue that anti-essentialism has in fact worked *against* theorizing lesbian difference, because the construct "difference" presupposes a disanalogy between sexual orientation and race, class, ethnicity. In the second part, I pursue the political boundaries around feminist representations of differences. There, using the lesbian feminist sex wars as a case in point, I argue that feminist values and goals have worked against representing lesbian difference. In the third part of this essay, I confront the underlying requirement of difference-sensitive feminism that lesbians be representable as different *women*. In Western culture, the lesbian as the bearer of a different, distinctive identity became thinkable, imaginable, largely by virtue of turn-of-the-century sexologists' construction of a nonbinary sex/gender system in which the lesbian was positioned as the third sex; or, as Monique Wittig describes her, "a not-woman, a not-man";[3] or as Judith Butler might describe her, as disruptively reconfiguring and redeploying the categories of sex.[4] If thinking the lesbian depends on thinking a position outside of "woman" and "man," then lesbian representation cannot be accomplished under the sign "women." Positioned in a lineup of womanly differences in race, class, and so forth, *lesbian* difference cannot appear. In short, "women" may operate as a lesbian closet.

The Promise of Anti-Essentialism

Feminist theorizing has dramatically changed since 1980 when Marilyn Frye charged women's studies with thoroughgoing heterosexism and urged lesbians to refrain from supporting it.[5] In particular, feminist theorizing no longer makes the essentializing assumptions that "woman" signifies a set of universal commonalities, that all women share a common oppression, and, thus that a single feminist agenda will equally address all women's needs. In an effort to combat the racism, classism, and other biases built into earlier feminist theorizing, "difference" has largely replaced "woman" as the category of analysis. "It would seem that dealing with the fact of differences is *the* project of women's studies today."[6] Dealing with differences promises an inclusiveness that would address both Marilyn Frye's charge of heterosexism in women's studies and Joan Nestle's conviction that lesbians inhabit a different geography. That promise, however, warrants scrutiny.

Lesbian Disappearance under "Difference." In her 1988 article on lesbian autobiography, Biddy Martin observes the potential political value for lesbians of focusing on lesbian difference from heterosexual women: "Claims to difference conceived in terms of different identities have operated and continue to operate as interventions in facile assumptions of 'sisterhood,' assumptions that have tended to mask the operation of white, middle-class, heterosexual, 'womanhood' as the hidden but hegemonic referent." Thus, "The isolation of lesbian autobiography . . . may have strategic political value, given the continued, or perhaps renewed, invisibility of lesbians even in feminist work." Autobiographical collections, such as *The Lesbian Path, The Coming Out Stories*, and *The New Lesbians*, challenge the assumption that women's normal trajectory is "toward adult heterosexuality, marriage, and motherhood." They also challenge the presumed continuity between biological sex, gender identity, and sexuality.[7] Because both assumptions are often at work in feminist writing, lesbian autobiography helps to bring lesbian difference back into view.

Martin, however, is ultimately critical of lesbian anthologies like *The Coming Out Stories*. In her view, they do not instantiate a difference-sensitive feminism. What she means by "sensitivity to difference" emerges in her critique of lesbian autobiographical writing. It is, paradoxically, a definition of "difference" that implicitly excludes the representation of *lesbian* difference.

Published during the 1970s and 1980s, *The Coming Out Stories*, *The Lesbian Path*, and *The New Lesbians* narrate a lesbian identity heavily influenced by the emergence of lesbian feminism, particularly its view of the lesbian as the truly woman-identified woman. "Lesbianism, understood to be first and foremost about love for other women and for oneself as a woman, becomes a profoundly live-saving, self-loving, political resistance to patriarchal definitions and limitations in these narratives." In keeping with this portrayal of lesbians a *women*-identified women, "sexual desire is often attenuated and appears as 'love' in these narratives," and the desirability of looking or acting like men or of engaging in butch-femme role playing is denied.[8]

Martin criticizes these narratives, first, for representing as an essential, true, discovered identity what was in fact the constructed, historical product of feminism itself. In her view, this essentializing, ahistorical, psychological approach to lesbian difference disqualifies these narratives from articulating a truly difference-sensitive perspective. "Difference sensitivity" requires that the identity in whose name difference is claimed be subject to historical and political investigation in a way that opens a space for agency between the subject and her identity. I agree.

Second, she criticizes these narratives for ultimately failing to represent lesbian *difference*. How do they go wrong? One might think (as I do, but Martin does not) that something has gone seriously wrong when lesbianism is desexualized. The woman-identified woman has no distinctive sexuality; one might say she has no sexuality at all. "In conventional terms, whatever is sexual about Political Lesbianism appears to be systematically attenuated: genitality will yield to a unspecified eroticism, eroticism to sensuality, sensuality to 'primary emotional intensity,' and emotional intensity to practical and political support."[9] When feminist woman loving replaces lesbian genital sexuality, lesbian identity disappears into feminist identity, and the *sexual* difference between heterosexual women and lesbians cannot be effectively represented. Moreover, when lesbian cross-dressing and role-playing are denied, a distinctively lesbian relation to (and I will argue, *outside of*) gender disappears into a feminist relation to gender. The woman-identified woman is incapable of either the femme's redeployment of femininity or the butch's gender crossing. As a result, the *gender* difference between heterosexual women and lesbians cannot be effectively represented, indeed is repressed, under her image.

Although Martin does observe that lesbian specificity cannot be represented via a desexualized woman-identified woman, it becomes clear that she does not take this as the problem to be solved. On the contrary, she appears to endorse the equation of lesbianism with "women's love for other women and for ourselves as women."[10] Lesbian desire remains desexualized as the desire for connection with other women. In short, representing lesbians' difference from heterosexual women is *not*, in her account, critical to successfully representing lesbians within a difference-sensitive frame.

If "difference" does not in part mean *lesbian* difference, what difference does matter in a difference-sensitive frame?—lesbians' difference from each other. In Martin's view—and she is not alone here—"difference sensitivity" requires that any representation of women must recognize the boundaries imposed between women by race, class, ethnicity, and nationality. What Martin admires in the autobiographical anthologies *This Bridge Called My Back: Writings by Radical Women of Color* and, to a lesser extent, *Nice Jewish Girls: A Lesbian Anthology*, is the way their narratives repeatedly insist that neither "woman" nor "lesbian" constitute a unified category. Unity, rather than being the result of shared identity, is something that must be achieved without erasing differences between women or between lesbians. Thus, Martin does not object to the woman-identified woman because it erases lesbian differences from heterosexual women. She objects because it erases race, class, ethnic, and national differences between women and between lesbians by implying that a mere consciousness of being women (or lesbians) together is sufficient to produce unity among women. "[T]he feminist dream of a new world of women simply reproduces the demand that women of color (and women more generally) abandon their histories, the histories of their communities, their complex locations and selves, in the name of a unity that barely masks its white, middle-class cultural reference/referent."[11]

Something is right and something is very wrong about this picture. It is surely right to deny that an essential lesbian identity can be distilled out from all other differences—in race, class, ethnicity, and nationality—and shared, in this pure form, by all lesbians. What Elizabeth V. Spelman called "tootsie roll metaphysics" or "pop-bead metaphysics" is simply wrong. It is not true that "each part of my identity is separable from every other part, and the significance of each part is unaffected by the other parts."[12] Nor can heterosexist oppression be cleanly isolated from gender, race, class, and ethnic oppressions. But it is surely equally wrong to *eliminate* lesbians and heterosexist oppression from the picture. And this is exactly what has happened. The one difference that is not allowed to appear as such is the difference between lesbians and heterosexual women. The one structural and institutional barrier between women that is not allowed to appear is institutionalized heterosexist oppression. Because of that, there are no lesbians in Martin's account of difference-sensitive lesbian narratives. What appears in the place of the woman-identified woman is, in effect, the difference-identified woman. In her words, but echoing Cherríe Moraga, lesbianism is

> a desire that transgresses the boundaries imposed by structures of race, class, ethnicity, nationality; it figures not as a desire that can efface or ignore the effects of those boundaries but as a provocation to take responsibility for them out of the desire for different kinds of connections.

Almost immediately following this passage, it becomes clear that what really matters to lesbian autobiography is the desire to connect across difference, not lesbianism.

> For a number of contributors, lesbian *and not*, the love of women, the pleasure in women's company, is said to sustain political analysis and struggle across divisions. This sense of a desire for connection, however partial and provisional, gives the pieces a particular force.[13]

"Lesbian" ceases to signify lesbians in their specific difference from heterosexual women. "Lesbian" now signifies a kind of ideal (feminist) woman, *to whom* differences matter, but *whose own* difference does not. It is tempting at this point to paraphrase Martin's critique of lesbian feminism quoted above. The difference-sensitive feminist dream of a new world of women negotiating unity across race, class, ethnic, and national differences simply reproduces the demand that lesbians abandon their histories, the histories of their communities, their complex locations and selves, in the name of an acknowledgment of difference.

I have spent a long time on Biddy Martin's article because it is an excellent piece of work in what I am calling the "difference-sensitive feminist frame." It is because this piece represents that frame so well that it so usefully illustrates why the anti-essentialist move to difference has worked against, rather than for, representing lesbian difference.[14] Feminism has moved straight from "There is no essential Woman identity" to "There is no essential Lesbian identity." In both cases, it is the appeal to race, class, ethnic, and national structures that enables the anti-essentialist point to be made. Missing is a crucial intermediate step: One reason why there is no essential Woman identity is because institutionalized heterosexist structures create critical differences (and barriers) between heterosexual and nonheterosexual women. Tarrying first over the contrast between heterosexual and nonheterosexual women would have made it clear why it makes sense, and why it is not necessarily essentializing, to speak categorically of "lesbians" in the same way it makes sense to speak categorically of "Black women" or "women of color." Because that did not happen, invoking the differences between lesbians has the effect of causing lesbians to disappear. A similar de-essentializing move performed on the identity Black woman would not have this effect. It would instead reveal the intersection of race with other structural difference, such as class. In the case of lesbians, however, given the absence of extensive sociopolitical analyses of institutionalized heterosexist oppression and of the socially constructed category "lesbian," there is nothing *lesbian* for structural differences of race, class, ethnicity, and nationality to intersect *with*.[15]

The Promise of Gender *and* . . . Analyses

The disappearance of lesbians under "difference" is strikingly odd. After all, difference-sensitive feminism is predicated on the assumption that gender is not the sole determinant of woman's fate. Although historically the first demand was that "[r]ace and class oppression . . . be recognized as feminist issues with as much relevance as sexism,"[16] recognizing the oppression of lesbians (and gay men) seems a natural next step. Race and class constitute only two important factors with which gender must be integrated in a difference-sensitive analysis. The logical implication of any difference-sensitive feminism is that gender must also be integrated with sexuality analyses.

Elizabeth Spelman's construction of the difference-sensitive feminist frame brings the oddity of closeting lesbians under "difference" into particularly clear view. She argues that the most fruitful and accurate way of performing integrated analyses is to begin thinking in terms of multiple genders, that is, multiple kinds of women.[17] This has the advantage of short-circuiting the temptation to imagine that one's gender, or what it means to be a woman, is something that can be described independently of one's race, class, *or* one's sexual orientation. The image of different (woman-)genders also reminds us that feminism cannot be centrally about gender oppression unless it is at the same time centrally about racism, classism, and heterosexism.

Focusing on lesbians as a distinctive (woman-)gender produced at the intersection of gender and sexual orientation should have sparked reflection on *lesbian* difference in addition to the differences between lesbians. What I want to explore is the possibility that what Spelman calls the ampersand problem (for example, gender *and* race) may be a uniquely difficult problem when the ampersand conjoins gender with sexual orientation. In this section, I will examine feminist political motives for resisting the conjunction of "woman" with "sexual orientation." In the following section, I will question whether lesbians can be represented as a (*woman*-)gender at all.

Lesbian Disappearance under "Gender." Although largely antedating the emergence of difference-sensitive feminism, the sex wars over lesbian sadomasochism illuminate some of the political motives for *not* representing lesbian difference within a feminist frame. The sex wars constitute one of the few arenas in which lesbianism has been the explicit focus of feminist theorizing. Both opponents and proponents of lesbian sadomasochism claimed to speak from a feminist point of view.[18] Because both sides focused on the *gender* of lesbians as women in the context of rethinking lesbian *sexuality*, one might expect the entire debate to have been a concerted attempt to work out the ampersand conjoining gender with sexual orientation. It was not. One of the most remarkable features of the debate is the way that *lesbian* sexuality continuously disappears into *women's* sexuality.

Proponents of lesbian sadomasochism argued that, contrary to appearances, lesbian sadomasochism does not conflict with feminist goals, because it substantially differs from heterosexual male-dominant, female-subordinate sexual relations which also eroticize violence. Because lesbians belong to the same sexual caste, lesbian sadomasochism occurs outside of the larger frame of gender inegalitarian relations, and because the lesbian masochist consents to and controls the scene, she retains the right to determine what happens to her body. Moreover, lesbian sadomasochistic fantasies are clearly understood as just fantasies, and freedom to explore such fantasies and women's sexual pleasure is critical to women's liberation from repressive restrictions on women's sexuality. Finally, dominant-submissive scripts enable women safely to explore their own feelings about power relations and, possibly also, to explore an inevitable feature of human relations.

Opponents responded with skepticism about the alleged disanalogy between inegalitarian heterosexual relations and lesbian sadomasochism. Lesbian sadomasochism is a product of the larger, heterosexual culture which constructs sexuality as naturally sadomasochistic by eroticizing violence and humiliation.[19] The attraction of sadomasochism is not natural but culturally produced; and lesbian sadomasochists, far from exploring a new, liberating sexuality, simply mirror the inegalitarian and sadomasochistic form that heterosexual relations take in a society where men are powerful and women powerless. To claim that, simply by virtue of its lesbian context, lesbian sadomasochism does not carry the connotations of male dominance over and violence against women is to indulge in objective idealism: the belief that the meaning of symbols and actions "can be amputated from their historical and social context" and made to mean whatever one likes.[20] Rather, lesbian sadomasochistic fantasies endorse and perpetuate the values and systems of oppression that feminists are committed to undermine. Moreover the masochist's claim to have given consent is suspect given that "[f]or women, love is structured as masochism. For women, sex is structured as masochism. None of us escapes this message, not even lesbian feminists."[21]

What I find interesting about these debates is that they proceed curiously unencumbered by the thought that *lesbianism* might complicate the analysis of sadomasochism between women. Indeed, one could almost forget that lesbian sexuality is the issue. And for good reason. The entire debate takes place on the backdrop and avails itself of arguments used in debates about heterosexual women's sexuality. On the one hand is the (hetero)sexual revolution of the 1970s with its revolt against sexual repression and advocacy of unrestricted sexual experimentation. On the other hand is the anti-(heterosexual) pornography movement with its condemnation of (hetero)sexual objectification of and violence against women. At issue in both the larger pro- versus anti-sex debates and the smaller lesbian sadomasochism debates is the disposition of *women's* sexuality, with heterosexual women's sexuality setting the terms of the debate.

Opponents assumed that lesbian sadomasochism could be nothing but an imitation of the worst forms of heterosexuality. Proponents assumed that the value of sadomasochism for lesbians could be nothing but the sexually liberating value it had for women. Neither side in the sex wars imagined that lesbianism had much to do with the issue. Why should lesbianism have complicated the analysis of lesbian sadomasochism? And why might that complication have been resisted?

Imitation versus Solving Representational Problems. The idea that sadomasochism (and butch-femme roles, pornography, dildos, etc.) gets into lesbian relations simply via imitation warrants scrutiny. Imitation implies that what lesbians find erotic in sadomasochism, butch-femme, pornography, dildos, and so forth, is exactly what heterosexuals find erotic in these same things: violence, power differences, sexual objectification, penetration. Hence, opponents concluded that lesbian sadomasochism conflicts with feminist values. But why assume in the first place that sadomasochism has no meaning for lesbians *beyond* what it does for heterosexuals? Given that the taboo on lesbian sexuality is itself a source of erotic charge, one might ask what connection sadomasochism bears to the eroticism of the lesbian taboo. Does its attraction for lesbians lie not just in eroticized violence but more centrally in the power of sadomasochism to represent the lesbian taboo? Moreover, given that "lesbian" is a sexual identity, one might ask what connection sadomasochism bears to the representation of lesbian identity. Does its attraction for lesbians lie in its power to represent lesbian difference from heterosexual women?

B. Ruby Rich has suggested that one result of feminism was that the

> lesbian moved from a position of outlaw to one of respectable citizen. Yet in the pre-Stonewall era prior to 1969, the lesbian was a far more criminal figure, her very sexuality criminalized in many laws, her desires unacceptable, and her clothing taboo (at least for the butch, who was the only visible lesbian in this period). . . . Thus, there was a very real sense of loss associated with the hard-won respectability: a loss of taboo and its eroticism.[22]

That respectability resulted partly from arguments to the effect that lesbians, from a feminist political point of view, are the truly woman-identified women. Partly it resulted from lesbian feminists cultivating (feminist) respectability by eschewing roles, conducting egalitarian relations, and practicing nonpenetrative sex. Partly it resulted from suggestions that lesbianism is natural to women, and heterosexuality is the cultural product of compulsory heterosexuality.[23] Thus, Gayle Rubin could say of her experience of seventies' feminism, "One could luxuriate in the knowledge that not only was one not a slimy pervert, but one's sexuality was especially blessed on political grounds. As a result, I never quite understood the experience of being gay in the face of unrelenting contempt."[24] But this blessing was mixed, and its price tag was the eroticism of the lesbian taboo. Reinvesting lesbianism with the eroticism of the taboo required importing tabooed practices into lesbianism. But where was a lesbian feminist to find a tabooed practice? In feminism itself—specifically, in the feminist prohibition of power-structured sexual practices. Hence, the particularly strong endorsement of sadomasochism by lesbian *feminists*.[25]

Feminist theorizing, however, did more than render lesbian sexuality respectable. It eroded the distinction between lesbians and (feminist) heterosexual women, thereby undermining the possibility for *lesbian* representation. The Radicalesbians, Charlotte Bunch, and Adrienne Rich all offered desexualized and politicized readings of lesbianism as a matter of emotional commitment to women and resistance to patriarchally structured personal relations between women and men. The lesbian is the woman-identified woman. Thus, the mark of the lesbian ceases to be her sexual outlaw status in heterosexual society and becomes her gender outlaw status in a patriarchal society. Economically, socially, emotionally, and sexually she refuses to behave like a woman in relation to men. But even (careful) heterosexual women can claim this gender outlaw status. As a result, lesbian difference becomes unrepresentable under the gender sign "woman-identified woman."

Feminist reconstructions of the erotic exacerbated the problem by eroding the line between heterosexual women's and lesbians' erotic relations to women. Aimed at distinguishing *women's* sexuality from men's, the new feminist eroticism stressed the deep satisfaction of acting on one's own needs for sharing and creativity, a passion for friends and shared work, and the quality of attention brought to both love and friendship.[26] On this conception of the erotic, heterosexual women and lesbians obviously can—and presumably *should* insofar as they are woman-identified—have the same erotic relations to women. The new feminist eroticism also equated heterosexuality with the male-identified and oppositionally positioned heterosexuality, not against homosexuality but against *women's* egalitarian, passionate, attentive, "erotic" relations. Thus, the contrast between heterosexuality and homosexuality, which is crucial to thinking about lesbian difference, disappeared from view.

Barred from using her desire for women to represent lesbian difference, how could a lesbian feminist represent lesbian difference and the difference of lesbian eroticism?—by deploying male-identified heterosexual forms in lesbian feminist sexual practices. She could then claim that what distinguishes the lesbian is her power to appropriate seemingly male-identified sexual forms and use them for woman-identified purposes—something heterosexual women cannot do.

The problem created for lesbian representation by "the woman-identified woman" and her nonsexual eroticism interestingly echoes the problem created for lesbian representation during the first decades of the twentieth century by the Victorian image of romantic friendships. In "The Mythic Mannish Lesbian: Radclyffe Hall and the New Woman," Esther Newton argues that Radclyffe Hall uses the mannish lesbian Stephen Gordon as the protagonist in *The Well of Loneliness* for the purpose of representing lesbian sexuality and that she could not have achieved this aim by using a less mannish figure. As Newton points out, Victorian wisdom held that women are not sexual beings. Thus, the first generation of New Women in the late 1800s who sought out romantic friendships with other women rather than marrying lacked a conceptual framework to envision their relations as sexual ones. "[W]hat 'pure' women did with each other, no matter how good it felt, could not be conceived as sexual within the terms of the nineteenth-century romantic discourse." Unlike the first generation who equated liberation with autonomy from family, the second generation of New Women, which included Radclyffe Hall, equated liberation with sexual freedom. But how was a lesbian to represent her sexuality given the construction of romantic friendships between women as asexual and the equation of sexual desire with male?—by deploying *masculine* gender images within her relation to women. Thus Newton concludes that "Hall and many other feminists like her embraced, sometimes with ambivalence, the image of the mannish lesbian and the discourse of the sexologists about inversion primarily because they desperately wanted to break out of the asexual model of romantic friendship."[27] Mannishness in the early 1900s and male-identified sexual forms in the 1970s and 1980s can, then, both be read as lesbian representational strategies, aimed at solving different problems of lesbian representation. For Radclyffe Hall, the problem was how to represent lesbian *sexuality* in a world that equated "sexual" with "male." For lesbian feminists, the problem was how to represent *lesbian* sexuality in a world of erotic woman bonding that includes both heterosexual women and lesbians.

The point of these observations is threefold. First, in the sex war debates, gender operated as a lesbian closet in spite of the debates' focus on lesbian sexual practice. Cast as a debate over *women's* sexuality, the arguments rendered invisible the problems posed by feminism for lesbian eroticism and lesbian representation. Second, feminist political investment in distinguishing *women's* sexuality from men's motivated the denial of sexual differences between heterosexual women and lesbians. Third, the distinctively lesbian deployment (even, or especially, within feminism) of male sexual roles and male-identified sexual forms suggests that any conjunction of "sexual orientation" with "woman" will be an uneasy one. Lesbian slippage between "woman" and "man" suggests that the lesbian is not just another (woman-) gender.

The Dangers of Gender

I have argued that, because "woman-identified woman" elides the difference between heterosexual women and lesbians, theorizing that takes as its subject the woman-identified woman is unlikely to represent lesbian difference effectively. If theorizing about lesbians is to be possible within a feminist frame, then we need to bring them into this frame as *lesbians*, not women-identified, or difference-identified, women. But what does bringing them in "as lesbians" mean?

One of the interesting features of lesbian history, as opposed to women's history, is the seemingly irresolvable ambiguity of the subject of lesbian history. That ambiguity is partly attributable to the fact that the lesbian (and the homosexual) as a distinct sort of person appear to have been the creation of late 1800s' medical and psychiatric discourse. As a culturally constructed subject, the lesbian does not exist prior to that time. Thus, of the women who cross-dressed, married other women, had sex with women, and formed intensely romantic but non-sexual friendships with women before the late 1800s, one may reasonably ask, "But were they lesbians?" Their ambiguous status reflects not only the relatively recent invention of the lesbian but also the absence today of consensus on any single definition of what it means to be a lesbian. Even the centrality of sexual desire to lesbianism can be called into question, as it was in the equation of lesbianism with woman identification.

We cannot, it would seem, get at lesbian difference by asking "Who *is* a lesbian?" Nor perhaps should we, since the "who is" question invites a set of troubling assumptions: that identity is an interior essence, that one is definitively and permanently either a lesbian or not a lesbian, and that real lesbians can never be correctly read for traces of heterosexuality (and vice versa). But perhaps we can get at lesbian difference, and do so without inviting these troubling assumptions, by instead asking "Who *represents* the lesbian?" Through what images does the lesbian become most thinkable? What images invite a lesbian reading?

Martha Vicinus opens her erudite essay on the history of lesbianism with the image of Rosa Bonheur, a woman who dressed like a man and lived with a woman and who wrote her sister in 1884, "It amuses me to see how puzzled the people are. They wonder to which sex I belong. The ladies especially lose themselves in conjectures about 'the little old man who looks so lively.' "[28] Vicinus introduces Bonheur in order to pose the problem of doing lesbian history: we know nothing of Bonheur's sexuality, only that she enjoyed her gender ambiguity and her passionate friendship with Nathalie Micas. What about Bonheur represents the lesbian and invites us to see her as a lesbian? On the one hand, there is her passionate friendship and devotion to another woman. She is one among many women in the second half of the nineteenth century who sustained a long-term, emotionally intense relation to another woman. But why choose Bonheur rather than Micas to pose the problem of doing lesbian history? Why ask whether the *cross-dressed* Bonheur is a lesbian as though she, but not Micas, were an especially tantalizing candidate?

Bonheur is one among many cross-dressing women who lived with, married, or had sexual affairs with women. In the eighteenth century, there are Mary East who passed as James How and had a wife for thirty-five years, the curious Ladies of Llangollen who lived together and attired themselves in a cross between women's and men's styles, and Catharina Margaretha Linck who passed as a man and was executed when her wife revealed that Linck was a woman.[29] In the nineteenth century, there are Rosa Bonheur, Louisa Lumsden, who although not crossed dressed was the "husband" of Constance Maynard in their Boston marriage, and the tie-and-top-hat-sporting George Sand. In the twentieth century there are Gertrude Stein, clad in a large overcoat, Greek sandals, loose skirts, and cropped hair, married to the more feminine Alice B. Toklas; and Radclyffe Hall, passing as "John"; and Hall's fictional creation, mannish Stephen Gordon, whose lover was the feminine Mary. And more recently, there are the butch lesbians of the forties and fifties with their femme cohorts.

Who among these women have the most power to represent, make think-able, the lesbian—the feminine women (the wives) or the cross-dressed women (the husbands)? It would seem to be the latter. Bonheur, Stein, Gordon, and butches figure the lesbian in ways their more feminine counterparts can not. In their power to generate the question "To which sex does s/he belong?" they in-vite a reading of them as lesbians.

I am not here suggesting that the mannish lesbian, the butch, is a "real" lesbian in ways the feminine lesbian, the femme, is not. On the contrary, to take mannishness itself as the marker of the lesbian is to read literally what is merely symbolic.[30] It is to fail to see that mannishness figures the lesbian only because, and only so long as, it successfully raises the question "To which sex does s/he belong?" The more vigorously one attempts to read the cross-dressed or man-nish female for signs that she is unambiguously a woman, the less powerful be-comes cross-dressing and mannishness as symbols for the lesbian. Similarly the more vigorously one attempts to read femme lesbian sexuality for sex/gender ambiguity, the more powerfully femme sexuality figures the lesbian.[31]

What I am suggesting is that same-sex desire does not by itself represent the lesbian and make her thinkable, that sexuality must in some way raise for us the question of sex/gender categorization before it can effectively represent the lesbian. For example, as one lesbian observed,

> When lesbians sponsor strip shows, or other fem erotic performances, it is very difficult to "code" it as lesbian, to make it feel queer. The result looks just like a heterosexual performance, and lesbian audiences don't re-spond to it as subversively sexual, specifically ours.[32]

Her sex performance for women fails to represent the lesbian, because it "looks just like a heterosexual performance." That is, *she* looks just like a heterosexual, about whom one would never ask "To which sex does s/he belong?"

Some lesbians have made use of the powerlessness of same-sex desire to represent the lesbian in their bid for heterosexual acceptance. In Celia Kitzin-ger's study of lesbian identity, some lesbians argued that they are just *persons* who happen to desire women sexually. Their sexuality is a private, personal matter, constituting "only a small and relatively insignificant part of the 'whole person.' "[33] In this construction, sex takes place between people, and thus same-sex activity need not mark one out as different, a lesbian. The affirmation of same-sex desire can coexist with a denial of lesbian difference only because same-sex desire does not itself represent lesbian difference.[34]

The powerlessness of same-sex desire and activity by itself to figure the les-bian is perhaps most strikingly evidenced by one study of lesbian identity for-mation. A full 45 percent of the lesbians in this study did not conclude from their first sexual experiences with women that they were lesbians. The researchers explained this by suggesting that "a woman's first homosexual relationship . . . is seen as 'special' and she thinks of herself as a person who loves a particular woman, without that having any particular implications for identity."[35]

If it is not same-sex desire, but an ambiguous relation to the categories "woman" and "man" that most powerfully represents the lesbian, then the most common objection to the woman-identified woman—namely, that this image *desexualizes* lesbians—may be misplaced. The elision of lesbian difference may result less from desexualizing lesbian desire than form the firm insistence that lesbians are unambiguously *women*. Both the liberal stress on lesbians' personhood and the feminist stress on their authentic womanhood have much the same effect—the erasure of lesbian difference. Rosa Bonheur's sex/gender ambiguity disappears under the categories "person" and "woman."[36]

The Third Sex. The power of sex/gender ambiguity to represent the lesbian dates from Carl von Westphal's case study of the congenital invert published in 1869. Westphal's case brought the lesbian as a distinct kind of person into being and inaugurated an explosion of psychiatric studies of the "invert," the "third sex," the woman with "a touch of the hermaphrodite," the "male soul trapped in a female body," the "unsexed," the "semi-women." Havelock Ellis and Richard von Krafft-Ebing were two of his more famous disciples.

Westphal, Ellis, Krafft-Ebing, and others transformed the *act* of sodomy which had long been criminalized into the sodomitical *person*. They created (or at least officialized) lesbian and homosexual difference. But as the above list of referring terms suggests, and as Michel Foucault warns,

> [w]e must not forget that the psychological, psychiatric, medical category of homosexuality was constituted from the moment it was characterized . . . less by a type of sexual relations than by a certain quality of sexual sensibility, a certain way of inverting the masculine and the feminine in oneself. Homosexuality appeared as one of the forms of sexuality when it was transposed from the practice of sodomy onto a kind of interior androgyny, a hermaphrodism of the soul.[37]

Ellis, for example, described the sexually inverted woman as someone in whom some trace of masculinity or boyishness is to be found. She elicits, often subtly, the thought, "she ought to have been a man." She has a masculine straightforwardness and sense of honor, wears male attire when practicable, has a penchant for cigarettes and cigars, is a good whistler (male inverts cannot whistle), likes athletics but not needlework, is aggressive (sometimes committing violent crimes like men), and may be both muscular and hairy.[38] Although obviously intrigued by lesbian sexual desire, Ellis makes sexual desire take a backseat to gender inversion. Indeed, sex and desire between women do not differentiate the invert from either the "normal" woman or the "class of women" to whom the sexual invert is attracted. Normal women may sexually interact when segregated from men in prisons, convents, girls' and women's schools, or harems; and, in Ellis's view, pubescent girls normally experience attractions to other girls. The class of women to whom inverts are attracted, although not quite normal, he thought, are typically "womanly" and not true inverts.

Krafft-Ebing, although not equating lesbianism with inverted gender style, did equate the most degenerate forms of lesbianism with an inverted gender style. In his view, lesbianism took four increasingly degenerate forms: psychical hermaphroditism, or what we might now call bisexuality; homo-sexuality, or, sexual desire oriented toward the same sex; viraginity, where lesbian desire is coupled with a preference for the masculine role; and gynandry, or "men-women," in which the body itself appears masculine (she "possesses of the feminine qualities only the genital organs"). In describing viraginity, Krafft-Ebing focuses on the women's tomboyish childhood; their preference for playing with soldiers; and their inclination for male garments, science, smoking, drinking, and imagining themselves men in relation to women. "The masculine soul, heaving in the female bosom," he remarks, "finds pleasure in the pursuit of manly sports and in manifestations of courage and bravado." He adds: "Uranism may nearly always be suspected in females wearing their hair short of who dress in the fashion of men, or pursue the sports and pasttimes of their male acquaintances."[39]

In his descriptions of "homo-sexuality," Krafft-Ebing, unlike Ellis, appears on the surface to conceptualize lesbian sexual desire independently of gender images, because gender crossing characterizes only the more degenerative stages. But this is only a surface appearance. In an effort to explain same-sex desire, Krafft-Ebing posits a psychosexual cerebral center which would normally develop homologous to the "sexual glands" but which in lesbians develops contrary to them. The result is a masculine psychosexual center in a feminine brain.[40] Thus, even if some lesbians are not masculine in character, they are nevertheless not fully women.

The Instability of Lesbian Representation. In returning to the sexological literature on lesbians, my aim is not to endorse its particular pathologizing, biologizing, and masculinizing descriptions. My point instead is that the *lesbian* became and remains conceivable, representable, by virtue of the creation of a new category of individuals who were *outside* of the sex/gender categories "woman" and "man."[41] If she has a sex or gender it is neither female nor male. As I read the

sexologists, the lesbian is not constituted by her mannishness but more fundamentally by her externality to binary sex/gender categories. Magnus Hirschfeld's image of the male soul trapped in a female body, Ellis's image of the boyish woman, and Krafft-Ebing's image of the masculine psychosexual center in
a feminine brain are multiple efforts to represent the possibility of being someone who is not-woman, not-man.

It is no surprise that in the wake of sexology's particular strategy for representing the not-woman, not-man, cross-dressing became the vehicle for articulating lesbian personhood. In 1920s Paris, for instance, cigarette smoking,
cropped hair, monocle-wearing, top hats and tails signaled lesbian "sexual difference *within*." Nor is it surprising that Radclyffe Hall chose mannish Stephen
Gordon rather than womanly Mary to represent the lesbian. But as Marjorie
Garber points out, gender-crossing strategies of lesbian representation are in-
herently unstable because they are perpetually open to being appropriated by
and for heterosexual women. Smoking, which both Ellis and Krafft-Ebing associated with lesbianism was, by the 1940s taken over by heterosexual women.[42]
And "[l]esbian styles of the 20s—men's formal dress, top hats and tails—popularized on stage by entertainers like Marlene Dietrich and Judy Garland, became
high fashion statements, menswear for women resexualized as straight (as
well as gay) styles." According to Newton, Hall's cross-dressing and the cross-
dressed figure of Stephen Gordon represented not only the lesbian inner self
but also "the New Woman's rebellion against the male order," and was thus
open to appropriation by heterosexual feminists who had their own interests in
gender-deviant representational strategies.[43] Butch lesbian style of the 1940s and
1950s also proved unstable. In a somewhat toned-down form, lesbian butch style
became, via feminist PC dress codes, *the* feminist style and the symbol for the
authentic, non-male-identified woman.[44] Contemporary marketing strategies
contribute to the instability of lesbian representation. Danae Clark, for example,
argues that advertisers are now employing dual marketing strategies that offer
to lesbian consumers styles and images that are coded "lesbian" but that heterosexual consumers will not detect.[45]

Cross-dressing, however, is not the only possible representational strategy.
Monique Wittig argued that lesbians are not-women, not-men, because they, unlike members of the category "woman," are economically and socially independent of men.[46] She figures lesbians' position outside the binary gender system by means of their economic and social relations, not their cross-dress.
But like earlier lesbian representational strategies, this one too proved unstable.
Wittig's symbol of the lesbian becomes in later feminist work the symbol of
the (straight) feminist, the liberated woman. This instability of lesbian repre-

sentation is exactly what one would expect given the social construction of gender itself.

The Disappearance of the Lesbian under the De-essentialized Woman. We are now in a position to see why the de-essentializing of the category "woman" might endanger lesbian representation. So long as "woman" remains substantively filled in, lesbians can representationally position themselves outside of that category, although those representations will have to shift continually to accommodate shifts in the meaning of "woman." The de-essentialist, difference-sensitive turn in feminism presents a vastly new and more difficult challenge for lesbian representation. If "woman" has no essential meaning, but there are, instead, multiple and open-ended ways that women can be, how does one go about representing oneself *outside* "woman" rather than differently *inside* "woman"? After all, it seems that being the sort of person who sexually desires women is one of the ways a woman can be and so is being mannish, butch, using a dildo, engaging in sadomasochism, marrying a woman, and so on.

Judith Butler's particular de-essentializing strategy helps pose the problem in an acute form. "Woman," in her view, is something one can never fully *be*, because there are no natural women. The illusion of a natural binarism of gender categories into "woman" and "man" is the result of repetitive (and panicked) performances of a unity between body, gender, and (heterosexual) desire. One consequence of this view is that neither femininity nor masculinity naturally belong to a particular sex. The illusion that femininity belongs to women in a way masculinity does not is simply the result of the compulsoriness of that particular gender performance for women. But it is open to women to perform otherwise. The "mannish" lesbian is, on this reading, neither imitating a man (because there is no real or natural man to imitate) nor necessarily being unwomanly. Butler notes that "in acting in a masculine way, *she changes the very meaning of what it is to be a woman*; indeed, she expands the meaning of what it means to be a woman to include a cultural possibility that it previously excluded."[47]

Once "woman" is denaturalized and opened up in this way, the lesbian may well find herself in a hopeless representational position. *Nothing* she does may count as positioning her outside of the category "woman." *Everything* she does may be read simply as expanding the meaning of "woman." What was originally intended within feminism as a move away from a totalizing conception of "woman" that was incapable of admitting differences between women now becomes totalizing in a quite different way. Although virtually any self-representation may be permitted within the category "woman," and the meaning of "woman" remains perpetually open to contestation, the one thing that may not be possible is self-representation *outside* of that category.

Butler herself does not come to this conclusion. In her view "the effect of this carnival of gender [that becomes possible when the meanings of "masculine" and "feminine" become fluid] can be conceptualized in one of two ways, either as an internal expansion of existing gender categories or as a proliferation of gender itself beyond the usual two."[48] That is, the denaturalization of "woman" and "man" could facilitate lesbian representation by underscoring the plausibility of constructing a third (or fourth, etc.) sex. Rather than being perpetually accused of being a woman who imitates men, the lesbian could claim to be a distinct gender.

However, the imperative driving difference-sensitive feminism—to acknowledge differences between women and to frame a nonexclusionary feminist agenda—militates against this option. If feminists are to theorize the lesbian and include lesbian rights among feminist political goals, the lesbian must first be brought under the sign "woman." There, she may contest the meaning of woman. What she may not do is announce her defection from the category "woman" altogether. If this is in fact, as I think it is, the compulsory effect of a difference-sensitive feminist frame, then "gender" will operate within feminism as a lesbian closet. The lesbian becomes the lesbian *woman*. This means that we must read her sexuality much the way liberal defenders of lesbian and gay rights do: her sexuality constitutes only an accidental difference. Within liberalism, she is essentially a person; within difference-sensitive feminism, she is "essentially" a woman. Stripped of the monstrous image of the third sex—not-woman, not-man—lesbian sexuality becomes just sex, a woman's sexuality, and as such simply a set of acts or practices which cannot challenge the binarism of gender. In addition, having subsumed the lesbian under "women," it would seem that we must read heterosexist oppression as a set of penalties addressed to the lesbian for her failure to conform to an essentializing cultural definition of Woman. Within this feminist frame, we may not read heterosexist oppression as addressed to her failure to be a woman of any sort at all.

Conclusion

I have argued, in the first part of this article that feminist theorizing has failed to capture lesbian difference, because it has not begun with a full-blown theory of heterosexist oppression fully parallel to race and class oppression. In order to theorize the lesbian within a feminist frame we would need an analysis of the distinctive material, social, legal, and ideological position of the lesbian under institutionalized heterosexist oppression. This would mean, among other things, examining the ways that heterosexuals and nonheterosexuals constitute opposing political classes.[49] Undertheorizing heterosexist oppression resulted in feminist constructions of lesbian identity that served more to obscure lesbian difference than to illuminate it: first, the woman-identified woman, then more recently, the difference-identified woman.

In the second part, I suggested that the problem runs deeper than simple undertheorizing. The feminist goals of emancipating women's sexuality from patriarchy and of specifying a distinctive (nongenital) women's eroticism necessitates blurring the distinction between lesbian and heterosexual women's sexuality. Thus, feminist political commitments may motivate suppressing lesbian difference.

In the third part, I have argued that even if the ampersand between gender and lesbianism were fully articulated, gender may continue operating as a lesbian closet. Lesbian difference was originally made conceivable and representable through the image of the third sex, the not-woman, not-man. To place lesbians within the category "woman" (or "women") is, then, in a real sense not to see lesbians but only women with a different sexuality. My point here is directly parallel to Marjorie Garber's critique of feminist reading of transvestites like Michael/Dorothy in *Tootsie*. To see him/her as just a man dressed in women's clothes (and so, for example, to criticize him for posturing as a better woman than "real" women are) is to fail to see the cross-dresser. Within a world populated solely by women and men, the cross-dresser *as a cross-dresser* disappears. "This tendency to erase the third term, to appropriate the cross-dresser 'as' one of the two sexes, is," Garber notes, "emblematic of a fairly consistent critical desire to look away from the transvestite as transvestite, not to see cross-dressing except as male or female manqué. . . . And this tendency might be called an *underestimation* of the object."[50] To appropriate the lesbian as a woman similarly underestimates the lesbian.

Can one theorize the lesbian within a feminist frame? This, I think, depends on whether "woman" delimits the feminist frame. If feminism is about women, then lesbians cannot adequately be theorized within that frame.[51] If instead feminism is about women *and* the open space of possibilities signified by "the third sex," then lesbians can be theorized within a feminist frame. But the cost of opening the feminist frame this way is quite high. With the lesbian not-woman enter the gay man, the heterosexual and gay male transvestite, the male-to-female transsexual, the male lesbian and the like—this time *not* as men or imitation women but as the third term between gender binaries. In an opened frame, these male bodies could no longer be constructed as the Other to women. They would be fully feminist subjects. I suspect that this transformation of males into feminist subjects is a move many feminists would reject. If so, the lesbian will remain not only outside "woman" but outside feminism.

Notes

This essay develops the claim in my "Separating Lesbian Theory from Feminist Theory" (*Ethics* 104 [April 1994]: 558–81) that lesbians are not-women. I want to credit and thank Cheryl Hall for articulating such deep skepticism about my view that feminism has not and cannot deal adequately with lesbianism that I was motivated to write this essay and had a sense of where I needed to go with it. For those interested in what I take to be the practical and political implications of assigning lesbians not-woman status, I suggest "Separating Lesbian Theory from Feminist Theory." My focus there is on the difference and conflict between feminist politics and lesbian politics. Quotations at the beginning of this essay are from Marilyn Frye's "A Lesbian's Perspective on Women's Studies, 1980," in her volume *Willful Virgin: Essays in Feminism, 1976–1992* (Freedom, Calif.: Crossing Press, 1992), 51–58; Joan Nestle's "Butch-Femme Relationships: Sexual Courage in the 1950s," in her book, *A Restricted Country* (Ithaca, N.Y.: Firebrand Books, 1987), 100–109; and Sue-Ellen Case's "Toward a Butch-Femme Aesthetic," in *The Lesbian and Gay Studies Reader*, ed. Henry Abelove, Michèle Aina Barale, and David M. Halperin (New York: Routledge, 1993), 294–306.

1. See Case, 295.

2. Consider, for example, Susan Moller Okin's excellently researched *Justice, Gender, and the Family* (New York: Basic Books, 1989), which completely omits the justice issues regarding the family that lesbians find themselves up against.

3. Monique Wittig, "One Is Not Born a Woman," in her book, *The Straight Mind and Other Essays* (Boston: Beacon Press, 1992).

4. Judith Butler, *Gender Trouble: Feminism and the Subversion of Identity* (New York: Routledge, 1990). Havelock Ellis and Richard von Krafft-Ebing, Monique Wittig, and Judith Butler obviously differ substantially in their specific understandings of what it means for the lesbian to be outside the category "woman." In this essay, however, I want to take seriously the significance of their agreeing that she is "outside."

5. The specific change that Frye hoped for has not, however, come about. She asked that heterosexual feminists cease presenting heterosexuality as an inevitability to be "coped with" and that they defend the rationality of their own choice to continue to be heterosexual.

6. Christina Crosby, "Dealing with Differences," in *Feminists Theorize the Political*, ed. Judith Butler and Joan W. Scott (New York: Routledge, 1992), 131.

7. Biddy Martin, "Lesbian Identity and Autobiographical Difference[s]," in *The Lesbian and Gay Studies Reader*, 275, 278, 280.

8. Ibid., 280, 281.

9. Hilary Allen, "Political Lesbianism and Feminism—Space for a Sexual Politics?" quoted in Martin, "Lesbian Identity and Autobiographical Difference[s]," 280.

10. Martin, "Lesbian Identity and Autobiographical Difference[s]," 284.

11. Ibid., 283.

12. Elizabeth V. Spelman, *Inessential Woman: Problems of Exclusion in Feminist Thought* (Boston: Beacon Press, 1988), 136.

13. Martin, "Lesbian Identity and Autobiographical Difference[s]," 284 (emphasis mine).

14. In a more recent piece ("Sexual Practice and Changing Lesbian Identities," in *Destabilizing Theory: Contemporary Feminist Debates*, ed. Michele Barrett and Anne Phillips [Stanford: Stanford University Press, 1992]), Biddy Martin takes a quite different approach to lesbian difference. Sensitive to race and class differences between lesbians as well as to the permeability of the lesbian-heterosexual opposition, Martin also focuses on lesbians' difference from hetero-

sexuals. In particular, she follows Butler in understanding homosexual practices (particularly drag and butch-femme) as ones that reconfigure sex and gender.

15. An analogy may help clarify what I am looking for in looking for "something lesbian." Consider what Patricia Hill Collins has called "controlling images" of Black women— the mammy, the matriarch, the Jezebel, and the welfare mother (*Black Feminist Thought: Knowledge, Consciousness, and the Politics of Empowerment* [New York: Routledge, 1990]). Without invoking an essentialized definition of "woman," we can say a lot about what makes these images gendered images, how they are connected across racial lines to other gendered images, and how they function in a general pattern of women's subordination. Similarly, without invoking an essentialized definition of "Black," we can say a lot about what makes these images raced images, how they are connected across gender lines to other raced images, and how they function in a general pattern of racial subordination. Consider now the sexual practice of butch-femme relations. Feminists have commented (largely negatively) on the *gendered* character of butch-femme relations and their similarity across sexuality lines to heterosexual gender relations. We could also say why the preference of Black butches for "beautiful" white femmes is *raced* (this example is from Martin, "Sexual Practice and Changing Lesbian Identities"). But what about butch-femme codes it *lesbian*? If we can talk meaningfully about the gendered and raced character of a practice without invoking essential definitions, then we should be able to talk equally meaningfully about the lesbian character of a practice. In looking for "something lesbian" I am looking for something to say about what might code a practice lesbian other than the unhelpful fact that lesbians do it.

16. bell hooks, *Feminist Theory: From Margin to Center* (Boston: South End Press, 1984), 24, 25.

17. Spelman, 175.

18. For helpful articles within this debate and summaries of that debate, see *Against Sadomasochism: A Radical Feminist Analysis*, ed. Robin Ruth Linden et al. (San Francisco: Frog in the Well, 1982); B. Ruby Rich, "Review Essay: Feminism and Sexuality in the 1980s," *Feminist Studies* 12 (fall 1986): 525–61; and Shane Phelan, "Sadomasochism and the Meaning of Feminism" in her *Identity Politics: Lesbian Feminism and the Limits of Community* (Philadelphia: Temple University Press, 1989).

19. Heterosexual sadomasochism, in Sally Roesch Wagner's words,

> is not a "kinky" deviation from normal heterosexual behavior. Rather, it is the defining quality of the power relationship between men and women. Sadism is the logical extension of behavior that arises out of male power. Self-will, dominance, unbridled anger and cold rationality: these qualities, bought at the expense of gentleness and concern for others, define the classic sadist as the "real" man. Selflessness, submission, lack of will and unbridled emotionalism: these qualities demanded of women, to the detriment of concern for self and independence, portray the classic masochist.

See her "Pornography and the Sexual Revolution: The Backlash of Sadomasochism," in *Against Sadomasochism*, 28.

20. Susan Leigh Star, "Swastikas: The Street and the University," in *Against Sadomasochism*, 133.

21. Wagner, 29.

22. Ruby Rich, 532.

23. I am thinking here of Adrienne Rich's interpretation of Nancy Chodorow in "Compulsory Heterosexuality and Lesbian Existence," in *The Signs Reader: Women, Gender, and Scholarship*, ed. Elizabeth Abel and Emily K. Abel (Chicago: University of Chicago Press, 1983), 139–168.

24. Gayle Rubin, "The Leather Menace," quoted in Phelan, 103.

25. This is a point Julia Creet stresses in "Daughter of the Movement: The Psychody-

namics of Lesbian S/M Fantasy," *Differences* 3 (summer 1991): 135–59. Although more evidence on this point would be a good thing, the ability of a thesis to do much-needed explanatory work is itself a form of evidence. What needs to be explained is why the principal advocates of sadomasochism were both lesbian and feminist. Some have argued that lesbian-feminist advocacy of sadomasochism, neo butch-femme, lesbian pornography, and public sex was a reaction to the sexually repressive prescriptivism of cultural feminism. (See, for example, Lillian Faderman, *Odd Girls and Twilight Lovers: A History of Lesbian Life in Twentieth-Century America* [New York: Penguin Books, 1992], chap. 10, and "A Return of Butch and Femme: A Phenomenon of Lesbian Sexuality of the 1980s and 1990s," *Journal of the History of Sexuality* 2, no. 4 [1992]: 578–96.) This "rebellion against repression" thesis, however, does not explain why it was specifically *lesbians* who rebelled. B. Ruby Rich's and Julia Creet's focus on the loss of the lesbian taboo does.

I do not mean to rule out alternative accounts of the lesbian-specific meaning of lesbian sadomasochism, butch-femme, and lesbian pornography. The truth may be that *lesbian*-feminist advocacy of these sexual forms was overdetermined. For instance, Judith Butler, and following her, Biddy Martin, Terralee Bensinger, and I have argued that the reconfigurations of femininity and masculinity in lesbian sexual practices denaturalizes gender and challenges the assumption of a natural gender binarism that underlies heterosexual society, and all too often feminist theory as well. See Butler, *Gender Trouble*, and "Imitation and Gender Insubordination," in *Inside/Out*, ed. Diana Fuss (New York: Routledge, 1990); Martin, "Sexual Practice and Changing Lesbian Identities"; Terralee Bensinger, "Lesbian Pornography: The Re/Making of (a) Community," *Discourse* 15 (fall 1992): 69–93; and Calhoun, "Separating Lesbian Theory from Feminist Theory."

26. I am thinking particularly of Audre Lorde, "Uses of the Erotic: The Erotic as Power" in *Sister Outsider: Essays and Speeches by Audre Lorde* (Freedom, Calif.: Crossing Press, 1984); Janice G. Raymond, *A Passion for Friends: Toward a Philosophy of Female Affection* (Boston: Beacon Press, 1986); and Sarah Lucia Hoagland, *Lesbian Ethics: Toward New Value* (Palo Alto: Institute of Lesbian Studies, 1988).

27. Esther Newton, "The Mythic Mannish Lesbian: Radclyffe Hall and the New Woman," *Signs* 9, no. 4 (summer 1984): 561, 560.

28. Martha Vicinus, " 'They Wonder to Which Sex I Belong': The Historical Roots of the Modern Lesbian Identity," in *The Lesbian and Gay Studies Reader*, 432.

29. All are mentioned by Vicinus. The history of cross-dressed women is also discussed by Lillian Faderman in *Surpassing the Love of Men: Romantic Friendship and Love between Women from the Renaissance to the Present* (New York: William Morrow & Co., 1981); and by Marjorie Garber, in *Vested Interests: Cross-Dressing and Cultural Anxiety* (New York: HarperPerennial, 1993).

30. An analogy may clarify the point. Suppose I present you with a picture of a person seated, reading in a library full of books and a picture of a person walking through a cornfield at dawn. I ask, "Which image more powerfully represents the scholar?" The library picture does. To infer from this that people in cornfields cannot be scholars or that everyone in libraries is a scholar would be a mistake—a mistake made possible by taking literally a symbolic image of the scholar.

31. Developing both Judith Butler's notion of "the logic of inversion," where what first appeared feminine in the femme inverts into the masculine ("Imitation and Gender Subordination") and Joan Nestle's descriptions of femme sexual power, Biddy Martin reads femme (and butch) sexuality as resisting categorization into the unambiguously feminine (or masculine). See Martin, "Sexual Practice and Changing Lesbian Identities."

32. Quoted in Garber, 153.

33. Celia Kitzinger, *The Social Construction of Lesbianism* (London: Sage Publications, 1987), 111.

34. Significantly, those same women adopted antifeminist stances, particularly toward

what they perceived as the unfeminine appearance of feminists. As one woman observes of feminist lesbians, "Once they have 'become lesbians' they are relieved to think they will never again have to wear pretty clothes or curl their hair. Nonsense!" (ibid., 142). They secure their status as people, rather than lesbians, by presenting themselves as possessors of a nonambiguously womanly femininity. My guess is that they would equally resist being read as femmes, that is, as possessors of an ambiguously womanly femininity.

35. Ibid., 105.

36. I deliberately use "sex/gender" here. Lesbian gender ambiguity—her openness to readings as masculine and feminine—is intimately connected with lesbian sex ambiguity, that is, to questions about whether she is "really" female at all and to suspicions about her anatomy. Although I do not endorse biologizing lesbianism, I do want to claim that reading a person as lesbian involves reading her as ambiguously gendered *and* ambiguously sexed.

37. Michel Foucault, *The History of Sexuality*, vol. 1, *An Introduction* (New York: Vintage Books, 1990), 43.

38. Havelock Ellis, *Studies in the Psychology of Sex*, vol. 2, *Sexual Inversion* (Philadelphia: F. A. Davis Co., 1928). See especially chap. 4.

39. Richard von Krafft-Ebing, *Psychopathia Sexualis: A Medico-Forensic Study* (New York: Pioneer Publications, 1947), 399, 336, 300, 398.

40. Ibid., 348–49.

41. Does this mean that one cannot do lesbian history prior to the late 1800s? I have argued elsewhere ("Denaturalizing and Desexualizing Lesbian and Gay Identity," *Virginia Law Review* 79 [October 1993]: 1859–75) that lesbian and gay history is essentially political: it aims to reveal the nonuniversality of taboos and what *we now* consider to be lesbianism and homosexuality. To accomplish that aim, lesbian and gay history must take as its subjects persons who fit *our* concepts of "lesbian" and "gay." Thus, the absence of a concept of "lesbianism" or "homosexuality" at earlier historical points is not a bar to doing lesbian and gay history.

42. Garber, 155–57.

43. Newton, 570.

44. Faderman, "The Return of Butch and Femme."

45. Danae Clark, "Commodity Lesbianism," in *The Lesbian and Gay Studies Reader*, 186–201.

46. Wittig.

47. Judith Butler, "Gendering the Body: Beauvoir's Philosophical Contribution," in *Women, Knowledge, and Reality: Explorations in Feminist Philosophy*, ed. Ann Garry and Marilyn Pearsall (Boston: Unwin Hyman, 1989), 260 (emphasis mine).

48. Ibid.

49. I have argued for this thesis in more detail in "Separating Lesbian Theory from Feminist Theory."

50. Garber, 10.

51. To be sure, lesbians are mistaken for women and oppressed as women. And as a "nonwoman," the lesbian is conceptually linked to "woman." Thus, quite a lot, even if not everything, can be said about lesbians within a feminist frame.

14

"They Wonder to Which Sex I Belong"

The Historical Roots
of the Modern Lesbian Identity

Martha Vicinus

IN 1884 THE aging French painter, Rosa Bonheur, wrote her sister, from Nice, where she had gone in her usual smock and trousers to sketch:

> It amuses me to see how puzzled the people are. They wonder to which sex I belong. The ladies especially lose themselves in conjectures about "the little old man who looks so lively." The men seem to conclude: "Oh, he's some aged singer from St. Peter's at Rome, who has turned to painting in his declining years to console himself for some misfortune." And they shake their beards triumphantly.[1]

Bonheur's bemused description of the impact her androgynous appearance had upon the general public pinpoints many of the major difficulties historians face in reconstructing the history of the lesbian. Bonheur spent her adult life living with a woman and wearing male attire, but she used a specifically Victorian vocabulary, reveling in her gender freedom, rather than her specific sexual identity. In describing her lifelong friendship with Nathalie Micas, Bonheur spoke appreciatively of those who understood that "two women may delight in an intense and passionate friendship, in which nothing can debase its purity."[2] Did she have an active sexual life with Micas? Was she a lesbian? Did she identify as a lesbian? Whom should we include and why in the history of the modern lesbian?

Lesbian history is in its initial stages, inhibited both by the suspect nature of the subject and the small number of individuals willing and able to pursue half-forgotten, half-destroyed, or half-neglected sources. Nevertheless, the past fifteen years have seen an encouraging efflorescence of work, breaking from the

Feminist Studies 18, no. 3 (Fall 1992). © 1992 by Feminist Studies, Inc.

old psychological paradigms and insisting upon the necessity of a historical understanding of women's same-sex sexual behavior. These studies have concentrated on issues of concern to contemporary lesbians, especially the origins of
an individual and group identity.

This attention to identity politics, past and present, has had two obvious
pitfalls. As the editors of *Signs* pointed out in the introduction to their 1984 special issue on lesbians, "Such focus on identity may in fact limit inquiry to those
cultures in which lesbian identity and survival *as lesbians* are crucial matters of
concern; it may hinder cross-cultural analysis, for example, because it provides
inadequate vocabulary for discussion of relationships among Third World
women. . . . Discussion of lesbianism in these terms has relevance only where
identity and sexuality are intertwined and where personal identity is itself a
cultural value."[3] Such pioneering collections as *This Bridge Called My Back: Writings by Radical Women of Color* (1981), edited by Cherríe Moraga and Gloria Anzaldúa; *Nice Jewish Girls: A Lesbian Anthology* (1982), edited by Evelyn Torton
Beck; and *Home Girls: A Black Feminist Anthology* (1984), edited by Barbara Smith
have problematized the contemporary relationship between a lesbian identity
and a racial identity in the United States. But possible role conflicts, personal
opportunities, or individual self-definition in the past remain largely unknown.
Moreover, the homosexual possibilities for women in the Third World, past or
present, are still little understood by Western writers.

Lesbian desire is everywhere, even as it may be nowhere. Put bluntly, we
lack any general agreement about what constitutes a lesbian. Jackie Stacey has
suggested one alternative to any rigid definition of the lesbian identity. In an
unpublished article questioning feminist psychoanalysis, she recommends instead that "it might be possible to consider questions of lesbian identity and desire within the models of fragmented subjectivity."

> The diversity of our experience of lesbianism is enormous. . . . We can-
> not assume any coherent or unified collective identity when we recognise
> the diversity of definitions and experiences of lesbians. . . . Lesbian expe-
> riences are not only fragmented within "lesbian cultures," but also within
> cultures dominated by heterosexuality, in which lesbians are ascribed the
> contradictory positions of the invisible presence.[4]

"Diversity" is a salutary reminder that not all questions can be answered, but
it hardly resolves the problems facing a historian. If we are to make sense of
our history, we must look for connections embedded in differences and contradictions.

Virtually every historian of sexuality has argued that the present-day sexual identity of both homosexuals and heterosexuals is socially constructed and

historically specific. Yet same-sex erotic attraction appears to be transhistorical and transcultural and to appear repeatedly in a limited range of behaviors. As Eve Kosofsky Sedgwick has pointed out, most of us hold contradictory notions in regard to sexual preference without attempting to resolve them. We recognize a distinct group of homosexual peoples or individuals and also understand that sexual behavior is unpredictable, various, and strongly affected by both same-sex and opposite-sex desires and influences.[5]

The history of lesbianism also demonstrates a continual jostling of two competing perspectives on the origins of homosexual feeling. Is it a product of social conditions or of one's innate propensity? Onlookers have usually chosen the former, and medical experts have chosen the latter, although by the twentieth century the two models are often postulated simultaneously. Lesbians themselves seem to use both explanations, but those privileging butch-femme relations lean toward a model of innate predisposition, and those preferring romantic friendships favor a conditioned, sexual continuum. Moreover, in spite of the many different forms of actual behavior, lesbians, past and present, are assigned to a few readily recognizable types. As Steven Epstein has pointed out, "Each society seems to have a limited range of potential storylines for its sexual scripts. . . . It may be that we're all acting out scripts—but most of us seem to be typecast. . . . To paraphrase Marx, people make their own identities, but they do not make them just as they please."[6] The remaining sections of this essay document the "scripts" of the modern Western lesbian.

The Parameters of Lesbian Historiography

Conceptual confusion is perhaps inevitable in regard to lesbians, given the historical suppression of female sexuality in general. All societies that I know of have denied, controlled, or muted the public expression of active female sexuality. We must first decode female sexual desire, and then within it, find same-sex desire. By necessity we need to be sensitive to nuance, masks, secrecy, and the unspoken. If we look to the margins, to the ruptures and breaks, we will be able to piece together a history of women speaking to each other. Nevertheless, lesbian history will remain a history of discontinuities: we rarely know precisely what women in the past did with each other in bed or out, and we are not able to reconstruct fully how and under what circumstances lesbian communities evolved. Our history includes teenage crushes, romantic friendships, Boston marriages, theatrical cross-dressing, passing women, bulldykes and prostitutes, butches and femmes, and numerous other identifications which may—and may not—include genital sex. When we can't even claim a specific

sexual expression as a key to our past, we must accept a fragmentary and confusing history.

To date, lesbian historiography has concentrated on three areas of research:
(1) the retrieval and reconstruction of both individual lesbians and lesbian communities; (2) the exploration of the two major paradigmatic forms of lesbian behavior, namely, romantic friendships and butch-femme roles; and (3) the question of when the modern lesbian identity arose and under what circumstances.
Although all three of these have generated valuable preliminary work, all have
weaknesses. Because scholars have spent so much time excavating a lost past,
few cross-cultural or cross-national comparisons have yet been made. We also
know all too little about the legal position of lesbians, in comparison with the
far richer documentation of the oppression of gay men.[7] In spite of the extensive
debates about the influence of the late nineteenth-century sexologists, we do not
yet have detailed studies of how their theories were popularized within and outside the medical profession.[8] And we are still woefully ignorant about women's
sexual behavior before the early modern period.[9]

The rediscovery of past lesbians has focused either upon the lives of well-
known writers, artists, and activists who have left extensive documentation;
upon an unproblematic celebration of the most famous lesbian communities;[10]
or, more recently, on oral histories of self-identified lesbians.[11] We look to the
personal life to define a woman, whether by her sexual acts or her sexual identity. Biddy Martin, in her literary deconstruction of contemporary lesbian coming-out stories, has shown the ways in which

> they assume a mimetic relationship between experience and writing and
> a relationship of identification between the reader and the autobiographi-
> cal subject. Moreover, they are explicitly committed to the political impor-
> tance of just such reading strategies for the creation of identity, commu-
> nity, and political solidarity.[12]

She recommends considering multiple roles, rather than a single overriding
identity, and points to recent autobiographies by American women of color who
have both used and problematized issues of identity and identity politics.[13]
Coming-out stories, with their affirmation of a personal self, seldom critique the
lesbian community which made this fulfillment possible. A shift in focus so that
both an individual's multiple roles and the communities that have sustained
(or rejected) her are examined may yield richer biographies and autobiographies.

Far too much energy has probably been consumed discussing a very American concern—whether romantic friendships or butch-femme relationships
are most characteristic of lesbianism. Following Lillian Faderman's pioneer-

ing work, *Surpassing the Love of Men: Romantic Friendships and Love between Women from the Renaissance to the Present* (1981), some scholars have privileged romantic friendships. Blanche Wiesen Cook and Adrienne Rich have pointed to the historical suppression of homosexuality and argued for the essential unity of all women-identified-women. Cook's definition, for example, has been influential in encouraging women to rethink the broader social and political context of their own lives and of women in the past: "Women who love women, who choose women to nurture and support and to create a living environment in which to work creatively and independently, are lesbians."[14] This definition usefully reminds us that women's sexuality is not a matter of either/or choices, but can be many things in different contexts. But for many lesbians, it neglects both the element of sexual object-choice and of marginal status that was (and continues to be) so important in lesbian relationships. Moreover, the different patterns of sexual behavior in the working class and aristocracy are neglected in favor of a middle class that closely resembles the present feminist movement.

Broad definitions have been largely rejected after several lesbians pointed out that scholars were in danger of draining sexuality from lesbians' lives. In an important special issue of *Heresies* (1981), several lesbians challenged the feminist vision of an egalitarian, "mutually orgasmic, struggle-free, trouble-free sex." Amber Hollibaugh insisted that "by focusing on roles in lesbian relationships, we can begin to unravel who we really are in bed. When you hide how profoundly roles can shape your sexuality, you can use that as an example of other things that get hidden."[15] Depending as it does upon self-definition and active sexuality, this definition can become insensitive to the very different lives of women in the past. How are we ever to know, definitively, what someone born a hundred or two hundred years ago did in bed? And as Cook has pointed out, does it really matter so much?[16]

The question of when and under what circumstances the modern lesbian identity arose is, perhaps, impossible to answer. If we turn to the larger historical context within which such an identity might have grown, all the usual criteria used by historians to explain social change do not seem sufficient. A lesbian identity did not result from economic independence or from an ideology of individualism or from the formation of women's communities, although all these elements were important for enhancing women's personal choices. In 1981 Ann Ferguson argued that financial independence was a necessary precondition for the formation of a lesbian identity, but this does not seem to be the case.[17] We have examples from the eighteenth and nineteenth centuries of women who were economically dependent upon their families and yet were successfully involved with women. The sexually active upper-class Anne Lister (1791–1840) was often frustrated that she had to live with her wealthy uncle and aunt in provincial Yorkshire, but she arranged her social life to take advantage of every sexual opportunity. Over the course of eight years she managed numerous meetings with her married lover and had several affairs.[18]

The onset of the industrial revolution appears to have had little impact upon the formation of a lesbian culture, although it led to more occupational opportunities for women of all social classes. The development of a mercantile economy in seventeenth- and eighteenth-century northern Europe may have encouraged some women to think of themselves as individuals apart from their families. Both religion and politics united to emphasize the importance of the individual's soul; those women who found strength through their religious beliefs to seek nontraditional roles may also have felt—and acted upon—nonconforming sexual desires.

The formation of self-conscious women's communities can be seen as a necessary precondition for a lesbian identity. But here again we find a tradition going back into the Middle Ages that yielded feminine and proto-feminist independence and bonding but hardly anything one could recognize as a lesbian identity. During the eighteenth and nineteenth centuries women organized salons, artistic coteries, religious organizations, and educational institutions. Although these were rarely self-consciously lesbian, such groups clearly provided opportunities for the development of intense friendships.[19]

Despite the weaknesses of all current explanatory models, fragmentary evidence and ghostly immanences tease scholars. The polymorphous, even amorphous sexuality of women is an invitation to multiple interpretative strategies. Discontinuity and reticence do not mean silence or absence. Many lesbian histories, contradictory, complicated, and perhaps uncomfortable, can be told.

The Seventeenth and Eighteenth Centuries: Theatrics or Nature?

By the late seventeenth and eighteenth centuries, when the traditional hierarchies of social order, private and public, were giving way, in Europe and among Europeans in the Americas, to ideas of individualism and egalitarianism, lesbian desire appears to have been defined in four dominant ways, closely linked to the social class of the women concerned. This correlation between class, public appearance, and sexual behavior suggests an effort to categorize women's deviancy in a satisfactory manner that did not threaten the dominant heterosexual and social paradigms of the age. Biological explanations seem to have been confined to educated, often medical, men, but the general public preferred a "social constructionist" approach that emphasized the individual's circumstances.

The most common figure of female deviance was the transvestite. Early modern Europeans took cross-dressed women in their stride, even as they excoriated the effeminate man.[20] Virtually all the examples of "passing women" that have survived (and many women must have died with their true identity unknown) are of working-class and peasant women who sought more job opportunities, better pay, and greater freedom.[21] Contemporaries accepted such economic necessity but often reinterpreted it in more romantic, heterosexual terms. Eighteenth-century broadside ballads praised the "female warrior" who went into battle in order to find her beloved. Most versions raised the possibility of sexual transgression but resolved matters in the final verse with a happy marriage or other appropriate female destiny.

The precursor to the modern "butch" cannot be traced back to those women who passed as "female soldiers." As Dianne Dugaw points out, such women retained their biological identity as women and simply donned the outward clothing of men. They managed to be courageous fighters, gentle helpers, and loyal wives simultaneously—and to be universally admired.[22] In her examination of the records of modern "military maids," Julie Wheelwright documents how many women depended upon the collusion of fellow soldiers to safeguard their secret.[23] When faced with a heterosexual proposition, the "soldier" either deserted or capitulated to a common-law marriage.

The female soldier's closest relative was the immensely popular cross-dressed actress of the eighteenth-century stage. Wandering actresses, or even less reputable vagrants, made up most of this group. Most of these women were notoriously heterosexual; only the infamous Londoner Charlotte Charke wore breeches in public. She delighted in playing with the possibilities of sexual transgression; her 1755 memoir robustly declared on the title page, "Her Adventures in Mens Cloaths, going by the Name of Mr. *Brown*, and being belov'd by a Lady of great Fortune, who intended to marry her."[24] However, she cast her autobiography in terms of a theatrical comedy, so as to mitigate the dangerous implications of her actions. Neither theatrical nor military dress implied a permanent identity but, rather, a temporary, if bold, seizing of opportunity.

More troubling, because more difficult to place, were those women who either appeared "mannish" or continued to cross-dress after the wars were over. Rudolph Dekker and Lottie van de Pol have argued that in Holland women who dressed as men did so because they could conceive of love for another woman only in terms of the existing heterosexual paradigm. If this was so, the highly risky marriages that so many cross-dressed women undertook make sense, for they were "the logical consequence of, on the one hand, the absence of a social role for lesbians and the existence of, on the other hand, a tradition of women in men's clothing."[25] Although this suggestion is attractive, we lack sufficient personal information to generalize with confidence about the many and complicated psychosocial reasons why a woman might have cross-dressed in the past.

Elaine Hobby has usefully reminded us that the modern lesbian identity may go further back than early critics admitted. Hobby argues that the types are familiar to us but that the explanatory models are different. Mannish women came from distant or past peoples; possessed an elongated clitoris, said to resemble a penis; were cursed by the stars or witchcraft; or, if all other explanations failed, might just be born that way. Hobby quotes a 1671 account of a German woman trader which illustrates these diverse explanations, in order to show the early existence of someone whose sexual identity appears to have been both self-determined and innate.

> [Gretta] loved the young daughters, went after them and bought them pedlars' goods; and she also used all bearing and manners, as if she had a masculine *affect*. She was often considered to be a hermaphrodite or androgyne, but this did not prove to be the case, for she was investigated by cunning, and was seen to be a true, proper woman. To note: She was said to be born under an inverted, unnatural constellation. But amongst the learned and well-read one finds that this sort of thing is often encountered amongst the Greeks and Romans, although this is to be ascribed rather to the evil customs of those corrupted nations, plagued by sins, than to the course of the heavens or stars.[26]

Rather than looking for a societal or economic explanation for Gretta's behavior, suitable for cross-dressers, commentators sought an "essentialist" argument rooted either in biology or birth. In effect, she was a precursor to the mannish lesbian.

Far more common, however, was the "free woman" who seemed to choose a flagrantly varied sexuality. Her appearance and behavior could signal an erotic interest in women, but at other times—as prostitute, courtesan, or mistress—she chose men. The subject of gossip or pornography, she was invariably portrayed as consuming both women and men. I would label this third category of publicly identified lesbian desire as the occasional lover of women. This woman was frequently attacked as a danger to the normal political hierarchies because of her undue influence upon male leaders. The evidence for her activities can be best described as "porn and politics," pamphlets, gossip, and similarly suspect sources describing flagrant sexual freedom. The connection between sexual deviance and political deviance is hardly unique to women; indeed, the libertine libertarian John Wilkes (1727–97) was the subject of an intense pamphlet war linking him with excessive freedoms of all sorts.[27]

The most famous example of this kind of political linkage is Marie Antoinette, who was repeatedly accused of political intrigue and bisexual debauchery.[28] Although her female lovers were of her own social class, she was accused of taking on male lovers from the lower classes. Much of the evidence against her was generated by those determined to destroy an effeminate aristocracy and to replace it with a purified masculine democracy. In several cases Marie Antoinette was woven into preexisting pornographic plots with little consideration for historical facts.[29] But we should not dismiss this material, for such culturally influential male fantasies, derived from both pornography and high art, had a lasting impact upon the public (and, occasionally, the private) image of the lesbian.

The fourth and increasingly common form that lesbian desire took is the romantic friendship. Nancy Cott has documented the ways in which the definition of "friend" changed in the eighteenth century to refer specifically to an elective, nonfamilial relationship of particular importance.[30] Maaike Meijer in her description of the friendship of two famous late eighteenth-century Dutch blue-stockings, Betje Wolff and Aagje Deken, points to the importance of a shared interest in learning, often in the face of family and public opposition, as a crucial element in romantic friendships.[31] A sense of being different, of wanting more than other young women, symbolized by a love of learning, characterizes many of the romantic friendships described by Faderman in *Surpassing the Love of Men*. Yet even here, women's friendships were tightly controlled by external definitions of respectability. All bourgeois families feared any emotions that would overturn the conventional hierarchies in the private and public spheres. The discipline of study was supposed to teach women friends to be rational, to control their love for each other. In actuality, it probably led to a desire for greater independence—and consequently, an increased labeling of such friendships as deviant.[32]

Elaine Marks has wittily labeled "the Sapphic fairy tale," the common variation on romantic friendship in which an older woman teaches a younger woman about sexual desire and life; in most cases the relationship is brief, as the younger woman outgrows her initial attraction.[33] The degree of sexual involvement in this relation has been a subject of some controversy among scholars. But descriptions by participants invariably include a combination of emotional and physical feelings, creating, in the words of Constance Maynard (1849–1935), founder, in the next century, of Westfield College, London, that delicious "long, long clasp of living love that needs no explanation."[34] Participants emphasized the totality of the relationship, rather than one's outward appearance or a sexual act.

These four forms of lesbian sexual desire were united less by the behavior or attitudes of the women than by the ways in which men interpreted women's same-sex desire. On the one hand, we have amusement, curiosity, and romanticization; on the other, we have horror, punishment, and expulsion. In either response, however, women's same-sex behavior remained marginal to male sexual and societal discourses.[35] The vocabulary used to define these visibly aberrant women, drawn from the classical world, emphasized either an unnatural act or a congenital defect. The Greek word "tribade" appears only in the sixteenth and early seventeenth centuries in France and England, as a description of a woman who rubbed her genitals against another woman's. Well before the pioneering sexologists of the late nineteenth century, medical theorists assigned an essentialist identity to same-sex behavior, arguing that it must be rooted in the individual's physiology. The most common medical term was "hermaphrodite." "Sapphic," the word used most frequently in memoirs, does not even merit a sexual definition in the *Oxford English Dictionary*.[36]

Only when a woman seemed to contravene directly masculine priorities and privileges was she punished. But even in these cases, sexual deviancy had to be compounded by a trespassing upon the male preserves of religion or politics in order to draw the full wrath of masculine authority. Lesbian sexuality remained a muted discourse. The usual punishment for a woman who married another woman was a public whipping and banishment. One notable exception, however, was the early eighteenth-century case of the respectable innkeeper, "James How." Mary East and her friend had opened a public house in the 1730s in a village north of London, and by dint of hard work and honesty they prospered. But East, known everywhere as "James How," had been forced to pay a blackmailer for years. Finally, after the death of her partner, she took her case to the magistrates; they did not arrest her for fraud but imprisoned the blackmailer. All surviving accounts of How treat her sympathetically.[37] The most acceptable model for understanding her thirty-five year "marriage" was the female-warrior ballad, and reports were circulated that she and her "wife" must have decided to join together after they had been jilted by men. Marjorie Garber has labeled this "normalization" of the transvestite as a "progress narrative," which recuperates an individual into a bourgeois tale of economic struggle and social success.[38] Ironically, it also bears close resemblance to the lesbian autobiography which Biddy Martin critiqued for its seamless movement toward self-actualization.

This casual and seeming indifference to women's relationships needs to be contrasted with those occasions when women clearly threatened the dominance of men or of the traditional family. The actress Charlotte Charke, in spite of her notoriety, was never a public threat because she remained a liminal figure of farce, but the multifarious sins of the German Catharina Margaretha Linck led to her trial for sodomy and her execution in 1721. She had joined an egalitarian, woman-led religion and later had converted to Roman Catholicism and then Lutheranism. Dressing as a man, she served in a Prussian volunteer corps, worked as a weaver, and married a woman with whom she had sex, using a homemade dildo. After hearing complaints from her daughter, Linck's mother-in-law and a neighbor "attacked her, took her sword, ripped open her pants, examined her, and discovered that she was indeed not a man but a woman."[39] In her defense, Linck insisted she had been deluded by Satan and that it was no sin for a maiden to wear men's clothes. Both reasons depend upon circumstances; Linck did not argue that she was biologically different or that she had been born "that way."

Women who avoided a direct confrontation with male prerogatives, whether sexual or political, fared best. The most famous example of romantic friendship in the eighteenth century was the upper-class "Ladies of Llangollen," who ran away from threats of marriage and the convent to live with each other in remote north Wales. Eleanor Butler (1739–1829) and Sarah Ponsonby (1755–1831) succeeded because they each had a small income and made a determined effort to reproduce a happy marriage in rural retirement. (James How and his "wife" had followed the working-class equivalent of this pattern in their moral probity, modesty, and hard work.) In their riding habits and short, powdered hair they looked like a pair of old men when seated (they still wore skirts), and their eccentricities were brushed aside by a wide circle of admirers. Yet even they were subject to gossip. In 1790 a journalist described Lady Eleanor as "tall and masculine" and appearing "in all respects a young man, if we except the petticoats she retains."[40] She was actually short, dumpy and fifty-one at the time. During their long lives they faced down snide comments by appearing intellectual, desexualized, and otherworldly.

Samuel Johnson's friend, the well-known gossip Mrs. Piozzi, made a distinction that was typical of the age, in respecting the intellectual Ladies of Llangollen and loathing the sexual antics of the aristocracy. In 1789 she noted, "The Queen of France is at the Head of a Set of Monsters call'd by each other *Sapphists*, who boast her example and deserve to be thrown with the *He* Demons that haunt each other likewise, into Mount Vesuvius. *That* Vice increases hourly in Extent—while expected *Parricides* frighten us no longer...."[41] The dislike of such behavior seems to have stemmed from the growing political hatred of the dissolute aristocracy as much as a distaste for their frolics. Nevertheless, the fear of active female sexuality in places of power was a potent threat, as Marie-Jo

Bonnet reminds us. She argues that the Revolutionary crowd's decapitation and mutilation of Mme. Lamballe's genitals was an effort to destroy lesbian friendships and not just the friend of the imprisoned queen.[42]

The Nineteenth and Twentieth Centuries: Natural Affection or *Femme Damnée?*

By the early years of the nineteenth century we can see two changes in same-sex relations. First, male commentary on occasional lesbian lovemaking, whether hearsay, journalism, or literature, became much more common. Public gossip shifted from Marie Antoinette's bedroom politics to the overtly sexual, unconventional women in artistic circles. Now women who were not necessarily prostitutes or well-connected could—at the price of respectability—choose to live a sexually free life. In addition, a few middle-class working women began to wear masculine (or simply practical) clothing. The active, mannish woman from the middle classes can be found throughout Europe and America by the 1820s. Most insisted upon their sexual respectability but also asserted their right to enter such predominantly male arenas as medicine, literature, art, and travel. While professional single women emphasized their emotional ties, the bohemians flaunted their sexuality. George Sand (1804–76) is the most important representative of the latter type, and Rosa Bonheur (1822–99) of the former; not coincidentally both were economically independent artists.

Sometime in the early nineteenth century the cross-dressed masculine woman (the mannish lesbian) appeared, whose primary emotional, and probably also her sexual, commitment, was to women—the Rosa Bonheurs about whom society wondered to which sex they belonged. In effect, these women combined the outward appearance of the cross-dressed woman and the inner, emotional life of a romantic friendship. The mannish lesbian, a forerunner of the twentieth-century "butch" is the result of this double inheritance. It is one which denied the theatricality of gender and instead inscribes it upon the body as a permanent identity. As I will discuss below, this figure became the identified deviant "invert" in the later-nineteenth- and early-twentieth-century work of such sexologists as Richard von Krafft-Ebing, Havelock Ellis, and Sigmund Freud. At the same time, both romantic friendships and passing women continued well into the twentieth century. In 1929, for example, in the midst of Radclyffe Hall's *The Well of Loneliness* obscenity trial, a Colonel Barker was arrested after passing as a World War I hero for over a decade; she had been "married" for three years before deserting her wife.[43] Romantic friendships flourished among women activists in the national Woman's Party in the 1940s and 1950s, according to Leila Rupp.[44]

None of these familiar types includes what we would now call the "femme" of the butch-femme couple.[45] Like the younger woman in a Sapphic romance, she was presumed to be only an occasional lover of women—someone who could, like Mary in *The Well of Loneliness* (1928), be lured away from her aberration by a handsome man. Teresa de Lauretis concludes: "Even today, in most representational contexts Mary would be either passing lesbian or passing straight, her (homo)sexuality being in the last instance what can not be seen. Unless . . . she enter the frame of vision *as* or *with* a lesbian in male body drag."[46] The impossibility of defining her by appearance or behavior baffled the sexologists. Havelock Ellis, by defining the sexual invert as someone who possessed the characteristics of the opposite sex, was unable to categorize the feminine invert. As Esther Newton has pointed out, he argued tentatively, "they are always womanly. One may perhaps say that they are the pick of the women whom the average man would pass by. . . . So far as they may be said to constitute a class they seem to possess a genuine, though not precisely sexual, preference for women over men."[47] Perhaps Ellis sensed that the "femme" was not a passive victim but an active agent in defining her own sexual preference. Certainly by the late 1950s, scandal sheets had identified her as the consummate actress who deceived unsuspecting husbands—in effect, she had overtaken the butch as the threatening female who undermined masculinity.[48] An instability of gender identity adheres to the feminine invert in spite of every effort to categorize her.

The recent publication of excerpts of Anne Lister's diaries for the years 1817–24 has given us new insight into the life of a self-consciously mannish lesbian.[49] Her entries reveal that many educated women had covert sexual relations with other women, often as a pleasurable interlude before or during marriage, sometimes as part of a long-term commitment. Lister, twenty-five when her published diary begins, spends little time analyzing why she preferred a masculine demeanor, even at the expense of public effrontery. But she was deeply distressed when her more conventional (and married) lover was uneasy about being seen with her at a small seaside resort because she looked "unnatural." Lister defended her carefully contrived appearance, recording in her diary that "her conduct & feelings [were] surely natural to me in as much as they are not taught, not fictious, but instinctive."[50] Lister was a forerunner of those women who sought to change their appearance to accord with their souls; she assumed that her behavior was innate and instinctual, even though she had gradually and self-consciously adopted more masculine accoutrements. Her lover, on the other hand, denied that she might be pursuing an adulterous affair with "Freddy" Lister; economic circumstances had driven her into marriage and emotional circumstances had led her into Lister's arms. Both were choices made under social constraints, but in no way were they part of her intrinsic identity.[51]

Within a self-consciously sexual couple, two conflicting justifications for their behavior coexisted uneasily.

George Sand dressed as a male student in order to sit in the cheap seats at the theater, and into her forties she wore informal male dress at home. She was also for a brief period madly in love with the actress Marie Dorval; each of the men in Sand's life was convinced that they were having an affair specifically to torment him.[52] Given her reputation as a sexually free woman, rumors swirled around Sand, inviting different interpretations of her identity then and now. Sand, as Isabelle de Courtivon has pointed out, fit male fantasies of the devouring lesbian, of the woman who is all body. When this remarkable woman cross-dressed, it represented not her soul but her all-too-dominating body.[53] The bisexual Sand symbolized the strong woman who devoured weak men and found her pleasure in the arms of other women. The 1830s in France spawned novels about monsters, of whom lesbians were among the most titillating. This male-generated image of sexual deviance proved to be especially powerful and one that would return repeatedly in twentieth-century portrayals of the lesbian *femme damnée*.[54]

We are now familiar with the public lives of numerous respectable professional women during the Victorian period. One of the most famous was the American sculptor Harriet Hosmer (1830–1908), who led a group of expatriate women artists in Rome. Charlotte Cushman (1816–76), an American actress of the period, frequently acted in male roles and wore men's clothes offstage. She and Hosmer, keen advocates of physical activity for women, took midnight horse rides, sat astride, and followed the hounds with the men.[55] The highly esteemed Rosa Bonheur was granted special permission to dress in trousers when she visited abattoirs and livestock auctions in order to study the anatomy of animals. She wore her trousers and smock, however, on all but formal occasions.

Lillian Faderman has defined the nineteenth-century as the heyday of romantic friendships, when women could love each other without fear of social stigma.[56] In New England the longevity and the erotic undertones of relations between women appear to have been publicly accepted, for "Boston marriages" were commonplace in literary circles; we have numerous other well-documented examples in every northern European country where women were making inroads into the professions. Most of these highly respectable couples had one partner who was more active and public, while the other was more retiring. The nineteenth-century English educational reformers, Constance Maynard and Louisa Lumsden, for example, spoke of each other as wife and husband, respectively; as headmistress of a girls' school, Lumsden expected her "wife" to support her decisions and to comfort her when difficulties arose.[57]

Lumsden was repeatedly described by her friends as assertive, even "leonine," although photographs reveal her to our eyes as an upper-class lady much like her peers in physical appearance.

The mannish Bonheur worked hard to keep the image of respectable independence which characterized romantic friendships. Nevertheless, her square, craggy features and men's clothes placed her in a suspect category. When French taste turned against her realistic paintings, she hinted to friends that the criticism was as much a personal attack on her life with Nathalie Micas as it was her artistry.[58] However proud she may have been of her androgynous appearance, Bonheur was also self-conscious enough to insist that her lifelong relations with Micas and Anna Klumpke were pure. Both Lister and George Sand, one moneyed, the other an aristocrat, were willing to risk public slander, but Bonheur needed public acceptance to succeed as a painter.

I think that we may have exaggerated the acceptability of romantic friendships. A fear of excess—whether of learning or of emotion—may well have been a cover for opposition to the erotic preference implied by a close friendship. The vituperation launched against Marie Antoinette and her best-known lovers had political roots, but it is only an extreme form of similar warnings found in etiquette books, medical tracts, and fiction, describing the dangers of over-heated friendships. The Queen could endanger the state; less lofty women could endanger the state of marriage. The notorious example of the feminist Emily Faithfull (1835–95) provided ample opportunity to editorialize against romantic friendships. In 1864 Admiral Henry Codrington petitioned for divorce on the grounds of his wife's adultery; in addition, Faithfull was accused of alienating his wife's affections. Helen Codrington, in turn, accused him of attempted rape upon Faithfull one night when the two women were sleeping together.[59] Faithfull herself first signed an affidavit claiming that this incident had taken place, but in court she refused to confirm it. The scandal permanently damaged her standing with other feminists, and she never regained the position of leadership she had held as the founder of the Victoria Press and The Victoria Magazine.

During the first half of the nineteenth century we can see the accelerating efforts of the medical and legal professions to define, codify, and control all forms of sexuality and thereby to replace the church as the arbiters of sin and morality. Women's deviant sexual behaviors, whether heterosexual prostitution or homosexuality, continued to be male-defined transgressions dominated by male language, theories, and traditions. Such narrow terms as "hermaphrodite" were replaced with a plethora of competing words, such as "urning," "lesbian," "third sex," and "invert." Writing in the 1830s, Alexandre Jean-Baptiste Parent-Duchâtelet, the pioneering French medical hygienist, linked the lives of prostitutes with those of cross-dressed lesbians. Both represented possibilities and fears for men, for each embodied an active, independent, uncontrollable sexuality.[60] Underneath their veneer of scientific language, the medical and legal tracts betray many of the same interests and biases as pornography and literature.

It has become a truism that the sexologists, such as Richard von Krafft-Ebing and Havelock Ellis, did not so much define a lesbian identity as describe and categorize what they saw about them. Ellis drew his small sample of six lesbians from his bisexual wife and her friends. All his other examples are either historical or literary; many are drawn from the French writers who had been so shocked by Sand's flamboyance. Like Krafft-Ebing, he identified lesbians by their "masculine" behavior, such as smoking, speaking loudly, and wearing comfortable clothes. Carroll Smith-Rosenberg has pointed out that "Krafft-Ebing's lesbians seemed to desire male privileges and power as ardently as, perhaps more ardently than, they sexually desired women."[61] However revolutionary these men may have thought their descriptions to be, both were simply confirming the long-standing representations of women's social transgression as both the symptom and the cause of their sexual transgression. The incipient biologism of an earlier generation of medical men now moved to the forefront. These theorists all insisted upon the primacy of the body as the definer of public, social behavior. The long-familiar descriptions of deviant sexual activity were now labeled innate characteristics, rather than immoral choices.

Several feminist historians in Britain, following the lead of Lillian Faderman, have argued that the sexologists created a climate of opinion that stigmatized single women and their relationships and favored heterosexuality.[62] Others have argued that the sexologists stimulated the formation of a lesbian identity[63] or that their influence has been greatly exaggerated.[64] All these scholars have, to date, looked almost exclusively at the medical debates, rather than placing these debates in a wider historical context. A host of competing sociobiological ideologies and disciplines grew at the end of the nineteenth century, including social Darwinism, eugenics, criminology, and anthropology; women's sexual relations could hardly remain unaffected by them.

Have we too readily categorized these early sexologists and their embarrassingly crude classifications of sexual behavior? Rather than labeling the sexologists' descriptions benighted misogyny, we might learn more from them about both contemporary lesbian mores and masculine attitudes. Esther Newton has suggested that Havelock Ellis's biological determinism at the very least made available a sexual discourse to middle-class women, who "had no developed female sexual discourse; there were only male discourses—pornographic, literary, medical—*about* female sexuality."[65] I would add that these three male discourses had long affected the traditional categories of transvestite, romantic friend, occasional lover, and androgynous woman; all four types had already been defined as suspect before they were taken up by Krafft-Ebing and Ellis. In effect, women's sexual behavior has never been isolated from or independent of the dominant male discourses of the age.

This dependence upon male theory can be seen in Germany, where lesbians—in spite of their very visible and active culture—remained quite marginal to the leading male theoreticians, Magnus Hirschfeld (1868–1935) and Benedict Friedlander (1866–1908). The former, a physician, worked all his life for the social acceptance of the congenital invert, which he defined as a female soul trapped in a male body or vice versa, and for the repeal of the German law criminalizing homosexuality. Women connected with his Scientific Humanitarian Committee played a minor role in their Association for the Legal Protection of Mothers and for Sexual Reform, which combined an emphasis upon better maternity and sexual choice. Friedlander's "Gemeinschaft der Eigenen" promoted male friendship, with a special focus on "pedagogical eros," modeled on Greek boy-man relations. Friedlander and his followers championed bisexuality in all people, arguing that women were meant to bear children, while men should bond together to create culture and lead the nation. The women connected with this movement saw themselves as closer to Nature than men and therefore as carriers of the spirit of Mother Nature.[66] They too promoted eroticized cross-age friendships, best exemplified by the film *Mädchen in Uniform* (1931), in which Manuela, in the climactic scene, is dressed as the hero in the school play and confesses her love for a favorite teacher before all the girls.[67]

By the end of the nineteenth century, wealthy and/or intrepid women had consciously migrated not only to Paris but also to Berlin, Amsterdam, New York, San Francisco, Chicago, and other cities, where they hoped to find other homosexuals.[68] They were specifically attracted to cities with bohemian subcultures, which promised to give women space to explore their sexuality, their bodies. An extraordinary number of homosexual clubs and bars—surviving photographs indicate a passion for elegant butch-femme attire—flourished in Berlin, Munich, Hamburg, and other German cities, attesting to the cultural richness of Weimar Germany; none survived the Nazi takeover of 1933.

Some of the excitement and fragility of Germany's lively gay night life was also characteristic of Harlem of the 1920s. As Lillian Faderman has argued, it was a decade when bisexuality was fashionable, and the sexually freer world of Harlem attracted both white and Black women.[69] The wealthy A'Lelia Walker threw large and popular cross-race, cross-gender, and cross-class parties; lesbian "marriages" were celebrated with exuberant panache. Ma Rainey, Bessie Smith, Alberta Hunter, Jackie "Moms" Mabley, Josephine Baker, Ethel Waters, and above all, Gladys Bentley, celebrated lesbian sex. Bentley, a star at the famous Clam House, performed in a white tuxedo and married a woman in a civil ceremony in New Jersey. Many of the blues songs she and others sang mocked male sexual anxieties and reveled in female sexual subjectivity:

> Went out last night with a crowd of my friends,
> They must've been women, 'cause I don't like no men . . .
> . . . .
> They say I do it, ain't nobody caught me,
> They sure got to prove it on me . . . [70]

But for literary English and American lesbians, Paris symbolized sexual freedom.[71] It was already known for its lesbian subculture, thanks not only to Sand's reputation but also to the poetry and fiction of such notable male writers as Balzac, Gautier, Baudelaire, Louÿs, Zola, Maupassant, and Daudet. In Paris the passing woman was embodied in the cross-dressed Marquise de Belbeuf, Colette's lover, or in Radclyffe Hall. The enthusiasm for learning languages and the arts so characteristic of earlier generations of romantic friends, continued. Renée Vivien and Natalie Barney took Greek lessons in order to read Sappho in the original; both made trips to Greece and participated in Greek theatricals. The Sapphic parties of Marie Antoinette were revived in Barney's famous entertainments. The militant respectability of Rosa Bonheur was transformed into the militant demand for recognition, best embodied in Hall's decision to write a book defending the "true invert." The bohemian world of George Sand did not need to be re-created because these women were living their own version of it.[72]

The most striking aspect of the lesbian coteries of the 1910s and 1920s was their self-conscious effort to create a new sexual language for themselves that included not only words but also gestures, costume, and behavior.[73] These women combined the essentialist biological explanation of lesbianism with a carefully constructed self-presentation. The parties, plays, and masquerades of the wealthy American Natalie Barney (1876–1970) are the best known "creations." They are commemorated in Djuna Barnes's privately published mock-heroic epic, *The Ladies' Almanack* (1928), in which Barney appears as Evangeline Musset. Although a "witty and learned Fifty," she was "so much in Demand, and so wide famed for her Genius at bringing up by Hand, and so noted and esteemed for her Slips of the Tongue that it finally brought her in the Hall of Fame. . . . "[74] Barney herself said: "Men have skins, but women have flesh—flesh that takes and gives light."[75]

An insistence upon the flesh, the very body of the lesbian, distinguished this generation. But if Barney celebrated the tactile delights of a woman's body, for Radclyffe Hall the lesbian body could be a curse because society refused to acknowledge its inherent validity. Without public, and especially family, acceptance, self-hatred was inevitable for her heroine Stephen in *The Well of Loneliness*: "She hated her body with its muscular shoulders, its small compact breasts, and its slender flanks of an athlete. All her life she must drag this body of hers like a monstrous fetter imposed on her spirit. This strangely ardent yet sterile body."[76] Moreover, contemporaries had the example of Renée Vivien (1877–1909) to remind them of the psychic dangers of lesbian love. Vivien embodied the doomed lesbian by changing her name, her religion, and her body, finally drinking and starving herself to death by the age of thirty-one.

The privileged Barney declared that a woman's body was her greatest pleasure, but Hall contended that a woman's body was her unavoidable destiny, sterile or fertile. Both positions have an altogether too familiar ring, for both had long been encoded in male discourse. This generation of extraordinary women could not escape a familiar paradox that feminists still confront: by privileging the body, positively or negatively, women necessarily became participants in an already defined language and debate. Woman as body had been a male trope for too long to be overcome by a spirited or tragic rejection.[77]

Newton has argued that Radclyffe Hall chose to portray Stephen as a congenital invert, based upon Havelock Ellis's theories, because it was her only alternative to the asexuality of romantic friendships. Actually, by the late 1920s Hall had numerous other alternatives, including Barney's hedonistic lesbianism, Vivien's self-created tragedy, Colette's theatrical affair with the marquise, and the many less colorful monogamous couples in Paris's literary world. For Hall, these women were either too secretive or too ostentatious and therefore too close to heterosexual fantasies about the life of the deviant.[78] Hall's militant demand for recognition made Ellis's congenital invert the most natural choice. This model, with its emphasis upon an innate, and therefore unchangeable, defect, also carried the status of scientific veracity. Ironically, as soon as a woman's body—specifically Stephen's "monstrous" body—became the focus of discussion, the book was legally banned in England. Only in 1968 was *The Well of Loneliness* available in England in a popular edition. A book that proclaimed a woman's free sexual choice as overtly as *The Well of Loneliness* was as dangerous as Catharina Margaretha Linck's dildo.

The demand for respect, for acceptance of one's innate difference, assumed a kind of sexual parity with men which has never been widely accepted. Hall's radical message was lost, but her portrait of Stephen remained. The complex heritage of the first generation of self-identified lesbians, experimental and flamboyant, collapsed into the public figure of the deprived and depraved *femme damnée*. The open-ended confidence and playfulness of the 1910s and 1920s did not survive the court case against *The Well of Loneliness*. The politically and economically turbulent 1930s narrowed women's sexual options. The lesbian community in Paris continued but shorn of its former glamor. Those who could find work often had to support relatives. The women's movement itself seemed increasingly irrelevant in the face of such competing ideologies as communism and fascism. Unfortunately, generalizations are difficult to make, for we know little about the isolated lesbian of the 1930s. Characteristic of the decade, class divisions appear to have increased, so that the middle-class lesbian disappeared into discreet house parties, the aristocratic lesbian popped up at favorite expatriate spas, and the working-class lesbian could be found among the unemployed hitchhikers described by Box-Car Bertha.[79] Our only evidence of her public role is fleeting references in popular psychology books—like Krafft-Ebing's—labeling her as dangerously independent.

The doomed lesbian was a remarkably durable image. By the 1950s everyone knew what a lesbian was; she had been assigned a clearly defined role. Defiance and loneliness marked her life, according to the pulp romances. The *femme damnée* was not simply a product of a fevered literary imagination; if her sexual preference became public knowledge during the witch-hunts of the McCarthy period she became literally outlawed. After acceptance during the labor-hungry years of World War II, lesbians and gays faced expulsion from military and government jobs.[80] Nevertheless, Elizabeth Wilson in England found the *femme damnée* an attractive alternative to bourgeois marriage in the 1950s; she was disappointed when progressive friends told her she was sick, not damned.[81]

In the 1950s both the general public and lesbians themselves privileged the predictable figure of the mannish lesbian. Romantic excess, forbidden desires, and social marginality were all represented by her cross-dressing. But, as I have demonstrated, she was also the product of a tangled history which embodied the outlawry of passing, the idealism of romantic friendship, and the theatricality of aristocratic play. What adhered to her identity most powerfully during these years, however, was a sense of being born different, of having a body that reflects a specific sexual identity. The femme who could pass had disappeared. Although the American Joan Nestle has argued forcefully for her importance, Wilson experienced being a woman's woman as "the lowest of the low" in the liberal heterosexual world she inhabited.[82]

But the old playfulness of an earlier generation never completely died. Now it has returned not to re-create the past but rather to celebrate the identification of homosexuality with defined, and inescapable, roles or to imagine a utopian world of transformed women. Like the women of the early twentieth century, many lesbians of our time have set themselves the task of creating a lesbian language, of defining lesbian desire, and of imagining a lesbian society. Monique Wittig, in *Les Guérillères* (1969), *Le Corps lesbien* (1973), and *Brouillon pour un dictionnaire des amantes* (1975), has presented the most sustained alternative world. Her wholesale rewriting of history, in which all mention of man is eliminated, makes it possible to imagine a woman's body outside male discourse. Even here, however, our history is incomplete. In their heroic comedy *Brouillon pour un dictionnaire des amantes*, Wittig and her coauthor, Sande Zeig, leave a blank page for the reader to fill in under Sappho. Dyke, butch, amazon, witch, and such "obsolete" words as woman and wife are included. But androgyne, femme, invert, and friendship are missing.[83] Rosa Bonheur, who so disliked rigid sex roles, is strangely absent from this world. And what about the occasional lover of women? Historians are more confined to their evidence than writers of fiction and cannot create utopias, but they can and do create myths. When we rewrite, indeed, re-create, our lost past, do we too readily drop those parts of our past that seem unattractive or confusing to us? Can (and should) utopian language and ideas help us recuperate a history full of contradictions?

Notes

This is a revised and updated version of a paper originally presented at the "Homosexuality, Which Homosexuality?" conference (Amsterdam, December 1987). The paper appears in Dennis Altman et al., *Homosexuality, Which Homosexuality?* (Amsterdam: An Dekker, 1989). I am indebted to Anja van Kooten Niekerk, Theo van der Meer, and the other organizers of the conference for providing such a supportive environment for the testing of new ideas. My thanks to Anna Davin, Karin Lützen, and Marlon Ross for their help; their probing questions and detailed suggestions have improved this essay immensely. Special thanks go to Alice Echols and Anne Herrmann, who read and critiqued each version with such encouragement and goodwill.

1. Theodore Stanton, ed., *Reminiscences of Rosa Bonheur* (1910; New York: Hacker Books, 1976), 199.

2. Anna Klumpke, *Rosa Bonheur, sa vie, son oeuvre* (Paris: Flammarion, 1908), 356: "Deux femmes peuvent sentir l'une pour l'autre le charme d'une amitié vive et passionée, sans que rien n'en altére la pureté." I am indebted to Karin Lützen for this reference.

3. Estelle B. Freedman et al., Editorial, The Lesbian Issue, *Signs* 9 (Summer 1984): 554.

4. Jackie Stacey, "The Invisible Difference: Lesbianism and Sexual Difference Theory" (unpublished paper delivered at the "Homosexuality, Which Homosexuality?" conference, Amsterdam, December 1987).

5. Eve Kosofsky Sedgwick, *Epistemology of the Closet* (Berkeley: University of California

Press, 1990), 85. See also Carole S. Vance, "Social Construction Theory: Problems in the History of Sexuality" in *Homosexuality, Which Homosexuality?* 13–34.

6. Steven Epstein, "Gay Politics, Ethnic Identity: The Limits of Social Constructionism," *Socialist Review*, no. 93/94 (May–August 1987): 24, 30.

7. There are, however, at least two case studies concerning women. See Brigitte Ericksson, trans., "A Lesbian Execution in Germany, 1721: The Trial Records," *Historical Perspectives on Homosexuality*, ed. Salvatore J. Licata and Robert P. Petersen (New York: Haworth Press, 1981), 33; for the notorious Miss Pirie and Miss Woods vs. Lady Cumming Gordon, see Lillian Faderman, *Scotch Verdict* (New York: Quill Press, 1983). See also Louis Crompton, "The Myth of Lesbian Impunity: Capital Laws from 1270 to 1791," in *Historical Perspectives on Homosexuality*, 11–26.

8. But see George Chauncy, Jr., "From Sexual Inversion to Homosexuality: Medicine and the Changing Conceptualization of Female Desire," *Salmagundi*, no. 58/59 (Fall/Winter 1982–83): 114–46; and Myriam Everard, "Lesbianism and Medical Practice in the Netherlands, 1897–1930" (unpublished paper delivered at the "Homosexuality, Which Homosexuality?" conference, Amsterdam, December 1987).

9. See Judith C. Brown's *Immodest Acts: The Life of a Lesbian Nun* (New York: Oxford University Press, 1986) for a case study of a seventeenth-century Italian nun. See also the preliminary study of Elaine Hobby, "Seventeenth-Century English Lesbianism: First Steps" (unpublished paper presented at the "Homosexuality, Which Homosexuality?" conference, Amsterdam, December 1987).

10. See the early Bertha Harris, "The More Profound Nationality of Their Lesbianism: Lesbian Society in Paris in the 1920's," *Amazon Expedition: A Lesbian Feminist Anthology* (New York: Times Change Press, 1973), 77–88; and Lillian Faderman and Brigitte Ericksson, eds. *Lesbian-Feminism in Turn-of-the-Century Germany* (Tallahassee: Naiad Press, 1980). But see also the pioneering literary history of Shari Benstock, *Women of the Left Bank, Paris, 1900–1940* (Austin: University of Texas Press, 1986). Blanche Wiesen Cook and Jane Marcus have always insisted upon the importance of a women's community during the 1920s. See Cook's "Female Support Networks and Political Activism: Lillian Wald, Crystal Eastman, Emma Goldman," in *A Heritage of Her Own: Toward a New Social History of American Women*, ed. Nancy Cott and Elizabeth Pleck (New York: Simon & Schuster, 1979), 412–44; and for Marcus on Virginia Woolf, see especially "The Niece of a Nun" and "Sapphistry: Narration as Lesbian Seduction" in Jane Marcus, *Virginia Woolf and the Languages of Patriarchy* (Bloomington: Indiana University Press, 1987).

11. See, for example, Hall-Carpenter Archives, Lesbian Oral History Group, *Inventing Ourselves: Lesbian Life Stories* (London: Routledge, 1989), as well as Elizabeth Lapovsky Kennedy and Madeline D. Davis, *Boots of Leather, Slippers of Gold: The History of a Lesbian Community* (New York: Routledge 1993).

12. Biddy Martin, "Lesbian Identity and Autobiographical Difference[s], *The Lesbian and Gay Studies Reader*, eds. Henry Abelove, Michèle Aina Barale and David Halperin (New York: Routledge, 1993), p. 278.

13. Biddy Martin specifically compares the life-stories in *This Bridge Called My Back: Writings by Radical Women of Color*, ed. Cherríe Moraga and Gloria Anzaldúa (Watertown, Mass.: Persephone Press, 1981) with those in the predominantly white and middle-class collections, *The Coming Out Stories*, eds. Julia Penelope Stanley and Susan J. Wolfe (Watertown, Mass.: Persephone Press, 1980); and *The Lesbian Path*, ed. Margaret Cruikshank (San Francisco: Grey Fox Press, 1985).

14. See my discussion of this debate in "Sexuality and Power: A Review of Current Work in the History of Sexuality," *Feminist Studies* 8 (Spring 1982): 133–56.

15. Amber Hollibaugh and Cherríe Moraga, "What We're Rollin Around in Bed With: Sexual Silences in Feminism: A Conversation toward Ending Them," *Heresies*, no. 12 (1981): 58.

16. Blanche Wiesen Cook, "The Historical Denial of Lesbianism," *Radical History Review*, no. 20 (Spring/Summer 1979): 64.

17. See Ann Ferguson, "Patriarchy, Sexual Identity, and the Sexual Revolution," *Signs* 7 (Autumn 1981): 158–72.

18. Anne Lister, *I Know My Own Heart: The Diaries of Anne Lister*, ed. Helena Whitbread (London: Virago, 1988). Lillian Faderman's *Surpassing the Love of Men: Romantic Friendship between Women from the Renaissance to the Present* (New York: William Morrow, 1981) contains the best account of the pleasure and limitations of romantic friendship without financial means.

19. I am indebted to Laurence Senelick for drawing my attention to Pidansat de Mairobert's pre-revolutionary quasi-pornographic romance, *Histoire d'une jeune fille* (Paris: Bibliothèque des Curieux, n.d. [1789]), in which a fictional "Secte des Anandrynes" meet for lesbian frolics under the leadership of a statuesque woman described as possessing "something of the masculine in her appearance" ("quelque chose d'hommasse dans toute sa personne"), 23.

20. Randolph Trumbach has documented the shift from the rake's bisexual freedom to the effeminate sodomite in "Gender and the Homosexual Role in Modern Western Culture: The Eighteenth and Nineteenth Centuries Compared," in *Homosexuality, Which Homosexuality?* 149–70.

21. The one obvious exception to this generalization is James Barry (1795?–1865), a well-known British army surgeon, whom contemporaries assumed was a hermaphrodite on account of her small stature, lack of beard, and high voice. See Isobel Rae, *The Strange Story of Dr. James Barry* (London: Longmans, 1958).

22. Dianne Dugaw, *Warrior Women and Popular Balladry, 1650–1850* (Cambridge: Cambridge University Press, 1989), 148–58.

23. See especially the case of the American Civil War volunteer Frank Thompson (Emma Edmonds) in Julie Wheelwright, *Amazons and Military Maids* (London: Pandora, 1989), 62–66.

24. See the facsimile reprint of the second edition (1755), *A Narrative of the Life of Charlotte Charke*, ed. Leonard R. N. Ashley (Gainesville, Fla.: Scholars' Facsimiles and Reprints, 1969).

25. Rudolph Dekker and Lottie van de Pol, *The Tradition of Female Transvestism in Early Modern Europe* (London: Macmillan, 1988), 54–55, 71.

26. See Hobby. She is currently writing a book on lesbianism in the early modern period.

27. See Richard Sennett's discussion of the ways in which John Wilkes's body—and sexual freedom—came to represent political freedom in *The Fall of the Public Man: On the Social Psychology of Capitalism* (New York: Vintage, 1978) 99–106.

28. Marie-Jo Bonnet, *Un Choix sans équivoque* (Paris: Denoël, 1981), 137–65. See also Faderman, *Surpassing the Love of Men*, 42–43.

29. See Lynn Hunt, "The Many Bodies of Marie Antoinette: Political Pornography and the Problem of the Feminine in the French Revolution," in *Eroticism and the Body Politic*, ed. Lynn Hunt (Baltimore: Johns Hopkins University Press, 1991), 108–30.

30. Nancy Cott, *The Bonds of Womanhood: "Woman's Sphere" in New England, 1780–1835* (New Haven: Yale University Press, 1977) 186.

31. Maaike Meijer, "Pious and Learned Female Bosomfriends in Holland in the Eighteenth Century" (Unpublished paper delivered at the "Among Men, Among Women" conference, Amsterdam, June 1983). These ideals also characterized the friendship of Ruth and Eva in *Dear Girls: The Diaries and Letters of Two Working Women, 1897–1917*, ed. Tierl Thompson (London: Women's Press, 1987), a century later.

32. These issues are touched on, but not completely developed, in Martha Vicinus, "Distance and Desire: English Boarding-School Friendships," in *Hidden from History: Reclaiming the Gay and Lesbian Past*, ed. Martin Bauml Duberman, Martha Vicinus, and George Chauncey, Jr. (New York: New American Library, 1989), 212–29.

33. Elaine Marks, "Lesbian Intertextuality," *Homosexualities and French Literature*, ed. George Stambolian and Elaine Marks (Ithaca: Cornell University Press, 1979), 356–58.

34. Constance Maynard describing her relationship with Louisa Lumsden, quoted in Martha Vicinus, *Independent Women: Work and Community for Single Women, 1850–1920* (Chicago: University of Chicago Press, 1985), 201.

35. Joanne Glasgow argues that "misogyny, thus, accounts in significant ways for the official neglect of lesbianism" in the Roman Catholic church. See her "What's a Nice Lesbian Like You Doing in the Church of Torquemada? Radclyffe Hall and Other Catholic Converts," *Lesbian Texts and Contexts: Radical Revisions*, ed. Karla Jay and Joanne Glasgow (New York: New York University Press, 1990), 249.

36. The *Oxford English Dictionary*, not always the most reliable source on sexual matters, records the first use of tribade in 1601; tribady in 1811–19, in reference to the famous Miss Woods and Miss Pirie vs. Lady Cumming Gordon trial of 1811. Hermaphrodite receives the most complete coverage, with the first reference to its use as 1398. Sapphic is defined simply as "of or pertaining to Sappho, the famous poetess of Lesbos," or "a meter used by Sappho or named after her." Sapphism is not mentioned. Bonnet traces a similar linguistic development in French, beginning with the sixteenth-century use of tribade, 25–67. She gives three examples from the *Dictionnaire érotique latin-français*, a seventeenth-century erotic dictionary (published only in the nineteenth century) which mentions tribade, lesbian, and *fricatrix* (someone who rubs/caresses another person "for pleasure or for health"). See p. 43.

37. Faderman, *Surpassing the Love of Men*, 56; and Bram Stoker, *Famous Imposters* (New York: Sturgis & Walton, 1910), 241–46. Similar revelations were always fair game for the prurient and pornographic. See, for example, Henry Fielding's titillating (and inaccurate) account of Mary Hamilton, *The Female Husband* (1746). The actual events are described by Sheridan Baker, "Henry Fielding's *The Female Husband*: Fact and Fiction," *PMLA* 74 (1959): 213–24.

38. Marjorie Garber, *Vested Interests: Cross-Dressing and Cultural Anxiety* (New York: Routledge, 1991), 69–70. Garber's discussion is in regard to the jazz musician Billy Tipton, whose sexual identity was revealed at "his" death in 1989.

39. Ericksson, 33. See also Theo van der Meer, "Tribades on Trial: Female Same-Sex Offenders in Late-Eighteenth-Century Amsterdam," *Journal of the History of Sexuality* 1 (January 1991): 424–45. These women, drawn from a similar class as Linck's, were seen as public nuisances and prostitutes, as well as tribades.

40. Butler's and Ponsonby's lives are recounted in Elizabeth Mavor, *The Ladies of Llangollen* (London: Michael Joseph, 1971), 74.

41. See *Thraliana: The Diary of Hester Lynch Thrale (Later Mrs. Piozzi)*, ed. Katharine Balderston, 2d ed. (Oxford: Clarendon Press, 1951), 1: 740. Randolph Trumbach, in "London's Sapphists: From Three Sexes to Four Genders in the Making of Modern Culture," *Body Guards: The Cultural Politics of Gender Ambiguity*, ed. Julia Epstein and Kristina Straub (New York: Routledge, 1991), 112–41, documents Mrs. Piozzi's growing awareness of English "sapphists" and the reference to them in slang as early as 1782 as "tommies."

42. Bonnet, 165. See also Terry Castle's recent examination of the continued interest in Marie Antoinette among lesbians, "Marie Antoinette Obsession," *Representations* 38 (Spring 1992): 1–38.

43. The fullest account of "Colonel" Barker can be found in Wheelwright, 1–11, 159. Wheelwright points out that Barker married only after her father-in-law caught the two women living together. In court "his" wife, Elfrida Haward, denied all knowledge of her husband's true sex. Characteristically, the judge was most concerned with Barker's deception of the Church of England. See also Michael Baker, *Our Three Selves: The Life of Radclyffe Hall* (London: Hamish Hamilton, 1985), 254.

44. See Leila Rupp's essay, " 'Imagine My Surprise': Women's Relationships in Mid-Twentieth Century America," in *Hidden from History*, 395–410.

45. But see Colette's attempt to define her in an evocative re-creation of Sarah Ponsonby in *The Pure and the Impure*, trans. Herma Briffault (New York: Farrar, Straus & Giroux, 1966), 114–29.

46. Teresa de Lauretis, "Sexual Indifference and Lesbian Representation," *Theatre Journal* 40 (May 1988): 177.

47. Quoted by Esther Newton, "The Mythic Mannish Lesbian: Radclyffe Hall and the New Woman," in *Hidden from History*, 288.

48. See, for example, "The Shocking Facts about Those Lesbians," *Hush-Hush* 5 (September 1959), unpaginated; "Do Lesbian Wives Swap Husbands?" *On the Q.T.* 5 (July 1961): 28–29, 56–57, 60; Sharon Tague, "How Many U.S. Wives Are Secret Lesbians?" *Uncensored* 14 (February 1965): 20–21, 58. I am indebted to Laurence Senelick and the Lesbian Herstory Archives, New York City, for these references.

49. See also the more elusive life described in Betty T. Bennett's biography, *Mary Diana Dods: A Gentleman and a Scholar* (New York: William Morrow, 1991). One of two illegitimate daughters of the fifteenth earl of Morton, Dods earned a precarious living as a writer using several different male pseudonyms. In 1827 Mary Shelley helped Dods escape from England to the continent as Walter Sholto Douglas, "husband" of the pregnant Isabel Robinson. Although they gained entry to the highest literary circles in Paris, the Douglases were totally dependent upon funds from their families. Dods appears to have died in penury in 1829, freeing her "wife" to make a highly respectable marriage to an Anglican minister resident in Florence, Italy.

50. Lister, 28. For examples of attacks on her by men, see 48–49, 106, 110, 113–15.

51. We have, of course, only Lister's interpretation of her behavior, but see Lister, 104: "I felt she was another man's wife. I shuddered at the thought & at the conviction that no soffistry [*sic*] could gloss over the criminality of our connection. It seemed not that the like had occurred to her." The use of a masculine (or androgynous) nickname for the more mannish partner can be found repeatedly in these relations.

52. As Ruth Jordan describes it, "George was credited with at least three simultaneous affairs [with men]: one with Sandeau, unwanted but still officiating, another with Latouche, who had retired to the country, and yet another with Gustave Planche, the unkempt, uncombed, unwashed brilliant critic of the *Revue des Deux Mondes*. Marie Dorval was the latest, most sensational addition to a cohort of unproven lovers." See her *George Sand: A Biography* (London: Constable, 1976), 68. Biographers of Sand fall into two camps, those who sensationalize her life and those who normalize it; the latter, of course, are most reluctant to identify her relationship with Dorval as sexual.

53. Isabelle de Courtivon, "Weak Men and Fatal Women: The Sand Image," in *Homosexualities and French Literature*, 224–16.

54. In addition to de Courtivon, see also Claire Goldberg Moses, "Difference in Historical Perspective: Saint-Simonian Feminism," in Moses and Leslie Wahl Rabine, *The Word and the Act: French Feminism in the Age of Romanticism* (Bloomington: Indiana University Press, forthcoming); Faderman, *Surpassing the Love of Men*, 274–99; and Dorelies Kraakman, "Sexual Ambivalence of Women Artists in early Nineteenth-Century France" (unpublished paper delivered at the "Homosexuality, Which Homosexuality?" conference, Amsterdam, December 1987). I am indebted to Dorelies Kraakman for discussing with me the importance of the 1830s and 1840s in France for understanding the formation of a new public discourse about women's sexuality.

55. See Emmanuel Cooper, *The Sexual Perspective: Homosexuality and Art in the Last 100 Years in the West* (London: Routledge & Kegan Paul, 1986), 55–58. See also the biography, Emma Stebbins, ed., *Charlotte Cushman: Her Life and Memories of Her Life* (Boston: Houghton Mifflin, 1991).

56. Faderman, *Surpassing the Love of Men*, 190–230. See also Lillian Faderman, "The Morbidification of Love between Women by Nineteenth-Century Sexologists," *Journal of Homosexuality* 4 (Fall 1978): 73–90.

57. Martha Vicinus, " 'One Life to Stand Beside Me': Emotional Conflicts in First-Generation College Women in England," *Feminist Studies* 8 (Fall 1982): 610–11.

58. Dore Ashton and Denise Browne Hare, *Rosa Bonheur: A Life and a Legend* (New York: Viking Press, 1981), 162.

59. The known facts are briefly outlined in Olive Banks, *The Biographical Dictionary of British Feminists, 1800–1930* (New York: New York University Press, 1985), 74. I am indebted to Gail Malmgreen for reminding me of this example.

60. A. J. B. Parent-Duchâtelet claimed that "lesbians have fallen to the last degree of vice to which a human creature can attain, and, for that very reason, they require a most particular surveillance on the part of those charged with the surveillance of prostitutes. . . . " (*La Prostitution dans la ville de Paris* [1836], 1: 170), quoted in *Homosexualities and French Literature*, 148. I am indebted to Marjan Sax for pointing out the connection between prostitutes and lesbians in medical and legal texts.

61. Carroll Smith-Rosenberg, "The New Woman as Androgyne: Social Disorder and Gender Crisis, 1870–1936," in *Disorderly Conduct: Visions of Gender in Victorian America* (New York: Alfred Knopf, 1985), 271–72.

62. See Lal Coveney et al., *The Sexuality Papers: Male Sexuality and the Sexual Control of Women* (London: Hutchinson, 1984); and Sheila Jeffreys, *The Spinster and Her Enemies: Feminism and Sexuality, 1880–1930* (London: Pandora, 1985). I am grateful for the opportunity to discuss these issues and their current popularity in England with Alison Oram.

63. Sonia Ruehl, "Inverts and Experts: Radclyffe Hall and the Lesbian Identity," in *Feminism, Culture, and Politics*, ed. Rosalind Brunt and Caroline Rowan (London: Lawrence & Wishart, 1982), 15–36.

64. See Chauncey; and Vicinus, "Distance and Desire."

65. Newton, 291.

66. See Heidi Schupmann, " 'Homosexuality' in the Journal *Die Neue Generation*" (unpublished paper delivered at the "Homosexuality, Which Homosexuality?" conference, Amsterdam, December 1987); and Marian de Ras, "The 'Tribadic Revolt': Hans Blüher and the Girls' Unions," (unpublished paper delivered at the "Homosexuality, Which Homosexuality?" conference, Amsterdam, December 1987). See also Lillian Faderman and Brigitte Ericksson, *Lesbians in Germany: 1890s–1920s* (Tallahassee: Naiad Press, 1990); and John Steakley, *The Homosexual Emancipation Movement in Germany* (New York: Arno Press, 1975).

67. For a discussion of the political implications of this lesbianism, see B. Ruby Rich, "*Maedchen in Uniform*: From Repressive Tolerance to Erotic Liberation," *Radical America* 15 (1981): 18–36.

68. Gayle Rubin has coined the phrase "sexual migrations" to describe "the movement of people to cities undertaken to explore specialized sexualities not available in the traditional family arrangements, and often smaller towns, where they grew up." Quoted by Rayna Rapp, "An Introduction to Elsa Gidlow: Memoirs," *Feminist Studies* 6 (Spring 1980): 106, n. 4. In her autobiography, *Elsa: I Come with My Songs* (San Francisco: Booklegger Press, 1986), Gidlow (1898–1986) makes clear that until the 1970s her homosexual community was comprised primarily of men and a few close women friends.

69. Lillian Faderman, *Odd Girls and Twilight Lovers: A History of Lesbian Life in Twentieth-Century America* (New York: Columbia University Press, 1991), 62–92. See also Eric Garber, "A Spectacle in Color: The Lesbian and Gay Subculture of Jazz Age Harlem," in *Hidden from History*, 318–31, and "Gladys Bentley: The Bulldagger Who Sang the Blues," *Out/Look* (Spring 1988): 52–61.

70. "Prove It on Me Blues," sung by Ma Rainey, cited in Faderman, *Odd Girls and Twilight Lovers*, 77. See also Hazel V. Carby, "It Jus Be's Dat Way Sometimes: The Sexual Politics of Women's Blues," *Radical America* 20 (1986): 9–22.

71. The literary relations in this subculture have been explored by Benstock; see also the numerous biographies of the most famous figures. Benstock quotes Elyse Blankley (p. 49) in characterizing Paris as "a double-edged sword, offering both free sexual expression and oppressive sexual stereotyping. It might cultivate lesbianism like an exotic vine, but it would

never nourish it. In front of [Renée] Vivien—and, indeed, every lesbian—yawned the immense, unbridgeable chasm separating men's perceptions of lesbian women and lesbian women's perceptions of themselves." See Elyse Blankley, "Return to Mytilène: Renée Vivien and the City of Women," in *Women Writers and the City*, ed. Susan Merrill Squier (Knoxville: University of Tennessee Press, 1984), 45–67.

72. We have very little evidence of a working-class lesbian subculture at this time. Elsa Gidlow's memoirs (pp. 68–71) seem to indicate a similar pattern of seeking out a bohemian artistic culture. During World War I, while working as a secretary and living at home, she started a literary group in Montreal which attracted a young gay man who introduced her to the Decadent writers of the late nineteenth century, avant-garde music, and modern art.

73. In her essay "The New Woman as Androgyne," Smith-Rosenberg discusses the revolutionary nature of this project—and its failure, which she attributes to the writers' unsuccessful effort to transform the male discourse on female sexuality (pp. 265–66, 285–96).

74. Quoted in Meryle Secrest, *Between Me and Life: A Biography of Romaine Brooks* (London: Macdonald & Jones, 1976), 335. See also George Wickes, *The Amazon of Letters: The Life and Loves of Natalie Barney* (London: W. H. Allen, 1977).

75. Secrest, 336.

76. Radclyffe Hall, *The Well of Loneliness* (London: Corgi Books, 1968), 217.

77. The feminist literature on this equation is vast, but see, most recently, Susan R. Suleiman, ed., *The Female Body in Western Culture: Contemporary Perspectives* (Cambridge: Harvard University Press, 1986).

78. This point is also made by Gillian Whitlock, " 'Everything Is Out of Place': Radclyffe Hall and the Lesbian Literary Tradition," *Feminist Studies* 13 (Fall 1987): 576. See also Benstock's comment (p. 59) about this generation of lesbian writers as a whole: "Without historical models, [their] writing was forced to take upon itself the double burden of creating a model of lesbian behavior while recording the personal experience of that behavior."

79. See Vern Bullough and Bonnie Bullough, "Lesbianism in the 1920s and 1930s: A Newfound Study," *Signs* 2 (1977): 895–904; Marion K. Sanders, *Dorothy Thompson, A Legend in Her Time* (Boston: Houghton Mifflin, 1973) [Thompson was the lover of Christa Winsloe, playwright and author of the play and novel upon which *Mädchen in Uniform* was based]; Box-Car Bertha, *Sister of the Road: An Autobiography*, as told to Ben L. Reitman (1937; New York: Harper & Row, 1975). See also Faderman, *Odd Girls*, 93–117; and Gidlow, 250–81.

80. See Allan Bérubé, *Coming Out under Fire: The History of Gay Men and Women in World War II* (New York: Free Press, 1990).

81. Elizabeth Wilson, "Forbidden Love," in *Hidden Agendas: Theory, Politics, and Experience in the Women's Movement* (London: Tavistock, 1986), 175.

82. Joan Nestle, "Butch-Femme Relationships: Sexual Courage in the 1950s," in *A Restricted Country* (Ithaca: Firebrand Books, 1987), 100–109; and Elizabeth Wilson, "Gayness and Liberalism" in *Hidden Agendas*, 141.

83. I am using the English translation, *Lesbian Peoples: Materials for a Dictionary* (London: Virago, 1980).

Contributors

Tessa Boffin staged scenes, with the consent of others, for a good deal of her life. Her missionary quest to promote cultural activism and sexual diversity took her into the realms of part-time teaching and collaborative projects. Her exhibition and book *Ecstatic Antibodies: Resisting the AIDS Mythology* was coordinated with Sunil Gupta. The exhibition toured Britain, where it faced censorship, and North America.

Susan K. Cahn is assistant professor of history at the State University of New York at Buffalo. Her book *Coming on Strong: Gender and Sexuality in Twentieth-Century Women's Sport* won the 1994 Best Book Award from the North American Society for Sports History. She is currently working on a study of female adolescence and sexuality in the modern South.

Cheshire Calhoun is associate professor of philosophy and director of Women's Studies at Colby College, Waterville, Maine. She works on the intersections between moral theory, feminist philosophy, and gay and lesbian studies. She has published essays on forgiveness, reproach, resistance to unjust practices, gender bias in ethics, lesbian/gay identity, and sexuality injustice.

Tee A. Corinne's images have been published in the U.S. Women's Movement press since 1974. She was a founding co-editor of *The Blatant Image, a Magazine of Feminist Photography*, a past co-chair of the Gay and Lesbian Caucus (an Affiliated Society of the College Art Association), and co-founder of the Lesbian and Bisexual Caucus of the Women's Caucus for Art. Her books include *The Body of Love, Lesbian Muse, The Cunt Coloring Book, Women Who Loved Women, Dreams of the Woman Who Loved Sex, The Sparkling Lavender Dust of Lust*, and *Mama, Rattlesnakes, and Key Lime Pie*. Images from her photo book *Yantras of Womanlove* have been included in exhibitions at the UC Berkeley Museum and the Armand Hammer Museum at UCLA.

Heather Findlay received her Ph.D. in English from Cornell University in 1992. Her most recent academic publication is "Queer Dora," in *GLQ* (Winter 1994).

She has also published "Is There a Lesbian in This Text?: Derrida, Wittig, and the Politics of the Three Women," in *Coming to Terms: Feminism, Theory, Politics,* and "Renaissance Pederasty and Pedagogy: The 'Case' of Shakespeare's Falstaff," *Yale Journal of Criticism* 3 (Fall 1989). She is currently the editor-in-chief of *Girlfriends* magazine.

Jean Fraser is a freelance photographer living in London. She curated *Same Difference* (Camerawork, 1986) with Sunil Gupta and has organized photographic workshops for lesbian and gay young people. Her own work has appeared in *Ten.8* and has been exhibited in conventional galleries and in lesbian and gay exhibitions opposing Section 28. She is a regular contributor to the gay and lesbian press.

Karen V. Hansen teaches sociology and feminist theory at Brandeis University. She recently published *A Very Social Time: Crafting Community in Antebellum New England* and co-edited *Women, Class, and the Feminist Imagination.*

Anne Herrmann is associate professor of English and women's studies at the University of Michigan, Ann Arbor. She is the author of *The Dialogic and Difference: "An/Other Woman" in Virginia Woolf and Christa Wolf* and co-editor (with Abigail Stewart) of *Theorizing Feminism: Parallel Trends in the Humanities and the Social Sciences.* She is currently working on the performative nature of cross-gender and cross-racial identities in modernist memoirs.

Akasha (Gloria) Hull is a professor of women's studies and literature at the University of California, Santa Cruz. Expanded work on Alice Dunbar-Nelson can be found in her *Give Us Each Day: The Diary of Alice Dunbar-Nelson* and *Color, Sex, and Poetry: Three Woman Writers of the Harlem Renaissance.*

Elizabeth Meese is professor of English and adjunct professor of women's studies at the University of Alabama. The essay included here is from her newest work, entitled *(Sem)erotics: Theorizing Lesbian: Writing.* She has written two other books, *Crossing the Double-Cross: The Practice of Feminist Literary Criticism* and *(Ex)Tensions: Re-Figuring Feminist Criticism,* and co-edited (with Alice Parker) two volumes of feminist critical scholarship—*The Difference Within: Feminism and Critical Theory* and *Feminist Critical Negotiations.*

Leisa D. Meyer is an assistant professor in the history department at the College of William and Mary, where she teaches U.S. women's history, history of sexuality, and U.S. military history. Her book *Creating G.I. Jane: Sexuality and Work in the Women's Army Corps, 1942–1945* is forthcoming.

Lisa Moore, assistant professor of English at the University of Texas at Austin, teaches feminist theory and eighteenth-century literature. Her publications include "Teledildonics: Virtual Lesbians in the Fiction of Jeanette Winterson," in *Sexy Bodies: The Strange Carnalities of Feminism,* and articles on feminist theory and lesbian representation in *diacritics* and *Textual Practice.* Her book *Dangerous Intimacies: Toward a Sapphic History of the British Novel* is under contract with Duke University Press.

Makeda Silvera, born in Jamaica, spent her early years in Kingston before immigrating to North America. She is the author of *Remembering G and Other Stories; Her Head a Village and Other Stories;* and *Silenced: Oral Histories of Domestic Workers in Canada.* She is also the editor of *The Other Woman; Women of Colour in Contemporary Canadian Literature; Piece of My Heart: A Lesbian of Colour Anthology;* and *Pearls of Passion: A Treasury of Lesbian Erotica.* She currently lives in Toronto, Canada, where she is co-founder and managing editor of Sister Vision Press, the first and only publishing house in Canada dedicated to publishing the work of women of color.

Martha Vicinus, Eliza M. Mosher Distinguished University Professor of English, Women's Studies, and History, is also currently Chair of the Department of English, University of Michigan, Ann Arbor. She has written on working-class literature, Victorian women, and the history of sexuality, including *Independent Women: Work and Community for Single Women, 1850–1920,* and she co-edited *Hidden from History: Reclaiming the Gay and Lesbian Past.* She is completing a book on different forms of same-sex desire among women, 1780–1930.

Elizabeth Wilson has lectured in social policy and women's studies at the Polytechnic of North London, England. Her publications include *Women and the Welfare State* (1977), *Only Halfway to Paradise: Women in Postwar Britain* (1980), *Mirror Writing* (1982), and *What Is to Be Done about Violence towards Women?* (1983). She has been actively involved for many years in the women's liberation movement in Britain and has worked as a member of the editorial collective of *Feminist Review.*

Index